"This book is a gem. I am not aware of anything quite like it in the Baptist tradition. Each chapter is well researched and well written. My mind and soul have been nourished. This work will serve the church for years to come. I am delighted to give it my highest commendation."

—**Daniel L. Akin**, president,
Southeastern Baptist Theological Seminary

"A fantastic collection of essays wrestling with theology from the Baptist tradition that strives to restate afresh what it means to do theology with and for the believing church with due regard for conscience, confession, and mission."

—**Michael F. Bird**, deputy principal, Ridley College,
Melbourne, Australia

"*Confessing Christ* sets forth a clear theological vision that invites readers into a complete life transformed by the presence of Christ. This book goes beyond dry theory by urging readers to embrace theology as a living, breathing way of life. Every chapter reminds the church that faith meets practice in confession. Each author bids us to come, meet with, and be in awe of the Father revealed through Jesus Christ by his Spirit. *Tolle lege!* May all pastors, seminarians, and laypersons take up and read."

—**T. Andrew Brown**, senior pastor, First Baptist Church,
Starkville, Mississippi

"Steve McKinion, Christy Thornton, and Keith Whitfield have gathered a gifted group of Baptist theologians, philosophers, and historians to join them in an initiative known as the Baptist Dogmatics roundtable. From this effort developed this volume titled *Confessing Christ*, which seeks to engage the discipline of dogmatics in a distinctively Baptistic manner. Readers will agree that the great strength of the book is not just the call for a fresh look at historical, covenantal, ecclesial, and confessional matters that have formed Baptist life, but also in the overall emphases and coherent themes, consistently echoed throughout the book, that stress the necessity of relating Baptist theology for the purposes of genuine edification, discipleship, and Christlikeness of the church."

—**David S. Dockery**, president and distinguished professor
of theology, Southwestern Baptist Theological Seminary

"*Confessing Christ* presents the distinct ecclesial, pragmatic, and methodological emphases in the Baptist theological tradition. This book offers essays on doctrines of the Christian confession of faith that are appropriately built from theology proper and for the edification of the church. It highlights the legacy of Baptist theology and passes that legacy on to the next generation of Baptists."

—**Sherelle Duckworth**, instructor of Christian studies,
Clamp Divinity School, Anderson University

"An important book written by a superb team of our brightest Baptist theologians. It brings together salient markers of Baptist identity in the context of the great tradition. This volume is a timely contribution to the renewal of Christian faith and life, and I recommend it warmly!"

—**Timothy S. George**, distinguished professor,
Beeson Divinity School

"*Confessing Christ* presents a constructive vision for Baptist dogmatics. It honors the Baptist tradition but also attends to modern scholarship and contemporary concerns, offering a relevant restating of Baptist convictions. This work should serve Baptists for years to come."

—**David Rathel**, associate professor of Christian theology,
Gateway Seminary

"On the basis of Holy Scripture and in the communion of saints, the discipline of dogmatics seeks to provide an orderly account of God and all things in relation to God: for the salvation of the world and the building up of the church to the glory of God. *Confessing Christ* is a welcome contribution to this discipline from a learned company of authors. Each essay directs the church's praise to its primary object, the triune God, and measures the church's praise by its primary standard, Holy Scripture, while highlighting the distinctive notes sounded by Baptist congregations within the catholic chorus of God's people."

—**Scott R. Swain**, president and James Woodrow Hassell Professor
of Systematic Theology, Reformed Theological Seminary, Orlando

# CONFESSING CHRIST

# CONFESSING CHRIST

# AN INVITATION TO BAPTIST DOGMATICS

### EDITORS

Steven A. McKinion, Christine E. Thornton, Keith S. Whitfield

ACADEMIC®
BRENTWOOD, TENNESSEE

To Fulga Pascu Dan, for her legacy, which embodies the convictions that have guided this project, and for her encouragement and support in this project when she joined us in June 2021 at the first Baptist Dogmatics roundtable.

# CONTENTS

# CONFESSING CHRIST: EDITORS' INTRODUCTION

## STEVEN A. McKINION, CHRISTINE E. THORNTON, KEITH S. WHITFIELD

This project emerges from the conviction that contemporary Baptist theology ought to serve the church and its witness as we grow together in the "grace and knowledge of our Lord and Savior, Jesus Christ" (2 Pet 3:18). As Baptists deepen our theological reflection and develop distinctive ways of confessing the Christian faith, we serve Baptist churches and contribute to the great tradition. Each generation of Baptists must shape its theological perspectives on the basis of its ecclesial experiences, participating in the communion of saints across time, and offering theological discourse relevant to its contemporary context.

To pursue this goal, in June 2021 a group of Baptist theologians convened in Wake Forest, North Carolina to explore the possibility of engaging the discipline of dogmatics in a distinctively Baptistic manner. Recognizing dogmatics as a subset of systematic theology that investigates the coherence of the faith within, by, and for the church, we seized the strategic opportunity to develop Baptist theology within this dogmatic framework.[1] Our aim has been to move beyond the misconception of Baptist theology as a mere supplement to other theological systems. *Instead, we assert that our baptistic ecclesial experience yields a unique mode of theologizing, offering a framework and emphasis consistent with our tradition, rather than introducing novel content.*

The Baptist Dogmatic roundtable discussions were marked by rigorous dialogue, occasional disagreements rooted in conviction, and loving collegiality as we collectively worked toward a clarified vision. Over the course of two years, we presented, shaped, and revised the core components of "The Baptist Dogmatics Manifesto" and developed the chapters presented in this book. The result is the product of a community with the hope to perpetuate that community, presenting a cohesive and united introduction to our project while preserving the unique voices and methods of each roundtable participant. Though the construction of Baptist dogmatics is ongoing, this book represents the first fruits of our collaborative labor. We invite you to join us on the journey towards a Baptist dogmatic theology and encourage you to view Christian theology through the Baptist lens.

To ensure a cohesive project, we established in "The Baptist Dogmatics Manifesto" four signposts that guide our doctrinal discourse: *historical*, *ecclesial*, *covenantal*, and *confessional*. While these signposts are doctrinal convictions in themselves, they also serve as orienting markers for a Baptistic way of theologizing. Each signpost is rooted in the fundamental Baptist conviction of the Lordship of Christ and distributed in the particular Baptistic way of knowing and being. The purpose for the manifesto is to provide an in-depth exposition of each signpost and its role in our overall project.

---

[1] Steven A. McKinion, Christine E. Thornton, and Keith S. Whitfield, "Toward a Baptist Dogmatics," *Southeastern Theological Review* 14, no. 2 (2023): 4–6, 12–20.

*Confessing Christ* is not a systematic theology textbook. We merely seek to introduce in this book our Baptist Dogmatics project through common doctrinal headings. Our goal is not to provide a comprehensive overview of the doctrine covered in each chapter but to highlight how the doctrines may be conceived according to our baptistic convictions and oriented within the four signposts.

To achieve this, each chapter is divided into three subsections. The first section offers a basic introduction to doctrine. It has some distinctive nuances, but it should resonate with readers familiar with traditional approaches. The second section delves into a particular aspect of the doctrine relevant to our project. The third and final section explains how the doctrine is distributed within Baptist dogmatics, providing the most pointed introduction to the distinct features of our proposal.

We hope that as Baptists read this book, they will identify with the shaping convictions of our heritage and be inspired to deepen their own theological vision. For Christians from other traditions, we hope this book fosters an appreciation for the unity we share and highlights the unique contribution of a thoroughly Christian theology presented in a distinctly Baptist voice.

As you hold this book, you are not merely encountering a collection of chapters; you are engaging with the collective voice of a community dedicated to shaping Baptist theology. Our aspiration is to move beyond the stereotype of Baptist theology as a mere supplement and showcase its distinctive mode of theologizing—a framework and emphasis consistent with our rich tradition.

The following chapters in the book offer a glimpse into the foundational importance of Scripture for practicing theology through a distinctively Baptist theological reflection. From discussions on the Trinity and human dignity to reflections on the virgin birth, each chapter unfolds a facet of Baptist theology, inviting readers to consider Christian theology through the Baptist lens.

In chapter 1, Steven McKinion and Brandon Smith establish the foundational importance of Scripture in the Baptist perspective, emphasizing its role in revealing God's work through communal reflection centered on Christ. They argue for its authority, rooted in inspiration by the triune God, and underscore Baptists' prioritization of Scripture over reason, experience, and ecclesial structures. Baptists recognize Scripture as the ultimate theological authority, but also seek to retrieve from the history of Christian doctrine readings of the Bible that properly shape theological reflection.

In chapter 2, Ross Inman and Stephen Presley delve into the concept of the Trinity, distributing the doctrine in a distinctively baptistic way. They highlight the baptismal formula in Matt 28:19 as a key expression of the triune nature of God and explore the relationship between the divine name, belief, and baptism. The chapter emphasizes the responsibility to honor and make known the triune name among the nations, tying together baptism, the divine name, and a believer's new identity and mission in the world.

Chapters 3–6 cover the doctrine of humanity, Christology, salvation, and the Christian life. Rhyne Putman and Malcolm Yarnell explore the concept of human dignity in Western thought, tracing its roots to biblical and Christian origins, particularly in Baptist and free church traditions. The chapter discusses the significance of the *imago Dei* and its historical development in the context of gender equality and racial issues. The authors reflect on Southern Baptist views on human dignity, urging a widespread reclamation of this concept in theological discourse. They provide constructive reflection on the themes of confession, conscience, and covenant in their relationship to the Baptist dogma of human dignity. Luke Stamps and Tyler Wittman focus on Christ's person and the virgin birth in chapter 4. They argue against the confusion of preexistence and pro-existence in Christological heresies and delve into the theological and doctrinal implications of the virgin birth. The chapter discusses the ecclesial implications of Baptist Christology, emphasizing the sole lordship of Christ and its implications for religious liberty. They conclude by highlighting that Baptist distinctives, including personal conversion, a believers' church, believers' baptism, and religious liberty, are downstream from their doctrine of Christ.

In chapter 5, Stefana Laing and John Laing rehearse various biblical images of salvation through the framing of John 3:16. They propose three key points to strengthen a distinctively Baptist soteriology, concluding with reflections on Baptist distinctives and theological trajectories, highlighting the historic Baptist commitment to religious liberty and advocating for a theologically responsible understanding of disestablishment. They also emphasize the importance of supporting individual freedom of faith and expression in a diverse society. In chapter 6, Nathan Finn and Keith Whitfield focus on the Christian life from the lens of Romans 5–8, with John Gill as a central reference. The chapter emphasizes the transformative practice of theology in the Baptist tradition, particularly through its ecclesial focus and baptismal practices. The chapter demonstrates how a Baptist approach to the Christian life is characterized by its ecclesial focus, with church covenants serving as guiding principles for members in their journey of sanctification.

Ecclesiology is the focus of chapters 7–8. Jason Lee and Benjamin Quinn present a vision for Baptist churches in chapter 7, establishing the nature of Baptist ecclesiology with a robust affirmation of Christ's headship over the church. The chapter highlights unique traditions of baptism, the Lord's Supper, and the preaching of the Word. It concludes by discussing the role of Baptist confessions and covenants in shaping ecclesial practices and mission, providing a theological basis for Baptist churches and a guide for their community life. Stephen Lorance and Christine Thornton highlight the significance of baptism in Baptist theology, emphasizing its role in defining the church's practices and dogmatic framework. The chapter connects Baptist distinctives to the ongoing work of the Holy Spirit in baptism and the Lord's Supper and presents how baptism aids believers in interpreting the Bible and understanding the rule of faith. The chapter concludes by weaving together the threads of baptism's sanctifying activity, its role in shaping Baptist ecclesial experiences, and its connection to the missional context of belief and practice.

The final chapter by Matt Emerson and Oren Martin explores Baptist eschatology, emphasizing Christ's role as the judge in the final judgment. The chapter traces the eschatological narrative from creation and the fall to redemption and fulfillment in Jesus, highlighting Baptist views on the bodily return of Christ, final judgment, and the renewal of all things.

Again, we are indebted to the group of Baptist scholars who comprise the Baptist Dogmatics Roundtable. Many contributors to the roundtable are authors in this volume, and we are thankful for their investment in this project. Others who contributed to the roundtable discussion include Ken Keathley, Dennis Greeson, David Rathel, Walter Strickland, Timothy George, and Scott Swain. Chris Hanna, David Rathel, and Timothy George each contributed to the Fall 2023 edition of the Southeastern Theological Review, presenting a collection of essays on the consideration of Baptist dogmatics that represented the first public artifacts from the work of the roundtable.[2]

We are also grateful for the support and careful guidance from the B&H Academic team. We appreciate Devin Maddox and Madison Trammel for taking on this book. They believed in the concept from the start and have been steady encouragers. Michael McEwen led the project through all the various publication stages. He did so with such professionalism—providing careful editing, advice on the process, and championing the project every step of the way.

This project would not be where it is today without Will Johnston, who attended each of the roundtable meetings, took copious notes, and

---

[2] Steven A. McKinion, Christine E. Thornton, and Keith S. Whitfield, eds., "Interview with Timothy George," *Southeastern Theological Review* 14, no. 2 (2023): 21–30; Christoper Hanna, "Retrieval for the Sake of Renewal: Timothy George's Methodology," *Southeastern Theological Review* 14, no. 2 (2023): 31–54; and David Rathel, "John Gill and the Rule of Faith: A Case Study in the Baptist Retrieval of Tradition," *Southeastern Theological Review* 14, no. 2 (2023): 55–72.

provided wise and thoughtful perspective along the way. Southeastern Baptist Theological Seminary students Chandler Collins and Faith Steele read, provided feedback, and contributed some research for "The Baptist Dogmatics Manifesto" and "Towards a Baptist Dogmatics."[3] We are grateful for their help. Finally, we thank Mary Jo Haselton, who coordinated each of the Baptist Dogmatic Roundtable meetings—managing travel, housing, food, and room setup. None of this would be possible without her dedication.

May this book serve as an invitation—to Baptists, an invitation to deepen their theological vision; to Christians from other traditions, an invitation to appreciate unity and unique contributions in a distinctly Baptist voice. As we navigate the pages ahead, may the dialogue continue and the community of exploration thrive.

---

[3] McKinion, Thornton, and Whitfield, "Toward a Baptist Dogmatics": 3–20.

# A BIOGRAPHY IN HONOR OF FULGA PASCU DAN

Born in Arad, Romania, in 1936, Mrs. Fulga Pascu Dan is the grand-daughter and the grandniece of two brothers, Atanasie (Athanasius) Pascu and Timotei Pascu, both pastors in Timiş County. A century ago, her paternal grandfather, Atanasie, served as a home missionary and church planter, establishing the First Baptist Church (now "Betel") of Timisoara in 1923. His son (Fulga's father) Dănilă Pascu established the church choir, which has led the church in worship for 100 years without hiatus. After 1927, Fulga's father, Dănilă, undertook seminary studies in Bucharest (the Baptist seminary built on property owned by the WMU). He married in 1935 and pastored a large Baptist church in Buteni until 1939. That year, just before Fulga turned three, her father was invited to the Baptist World Alliance Congress in Atlanta, Georgia, to repre-sent Romanian Baptists and to lead in a prayer. George Truett presided, and L. R. Scarborough preached in that session. Baptists were especially concerned about the impending war in Europe, as well as about religious freedom for European Baptists. While Dănilă was still in the US, World War II broke out, and he was unable to return to Romania. The BWA sponsored him to remain in the US and find employment, while Fulga, her mother, and her younger brother, Dan, were sponsored to emigrate to America, traveling by plane and a ship out of Bilbao, Spain, and arriving in New York on March 25, 1941.

Fulga's life and work reflect a merging of two deeply held Baptist values: religious freedom and the work of missions and evangelism. Fulga grew up in Cleveland, Ohio, as a preacher's kid at the First Romanian Baptist Church. She was active in youth and music ministries, becoming the church pianist and a sought-after accompanist, having studied piano at Baldwin-Wallace College and Conservatory.

Fulga was fully aware of the persecution of Baptists overseas. She watched her father—a leader in the Romanian community in Cleveland and a well-known figure among Romanians in America—minister to the diaspora Romanians through preaching, pastoral care, and hospitality; through an evangelistic radio ministry' and more practically, by lobbying for immigration reform and religious freedom. Dănilă found sponsors for many professionals, artists, and religious and literary figures to visit or remain in the US, among them Mircea Eliade and Fr. Dumitru Cornilescu, the translator of the Bible into Romanian (1921; rev. 1924). He modeled historic Baptist political activism in the interests of religious freedom by appealing directly and personally to governing authorities: in 1952 pleading on behalf of persecuted Baptists in an audience with President Harry Truman, and in 1965 lobbying Cleveland congressman Michael Feighan to ease legal hurdles to family reunification for immigrants. Pascu urged the congressman to approve the Immigration Act of 1965 (which Rep. Michael Feighan had opposed for five years), signed into law by President Lyndon B. Johnson.

In her turn, Fulga was invited to participate in several traveling exhibitions of American modern and realist art that toured in politically, socially and religiously repressive countries in the 1960s as a form of soft diplomacy. Fluent in English, Romanian, and French, and sponsored by the State Department, she traveled to Romania with these "Art in Embassies" exhibitions in 1964, 1967 and 1969, eventually meeting her husband, Emanuel Titus Dan, a mechanical engineer and son of a Baptist pastor, whose family members had suffered humiliation, threats, intimidation, and various injustices as they faithfully planted and served Baptist churches in Cluj-Napoca and throughout the region of Ardeal/Transylvania.

In December 1970, Fulga and Titus wed in Cleveland, and within a few years Titus enrolled as a seminary student at The Southern Baptist Theological Seminary. Fulga found herself the main breadwinner as she continued her weekday job teaching French in the Cleveland Public School system and took on the weekend task of translator, editor, and typist of Titus's seminary term papers and essays.

As Titus pursued his doctor of ministry in evangelism under Lewis Drummond, Fulga took up along with Titus the mantle of bi-vocational ministry. Upon Titus's graduation in 1980, the couple taught ESL to Romanian students and their families in Cleveland. Additionally, partly sponsored by the Home Mission Board (NAMB), they revitalized the Romanian Baptist Church of Akron and planted a second Baptist church in the Cleveland suburb of Parma, all the while wrangling into sanctification three sometimes ornery and reluctant PKs (preacher's kids).

In 1985, their vocational giftings were called upon as Fulga and Titus were appointed by the International Mission Board of the Southern Baptist Convention (SBC) as church planting missionaries to the Romanian community in Sydney, Australia, which consisted of many expats for whom communist injustices and human rights violations in their beloved Romania were never out of sight, especially with the consistent influx of refugees fleeing Nicolae Ceausescu's dictatorial regime.

In those years of pastoral and social ministry in Sydney, and later in Melbourne (1986–2012), a generational Baptist legacy was lived out. The church-planting, pastoring, and music ministries of Athanasius and Dănilă Pascu were revitalized and distributed to reach and bless a new generation of Romanians. Fulga and Titus, both musically trained, poured into children and parents alike the gifts of the gospel, of instrumental and vocal music, hymns and spiritual songs, and of hospitality and discipleship. Further, they instilled in these brave refugees a sense of gratitude and hope for a new life in a free country, and an impulse to bless others as they had been blessed with freedom to believe and worship and love neighbor as self.

And so, this volume has been lovingly dedicated to a Baptist woman who carries on the legacy of promoting religious freedom and engaging in missional activity as a granddaughter, great-niece, daughter, niece, sister-in-law, daughter-in-law, aunt, and wife of Baptist pastors and missionaries. May this exemplar and this book encourage, instruct, and spiritually fortify all who read it.

Stefana Dan Laing

# A MANIFESTO FOR BAPTIST DOGMATICS

"A Manifesto for Baptist Dogmatics" is the product of the Baptist Dogmatic roundtable. Since June 2021, we met four times to discuss the core components found in this document. As is expressed in the Editor's Introduction, "The result is the product of a community with the hope to perpetuate that community, presenting a cohesive and united introduction to our project while preserving the unique voices and methods of each roundtable participant. Though the construction of Baptist dogmatics is ongoing, this book represents the first fruits of our collaborative labor. We invite you to join us on the journey towards a Baptist dogmatic theology and encourage you to view Christian theology through the Baptist lens."

Contemporary Baptists are actively contributing to the great tradition while simultaneously exploring and elucidating the Baptist faith to their congregations. In the early decades of the twenty-first century, there has been a renewed emphasis on our shared commitment to the apostolic faith, experienced in distinctively Baptist ways.[1] This theological revival within the Baptist tradition leads us to pray for a corresponding renewal within churches—a reinvigorated dedication to the lordship of Christ, the Scriptures, Baptist church practices, and a missional identity in the world. As theologians within the Baptist tradition, we welcome the abundance of theological discourse and pledge to be active contributors.

Since our inception out of the Protestant Reformations in England and continental Europe, Baptists have emphasized our participation in the one apostolic church through a shared confession of the gospel of Jesus Christ based on Scripture.[2] In the opening lines of the Orthodox Creed (1679), the framers of the statement make it clear that "the truly Ancient and Apostolical Faith, that was once delivered unto the Saints" is being carried forward in this present confession, and it is "our duty

---

[1] There are numerous examples of this development. In 2017, Matthew Emerson, Winston Hottman, Brandon Smith, and Luke Stamps started *The Center for Baptist Renewal* to "equip today's Baptists with the resources of the Baptist and broader Christian tradition so they might incorporate these beliefs and practices into the life of the local church." Emerson and Stamps collaborate with Christopher Morgan in an edited work on this topic. See Matthew Y. Emerson, Christopher W. Morgan, and R. Lucas Stamps, *Baptists and the Christian Tradition: Toward an Evangelical Baptist Catholicity* (Nashville, TN: B&H Academics, 2020). Curtis W. Freeman Freeman narrates the Baptist story as a movement that engages the convictions of the church catholic in *Contesting Catholicity: Theology for Other Baptists* (Waco, TX: Baylor University Press, 2014), 134. Christopher R. Hanna recently published a monograph on Timothy George's the vision and practice of retrieval for renewal. See *Retrieval for the Sake of Renewal: Timothy George as a Historical Theologian* (Eugene, OR: Wipf and Stock, 2022). Steven R. Harmon in *Baptist Identity and the Ecumenical Future: Story, Tradition, and the Recovery of Community* (Waco, TX: Baylor University Press, 2016) explores how the Baptist calling to be a pilgrim community relates to the ecumenical movement. In Fall 2023, the *Southeastern Theological Review* was dedicated to introducing the Baptist Dogmatics project. In that edition, there are essays on how Baptist have retrieved doctrine, as well as examples of contemporary Baptist theological retrieval. See *Southeastern Theological Review* 14 (2023): 1–129.

[2] For an exposition on how Baptists relate to eras and movements within the Christian faith, see Tom Nettles, *The Baptists: Key People Involved in Forming a Baptist Identity*, vol. 1, *Beginnings in Britain* (Fearn, UK: Mentor, 2008), 35–50.

to believe it, and thereby come through Faith, not only to have a sav-ing, but a satisfactory knowledg [*sic*] of those foundation and funda-mental Truths, which have been the same in all Generations; have been and shall be transmitted more clear from Age to Age in the times of Reformation."[3] The statement was written for the purpose of demon-strating that the faith of Baptists was consistent with the "Ancient" and "the main Points of the Protestant Religion."[4] Likewise, in the preface of *The Second London Confession of Faith* (1689), the framers declared the desire to demonstrate their agreement with the foundational state-ment of the Christian faith found in the historic, orthodox statements, as well as later published statement by various Protestants.[5] As faithful members of the universal body of Christ, Baptists have engaged in dia-logue with believers of other Christian traditions, as well as those outside of Christianity, sharing the message of God's work in Christ reconcil-ing the world to himself. Despite our theological and ecclesial emphases, Baptists recognize ourselves as Christians united by faith and tradition with other Christians. At the heart of the project we will describe lies an attempt to explore the nature of this unity in faith and tradition, along with unique Baptist contributions to the faith.

The common commitments to the faith expressed in early Christian confessions, such as the Nicene Creed and the Definition of Chalcedon, have seldom been sources of division among Baptists. While Baptists have debated the role of these creeds as standards for the faith, we have historically affirmed their orthodox conclusions.[6] Baptists have freely

---

[3] "An Orthodox Creed: Or, A Protestant Confession of Faith," transcribed by Madison Grace, http://www.baptiststudiesonline.com, accessed December 6, 2023, 1.

[4] "An Orthodox Creed," 2–3.

[5] *The Second London Confession*, http://baptiststudiesonline.com/wp-content/uploads/2008/08/the-second-london-confession.pdf, accessed December 6, 2023.

[6] Even calls of "No creed but the Bible" are meant to emphasize the author-ity and sufficiency of Scripture among Baptists more than to intimate a rejection of the expression of Christianity in church history.

utilized theological tools, such as early baptismal formulae, expressions of the rule of faith, creeds, and confessions, as means to comprehend and transmit the teachings of Scripture and the apostolic faith.[7]

In addition, Baptists have made significant contributions to the rich tradition of Christian theology based on our radical commitment to the sole authority of Scripture and to the Lordship of Christ over every individual soul, as well as our distinct positions on believers' baptism, a regenerate church, local church autonomy, and religious liberty. These theological commitments provide Baptists with a voice within the great tradition, often diverging from other traditions that emerged from the European Reformations. In other words, Baptists possess a theological voice that is distinctly Baptist in areas of theology beyond ecclesiology. However, it is worth noting that believers' baptism, the cornerstone of Baptist identity, sheds light on the particular perspective that encapsulates the essence of Baptist theology, identity, and practice. As Stephen Holmes suggests, this doctrine generates Baptist theology.[8] His observation is the case because baptism shapes Baptist churches around the core reality of Baptist faith: confessing Jesus as Lord. When engaging in the task of dogmatics, a covenantal community of faith embracing believer's baptism will situate and express Christology or trinitarian theology in unique ways, while also affirming the orthodox faith.

---

[7] See Christopher Hanna, *Retrieval for the Sake of Renewal*; David Rathel, "John Gill and The Rule of Faith: A Case Study in the Baptist Retrieval," *Southeastern Theological Review* 14 (2023): 55–72; Malcolm B. Yarnell III, "The Free Church Form of Dogmatics: Covenant and Conscience under Christ," *Southeastern Theological Review* 14 (2023): 115–129; Christine E. Thornton, "The Possibility of Baptismal Baptist Theology: Retrieving Irenaeus for Contemporary Baptists," *Southeastern Theological Review* 14 (2023): 97–113; and Matthew Y. Emerson and R. Luke Stamps, "On Trinitarian Theological Methods," in *Trinitarian Theology: Theological Models and Doctrinal Application*, ed. Keith S. Whitfield (Nashville, TN: B&H, 2019), 60–80.

[8] Stephen Holmes, "Toward a Typology of Baptist Theology," *Pacific Journal for Baptist Research* 14 (2019): 2–3.

Dogmatics serves as both an explanatory and exploratory discipline. This manifesto represents our initial endeavor to elucidate and delve into the realm of Baptist dogmatics. A revival of Baptist life and mission, both presently and in the future, necessitates a retrieval of the rich Baptist theological heritage.[9] Today's Baptists are the result of centuries of Baptist faith and practice. Understanding and exploring that tradition will enable us to confess our faith more faithfully in the present and future. Likewise, reclaiming the apostolic faith as it has been lived and proclaimed in other times, places, and traditions will further deepen our own Baptist mission.

## The Method, End, and Terrain of Baptist Dogmatics

Defining Baptist Dogmatics necessitates a clear understanding of both the discipline of dogmatics within systematic theology and the unique perspective that emerges when approaching it from a Baptist standpoint. In the following two sections, we articulate the nature of dogmatics as a systematic theological discipline and highlight the specific Baptist perspective that informs its exploration.

### Working Conception of Dogmatics

Following David Yeago's "The New Testament and the Nicene Dogma," we speak of dogmatics as a biblical discipline rooted in the biblical gospel that employs appropriate conceptual terms to make accurate judgments about patterns of biblical language.[10] In dogmatics, Scripture serves as the primary locus for the revelation of the triune God in the person of Jesus Christ the Son, through the power of the Holy Spirit. This ontological

---

[9] Throughout this document, we cite historical Baptist documents to demonstrate theological continuity between the touchstones of this manifesto and what Baptists have confessed since the earliest days of the Baptist movement.

[10] David Yeago, "The New Testament and the Nicene Dogma," *Pro Ecclesia* 3, no. 2 (1994): 152–64.

principle recognizes that the Scriptures are intended to instruct the church within its specific context. Reading the Scriptures theologically involves recognizing the theological unity of the text, the interconnectedness of theological concepts and categories within the text, and the epistemological purpose of the text. The Scriptures constitute the theological foundation and primary source of knowledge for dogmatics.

In addition to Yeago's perspective, we also acknowledge that dogmatics is an ecclesial discipline since it seeks to explicate the content of the church's confession. Jaroslav Pelikan's description of the church's theology says it well; it is what the church "believes, teaches, and confesses as it prays and suffers, serves and obeys, celebrates and awaits the coming of the Kingdom of God."[11] Dogmatics is not speculative theology, nor is it a mere cataloging and categorizing of biblical teachings on theological questions. Rather, it entails the church's engagement with Scripture as a confessing and praying community of God's people. Drawing on the theological history of the church's witness to God's work in Jesus Christ through the Holy Spirit, dogmatics seeks to understand and articulate what the church believes, confesses, and proclaims in its worship and preaching. While dogmatics explains and summarizes the overarching pattern of Scripture as a theological unity, it also aims to proclaim what the church has believed and ought to believe to remain faithful to the apostolic faith. Dogmatics employs theological terminology that conveys the church's understanding of Scripture. It does not replace the Scriptures themselves as divine revelation. Whether viewed as a subset of systematic theology or as a distinct discipline, dogmatics elucidates the faith confessed by the believing community of God's people. It is not simply systematic theology practiced within the church but rather a faithful rehearsal of the church's reading of Scripture.

The task of dogmatics extends beyond a mere restatement of biblical language or the church's confession and teaching. It also serves as a

---

[11] Jaroslav Pelikan, *Development of Christian Doctrine: Some Historical Prolegomena* (New Haven: CT: Yale University Press, 1969), 143.

guide for Christians, explaining and exploring the profound riches of the gospel and how it should shape both our personal and corporate lives. In this sense, dogmatics is a theological discipline that utilizes theological vocabulary to explain and communicate the patterns of biblical language. This theological language must accurately convey the comprehensive pattern of Scripture, read in its theological unity. The goal is to move beyond the terminology of the Bible and express the deposit of faith that the Bible conveys. Dogmatics requires an explanation of the scriptural faith and a summary of that faith using terms that are both meaningful and effective in conveying its message to the listeners. These terms can be found in the church's confessions, creeds, prayers, and sermons. Dogmatics is a coherent retelling of Scripture infused with a theo-logic, a concern for both the implicit and explicit knowledge of God derived from his self-revelation.[12]

Theology proper pertains to language about God in his eternal being. Through his saving work, God reveals himself to humanity as Father, Son, and Holy Spirit through the revelation of the Son, the Lord Jesus Christ. The theological nature of dogmatics directs our activities and governs our conclusions. Our ultimate concern lies with the God who has reconciled us to himself in Jesus Christ. It involves discussing the being of God and his actions in the world to fulfill his purposes. Therefore, dogmatics is inherently trinitarian and Christocentric. Its foundation rests on God's self-revelation and upholds the authority of that revelation. It is through the knowledge of this God that we come to know him and grow in that knowledge. Furthermore, it is this triune God of Scripture whom we confess to the world for their salvation. This theological aim dictates the method of dogmatics. Like other theological disciplines, dogmatics is explanatory, providing understanding of

---

[12] See Karl Barth's *Church Dogmatics*, I.1, sec.1 (p.16). Barth writes, "Therefore dogmatics as such does not inquire what the Apostles and Prophets have said, but what we ourselves must say 'on the basis of the Apostles and Prophets.' This task cannot be taken from us, even by the knowledge of the 'Scripture basis' which necessarily precedes it."

the Christian faith to its adherents. A proper understanding of the gospel of Jesus Christ is vital for Christian life and practice, including life within Christian community. Explaining the message of Scripture at the level of individual passages, books, and the canon is an essential part of our methodology.

Barth describes dogmatics as the church's "task of self-testing in respect to the language proper to her in speaking about God." This includes evaluating the "responsibility" of the church's language, measured by its consistency with the Word of God that it claims to proclaim.[13] Dogmatics represents the church's responsibility to explore the coherence of its faith with ideas that are appropriate to biblical teaching. It does so within its specific time and place to faithfully confess the faith within its cultural context.

When Christians "believe," they affirm the conceptual truth of a statement, but they also practice the truth through their lives before God and in relation to the rest of creation. Dogmatic theology helps establish propositional and explicit theological knowledge that is believed by Christians. Additionally, "belief" entails a relational and implicit knowledge; we participate in the truth and come to know the Father through our union with Christ by the power of the Spirit. Both the propositional and relational aspects of knowledge of God must be considered in dogmatic reflection. Therefore, it is important to recognize and acknowledge both the propositional nature of theological discourse and the narrative nature of theological discourse in dogmatics. Believers' worship and prayers are shaped by both modes, conforming to the truth conveyed in both. Dogmatics provides appropriate language to ensure that what we acknowledge corresponds to the reality of God, his work, and the world. Consequently, the pursuit of dogmatics holds the promise of enriching Christian communities in their spiritual and missional health.

---

[13] Barth, I.1, sec.7 (p.286).

## *Mapping the Terrain of* Baptist *Dogmatics*

This Baptist dogmatics initiative marks its task with four signposts: *historical, ecclesial, covenantal,* and *confessional.* The existence of numerous Baptists and Baptist congregations worldwide suggests a need for Baptist dogmatics within Baptist churches. Now, our attention shifts toward defining the Baptist descriptor to understand how dogmatics can be conceived in a Baptist mode. In truth, we seek to determine the feasibility of this project. Baptists have historically maintained a degree of independence and, as a whole, have not embraced a specific confessional tradition within their broader movement. The preamble for the Baptist Faith and Message, the statement of faith for Southern Baptist entities and ministries, acknowledges this confessional peculiarity by stating that "any group of Baptists, large or small, have the inherent right to draw up for themselves and publish to the world a confession of their faith whenever they may think it is advisable to do so." This observation leads us to question what constitutes a *Baptist* dogmatic enterprise.[14]

It is commonly believed that Baptists have primarily contributed insights on ecclesiology to the Christian tradition and have relied on non-Baptists for other elements of Christian doctrine. While this perspective may not capture the complete picture, it is fair to recognize that the theological identity of Baptists revolves around matters related to ecclesiology. The following sections will outline a Baptist dogmatics project that is primarily informed by the nature of the believers' church. The Baptist confessional tradition represents a specific expression of the apostolic faith that has benefited from four centuries of Baptist theological endeavors, including evangelical preaching, intentional local gatherings, and missional commitments. This project strives to reflect the uniqueness and value of Baptist dogmatics.

---

[14] "Baptist Faith and Message," https://bfm.sbc.net/preamble/ (accessed December 6, 2023).

Because Baptist dogmatics is theological, its aim is spiritual maturity—transformation into the image of the One who created each believer.[15] The task of Baptist dogmatics belongs to the church and takes place within the church, enabling its members to be conformed to the likeness of Christ, the hope of glory. The Baptist dogmatics outlined below also strives for comprehensiveness. The Baptist beliefs and practices that shape Baptist churches play a formative role in a Baptist dogmatics project. In other words, there is a "Baptist lens" through which church doctrine is explained and explored, inflecting all major tenets of the faith from Baptist commitments, so we can discover the coherence within those commitments for the believing church. Just as dogmatics should not be overly simplified as merely "Bible doctrine," Baptist dogmatics should not be reduced to a narrow focus on how believers' baptism impacts all aspects of doctrine or a combination of evangelical theology with believers' baptism and a believers' church. To avoid these oversimplifications, this Baptist dogmatics project will be guided by the aforementioned four "signposts" that serve as points of orientation, addressing all aspects of the Christian faith from a Baptist perspective. These signposts—*historical, ecclesial, covenantal,* and *confessional*—remind the Baptist dogmatician of the unique terrain of Baptist faith and practice. Each signpost will be shaped by the theological and confessional core of the Baptist tradition—the lordship of Christ—in corresponding, yet distinct, ways. It is from this confession that specific theological insights emerge, shaping the way dogmatics is approached from a Baptist perspective.

## 1. Historical Signpost

The method for Baptist dogmatics is guided by the *historical* signpost. The centrality of Christ in the Christian faith is based on the historical reality of the incarnation of the Son, encompassing his birth, life, death, burial, and resurrection. As a result, the historical confession of the church

---

[15] See Col 1:24–29 and 3:10–16.

echoes Thomas' declaration about Jesus, "My Lord and my God" (John 20:28). These historical realities form the foundation of the living faith that the church both explains and explores.[16] The script for the church's life and message is the Scriptures. Thus, the church has inherited from the apostles a way of reading these biblical texts as a historically situated, textual community.[17] The Scriptures proclaim, explain and interpret for us the person and work of Jesus Christ within a historical context.[18]

---

[16] "The rule of this Knowledge, Faith, and Obedience, concerning the worship and service of God, and all other Christian duties is not mans inventions, opinions, devices, lawes, constitutions, or traditions unwritten whatsoever, but onely the word of God contained in the Canonicall Scriptures (Joh. 5.39; 2 Tim. 3.15–16, 17. Col. 21.18, 23. [*sic*] Matth. 15.9)." "First London Confession 1644: Article VII," in *Baptist Confessions of Faith*, ed. Williams Lumpkin (Valley Forge, PA: Judson, 1959), 158. Parentheses around references added.

[17] "Whosoever reads and impartially considers what we have in our forgoing confession declared may readily perceive that we do not only concenter with all other true Christians on the Word of God (revealed in the Scriptures of truth) as the foundation and rule of our faith and worship, but that we have also industriously endeavoured to manifest that in the fundamental Articles of Christianity, we mind the same things—and have therefore expressed our belief in the same words that have on the like occasion been spoken by other societies of Christians before us." "An Appendix," CCEL, accessed February 12, 2024, https://www.ccel.org/creeds/bcf/bcfapdx.htm.

[18] "Although God did not speak to the Fathers in times past by his Son, as now he doth in these last Days to us, who have his Sacred Doctrine to contemplate at all times, and in all cases, yet was he made known to such as enquired after him; as it is written, 1 *Pet.* 1. 10, 11, 12. *Of which Salvation the Prophets have diligently enquired, who prophesied of the Grace that should come unto you; searching what, and what manner of time the Spirit of Christ which was in them did signifie, when it testified beforehand the Sufferings of Christ, and the Glory that should follow.* And unto *Adam* was a gracious Promise made of the overthrow of the Serpent, whose Head (or Power) God declared should be broken, *i. e.* His Victory made null and void, and the Conquest given to the Womans Seed; which is most fitly referr'd to Christ, who was manifested to destroy the works of the Devil. And as in the beginning of the Old World, God thus provided that Men might have hope of Salvation; so he left not himself without Witness, as *Abel, Enoch,* &c. Yea, in the very end of that World, we know *Noah* was a Preacher of Righteousness. And Christ is said to preach by his Spirit, to them. And thus

Baptist dogmatics, therefore, must operate with a sense of critical realism, recognizing that to truly know the apostolic faith, ongoing dialogue and conversation with those who have received, confessed, and continue to explore that faith is necessary. The deposit of faith is not merely a set of objects to be known and studied; it is the ongoing truth of God's work in Christ and the Spirit to bring about the great mystery: "Christ in you, the hope of glory" (Col 1:27).

Baptist dogmatics involves hearing from, living within, and passing on the Deposit of Faith that Jesus entrusted to the apostles and that the apostles conveyed to the Spirit-filled community of those who confessed (and continue to confess) Jesus as the Christ of the Hebrew Bible.[19] Luke 24:19–27 depicts two disciples recounting the "things" that had taken place around them and their incomplete understanding of the significance of those events. Jesus entrusts them with faithfully explaining those "things" and how "all the Scriptures" point to him. In another instance, in Luke 24:44–48, Christ provides a summary of the faith recorded in "the Scriptures" and gives the content of the apostolic witness. Verse 49 indicates that the promised Spirit will empower them for the dogmatic task ahead. Enabled by the Spirit, the apostles and early believers who followed them proclaimed Christ according to the Scriptures, enabling people from every nation to come to a true knowledge of their Creator.[20] The Christian faith is firmly rooted in the historical reality of God's work in Christ, reconciling the world to himself from creation to re-creation. The apostolic witness to Jesus Christ

---

was the *Gospel preached to them that are Dead, that they might be judged according to Men in the Flesh but live according to God in the Spirit.*" Thomas Grantham, *Christismus Primitivus* (London: Printed for Francis Smith, 1678), 57. Available on the Internet Archive at archive.org.

[19] Rom 1:1–6 and 16:25–27; 1 Cor 15:1–4; 2 Tim 1:11–14 and 3:14–17; 1 Pet 1:10–12.

[20] This universal knowledge of God is a promised component of the new covenant (Jeremiah 31) and is assured by the Spirit's presence (Ezekiel 36), as seen in the narratives of the book of Acts.

affirms his person and work, as promised in the Hebrew Scriptures and fulfilled in their own time—beginning with his virgin birth, continuing with his obedient life, culminating in his atoning death on the cross, followed by his burial, resurrection, and exaltation. The gospel of Jesus Christ is deeply rooted in God's activity among the Israelites, delivering them from Egypt and promising them a king with dominion over heaven and earth (Acts 7:2–53). Jesus accomplishes this work within a specific historical context (Acts 4:1–22).

Baptist dogmatics is a method of theologizing that recognizes the voice of Baptist Christians and Baptist theology without succumbing to sectarianism. Engaging in theology within the great tradition of Christians throughout time and space does not diminish the specific appropriation of the one Lord, one Faith, and one Baptism within a participatory Christian tradition.[21] The *historical* signpost is essential for Baptist dogmatics because it emphasizes that theology draws from the great tradition while locating the ultimate source of theology in the Scriptures. Engaging with Scripture is vital, but it should be done in ongoing conversation with the church. The concept of the great apostolic tradition—a faith in the Lord Jesus Christ according to the Scriptures, fully contained in the New Testament and expressed in our baptismal formula—finds expression in the life and worship of the church.

As Baptists, we navigate the Strait of Messina. On one side of the bank lies the doctrine of liberty of conscience, which is the theological affirmation that every person is accountable to God alone. At its core, this doctrine rests on the confession that Christ alone is the Lord of the human soul. This commitment manifests in a devotion to the authority of Scripture and a reliance on the guidance of the Holy Spirit in

---

[21] "The supreme judge, by which all controversies of religion are to be determined, and all decrees of councils, options of ancient writers, doctrines of men, and private, spirits, are to be examined, and in whose sentence we are to rest, can be no other but the Holy Scripture delivered by the Spirit, into which Scripture so delivered, out faith is finally resolved." 1689 London Baptist Confession of Faith, 1.10, https://reformedstandards.com/second-london/1689-confession.html.

interpreting the biblical text. However, we must avoid falling into the trap of relying solely on soul competency. On the other side of the bank lies a theological approach more aligned with Christian traditions where tradition serves as a complementary or supplementary source of truth.

We seek a dogmatic method in which Baptists participate within the great tradition and confess the faith of the great tradition in a manner that is distinctly, though not necessarily uniquely, Baptist in its approach and explanation. As recipients of the apostolic faith, we participate in historically defined contexts and communities. Therefore, we must listen to the voices of those who have come before us while engaging with Scripture in our own historical context, faithfully confessing the one apostolic faith. Creeds, confessions of faith, and other recognized documents articulating the apostolic faith serve as valuable guides for understanding the gospel found in the Bible. Recognizing the faithfulness of creeds and confessions of the Christian faith, especially those widely recognized by Christians, is a valid commitment for Baptists.[22] In fact, failing to listen to these voices poses a significant threat to the task of theology.

Confessing the apostolic faith alongside Christians from centuries past as Baptist Christians allows us to join in the universal confession that Jesus is Lord, alongside the faithful chorus of witnesses to the one gospel of Jesus Christ. Various Baptist confessions of faith are also crucial to understanding the faith that Baptists have practiced and proclaimed. For Baptist dogmatics, these historical documents are not merely explorations of "what other people believed"; they represent proper ways to confess the "Faith once for all delivered to the saints" within a specific historical context (Jude 3).[23] Creeds and confessions serve to guide the con-

---

[22] *The Orthodox Creed*, see http://baptiststudiesonline.com/wp-content/uploads/2007/02/orthodox-creed.pdf, accessed July 10, 2023, 1–2.

[23] "The truly Ancient and Apostolical Faith, that was on[c]e deliver[ed] unt[o] the Saints, by your Lord Jesus Christ, and miraculously confirmed unto us, by Signs and Wonders and divers Gifts of the Holy Ghost, according to the good pleasure of Almighty God. Which said Faith, and Practice, recorded in the only Oracles of Truth, and miraculously preserved from Age to Age, even in

temporary scriptural community by demonstrating how prior Christian communities read and received the biblical faith. Instead of viewing these documents as artifacts that determine the church's interpretation of Scripture, Baptist dogmaticians receive them as faithful engagements with Scripture from the perspective of the gospel of Jesus Christ, serving as guides for faithful scriptural engagement.

Embracing a robust, historically oriented dogmatic theology raises questions of authority. Baptist dogmatics locates authority in the text of Scripture, not solely in the church or its interpretation of Scripture. This poses a challenge for Baptist dogmaticians, as it requires avoiding an overreliance on soul competency. Baptist dogmatics navigates the Strait of Messina, steering clear of both extreme individualism and an excessive reliance on the church's authority in biblical interpretation. Rather than attempting to replicate the faith of the early church fathers or their particular modes of expression, we aim to draw from their patterns of living, speaking, understanding, and expressing that faith. We propose a retrieval not of the ancient church itself (as if that were even possible), but a retrieval of the faith that the ancient church lived. We have received this Faith from many living voices that have sought to preserve the apostolic

---

the darkest times of Popery, and Apostacy, by the infinite Wisdom, Mercy, and Goodness of God, is yet remaining, and to be continued to the end of the World; and hath been manifested in all, or most Nations for the obedience of Faith; the which Preservations of the Sacred Scriptures, or revelation of Gospel-Light therein contained, (of which this Nation hath had a grate share, especially within this last Hundred Years) is undoubtably a very great Evidence, of the Divine Verity, and Authority of the same: And the End of God in revealing this Light of the holy Scriptures, or Gospel of Christ, is that it might be read and known of all men, and its our duty to believe it, and thereby come through Faith, not only to have a saving, but a satisfactory knowledge of those foundation and fundamental Truths, which have been the same in all Generations; have been and shall be transmitted more clear from Age to Age in the times of Reformation, until that which is Perfect to come, and that which is Imperfect is done away; such addition is no Innovation, but Illustration; not a new Light, but a new Sight: The Looking-Glass slurs and cleared more or less, is the same Glass." "An Orthodox Creed: Or, A Protestant Confession of Faith Confession of Faith," 1.

faith. What we have received is not merely a set of ideas to affirm and acknowledge, but a way of theological exploration that must be undertaken afresh by the church today. Our doxological and formal language must yield to this Spirit-led theological exploration.

The universal church is the textual community produced by the canonical texts, not merely the community that produced the canon. While this holds true for the church as a whole, it is particularly relevant for Baptist churches (perhaps to a greater degree). These texts embody the authority of Christ and the message intended by the Spirit. The identity of this textual community guides Baptist dogmatics to adopt a textual hermeneutic that closely considers the biblical authors' compositional efforts.[24] The same Spirit that guided the biblical authors also empowers biblical readers to live the text as an ongoing authoritative Word. Historically, Baptists are committed to seeking the Spirit's help in interpreting the Bible. Rather than emphasizing an individual's soul competency to "search the Scriptures," a more appropriate implication of the Spirit's presence is that the life-giving Spirit connects readers to the subject matter of the text (God himself) and draws individual believers into the textual community as faithful readers, not necessarily as autonomous interpreters. The Spirit-filled believer is one who reads the Bible faithfully, recognizing Christ's authority in the biblical literature and participating in a textual community shaped by that authority.

## 2. Ecclesial Signpost

Dogmatics is a crucial task within the church. When embarking on a Baptist dogmatics project, one would expect an ecclesial focus. The *ecclesial* signpost for this project highlights a slightly different connotation than Pelikan's definition that refers to the content of the doctrine

---

[24] This hermeneutic is also confessional in that the church reads these canonical texts as a community under the texts' authority and as the direct addressees of their revelation (meaning/theological truth).

confessed by the church. The *ecclesial* signpost reminds us where Baptist dogmatics originates and that its theological discourse exists *within* as well as *for* the Baptist church. This signpost signifies that Baptist dogmatics is a theological expression specifically shaped to convey Baptist thinking and guide Baptist churches in their beliefs. It integrates biblical insights, orthodox teaching, Baptist confessions, and Baptist practices with the foundational Baptist theological impulse—the acknowledgment of Christ's lordship over every human soul—to articulate a distinctive Baptist way of expressing true Christian belief.[25]

Baptist dogmatics serves the church by informing and influencing the forms and functions of Baptist ecclesial practices and mission. It exists within the church, as Baptist dogmaticians embrace a faith that stems from their own baptism and is nurtured within local Baptist congregations where they gather to confess Christ and submit to his lordship.[26] Baptist dogmatics

---

[25] "In the execution of this power wherewith he is so I trusted, the Lord Jesus calleth out of the world unto himself, through the ministry of his Word, by his Spirit, those that are given unto him by his Father, that they may walk before him in all the ways of obedience, which he prescribeth to them in his Word. Those thus called, he commandeth to walk together in particular societies, or churches, for their mutual edification, and the due performance of that public worship, which he requireth of them in the world." "Second London Confession: Chapter 26, Article 5," 34.

[26] "Nor is this wisdom of God less, in pitching upon such a service, that as to outward appearance, hath but little beauty or excellency in it, and to place it among the beginnings of Christian religion; but rather very great, seeing by this means he makes manifest the loftyness of many hearts, calling hereby for such kind of abasement as that we find more to follow the example of the Pharisees and lawyers, *Luke* 7. 30. then follows the example of the *Publicans. verse the* 29. the former *rejected the Councel of God, being not Baptized,* the latter *justified God being Baptized.*

"And indeed, he that comes rightly to this path of Christianity, doth openly acknowledge (even in this very act) before God and man that he is a poor unclean Creature, and therefore doth wholly cast himself upon the free grace of God, for remission of his Trespasses; and though never so high, is glad to receive this low pledge of Gods mercy, at the hands of a despised Minister of Christ, and this in the ablution or washing in the River after the example of the Chamberlain, or

enriches the faith of Baptist churches that surrender wholly to the authority of Christ and grow in their relationships with him. These essential qualities form the *ecclesial* signpost for Baptist dogmatics, highlighting how Baptist churches are theological, textual, and living communities.[27]

Just as Baptist churches differ from churches of other traditions, Baptist dogmatics distinguishes itself from other dogmatic traditions. Being rooted in and for the Baptist church does not mean there is no interaction or overlap with dogmatics from other traditions, such as Roman Catholic or Reformed, or that there are not touch points ecclesial with other traditions. As we have seen in the *historic* signpost, the core of Baptist dogmatics lies in affirming orthodoxy as expressed in the ancient creeds and the authoritative biblical canon that shapes the church universal as well of ecclesial traditions. Indeed, recognizing the church as one, holy, catholic, and apostolic is a common ground for most Christian traditions.[28]

---

*Lord Treasurer* of the *Queen* of *Candice.* All which proud Flesh observing, streight through Satans Instigation, abhorreth this as a low and base performance, and though they be convinced, there is none to save them but Christ, and therefore are willing he should serve with their sins, and to be laden with their iniquities, yet will they not have him here in their Lord, or leader though himself hath gon this path before them: and exciting them after this manner. *Thus it becometh us to full fill all righteousness* Matth. 3. 15." Grantham, *Christismus Primitivus,* 23–24.

[27] "General councils, or Assemblies, consisting of Bishops, Elders, and Brethren, of the several Churches of Christ, and being legally convened, and meet together out of all the Churches; and have lawful right and suffrage in the General Meetings; or Assembly, to act in the Name of Christ; It being of Divine Authority, and is the best means under Heaven to preserver Unity, to prevent Heresie, and Superintendency among, or in any Congregation whatsoever within its own Limits, or Jurisdiction. And to such a Meeting, or Assembly, Appeals ought to be made, in case any Injustice be done, or Heresie, and Schism countenanced, in any particular Congregation of Christ; and the Decisive Voice in such General Assemblies is the Major part, and such General Assemblies have lawful power to Hear, and Determine, as also to Excommunicate." "An Orthodox Creed: Article XXXIX," 38.

[28] "There is one holy Catholick Church, consisting of, or made up of the whole number of the Elect; that have been, are, or shall be, gathered, in one Body under Christ, the only Head thereof: Which Church is gathered by Special

All Christian traditions acknowledge that theology for the church entails certain commitments to the Trinity, Christology, pneumatology, and mission. It is through the common confession of these theological truths that the church community, both global and local, is formed. Each of these, however, have particular Baptist modes of expression. Baptist ecclesiology emphasizes the autonomy of the local church on both Christological and pneumatological grounds. Christ is the head, and the only head, of the church, and therefore he is the sole head of any particular congregation. Additionally, each individual believer is equally indwelt by Christ's Holy Spirit and is thus competent to participate in the decision-making process of a local congregation under the authority of Christ as expressed in his rightly interpreted Word. And each local congregation is responsible for its mission to the world around it, accomplished in part by its faithful expression and teaching of sound theology. Baptist theology in an eccesial mode thus recognizes within the Christian tradition the Christological, pneumatological, and missional character of theology while emphasizing those realities at the level of the local congregation composed only of properly baptized believers.

Baptists share a commitment with the rest of the Christian tradition to the doxological character of theology, where the proper worship

---

Grace, and the Powerful and Internal Work of the Spirit; and are effectually united unto Christ their Head, and can never fall away" (Article XXIX).

"Nevertheless, we believe the Visible Church of Christ on Earth, is made up of several distinct Congregations, which make up that one Catholick church, or Mystical Body of Christ. And the Marks by which She is known to be the true Spouse of Christ, are these, viz. Where the Word of God is rightly Preached, and the Sacraments truly Administred, according to Christ's Institution, and the Practice of the Primitive Church; . . . And although there may be many Errors in such a Visible Church, or Congregations, they being not Infallible, yet those Errors being not Fundamental, and the Church in the major, or Governing part, being not Guilty, she is not thereby unchurched; nevertheless She ought to detect those Errors, and to Reform, according to God's holy Word, and from such Visible Church, or Congregations, no Man ought by any pretence whatever, schismatically to separate" (Arielle XXX). "An Orthodox Creed: Article XXIX and XXX," 28–29.

of the Triune God is central.[29] With respect to the doxological character
of theology, we should briefly acknowledge, however, the shift from a
more traditional liturgy of Word and sacrament, as expressed in the broad
history of the Christian tradition, to the "frontier liturgy" of "Song and
Sermon" prompted by the expansion of Christianity into the American
West and by nineteenth century revivalism. This shift in Baptist liturgy
is no doubt related to particular features of Baptist theology.[30] Regarding
theology's doxological function, we note the robust history of Baptist
hymnody. Other traditions have, of course, contributed to the hymnody
of the entire church, but certain Baptists have made an outsized contribution. Hymn writers like Fanny Crosby, for instance, exhibit a particularly Baptist outlook, namely one that is evangelistically and missionally
oriented. Baptists emphasize not only the act of confessing faith but also
the content and context of that faith.[31] They regularly affirm that a pro-

---

[29] "And thus by a parity of the Cases of Preaching and Praying, with that
of Singing in the Christian Church, together with a parity of the Reasons
going along therewith; It's evident, that he only hath a Doctrine, hath a Prayer,
hath a Psalm, fit for publick use in the Church of Christ, who understands the
Scriptures, and the Nature of these Services respectively, and gifted by God's
holy Spirit to exercise himself therein, after a publick manner. And hence we
fairly assume, that as he only that hath a Doctrine, or a Gift to teach, &c. ought
(in a modest way) to preach in the Church; Even so he that hath a Psalm, or Gift
to praise God in his Church, ought to sing there to edify others; For *as every man
hath received the Gift, so let him minister,* &c." Thomas Grantham, *Christismus
Primitivus,* 112.

[30] While there is much to say about this shift and what it means for Baptists
today, at the very least, we can note that a Baptist way of theologizing and practicing the faith gave rise to it. See Matthew Y. Emerson and R. Lucas Stamps,
"Liturgy for Low-Church Baptists," *Criswell Theological Review* 14, no. 2 (2017):
71–88.

[31] Baptist theology has particular expressions that indicate its teleologi-
cal character. While all traditions have used catechesis in one form or another,
Baptists have adapted the practice to their own polity and confessional outlook.
Rather than, for instance, having common catechisms used across an individual
denomination (e.g. the Westminster Catechism and Heidelberg Catechism for
Presbyterians), many individual Baptists and individual Baptist congregations

fession of faith in the Father, Son, and Spirit leads to a ministry of con-textualized disciple-making, fulfilling the Great Commission.

However, the theological nature of the Baptist ecclesial community anticipates at least three key points. First, Baptist churches, as theological communities, may not always express what is uniquely Baptist, but they express what is distinctively Baptist—bearing the distinguishing Baptist characteristics. In other words, Baptist dogmatics does not aim to highlight what makes Baptist theology unique, but rather how Baptist theology is exercised in a way that is fitting to its Baptist context.[32] Second, these Baptist distinctions are mostly differences in degree rather than kind. For example, key theological commitments that shape Baptist dogmatics within a Baptist ecclesial framework include Christology and pneumatology. Christ is the head and authority of each local church, and the Spirit indwells the community when it gathers, as each believer is indwelt by the Spirit. These understandings shape the Baptist doctrine of the priesthood of all believers and informs the communal life of the local church, where Spirit-indwelled members are competent in decision-making due to the Spirit's indwelling and Christ's authority.[33]

----

have written and published their own catechisms (e.g. Keach's catechism). These can be and are shared with other local congregations, but the point is that even the general practice of catechesis is translated into a congregational expression in Baptist theology.

[32] See "The Second London Confession: Appendix 1: On Baptism" for an example, 58–68.

[33] "Now when Christ thus ascended, he received Gifts for Men, and sent down the Gifts which he received, to continue in the Church (being such as fit Men for the Work of the Ministry, *Ephes.* 4.) to the end of the World, or till the perfecting of the Saints, (which Gifts are mistaken by some for Christ himself); nay, worse than this, a false Gift, or a confident perswasion of anything, is too commonly thought, by deceived Souls, to be the Voice of Christ, whom they suppose dwelleth in them. This is doubtless a part of the fulfilling of Christ's Prediction, that many false Christs shall arise and deceive many. Remember that *Peter,* that had received largely of Christs Spiritual Gifts, yet teacheth no such thing to be the Ascension of Christ; as the receiving of Gifts and Graces, to give a raisedness of Soul to the Saints, which it may well be feared many suppose

Therefore, these theological affirmations are often connected to ecclesial commitments such as congregationalism. Third, in a Baptist theological community (the church), these preceding theological commitments give rise to a missional purpose. Thus, local Baptist churches, theologically constituted, are on a mission guided by their theology and connected with their theological community.[34] Thus, ecclesiology is not only about polity; it is more fundamentally about ontology. These two are not mutually exclusive, of course, since a right understanding of ecclesiological ontology will lead to proper polity.[35]

Baptist pastors and theologians often emphasize a set of theological commitments that distinguish Baptist church ontology. Believers' baptism, understood as an act of dying with and rising with Christ and as an act of covenanting with other believers as a church, are foundational in Baptist communities. These ecclesial practices give rise to a central pairing that defines Baptist ecclesiological identity: regenerate church membership and congregationalism.[36] These two emphases capture key biblical metaphors for the church. The metaphor of the body (1 Corinthians 12), with its various members, portrays a congregational whole composed of individual parts. The metaphor of a building (1 Pet 2), built with living stones (individual believers) upon the foundation stone (Christ), represents regenerate church membership. This defining commitment to regenerate church membership typically sets Baptists apart from other

---

to have, which are really ignorant of them. However these Gifts are precious, but Christ the Giver, far more precious; who dwelleth in that Light whom no Man in his mortal state hath seen, nor can approach unto." Thomas, *Christismus Primitivus*, 72–73.

[34] See D. Scott Hildreth, *Together on God's Mission* (Nashville: B&H Academic, 2018) for more on the historical and theological support for cooperative missions among Baptists.

[35] See, for instance, Matthew Bingham, *Orthodox Radicals: Baptist Identity in the English Revolution* (Oxford: Oxford University Press, 2019).

[36] At some level, the "Baptist" part of the Baptist dogmatics project as a consideration of these blended commitments produces a uniquely Baptist dogmatic.

traditions. Congregationalism, as a logical consequence of regenerate church membership, affirms the participation of each member in the life of the church, including its theological task.

A significant question related to the *ecclesial* signpost revolves around different understandings of Baptist ontology, which is to establish that Baptists' ways of being are conditioned by their personal confession to lordship of Christ, conversion by God's saving power in the gospel, testimony of God's redeeming grace, and participation in the life of Christ and the church through baptism.[37] The teachings and practices specific to Baptist ecclesiology are shaped by this ontological understanding. Throughout history, Baptists have regularly revisited core considerations such as the ways in which Christ's lordship entails believers' baptism, regenerate church membership, congregationalism, personal discipleship,

---

[37] "For the definition of the Christian Church, we shall not much vary from that which hath therein been done by the ancient or modern Writers. *Lactantius* gives this brief definition of the Church, *Sola Catholica Ecclesia est,* &c. *It is only the Catholick Church which hath the true worship and service of God.* Our modern Protestants usually define the Church thus, *Where the Word of God is sincerely taught, and the Sacraments rightly administred, there is the true Church.* Dr. *Wollebius* gives it thus, *The visible Church is a visible society of Men, called to the state of Grace, by the Word and Sacraments.*

"Again, The definition of Christ's Church may be taken out of the word, or *Kahal, Ecclesia, evocare,* to call, or *Evocatus per Evangelium,* to call, or called out by the Gospel, and then the Church is defin'd, *A company of Men called out of the World, by the voice or Doctrine of Christ, to worship one true God according to his will.* But if the definition be made of the thing it self according to the largest consideration, then it may be this, *The whole number of the saved ones, from the beginning of the World to the end thereof.* This is that Body whereof Christ is said to be the Saviour, *Eph.* 5. 23. called the *general Assembly or Church of the first-born who are written in Heaven,* which in respect of all the individuals is not known in this World by Men, *God only knowing who are his;* yet thus much we may say in general, that such as only fell in *Adam,* and have no personal guilt of their own, together with all such in every Age and Nation as fear the God of Heaven, and work Righteousness, are rationally supposed to be within the verge of this vast Body, and may by the Grace of God be Heirs of Salvation." Thomas Grantham, *Christismus Primitivus,* 2–3.

and the role of scriptural authority. These considerations form the foundation for understanding Baptist identity, and Baptist dogmatics must engage and inform these core discussions. The *ecclesial* signpost serves to guide the task of Baptist dogmatics, anchoring it in these defining features of the Baptist way. In Baptist dogmatics, the ontology of the church as a believing and submitted community places Christ's lordship at the forefront. The lordship of Christ is expressed through Baptist churches constantly returning to Scripture, which defines their existence and even well-being. Historically, Baptists have demonstrated a willingness to revise their beliefs and practices in light of the Word. Consequently, being a submitted disciple means being a faithful reader of the Scriptures in covenant with other faithful readers.[38]

Both Baptist dogmatics and Baptist churches benefit from being more self-aware of their identity as a community founded and shaped by the reading and teaching of the Word. A theology for, in, and from the church should be grounded in the text of Scripture, preached, interpreted, and applied within the church. Recognizing the Word as rightly preached prompts a living faith or embodied theology within the life of the church. This embodied theology, rooted in the Word, lies at the heart of Baptist dogmatics, as the proclaimed Word of Christ dwells richly within the people of God. Baptist dogmatics is Christological and textual, affirming that "Christ's rule over theology" comes through His Word as rightly preached, interpreted, understood, and applied in the local church.

The reading of Scripture shapes the essential life of the text community—the church. The church becomes a worshipping community engaged in its present culture in accordance with the script of the biblical text and embodied theology. This vision necessitates a high view of Scripture's authority and a commitment to reading it with trained eyes and softened hearts. It results in a localized community, in the local church, in Baptist churches as living communities. As emissaries

---

[38] See Matt 13:52. See also 2 Pet 3:1–2.

of the message of reconciliation, Baptist churches live out the scriptural life by engaging in congregational practices that align with their theology and mission. Throughout the Baptist tradition, one crucial aspect of the congregation's participation in the theological task, which is also integral to living out the scriptural life, is congregational singing. The embodied theology found in songs, hymns, and spiritual songs allows all members to proclaim scriptural truths and reflect on the testimonies of other believers striving to live in submission to Christ. Musical reflections often revolve around central communal practices such as baptism, communion, and the preached Word. The goal of these communal theological recitations is the sanctification of believers, their formation into the image of Christ, and the rich dwelling of the word of Christ in the corporate life of the church.[39] Baptist dogmatics, when firmly rooted in the biblical text, enhances the church's missional purpose by considering the contemporary church as a text community that recognizes the vibrancy and relevance of the Bible in the present culture. The living community of the church is where the Bible comes to bear on culture. Even more significantly, the Bible breathes life into the church through it the church's head, Jesus Christ.

Baptist dogmatics encourages a life in the Spirit. Dogmatic conversations foster the maturity of believers. As noted in Col 1:24, Paul labored for the sake of Christ's "body, that is, the church," and his ministry included teaching with wisdom to present everyone mature in Christ. This body, which Paul teaches, refers to the community of faith now living by the power of the Spirit. Dogmatics describes and prescribes the life of faith for the believing community. In Ephesians 4, Paul mentions several marks of this living community of faith. They pursue the unity of faith and knowledge of the Son of God, indicating the necessary doctrinal content for growing into maturity. This growth not only leads to maturity but also draws believers closer to Christ, who is the head. These new believers are new creations, living a new life as members of

---

[39] Col 3:16.

one another. Baptist dogmatics aims to build up the body of Christ by fostering a living community—the church.

The *ecclesial* signpost positions Baptist dogmatics within the theological, textual, and living communities of Baptist churches. In other words, Baptist churches are reading communities that embody the biblical text in their daily lives and corporate confessions. Negatively, resistance to being guided by and conformed to the biblical text, both in life and doctrine, diminishes a church's "Baptist" nature and may even diminish its status as a "church."

## 3. Covenantal Signpost

The third signpost of Baptist dogmatics is *covenantal*, which frames the theological identity of Baptists. Baptist churches are covenanted bodies comprising individuals saved by God's covenant love and integrated into his covenantal plan for all people. The concept and practice of covenant have a profound impact on the shape, scope, and value of Baptist dogmatics. A survey of historical Baptist dogmatics reveals its covenantal nature, with three interrelated concepts of covenant forming the core contours of Baptist theology: covenant theology, covenant soteriology, and covenant ecclesiology.[40]

Historically, the earliest shape of Baptist dogmatics centered around two facets of covenantal life. John Smyth, the first Baptist theologian and pastor, identified them as "respecting God and the faithful" and "respecting the faithful mutually."[41] These two parts of the covenant, the vertical and horizontal dimensions, were also referred to as the eternal "covenant

---

[40] The term "covenant theology" should not be confused with the "covenant theology" or "federal theology" system of thinking of Johannes Cocceius in Reformed thought or William Ames in English Puritanism.

[41] John Smyth, *Principles and Inferences,* 1:254; cited in Jason K. Lee, "Baptism and Covenant," in *Restoring Integrity in Baptist Churches*, ed. Thomas White, Jason G. Duesing, and Malcolm B. Yarnell III (Grand Rapids: Kregel, 2008), 127.

of grace" and the earthly "local church covenant."[42] The connection between the two was later established by John Smyth, fusing the theological covenant with the ecclesial covenant as both are applied in time. Thomas Helwys, the first Baptist pastor in England, further united the practice of believers' baptism with the realities of the covenants, shaping the identity of Baptists.[43] The shape of the covenant necessitates a connection between the doctrine of the eternal covenant (covenant theology) and the doctrine of the local church covenant (covenant ecclesiology), which is embodied in personal conversion (covenant soteriology) and water baptism.

Baptist covenant ecclesiology is based on the biblical revelation of God's covenant love (covenant theology) and the personal relationship made possible through his covenant offer (covenant soteriology). Baptist ecclesiology rests not on a person's goodwill towards others, but on God's goodwill toward humanity. The mutual love displayed within the covenantal expression of a local church starts with God's revelation of his covenantal action towards his creation. This covenantal work becomes an individual experience when someone hears the promise of the gospel (God's covenant to save those who believe in Christ) and submits to Christ as Lord. Through the indwelling of the Spirit, the new believer is united with Christ and other believers in one body. The local church covenant then becomes the external confession of this "unity of the Spirit in the bond of peace," just as water baptism becomes the external confession of the internal baptism of the Spirit. Baptist dogmatics begins with the Triune God, who reveals himself through his Word and Spirit.

---

[42] Paul S. Fiddes, *Tracks and Traces: Baptist Identity in Church and Theology*, Studies in Baptist History and Thought (Carlisle: Paternoster Press, 2003), 22.

[43] Paul Fiddes, "Covenant and the Inheritance of Separatism," in Paul Fiddes, ed., *The Fourth Strand of the Reformation: The Covenant Ecclesiology of Anabaptists, English Separatists, and Early General Baptists* (Oxford: Centre for Baptist History and Heritage, 2018), 78. Fiddes follows B.R. White in the assertion about Browne developing the idea of the local church covenant for English Separatism.

his self-revelation sets the scope of Baptist dogmatics. Baptists have utilized the three covenantal concepts (theology, soteriology, ecclesiology)
to understand, explain, and participate in God's revelation.[44]

---

[44] "The worthy Receiver of the Lords Supper, does not only put away sin by
the power of Christ, but he must approach nigh to God with the whole heart *in
this* service. *My Son give me thy Heart, and let thine eyes observe my ways*, Prov. 23.
26. And again, *Lift up your heart with your hands to God in the Heavens:* Without
which hearty devotion all external services are but a mockery and not the worship of God; and the Lord detects services by the Prophet, *They sit before me as
my People, and with their Lips they shew much love, but their Hearts are far from me.*

"Some serious Christians being under a sense of their imperfections, do
greatly fear to approach the Holy Table of the Lord, because they apprehend
not themselves to be worthy: But surely such are in the most hopeful way to be
worthy Guests, and accepted of the Lord; For *to this man will I look (saith God)
to him that is poor, and of a contrite heart and trembleth at my word*, Isa. 66. 2. The
Holy Apostle saith, *We are not sufficient of our selves to think a good thought:* It was
God that counted the Apostle worthy to serve him in the Ministery, and the
humble soul he counts worthy, and will exalt him, *Luke* 14. 11. It is the hungering
soul after righteousness, that hath the promise of being filled. He therefore that
comes to this holy table without a sense of his wants, is most likely to go away
without refreshment.

Again, the worthy Receiver must come in charity. This is the bond of perfection among Christians, whose prayers are not heard, unless from *the heart they
shall forgive those that trespass against them,* Mat. 6. But in this holy ordinance,
both prayer and praises wait for God in his Churches; therefore it behoveth, that
all wrath, anger, and clamour be put away with all malice.

To discern the Lords Body is necessary in all that approach this solemn
*Manducation;* which standeth not only in making a difference between this
and our common Tables, for the refreshment of our bodies, which yet must be
done; But also First, that we believe the reality of his humanity, represented
in that holy ordinance, and that therein he did the Will of God, and by that
will, which he fulfilled, we are sanctified, as it is written, *Heb.* 10. 10. And
that God hath accepted humane nature to a state of glory, giving the earnest
thereof to us in the exaltation of Christs Body at his own right hand, being
there our High-Priest to make intercession for us; and finally to usher us into
the holy places not made with hands, Eternal in the Heavens, where he is
for us entred. Secondly, that this ordinance is not a Sacrifice propitiatory, but
commemorative only of that one only sacrifice which takes away sin; *Do this in
remembrance of me,* saith Christ, which is needless if he were there corporally
present, as some do vainly pretend, *For if he were on earth, he should not be a*

*Covenant theology* has been approached in various ways within Baptist dogmatics. Some Baptists have expressed the grand purposes of God through classically Reformed covenant theology, utilizing a "covenant of works" and "covenant of grace" framework.[45] Others have distinguished among the biblical covenants that appear in the Scriptures, associating baptism and communion with the new covenant as distinct from circumcision and the sacrificial system of the Abrahamic and Mosaic covenants.[46] By understanding the entire biblical revelation through a theological covenantal framework, Baptist dogmatics pivots to a personal, saving covenantal relationship for each believer.

*Covenant soteriology* unites God with those who believe in Christ, fulfilling his promise to save those who trust in him and adopt them as his children. The covenant of adoption imagery depicts the change of status and relationship that occurs through the covenant of salvation. Covenant soteriology also necessitates a Christological core in Baptist dogmatics and implies the new life lived in relationship to Christ as Lord through the indwelling of the Spirit. The believer's water baptism visually represents the hidden baptism of the Spirit that initiates this new life. The two-testament revelation of God (covenant theology) proclaimed in the gospel offer (covenant soteriology) establishes the opportunity for a relationship with the triune God.

---

*Priest, Heb.* 8. 4. Thirdly, the Body of Christ mystical is here to be discerned, as this is the evidence of that unity between the *Head* and the *Members, We being many, are one Body and one Bread, for we are all Partakers of that one Bread:* By Faith we herein eat the Flesh of the Son of God, and drink his Blood; and without this Faith it is impossible herein to please God. Rightly therefore it is said by Mr. *Perkins, Without Faith the Sacraments profit nothing.*" Grantham, *Christismus Primitivus,* 92–93.

[45] Some Baptist covenant theologians made their own contribution to the covenant theology discussions but still relied on the Reformed "covenant of works" and "covenant of grace" schema. See Thomas Grantham's *Infants Advocate,* 19–20, and *Truth and Peace,* 2–8, as an example.

[46] See John Smyth's *Character of the Beast* in W. T. Whitley, *The Works of John Smyth,* 605–610.

*Covenant ecclesiology* embodies the call for believers to live out this new life in unified relationships with other believers as a church. The covenant to live out the gospel's new life is paired with a covenant to exist in reconciled relationships with other believers within the church. The Christological emphasis of covenant theology and covenant soteriology extends to the body life of the local church, where Christ is the head. The mutual submission of believers to one another is a result of their submission to Christ as Lord.[47]

Within this covenantal framework, Baptist dogmatics finds its value not as an end, but as integral to the process of Christian maturity. Baptist dogmatics fuels the discipleship initiative of the covenantal life of Baptist churches. It is participatory, drawing on the shared faith of the covenanted congregation. The unity of the Spirit in the bond of peace is made evident in the church's covenantal life. For example, the Christian practice of forgiving others reflects the covenant theme of forgiveness in Christ. Displaying God's gracious purposes (covenant theology) in Christ, made available to individual believers (covenant soteriology), fosters reconciled relationships (covenant ecclesiology). Forgiveness is a manifestation of the theology of Christ's rule in the lives and churches of believers, and it is one of the blessings of covenantal dogmatics.

Baptist dogmatics informs and inspires the Baptist practice of covenant, often reflected in the wording of historical Baptist church covenants. Early Baptist covenants indicate that the content and practice of covenant making were derived from their reading of the Scriptures. The Great Ellingham Baptist Church (1699) wrote: "We likewise find in Holy Writ, that an explicit covenanting with, and giving up ourselves to the Lord and one another, is the formal cause of particular visible gospel church."[48] Similarly, the Baptist church in Horse Fair, Stony Stratford,

---

[47] Ephesians 4:15–16 and 1 Corinthians 12.

[48] Timothy George and Denise George, eds., *Baptist Confessions, Covenants, and Catechisms* (Nashville: B&H Academic, 1996), 181.

Bucks, England (1790) declared that they embraced "the Word of God as our only guide in matters of religion and acknowledge no other authority whatever as binding upon the conscience." They continued by stating, "On looking into the sacred Scripture, we find it was common in the first ages of Christianity for such as professed repentance towards God and faith in our Lord Jesus Christ, voluntarily to unite together in Christian societies called in the New Testament, churches."[49] These covenants affirm the authority of God's Word alongside other theological commitments as essential parts of covenant making. The Kiokee Baptist Church (in 1771, with revisions in 1826) wrote:

> According to God's appointment in His Word, we do hereby in His name and strength covenant and promise to keep up and defend all the articles of faith, according to God's Word, such as the great doctrine of election, effectual calling, particular redemption, justification by the imputed righteousness of Christ alone, sanctification by the spirit of God, believers' baptism by immersion, the saints' absolute final perseverance in grace, the resurrection of the dead, future rewards and punishments, etc., all according to Scripture which we take as the rule of our faith and practice, with some other doctrines herein not mentioned.[50]

The relationship between Baptist dogmatics and church covenants is reciprocal, as Baptists commit to covenant practices based on their dogmatics drawn from the biblical text and biblical authority. Simultaneously, the covenants prescribe an ongoing role for biblical dogmatics in congregational life. The Meherrin Baptist church (1779) added the following to their church covenant:

> [A]s we believe the Scriptures of the Old and New Testament is the only standard of truth by which the church is to conduct

---

[49] George and George, 187.
[50] George and George, 205.

herself (whatever respect she may have to good human composition) for that we believe the church of Christ will now grow
and make more discovery of light into the glorious treasure
of God's Word while she continues here militant state, and so
consequently it would be presumption before God and forming chains to fetter our consciences to bind ourselves unalter-
ably and unchangeably to any set of principles whatever, except
what is written and contained in the glorious unchangeable
Word of God.[51]

The trajectory of the dogmatic enterprise is informed by the authoritative
Scriptures and accomplished in the covenant relationships of the church.
This mutuality between dogmatics and the church context is in keeping
with the Baptist practice of dogmatics in deference to the Scriptures and
for the health of the church.

Addressing contemporary challenges, Baptist dogmatics faces
an anthropological challenge. Human beings are interconnected as
descendants of the single human couple God created. Baptist dogmatics explores how God's love for all people determines how we should
love, care for, and minister to one another.[52] Through the incarnation
of God the Son, who took on full humanity to redeem humanity, we
see the basis for our love and ministry towards others. His divine nature
and redemptive work declare him as Lord over all things, and one day
all human suffering will be subjected and removed under his reign.[53]
Baptist dogmatics recognizes God's work for humanity and his ongoing
work among human beings as relevant to our present challenges and
as the foundation of our future hope. It entails a calling from the Lord
Jesus Christ to be transformed by him and conformed to his image as
the head of his people.

---

[51] George and George, 211.
[52] See Col 3:14–17.
[53] See 1 Cor 15:20–28.

## 4. Confessional Signpost

The *confessional* signpost, our final marker, orients us to the practice of Baptist dogmatics. Dogmatics finds its expression not merely in describing the Christian faith, but also in the church confessing the gospel of Jesus Christ to one another and to the world. The discipline explicates the confession of a particular tradition to help that tradition continue to faithfully confess the faith. The confessional centrality to the task of dogmatics presumes the communicative purpose for theological language and the formative, Spirit-empowered action of speaking the Word to one another. Thus, the practice of this discipline is to confess the faith.

God reveals himself to us through his Word and in the power of his Spirit. We respond to the knowledge of him with our word by confessing Christ—who is himself the Word of God. Our confessional response is first, doxological; second, catechetical; and third, missional. The act of confessing is articulate, interpersonal, and empowered by God. Confessional dogmatics maintains the significance of articulate, true statements in theology and places those statements within their proper ecclesial locus and telos. As a result, this sense of confession introduces an experiential, interpersonal component to theological verbiage. When we speak our confession to one another, our words not only declare what is true, but through them, God works to grow our knowledge of him and form us into the image of the Son. God enlivens our communal confession by his personal presence through our speech.

The term "confessional" can be understood in multiple senses, two of which are pertinent to our purposes. In the first sense, confessional dogmatic theology can be defined as that which adheres to a binding document of Christian conviction or belief.[54] In this sense, confessional theology is synonymous with creedal theology. In the creedal model,

---

[54] For example, John Webster argues that in its propositional form "a creed or confessional formula is a public and binding indication of the gospel set before us in the scriptural witness." John Webster, *Confessing God: Essays in Christian Dogmatics II* (London, UK: T&T Clark, 2016), 73–74.

confessions of faith function with some level of authority for Christians and local churches. The idea of confessional authority external to the local church is quite common for evangelical dogmaticians functioning in other traditions and for many central to their dogmatic method.[55]

In a Baptist context, however, the authoritative sense of confessional becomes quite complex. Some Baptists reject any hint of an authoritative theological confession.[56] Other Baptists have argued for the potential to understand confessional/creedal authority on legitimate grounds while

---

[55] Michael Allen and Scott Swain provide a constructive proposal for a Reformed, biblically faithful approach to creedal authority in the *Reformed Catholicity*. See R. Michael Allen, and Scott R. Swain, *Reformed Catholicity: The Promise of Retrieval for Theology and Biblical Interpretation* (Grand Rapids, MI: Baker Academic, 2015). In another text, Michael Allen, engaging Kevin Vanhoozer's dramatic-linguistic approach states, "The traditions of the church—most especially its creeds and confessions—are Spirit-enabled guides to help the understudies go about their dramatic callings. They are binding guides: ecclesial expectations for worship and witness shaped by canonical speech of the Triune God." Michael Allen, Scott R. Swain, and Michael Allen, eds., "Knowledge of God," in *Christian Dogmatics: Reformed Theology for the Church Catholic* (Grand Rapids, MI: Baker Academic, 2016), 27–28.

[56] For example, Francis Wayland writes, "Whether an established confession of faith is desirable or not, with us it is impossible. We believe, in the fullest sense, in the independence of every individual church of Christ. We hold that each several church is a Christian society, on which is conferred by Christ the entire power of self-government. No church has any power over any other church. No minister has any authority in any church, except that which has called him to be its pastor. Every church, therefore, when it expresses its own belief, expresses the belief no other than its own members." Francis Wayland, *Notes on the Principles and Practices of Baptist Churches* (New York: Sheldon, 1867), 13–14. Wayland makes an argument for the impossibility of Baptist creedal commitments on the basis of the autonomy of the local church.

Still others have argued against Baptistic commitments to creeds on the basis of the sufficiency of Scripture. For example, in W. B. Johnson, first president of the SBC in the inaugural address stated, "We have constructed for our basis no new creed, acting in this manner upon a Baptist aversion for all creeds by the Bible." *Proceedings from the Southern Baptist Convention* (Richmond, VA: H. K. Ellyson, 1845).

seeking to maintain distinct Baptist convictions.[57] We can allow space for diversity in how we engage theological confessions within a broad view of Baptist distinctives.[58] Our proposal for a confessional Baptist dogmatic theology does not depend on the authoritative sense of "confessional," though it makes room for those who would include creeds and confessional documents. Creedal/confessional authority itself depends upon the second and primary sense of confessional. In the second sense, dogmatic confession is an act wherein the church confesses Christ to one another and to the world. Without doubt, these two senses of "confessional" overlap with one another.[59] The most significant distinguishing factor is the difference between words on a page and the Word in our mouths. While the confessional documents (words on a page) may guide the confessional practice of the church, without the church's present activity (the Word in our mouths), that creedal text remains an inert record of what Christians have confessed in the past. As a result, the church's active confession logically and historically precedes the written confessional documents, and

---

[57] Steve Harmon, Tom Nettles, and Curtis Freeman serve as 21st century examples of this argument. Harmon argues for a "magisterium-hood of all believers" through which he extends the Baptist conviction of the priesthood of all believers to create a space for some version of a magisterium. See Steven R. Harmon, *Baptist Identity and the Ecumenical Future*. Nettles also advocates for the value of confessions for Baptist discipleship and biblical interpretation. Tom J. Nettles, *Ready for Reformation: Bringing Authentic Reform to Southern Baptist Churches* (Nashville, TN: B&H, 2005), 14–15. Freeman argues that "the creeds surely are guides for reading the Scriptures with an eye to seeing how Christians have historically understood them." Curtis W. Freeman, *Contesting Catholicity*, 134. Thus, he concludes, "Because the canon of the Scripture and the creeds of the church developed together, neither can be grasped without reference to the other." Freeman, *Contesting Catholicity*, 134.

[58] Curtis Freeman provides a helpful overview of diverse, historic Baptist responses to creedal/confessional authority. See Freeman, *Contesting Catholicity*, 93–121.

[59] For example, the confessional document may serve as a guide for the act of confessing, and the confessional document is itself a record of that which has been confessed by the church.

the active register of confession is the primary sense we must consider in developing a Baptist dogmatic theology.[60]

In terms of dogmatic theology, we must consider our personal confession from within the Trinitarian, Christocentric economy of salvation, and not as outsiders to that reality. By the nature of our confession, our dogmatic theology cannot be viewed as a mere description (even if accurate and precise) of God and his work, but rather as our active participation in the reality we describe. In confessing Christ, we abide in God in the present. We do not peer into God's work in Christ according to the Scriptures as objective observers giving a neutral report of what we have observed. We participate in God's work in the world through the confession of our theology to one another and to those outside of faith in Christ.[61] In this way, our personal confession does not merely recite the words of Peter or Thomas (or Irenaeus or Athanasius) but joins them in their confession as we declare our own faith in Christ, our Lord and our God. Our confession is the articulate exhalation of the living breath of Christ in us.[62] Thus, our dogmatic language exists in the

---

[60] Webster helps articulate this idea when he writes, "The point of stressing this is to highlight how confession is act or event before it is document. Textual formulae are instruments of confession, but they do not in any way render the act of confession superfluous. This point is of considerable importance, not least because we are sometimes tempted to think that confessional formulae represent fixity, that they are a means of settling doctrinal disputes." John Webster, *Confessing God*, 69.

[61] Robert Louis Wilken notes this conviction characterized the theological practice of the early church fathers, as well. He writes, "Christian thinking is anchored in the church's life, sustained by such devotional practices as the daily recitation of the Psalms, and nurtured by the liturgy, in particular, the regular celebration of the Eucharist. Theory was not an end in itself, and concepts and abstractions were always put at the service of a deeper immersion in the *res*, the thing itself, the mystery of Christ and of the practice of the Christian life. The goal was not only understanding but love." Robert Louis Wilken, *The Spirit of Early Christian Thought: Seeking the Face of God* (New Haven, CT: Yale University Press, 2005), xviii.

[62] Here we are playing off of language from John Clifford, recorded in Freeman, *Contesting Catholicity*, 98.

context of God reconciling the world to himself. In short, the church confesses Christ, according to the Scripture, in the power of the Holy Spirit according to the Father's good purposes. Through that confession, we grow up into maturity in Christ and expand out to the coming eschatological reality of every nation, tribe, and tongue worshipping before the throne of God.

Christ reposes at the center of our confession.[63] The Scripture reveals Christ—the one through whom all things were made (John 1:3; Col 1:17) and in whom we are reconciled to God and one another (Col 1:22; Eph 2:13–14). He alone mediates between God and men (1 Tim 2:15). He died and was raised, and in him, we are raised to new life, seated with him in heavenly places (Eph 2:6). He himself is our salvation, and so it is him whom we confess. We confess Christ by the will of the Father and through the power of the Holy Spirit. In reaction to Peter's confession "You are the Messiah, the Son of the living God," Jesus exclaims, "Blessed are you, Simon son of Jonah, because flesh and blood did not reveal this to you, but my Father in heaven" (Matt 16:16–17). Peter's ability to confess Christ did not originate from within himself or his peers, but rather, his personal confession occurs according to the will of the Father in the Son through the Spirit.[64] We, too, confess Christ in the same way as Peter through the personal revelation of God, from the Father we confess Jesus Christ—the Son of the living God.

---

[63] For example, across the New Testament, we see the Christological centrality again and again—whether Peter's declaration, "You are the Messiah, the Son of living God," in Matt 16:16; Thomas's exclamation "My Lord and my God" in John 20:28; John's explanation of confession in 1 John 2:23, "He who confesses the Son has the Father as well"; or in 1 John 4:15, "Whoever confesses that Jesus is the Son of God—God remains in him and he in God."

[64] For example, John wrote, "This is how we know that we remain in him and he in us: He has given us of his Spirit. And we have seen and we testify that the Father has sent his Son as the world's Savior. Whoever confesses that Jesus is the Son of God—God remains in him and he in God" (1 John 4:13–15). Here, John ties our abiding in God ("He has given us of his Spirit") and our confession, ("Whoever confesses that Jesus is the Son of God—God remains in him").

As we confess Christ, we are saved. Our personal act of confessing Christ should be seen in light of regeneration in Christ through which we are saved (Rom 10:9–10). Theological knowledge is predicated upon our confession of Christ and our renewal in him.[65] In confessing Christ, we join the communion of the church. While this ecclesial sense of confession should be understood as different from the personal, salvific sense of confession, they bear the same essential quality of participating in Christ, in the power of the Holy Spirit according to the Father's good purpose. The confession that saves us is the same confession that sanctifies us. As a result, confession denotes both an identifying mark of the local church and its ongoing theological practice. This "confession" is expressed in distinctively baptistic ways. So, while we may have a common confession with other believers, we express our confession in believers' baptism, the Supper, church covenants, corporate worship centered on the Word, and congregational life and mission.

Confession is a defining mark of the church—or perhaps more to the point, confession is a defining mark of Baptist churches. A commitment to regenerate church membership sits at the center of our Baptist ecclesiology.[66] At the intersection of salvific confession and regenerate church membership, we can say that Baptist churches are confessional communities in essence. As we personally confess Christ, we share in a corporate confession within the local church's covenantal communion. In asserting that dogmatic theology should be both ecclesial and confessional, we are locating Baptist dogmatic theology within the context of historic Baptist convictions.

In terms of the ongoing theological practice, the church confesses Christ through informal and formal ministry to one another. Our informal confession occurs in a myriad of moments when the Spirit empowers

---

[65] John 17:3, 26, makes this connection clearly.

[66] John Hammett refers to regenerate church membership as *the* Baptist mark of the church. See John S. Hammett, *Biblical Foundations for Baptist Churches: A Contemporary Ecclesiology* (Grand Rapids, MI: Kregel, 2005), 81.

our words from one believer to the next. From moments around the dinner table where we encourage each other to hope in Christ, or when we speak spiritual comfort to a grieving family at the death of a loved one or express our joy in God's grace that a friend has come to faith—through our words in moments like these, we participate in God's work in the world. This type of theological ministry draws on Paul's admonishment to address "one another in psalms, hymns, and spiritual songs" (Eph 5:19) or to "encourage one another and build each other up" (1 Thess 5:11). Through such interpersonal dialogue, God accomplishes his purposes in and through the church together to grow us up into Christ's maturity. Our theological words fill us with teleological purpose, as the Word of Christ dwells in us richly (Col 3:16). In this sense, our informal, confessional conversations provide an integral component of the church's theological ministry.

Likewise, God works through the formal ministries of the church, namely the proclamation of the Word and the observance of the ordinances as we confess Christ. For centuries, the weekend gatherings of Baptist churches have centered around the proclamation of the Word in the form of a sermon. This unique teaching moment provides the ongoing opportunity for church leaders to nourish the Body by confessing Christ according to the Scripture.[67] The Spirit works through the words of the preacher, exposing the text of Scripture to build up his church. As we hear the Word of God confessed in the communion of the saints, we grow together in theological knowledge unto individual and corporate Christlikeness. Preaching is a primary, formal, dogmatic ministry of the church.

---

[67] Within Baptist churches, there is again some level of diversity regarding who is or is not qualified to give the sermon on Sunday mornings. While personally I see this act reserved for pastor/elders of the local church, for the purpose of Baptist dogmatic theology, we need not agree on a consensus. Regardless of the particulars, the confessing Christ in the sermon is a necessary component in dogmatic theology.

In the same way, the observance of the ordinances, baptism and the Lord's Supper, are formal confessional ministries of the church. As the church celebrates the baptism of new believers, we rejoice in their confession as we remember our own. We are together buried and raised in Christ and born again into the family of God. Baptism rehearses our life in Christ, not as a routine ritual but in actual participation in him. In baptism, the Spirit works to form the person who is baptized and the community into which they are reborn to Christian maturity. In observing the Lord's Supper, we confess Christ in the power of the Spirit. We respond to the preaching of the Word with the proclamatory performance of breaking bread and pouring wine. We act out our confession through eating and drinking in communion. In doing so, we remember the Lord and proclaim his death until he comes. We confess our ongoing, shared faith in him and the certainty of our conviction that he will return in glory. All the while, Christ is present and moving among his people through the Holy Spirit. In Christ, through the Spirit, God uses the ordinances as confessional means to grow us into Christ's fullness.

In its missional ministry, the church also professes Christ to the world. The Word of God spreads across the street and around the globe through Christian proclamation. God sends us out as participating ambassadors, through whom he makes his appeal (2 Cor 5:18–20). Christians do not simply relay the fact that God has come in the flesh, but we confess our regeneration in Christ, as we invite others to join our fellowship.[68] This evangelical proclamation trusts not in persuasive arguments but trusts in God to be about his work, as he empowers our confession in the Spirit to reveal Christ according to the Father's plan. Through this missional confession, God grows his church out to the eschatological reality of every

---

[68] Here we might see John's introduction to 1 John as instructive: "What we have seen and heard we declare to you, so that you may also have fellowship with us; and indeed our fellowship is with the Father and with his Son, Jesus Christ" (1 John 1:3).

nation, tribe, and tongue worshipping before the throne of God. In this way, Baptist dogmatics should consider itself a missional endeavor.

The return to the ecclesial centrality of confessional ministry in dogmatics retrieves the historic theological practice. As Robert Louis Wilken notes, this idea aligns with the early church's understanding of theological ministry. He writes, "By apprenticing themselves to the church's inner life, the bishops acquired skill in using the church's language, discovered anew the implications of biblical images trafficking in a world of things that could be seen and touched, not just opined, and in all, learning that what they taught had to do not only with words and ideas but palpable realities."[69] Through our lived experience in the community of the church, the words of our articulate confession and our personal experiences become inseparably fused together as we grow in wisdom. Thus, in proposing a *confessional* signpost of dogmatics, we reinforce the *historic, ecclesial,* and *covenantal* signposts that mark the terrain of Baptist dogmatics.

## Conclusion

Baptists, rooted in the free-church tradition, uphold the singular faith in harmony with Scripture, the great tradition, and their historical context. At the same time, they draw from their collective experience within the believing church, considering the realities of the new covenant and recognizing themselves as a people in union with Christ and one another. Baptist theology resists standardization, embracing diverse methods and conclusions within the community. Despite these differences, Baptists are unified by a shared gospel confession in baptism, a commitment to the authority of Scripture, and a communal tradition of confessing the Christian faith. The distinct hallmarks of Baptist dogmatics—*historical, ecclesial, covenantal,* and *confessional*—authentically reflect the tradition's unique identity within the broader Christian landscape.

---

[69] Wilken, *The Spirit of Early Christian Thought,* 42.

At the core of Baptist dogmatics lies a commitment to local churches worshiping under the lordship of Christ—a voluntary association marked by shared theology and practice, emphasizing the authority of Scripture, robust conversionism, the imperative of Christian mission, and the priesthood of believers. The mission of articulating this faith directs the theological task toward inviting people to know and experience the triune God through faith in Jesus Christ. Believers, recognized as priests of God, actively contribute to the ongoing confession of the common faith, bound covenantally among Baptist believers. This covenantal reality defines the vocation of Baptist theologians, compelling them to engage in the theological task for the sake of confession, formation, and missional faithfulness within the believing community. The overarching aim of this task is to deepen the understanding of the love of God in the Lord Jesus Christ and to extend the transformative invitation to the world, inviting others to partake in this profound knowledge.

CHAPTER 1

# SCRIPTURE

## Steven A. McKinion and Brandon D. Smith

### Introduction

This present chapter addresses the question of the doctrine of Scripture, offering a Baptist vision of submission to the rule of Christ through communal reflection on the text of the Scriptures themselves. Part one will offer an overview of the doctrine, answering the question, "What is Scripture?" Part two will give a justification of the need for "ruled readings" of Scripture, in which interpretation and articulation of the biblical text is understood in relation to received gospel summaries of the text. Part three distributes the doctrine throughout Baptist ecclesial communities, demonstrating the role the doctrine plays in the church operating under the rule of Christ mediated through the Scriptures.

### Part One: What Is Scripture?

Baptists join all Christians in acknowledging the Bible as the authoritative source of the knowledge of God, his will, and his work. The texts which comprise Scripture are those inspired writings by which God has communicated himself to humanity for the purpose of their knowing him and his will for their lives. The Christian doctrine of Scripture begins with God's self-revelation in and through Spirit-inspired, written texts by which humanity might know God through Jesus Christ. Baptist Christians recognize the Old Testament and the New Testament as the only inspired and authoritative texts.[1]

We begin with distinguishing those texts which are understood to be divine Scripture from other texts which either purport to be Scripture or which relate to the Christian community. While there are many texts which witness to the God of Israel or Jesus of Nazareth, Christians only recognize some of those texts as having divine authorship and therefore authority in Christian belief and practice. As theologians, we know that the source of our theological knowledge is the collection of those writings in particular. While Christians may find theological benefit in reflection upon other works of God or in human experience, the sole source of authority for the church's confession is the Bible. Proper readings of the texts of Scripture require the Spirit's illumination along with benefit of the community of believers throughout space and time. The Christian theologian does not read within a vacuum of soul competency but within the community of faithful witnesses to the gospel throughout history, as discussed below. But those faithful witnesses do not constitute an authority either as a body (in synod) or as a collective. The ultimate authority for Christian belief is the Scriptures.

Delimiting the Scriptures from other texts begins with the interaction of the risen Christ with his disciples in Luke 24. In this passage, Jesus

---

[1] Irenaeus of Lyons refers to the texts we call the Old Testament as "the Scriptures" and those we call the New Testament as "the apostles." In early Christianity, the "Testaments" referred to the two covenants in the Bible, the Sinai covenant in Moses and the new covenant in Christ. Gradually these terms Old Testament and New Testament came to refer to the two collections of texts rather than the two covenants describe in those texts. Both the Scriptures and the apostles described the old and new covenants.

encounters two of his disciples on the road to Emmaus. The disciples do not recognize him but invite him to spend the night with them and the other disciples gathered together after Jesus's death. After the disciples recounted the events of Jesus' death and their response to it, Jesus chastised them for being "slow to believe all the prophets have spoken" about the Christ (v. 25). Who are these prophets who have spoken about the Christ? Verse 27 identifies them as "Moses and all the Prophets," which the author then calls, "the Scriptures." Later in the passage, Jesus identifies the Scriptures as "the Law of Moses, the Prophets, and the Psalms" (v. 44). These texts, the Scriptures, are about Christ, telling the story of God's work in Christ to bring repentance and the forgiveness of sins. To both understand the identity of Christ as God at work, reconciling the world to himself, and proclaim that message to the world for whom Jesus was sent, the disciples of Jesus must turn to the Scriptures.

Once Jesus explains his identity to the disciples "according to the Scriptures," the disciples' eyes are opened, and they finally recognize his true identity as the Christ. This unveiling of his person and work is through their reception of the scriptural message. They now see that the message of the prophets has been fulfilled in Jesus.

This unveiling is reminiscent of the encounter between Jesus and Peter in Matthew 16. Peter confesses Jesus to be the "Messiah, the Son of the Living God" (v. 16). Jesus responded by saying that "flesh and blood did not reveal this to you, but my Father in heaven" (v. 17). The revelation of Jesus' identity from the Father to Peter is followed by the narrative of the Mount of Transfiguration in which Moses and Elijah (the Law and the Prophets) bear witness to Jesus as the Son of God. Peter himself references this encounter in the passage from 2 Peter mentioned previously. It is obvious that Matthew is offering his readers the same revelation of Jesus as the Old Testament Christ that Peter received from the Father. Revelation comes from reading and reflecting on the Scriptures.

The Gospel of Mark opens with the statement, "The beginning of the gospel of Jesus Christ, as it is written in Isaiah the prophet" (Mark 1:1–2). He then quotes from Isa 40:3. Mark's claim that the gospel of Jesus Christ is written in Isaiah indicates the necessity of the Old Testament for understanding Christian belief. The gospel message finds it origin in the Scriptures, the Old Testament. When Paul summarizes the Christian gospel for his readers, he does so in reference to the Scriptures. First Corinthians 15:3–4 states, "Christ died for our sins according to the Scriptures, that he was buried, that he was raised on the third day according to the Scriptures."

What then of the New Testament writings? The gospel which Jesus delivered to the apostles was that proclaimed in the Law, the Prophets, and the Psalms. As the apostles preached this message of Jesus as the Christ of the Old Testament, their preaching was eventually written down. Second Peter 1 describes Peter's purpose of writing down the apostolic message of Jesus according to the Scriptures as an effort to ensure that his hearers are "able to recall these things at any time after my departure" (2 Pet 1:15). The gospel message that Peter had preached was written down for future generations to read that message. Peter's proclamation was the message of the Scriptures (v. 20), and not simply a recounting of his own experiences with Jesus, as majestic as those experiences were. In addition, the author exhorts his readers to also read the letters of the apostle Paul, which contain divine wisdom which false prophets twist like "the rest of the Scriptures" (2 Pet 3:16).

Christians recognize the inspired writings which contain the apostolic message of Jesus according to the Old Testament as divine Scripture along with the Old Testament. The content of the church's confession and the message which the church professes in her mission to the world is found in both the Old Testament and the New Testament, not as two separate witnesses to the truth of God and his work, but as a single collection of inspired texts. The Scriptures are texts, written documents that must be read and interpreted. The authors employ grammar, figures of speech, and linguistic tools to help communicate their divine message. Genres like narratives, proverbs, and epistolary literature all come together to form a single witness to Jesus Christ as the eternal Son of God.

Scripture is the self-revelation of the triune God. And the inspiration and (therefore) authority of Scripture shapes and rules Christian reading of Scripture. This affirmation has been shared among Christians since the beginning, from the apostles themselves and throughout the Christian tradition of which Baptists are a part. This affirmation can be articulated in two main contentions.

### Scripture Is Inspired and (Thus) Authoritative

The Bible is of divine origin. God inspired the writers of Scripture so that a written and reliable source of God's self-revelation might enable humanity to know God and obey him (2 Pet 1:16–21). While experience within creation might demonstrate to humanity their need for a salvation outside of themselves or offer a glimpse of God's power or character (Ps 19:1; Rom 1:20–21), only the Scriptures contain the self-revelation of God such that humans might come to know him and his salvation. Scripture also provides us with what we are to obey, providing guidance for ethical decision-making, spiritual growth, and the formation of Christian beliefs. While Baptists value the insights of tradition, reason, and experience, we view Scripture as the ultimate and final authority of the revelation of God and his will.

Christians accept that Scripture is our authority, and we submit our lives to it because, as the inspired Word of God, Scripture itself demands it. Put another way, we do not make Scripture authoritative because we accept it as such; rather, we accept Scripture as authoritative *because* it is inspired by God and thus carries with it his authority. Consider Josh 23:6, "Be very strong and continue obeying all that is written in the book of the law of Moses," and 2 Tim 3:16–17, "All Scripture is inspired by God and is profitable for teaching, for rebuking, for correcting, for training in righteousness, so that the man of God may be complete, equipped for every good work." If these two examples (of many) are any indication, Scripture does not present itself as a mere set of facts to accept; rather, it presents itself as the very words of God that demand our allegiance, if we are to know and love God rightly.

### Scripture Requires Interpretation

We also recognize that Scripture must be interpreted rightly. In Jesus's temptation in Matthew 4, Satan quotes Scripture, but he does not quote it rightly. Jesus, however, interprets Scripture rightly by placing it in its proper context. For instance, Satan uses Psalm 91 to tempt Jesus to jump off the temple and trust God to send angels to catch him. But Jesus knew that this passage must be interpreted alongside Deut 6:16, which he quotes back to Satan: "Do not test the Lord your God" (Matt 4:7). This interaction assumes the inspiration and authority of Scripture since Scripture is at the center of back-and-forth. Peter also marries together the ideas of divine inspiration, authority, and interpretation in his second epistle. In 2 Pet 1:20–21, he says, "Above all, you know this: No prophecy of Scripture comes from the prophet's own interpretation, because no prophecy ever came by the will of man; instead, men spoke from God as they were carried along by the Holy Spirit." Later, he notes that Paul's letters are being twisted—along with "the rest of the Scriptures"—because they can be "hard to understand," which seems to indicate that they are being interpreted and taught incorrectly (2 Pet 3:16). More broadly, Scripture's seemingly endless intertextuality, repeated themes, and Christological centrality (Luke 22:44) lay the groundwork for a self-governed (or ruled) reading that does not allow for endless legitimate interpretations. Simply put, the inspiration and authority of Scripture requires a canonical sensitivity that treats all of Scripture as a unified witness to the triune God, even with all of its diversity.[2]

---

[2] The idea of a particular set of canonical texts shaping Christian thought and living is a consistent concern in the Christian tradition. See Edmon L. Gallagher and John D. Meade, *The Biblical Canon Lists from Early Christianity: Texts and Analysis* (Oxford: Oxford University Press, 2017) and

Of course, this conviction about the unity of the biblical canon is centered on the revelation of the triune God, unveiled in the Old and New Testament through human authors inspired by the Holy Spirit in witness to the incarnation of the Son (2 Pet 1:12–21; Heb 1:1). These Spirit-inspired authors left us a two-Testament witness so that we, as Spirit-illuminated readers, may be taught by God, as it were (Isa 54:13; John 6:45; 1 Corinthians 2). This illumination does not guarantee an inerrant interpretation on our part, we nonetheless can open our eyes to the things of God through the Scriptures, to understand who this God is who reveals and saves. So, through the Spirit's illumination and the Spirit's work in the church for two millennia, we can have confidence that we can understand and be transformed by the Scriptures as we read them with the church past and present.

With these parameters in place, Part two of this essay will proceed in two sections. First, we will discuss how the Christian tradition has expressed its dependence on Scripture as divinely inspired and authoritative for Christian thought and living, particularly the way in which Christians throughout history have developed ruled readings and creeds and confessions as interpretive guidelines for understanding and interpreting Scripture rightly. Then, we will return to the notion of authority in a Baptist dogmatic approach to Scripture and its interpretation.

## Part Two: Ruled Readings, Creeds, and Confessions in Biblical Interpretation

As we discussed above, the inspiration, authority, and interpretation of Scripture are closely related and, one could argue, inseparable. If Scripture is inspired by God and God's self-revelation, then it carries with it God's authority. Thus, it must be interpreted rightly to

---

John D. Meade and Peter J. Gurry, *Scribes and Scripture: The Amazing Story of How We Got the Bible* (Wheaton, IL: Crossway, 2022).

understand it and submit to it rightly. This does not mean, of course, that we can expect infallible interpretations of Scripture. We are fallen creatures, reading Scripture with the Spirit's help and looking "through a glass darkly," awaiting the day we will see God "face to face" (1 Cor 13:12 KJV). As Augustine of Hippo once said, we are sometimes perplexed by Scripture not because it is faulty, but because we "have failed to understand it."[3] That said, there is hope for our finite attempts at biblical interpretation. As the 1689 Second London Baptist Confession of Faith reminds us, "All things in Scripture are not alike plain in themselves, nor alike clear unto all; yet those things which are necessary to be known, believed and observed for salvation, are so clearly propounded and opened in some place of Scripture or other, that not only the learned, but the unlearned, in a due use of ordinary means, may attain to a sufficient understanding of them."

One does not need a PhD to understand Scripture unto salvation. A basic Reformational impulse is that Scripture can be understood by anyone who has the Spirit, without authoritative interpretation from a magisterium or some other extrabiblical authority. However, this Reformational impulse did cause an overreaction against traditional or extrabiblical sources, insofar as they were faithful to Scripture. Indeed, the church before and after the Reformation has generally sought to interpret Scripture rightly through ruled readings (guidelines and parameters regarding Scripture's unity and flow) and creeds and confessions (summaries of Scripture's teaching). A few examples from church history must suffice to drive home the point.[4]

---

[3] Augustine of Hippo, "Letter 83," in *The Nicene and Post-Nicene Fathers* vol. 1, ed. Philip Schaff, trans. J. G. Cunningham, First Series (Buffalo, NY: Christian Literature Company, 1886), 350.

[4] For a broader survey of the shared sensibilities of the Christian tradition, see Brandon D. Smith, *Taught By God: Ancient Hermeneutics for the Modern Church* (Brentwood, TN: B&H Academic, 2024), 65–85. Some of the work in this section is borne of the research in that book.

## *The Rule of Faith in the Early Church*

Two examples from the patristic period—Irenaeus of Lyons and Athanasius of Alexandria—serve as paradigmatic voices in the defense and development of ruled readings of Scripture. Though no formal ecumenical creeds existed in Irenaeus's day, he understood that doctrine and interpretation were not a free-for-all, but rather built upon the authority and unity of Scripture. His "rule of faith" or "truth" featured both a basic affirmation of the Father, Son, and Holy Spirit's work in revelation and salvation and a basic affirmation of Scripture's unity from the prophets to the apostles:

> And this is the order of our faith, the foundation of [the] edifice and the support of [our] conduct: God, the Father, uncreated, uncontainable, invisible, one God, the Creator of all: this is the first article (κεφάλαιον) of our faith. And the second article: the Word of God, the Son of God, Christ Jesus our Lord, who was revealed by the prophets according to the nature of the economies of the Father, by whom all things were made, and who, in the last times, to recapitulate all things, became a man amongst men, visible and palpable, in order to abolish death, to demonstrate life, and to effect communion between God and man. And the third article: the Holy Spirit, through whom the prophets prophesied and the patriarchs learnt the things of God and the righteous were led in the path of righteousness, and who, in the last times, was poured out in a new fashion upon the human race renewing man, throughout the world, to God.[5]

Here, Irenaeus draws an inseparable link between Christian confession and the inspiration and authority of the Scriptures.

---

[5] Irenaeus of Lyons, *On the Apostolic Preaching* 6, trans. John Behr (Crestwood, NY: St Vladimir's Seminary Press, 1997), 42–43.

This rule of faith summarizes much of his work in defending a right reading of Scripture over and against dissident groups like the so-called "Gnostics."[6] While the debates are legion, surrounding the stability of a biblical "canon" in the first few centuries of the church, Irenaeus nonetheless "works with a concept of the canonical context that is flexible but clearly discernable" as he quotes widely from Scripture and speaks of "the entire Scriptures" as the context for right interpretation.[7] The mosaic of the beautiful King is perhaps his most famous illustration for the unity and right reading of Scripture.

For Irenaeus, the Scriptures are like a mosaic made up of various precious jewels. If these jewels are arranged correctly, the mosaic ends up portraying the image of a beautiful king (Christ Jesus).[8] The "Gnostics," however, "re-arrange the gems, and so fit them together as to make them into the form of a dog or of a fox, and even that but poorly executed; and should then maintain and declare that this was the beautiful image of the king which the skillful artist constructed."[9] If people join the "Gnostics" in adding and taking away from the Scriptures handed down by the apostles, the rule of faith would be abandoned and people would instead believe all kinds of false doctrines.[10] Irenaeus demonstrates that, among the earliest Christians who received the Scriptures, there was already an understanding that the church was called to "guard the good deposit"

---

[6] "Gnostics" is a broad label for various groups. In his opening salvo in *Against Heresies*, he identifies these groups with specificity. For our purposes here, we will use "Gnostics" generally to describe the various opponents Irenaeus engages in his writings.

[7] Ched Spellman, *Irenaeus: Essential Readings* (Dallas, TX: Fontes Press, 2023), 15. See, e.g., Irenaeus, *Against Heresies* 2.27.2.

[8] Irenaeus, *Against Heresies* 1.8.1.

[9] Irenaeus, 1.8.1. English translation from *The Ante-Nicene Fathers*, vol. 1, eds. Alexander Roberts, James Donaldson, and A. Cleveland Coxe, trans. Alexander Roberts and William Rambaut (New York: Christian Literature, 1885), 326

[10] Irenaeus, 2.27.1

(2 Tim 1:14) by accepting the authority of the Scriptures and, in turn, learning to read them properly.

Just a few centuries later, ruled readings—and now an ecumenical creed—continued to help the church norm and protect correct biblical doctrine and interpretation. Although Athanasius did not articulate his rule of faith in the same way as Irenaeus, his doctrinal and interpretive sensibilities still functioned the same way. For example, an important part of Athanasius's career as a bishop and theologian was defending the Nicene Creed (AD 325) against various dissident theologies that developed or resurfaced between Nicaea and the Council of Constantinople (AD 381).[11]

In his defense of the Nicene Creed, Athanasius recognized that biblical interpretation was at the center of the disagreements. This makes sense, of course, given that the Nicene Creed was meant to be a summary of biblical teaching, with special focus on the doctrines of God and Christ. But as these false doctrines arose, Athanasius did not merely defend the content of the creed, but also the interpretive rules required to affirm it properly. One such interpretive rule was the "scope" or "character" (σκοπός) of Scripture:

> Now the scope and character of Holy Scripture, as we have often said, is this,—it contains a double account of the Saviour; that He was ever God, and is the Son, being the Father's Word and Radiance and Wisdom; and that afterwards for us He took flesh of a Virgin, Mary Bearer of God, and was made man. And this scope is to be found throughout inspired Scripture, as the Lord Himself has said, 'Search the Scriptures, for they are they which testify of Me.'[12]

---

[11] Athanasius's career is almost a timestamp of this period, as he likely was made a bishop in AD 328 and died in 373.

[12] *Against the Arians* 3.29. English translations from *The Nicene and Post-Nicene Fathers*, vol. 4, ed. Philip Schaff and Henry Wace, trans. John Henry Newman and Archibald T. Robertson (New York: Christian Literature Co., 1892).

Athanasius also called this scope a "rule" ultimately rooted in the teaching of the Apostles and the divinely inspired Scriptures, which his opponents had missed and thus "wandered from the way of truth [and] stumbled on a stone of stumbling."[13] Athanasius's language above is saturated with biblical language. He speaks about Christ as Word (John 1:1), Radiance (Heb 1:3), and Wisdom (1 Cor 1:24), his virgin birth (Matt 1:18–27), and his own words in John 5:39.

For Athanasius, all of Scripture can be summed up in the divinity and humanity of the eternal Son of God who put on flesh and dwelt among us. This basic rule is not Athanasius's only interpretive rule and perhaps not even the "center" of his hermeneutics,[14] but it does significant heavy lifting in his Christological polemics. For example, some opposing groups used Prov 8:22—"The Lord acquired [or 'created,' LXX] me at the beginning of his creation, before his works of long ago"—to say that the Son was created, since this passage seems to teach that Wisdom was created. Athanasius's scope, however, offers a way to speak partitively about the Son's two natures, as well as a way to privilege the unity of Scripture as God's inspired and authoritative word.

Within the context of Proverbs, Athanasius points out that Wisdom is spoken of as the Creator.[15] In the broader context of the Scriptures, Paul says in 1 Cor 3:10–11 that Christ is the foundation upon which all things are built.[16] Alongside textual evidence that the Son is God's Wisdom and, therefore, the Creator, he also affirms the biblical patterns and titles that the Son being the Word, Radiance, and Wisdom of God speaks of his eternity, since God was never without his Word, Radiance, or Wisdom.[17] As God's Word, Radiance, and Wisdom and as Creator,

---

[13] *Against the Arians* 3.28.

[14] James D. Ernest, *The Bible in Athanasius of Alexandria* (Atlanta, GA: Society of Biblical Literature, 2010), 1–42 summarizes various proposals for Athanasius's exegetical "center."

[15] *Against the Arians* 2.73.

[16] *Against the Arians* 2.74.

[17] See also *Against the Arians* 1.14.

the whole counsel of Scripture teaches that the Son is not created, but rather truly divine and thus eternal. The Nicene Creed teaches the same thing as a faithful summary of the Son's divinity: "Lord Jesus Christ, the Son of God, the only-begotten, begotten of the Father before all ages. Light of Light, true God of true God, begotten not made, of one essence with the Father by whom all things were made." Prov 8:22, then, could not be teaching that the Son is a created being and thus was not with the Father "before all ages." A more fitting biblical and theological interpretation of Prov 8:22 is that it speaks about the created human nature that the Son assumed in his incarnation.[18]

Similar to Irenaeus, then, Athanasius assumes that Scripture tells a unified story about God and his work in the world, and this assumption guides a ruled reading of Scripture. Whereas Irenaeus's rule of faith acts as its own doctrinal confession or proto-creed with interpretive entailments for canonical unity, Athanasius combines creedal logic with a canonically sensitive interpretive approach. In the end, they both demonstrate the relationship between the inspiration and authority of Scripture and its need to be interpreted rightly.

For the sake of space, we must jump ahead over 1,000 years to the Reformation. It is worth noting, however, that ruled readings were a constant throughout the Christian tradition, including the late-patristic and medieval periods.[19] For example, sixth-century bishop Gregory the Great mentions a threefold method consisting of the literal-historical sense (the words and history of Scripture), the allegorical sense (theological-Christological), and the moral sense (contemplation, communion, and transformation).[20] Hugh of Saint Victor and his "school" engaged in painstaking interpretive methods that sought to protect the

---

[18] *Against the Arians* 2.74.

[19] See Ian Christopher Levy, *Introducing Medieval Biblical Interpretation: The Senses of Scripture in Pre-Modern Exegesis* (Grand Rapids: Baker Academic, 2018).

[20] *To Leander* 1.

"literal sense" of Scripture as a way to protect against "allegorical" excess and uphold the authoritative norming of Scripture for doctrine and life.[21] Thomas Aquinas, too, employed interpretive guidelines in an effort to read Scripture rightly by focusing on the "literal sense" as a ruled principle for "moral" and "anagogical" readings.[22]

## Reformational, Post-Reformational, and Baptist Confessions

The late-medieval church to which Martin Luther reacted had not totally abandoned the authority of Scripture. However, there can be no doubt that Luther and the Reformers responded strongly and correctly to the crisis of authority taking place in the late-medieval Roman Catholic Church. Scripture and the church's tradition had, at best, become co-equals. Whereas Catholic leaders like Sylvester Mazzolini and Johann Tetzel argued for papal authority and infallibility, Martin Luther was one among many who argued that the Roman Catholic Church had developed this position on the Pope contra Scripture and the tradition.[23] Indeed, the Reformers argued that the church fathers would have approved of their critique that the church had elevated tradition over Scripture.[24]

The Reformation renewed the church's emphasis on the authority of Scripture and its right interpretation, which the late-medieval church had baldly abandoned. Baptists carried on this sensibility as a type of renewal movement within the Protestant tradition, responding in part to the new Christian magisterium that had taken hold of the Church of England. While these later approaches differ in context and nuance from Irenaeus and Athanasius, they still reflect a similar sensibility about the inspiration, authority, and interpretation of Scripture. In particular, many

---

[21] See, for example, *On Sacred Scripture* 5.
[22] See, for example, *Summa Theologiae* I, q. 1, a. 9.
[23] See, for example, Luther's *Explanations*.
[24] Timothy George, *Reading Scripture with the Reformers* (Downers Grove, IL: IVP Academic, 2011), 81.

of the resulting confessions and catechisms of this period place a high view on Scripture, sometimes making Scripture the first article of the confession or catechism.

For instance, Luther's Small Catechism begins with a type of rule of faith—the Ten Commandments and the Lord's Prayer, along with the Apostles' Creed. A doctrine or interpretation that aligned with or did not contradict this rule of faith could be deemed credible. Luther was not alone among the Reformers and their inheritors in developing these types of rules of faith.[25] The Reformers recognized that certain biblical texts or principles and ancient creeds should function as guides for ruled readings as a way to explain the inspired, authoritative Scriptures. Just as the heretics of old went astray without ruled readings and creeds, the new heretics of the Reformers' day made the same mistakes.

The Westminster Confession of Faith also begins with the doctrine of Scripture as the guiding authority for the church:

> (1) Although the light of nature, and the works of creation and providence, do so far manifest the goodness, wisdom, and power of God, as to leave men inexcusable; yet are they not sufficient to give that knowledge of God, and of His will, which is necessary unto salvation . . . the holy Scripture to be most necessary; those former ways of God's revealing His will unto His people being now ceased. (2) Under the name of holy Scripture, or the Word of God written, are now contained all the books of the Old and New Testament. . . .

This first article ends with a word about interpretation:

---

[25] Richard A. Muller, *Post-Reformation Reformed Dogmatics: The Rise and Development of Reformed Orthodoxy* vol. 2, 2nd ed. (Grand Rapids: Baker Academic, 2003), 493–97, provides several examples of Reformation/Post-Reformation rules of faith. See also Todd R. Hains, *Martin Luther and the Rule of Faith: Reading God's Word for God's People* (Downers Grove: IVP Academic, 2022).

(3) The infallible rule of interpretation of Scripture, is the Scripture itself; and therefore, when there is a question about the true and full sense of any scripture (which is not manifold, but one), it may be searched and known by other places that speak more clearly. (4) The Supreme Judge, by which all controversies of religion are to be determined, and all decrees of councils, opinions of ancient writers, doctrines of men, and private spirits, are to be examined, and in whose sentence we are to rest, can be no other but the Holy Spirit speaking in the Scripture.

This statement is decidedly supportive of *sola Scriptura*, but it is not decidedly anti-creedal or anti-tradition. Because of the inspiration and authority of Scripture, we submit our interpretations (and indeed, our entire lives) to the work of the Spirit in both inspiration and illumination. Further, the rule of faith (if we may call it that) is canonical unity: Scripture must interpret Scripture. Extrabiblical sources, like creeds, are not prohibited by this confession, but they are submitted to the ultimate authority of Scripture and are only useful insofar as they are faithful to Scripture.

Throughout Baptist history, our confessions have shared this Protestant sensibility. Indeed, the 1689 Second London Baptist Confession mirrors the Westminster Confession with tweaks here and there. While all traditions certainly care about the Bible, Baptists have historically quadruple-downed on the authority and importance of Scripture. Interestingly, the Second London Confession adds an opening line to the Westminster Confession to drive home the point: "The Holy Scripture is the only sufficient, certain, and infallible rule of all saving knowledge, faith, and obedience."

The General Baptists' Orthodox Creed (1678) does not mention Scripture until Article 37, after focusing on particular issues related to the doctrine of God and soteriology. However, the introduction almost immediately sets the table with the affirmation that the Creed's contents are dependent on the authority and truth of the Scriptures. Article 37 then articulates both the authority of the Scriptures and their need to be interpreted according to the rule or "analogy of faith."[26] This Creed also makes explicit its desire to protect the orthodoxy that has been handed down by the Christian tradition by naming ancient heresies that were dismissed by early councils and creeds, including Macedonians, Marcionites, Valentinians, Apelles, Apollinarians, Eunomians, Ebionites, Nestorians, Eutychians, Arians, and Sabellians, and then later particularly affirms the goodness of the Apostles', Nicene, and Athanasian Creeds in Article 38:

> The Three Creeds, (viz.) Nicene Creed, Athanasius his Creed, and the Apostles Creed, (as they are commonly called) ought throughly to be received, and believed. For we believe they may be proved by most undoubted Authority of holy Scripture, and are necessary to be understood of all Christians; and to be instructed in the knowledg [*sic*] of them, by the Ministers of Christ, according to the Analogie of Faith, recorded in sacred Scriptures (upon which these Creeds are grounded), and Catechistically opened, and expounded in all Christian Families, for the edification of Young and Old; which might be a means to prevent Heresie in Doctrine, and Practice, these Creeds containing all things in a brief manner, that are necessary to be known, fundamentally, in order to our Salvation.

Notice, again, the emphasis on the importance of creeds as interpretive aids insofar as they are "grounded" in the Scriptures. The earliest Baptists, like their forebears, recognized the need for ruled readings for right interpretation of the inspired and authoritative Scriptures as a means of protecting right doctrine and catechizing the church. Many more examples of the inspiration and authority of Scripture occur in Baptist history, with the Philadelphia Confession (1742) using similar wording to the 1689

---

[26] *An Orthodox Creed*, transcribed by Madison Grace (Baptist Studies Online, 2006) at http://baptiststudiesonline.com/wp-content/uploads/2007/02/orthodox-creed.pdf.

Second London Confession; the brief set of principles of the Sandy Creek Association (1758); the New Hampshire Confession (1833); and the various editions of the Baptist Faith and Message (1925; 1963; and 2000).

## Part Three: Scripture and Authority in Baptist Dogmatics

Baptists hold that the Bible is the highest authority for Christian faith and practice because it is the Word of God. The London Baptist Confession of Faith states, "They are therefore true and authoritative, so that in all religious controversies the church must make their ultimate appeal to them."[27] While creeds and confessions may be faithful summaries of scriptural teaching, only Scripture itself governs all matters of belief, morality, and conduct as a trustworthy guide rooted in the very truth of God himself. It is not subject to the authority of any human institution or tradition. The authority of Scripture is grounded in its divine origin and its claim to be the Word of God. Second Timothy 3:16 states, "All Scripture is inspired by God, and is profitable for teaching, for rebuking, for correcting, for training in righteousness." The Bible governs the life of the Christian and the church as the means to mediate the rule of Christ.

In Baptist theology, the authority of Scripture is an especially pertinent aspect of the doctrine. Christians of various traditions have particular ways of addressing the question of authority. There is additionally the matter of locating authority in reason or experience. Some modern *biblicism* locates authority in the reader or the community of readers. More formally, some Christian traditions locate authority in the ecclesial realm, in places such as a synod of ecclesiastical leaders, a formally received *magisterium,* or in the leaders of a local congregation of believers. For Baptists, while the proper interpretation of Scripture in many matters requires attention to ruled readings, the authority for Christian theology and its proclamation in the community of faith is the Bible.

---

[27] *London Baptist Confession of Faith* 1:8.

Baptist theologians recognize the authority of Scripture in all necessary matters of saving faith and Christian practice. There may be many sources of truth, but only Scripture contains the message of the church's confession. The London Baptist Confession of Faith states it clearly and succinctly: "everything essential for [God's] own glory and man's salvation, faith, and life is either explicitly stated or by necessary inference contained in the Holy Scriptures."[28] As Baptist theologians, we reflect on the Scriptures to discover and contemplate the glory of God, his nature and character, and his work. Because "everything essential" for the glory of God is contained in the Bible, the theologian's work is ultimately textual work. The church's confession of God's being and work is derived from the Scriptures as the *locus* of God's self-revelation in Christ. Baptist dogmatics recognizes the Bible as this *locus* and therefore determines to articulate doctrines as they are derived from the text of Scripture.

Scripture likewise provides sufficient guidance for knowing God, ethical decision-making, spiritual growth, and the formation of Christian beliefs in the life of the believer as a part of the community of faith. While Baptists value the insights of tradition, reason, and experience, they view Scripture as the ultimate and final authority of the revelation of God and his will for the lives of all human beings. Baptist churches confess a faith which forms and transforms believers ultimately by the power of the Spirit.

The Baptist Faith and Message 2000 states that the Bible is "the supreme standard by which all human conduct, creeds, and religious opinions should be tried."[29] As theologians develop language to articulate the faith, the value and truthfulness of that language is judged in relation to Scripture. To be authoritative in the life of the church or of an individual believer, a claim must be derive from and be consistent with the Bible. Theologians must regularly take note of the actual source of their

---

[28] *London Baptist Confession of Faith* 1:6.
[29] *Baptist Faith and Message,* Article 1.

theological claims. The *London Baptist Confession* again offers a warning: "Nothing is ever to be added to the Scriptures, either by new revelation of the Spirit or by human traditions."[30] The sufficiency of Scripture in Baptist theology means there is no further need, either by further revelation or human tradition, for additional source material for Christian doctrine. There is no later authority, church or tradition, which adds to the Bible's witness. As seen above, the church's tradition is a guide to reading Scripture, not an authority alongside or in addition to Scripture.

### Scriptural Authority and the Church

Baptist churches operate under the rule of Christ. No authority outside of the church, whether secular or ecclesiastical, supersedes the rule of Christ through Scripture. Neither governments nor synods determine church belief or practice. Christ does not, therefore, mediate his rule in Baptist churches through authoritative bodies. Instead, churches learn the rule of Christ and operate under that rule by becoming scriptural communities. What does biblical authority look like in Baptist dogmatics for Baptist churches?

If the first principle of the Baptist doctrine of Scripture is that God is the author of the text, it follows from that first principle that Scripture is the means by which Christ mediates his headship within the congregation. The London Baptist Confession guides churches in reminding them, "The authority of the Holy Scriptures obligates belief in them. This authority does not depend on the testimony of any person or church but on God the author alone, who is truth itself. Therefore, the Scriptures are to be received because they are the Word of God." The Orthodox Creed states, "The Authority of the holy Scripture, dependeth not upon the Authority of any Man, but only upon the Authority of God."[31] Fundamental to the church's confession is the divine origin of

---

[30] *London Baptist Confession of Faith* 1:6.
[31] *Orthodox Creed*, Article 38.

the Scriptures in which the gospel is found. Having God as its author, Scripture sufficiently guides the church in its common confession, its Christian practice, and its mission within and to the wider world. As divine revelation, the Bible is the reliable source of knowledge of God's being and work in Jesus Christ.

Because Scripture is divinely authored, churches are primarily tasked with teaching the Bible to explain the faith derived from it. Rather than appealing to "new revelation of the Spirit or human traditions," the church appeals to the Scriptures for all matters related to faith and practice.[32] Through leading the church in reading and reflecting on the text in community, the teachers in churches lead them in submitting to the headship of Christ through submission to the Scriptures.

The church confesses, both within and without, the gospel as a summary and explanation of the message of the Scriptures. Therefore, what the church teaches, believes, and practices is determined by the message of the Bible. Scripture, as divine revelation, is the ultimate authority in what the church teaches and practices. The church is not the *locus* of authority, the Scriptures are. The church merely submits to the authority of Christ by recognizing the authority of the Scriptures. Where there are matters to which the church must attend that are not addressed in Scripture, those additional claims are judged according to conformity with Scripture.[33]

This commitment to the authority of Scripture is seen in the autonomy of the local church. Churches do not submit to the authority of associations or denominations. Synods or counsels do not serve as authorities. While it may be the case that traditional readings of Scripture, confessions, creeds, and the like aid churches in the right reading of the Bible, those creeds and confessions are not authorities over the local church. Confessions are revisable, particular articulations of Christian belief that are amendable, provided those confessions and articulations conform

---

[32] *London Baptist Confession of Faith* 1:6.
[33] *London Baptist Confession of Faith* 1:6.

to Scripture. The Orthodox Creed explains, "no Decrees of Popes, or Councils, or Writings of any Person whatsoever, are of equal Authority with the sacred Scriptures."[34]

As Baptists practice theology in the long history of Christian faith and practice, there are numerous important sources of theological articulation of the Scripture faith. Ecumenical councils, local synods in antiquity, church doctors and other teachers, as well as current doctrinal formulations all seek to explain and confess the gospel. As theologians and churches evaluate the truthfulness and benefit of these theological contributions, they view Scripture as "the supreme judge for deciding all religious controversies and for evaluating all decrees of councils, opinions of ancient writers, human teachings, and individual interpretations."[35] This is not to say that sources within the history of the church are unimportant, as our section on rule readings makes clear. But rather, it is to say that the source of Christian doctrine, and therefore the church's final authority for our confession, is the Scriptures. In the words of the London Baptist Confession, "In this Scripture our faith finds its final word."[36]

## The Doctrine of Scripture Distributed in Baptist Theology

Baptist theology is grounded in the Christian reception of Scripture as "the only sufficient, certain, and infallible rule of all saving knowledge, faith, and obedience."[37] Baptists are not unique in their acceptance of Scripture as the revelation of God and of his will. However, Baptists have been intentional to let Scripture override tradition, particularly in

---

[34] *Orthodox Creed*, Article 38.
[35] *London Baptist Confession of Faith* 1:10.
[36] *London Baptist Confession of Faith* 1:10.
[37] *London Baptist Confession of* Faith 1:1.

matters of practice. One might say that Baptists have a certain sensitivity or ethos that drives them to run any doctrine through the litmus test of rigorous biblical warrant. For example, Baptists' acceptance of believer's baptism is grounded in our reading of Scripture, even when much of the church's history has been otherwise. Likewise with Baptist ecclesial structure. Plenty of Christian traditions practice a polity otherwise from Baptists. But Baptists find justification for their polity in their own reading of the Bible. The justification, and therefore authority, for Baptist polity is not tradition, but reflection on Scripture. The Baptist movement was founded on this conviction. In this way, Baptists truly are a reformation within the Reformation, even while we closely identify with both the Christian tradition more broadly and the Protestant tradition more narrowly.

Most important to Baptist theology is the role of Scripture as the means to mediate the rule of Christ in the church. The believer's church is a textual community in which practice is derived from Baptist readings of Scripture just as confession is. Baptist theologians and theological confessions show unmistakable continuity with the Great Tradition. The *Orthodox Creed* affirmed belief in three historical creeds—the Nicene, Apostles', and Athanasian. Baptist theology is not narrowly sectarian, it is located squarely within the consensual tradition of the church. This is particularly the case in its commitment to the authority of the divine Scriptures. For Baptist dogmatics, the church is confessing a Scriptural faith, but in traditional terms. Baptist confessions use traditional grammar for the Trinity, the person and work of Christ, salvation, and the other major theological loci. Baptists must continue to affirm the doctrines of the faith with other Christians. But the role that Scripture plays in Baptist churches must guide our understanding of that grammar, whether the vocabulary or the syntax of theology. It is here that we see most clearly the *historical* signpost at work in Baptist dogmatics. Baptist theology is Christian theology practiced particularly within a Baptist context.

Baptists' commitments to Scripture include its divine authorship and therefore divine authority. All human theological constructions and practices are dependent on the Bible. Moreover, our confessions, whether formal or informal, are amendable when consistent with proper readings of Scripture. Locating authority singularly in the Scriptures ensures that Christ rules his church through the only source of divine revelation. Baptist theology requires articulation, and Scripture is the foundation and source of that articulation. Whether in hymnody, preaching, or common confessions of faith, the Baptist church practices theology when it practices the faith. Baptist theology is particularly committed to theology that forms mature followers of Christ. While there is obviously room for theology as contemplation, Baptists most often see theology as confession.

We additionally see the doctrine of Scripture as distributed through Baptist theology in the church's proclamation itself. When Baptists call themselves a "people of the Book," they often mean to highlight the nature of preaching in Baptist churches. Typically, the centerpiece of a Baptist congregation's liturgy is the sermon. We would prefer the elevation of other liturgical elements alongside the sermon. Baptist churches could benefit from confession of the gospel and biblical teaching in elements of public worship beyond the sermon, and not to the exclusion of it. For example, greater attention to the reading of Scripture in worship, biblical language and themes in prayers, and even symbolic acts which highlight Bible stories would center Scripture even more in the life of the church.

A final place where the doctrine of Scripture can be distributed through Baptist theology is in the church's reading of Scripture in community. While Baptists are sometimes known as private Bible readers (for better or worse), Baptists have always valued time spent reading the Bible in community, with other believers. If Christ mediates his rule through the Bible, the entire church should listen to those words. There is indeed a place for Bible "study," both in academic and devotional contexts. But there might also be more space given to Bible reading. Baptist dogmatics embraces the belief that the Scriptures are meant for all Christians. One reason given in the London Baptist Confession of Faith for the translation of the Scriptures into the vernacular is that the people of God are "commanded in the fear of God to read and search them." Communal reading of Scripture—itself, of course, ruled by the gospel—is a necessary part of Christian living. Baptists' confession of the authority of Scripture requires that regular reading.

In addition to the illumination of the Spirit in interpreting Scripture, the church's right understanding of the Bible requires reading in community. Ruled readings of Scripture are necessary to prevent illicit readings which locate authority in the reader or in the reading community rather than in the text. The "rule" which guides the church's reading of Scripture is not an imposition on the text, but the necessary and demonstrable proper reading of the text. Christ himself, as God at work reconciling the world to him, is the testimony or criterion of Scripture. The biblical gospel which has formed and continues to form the church also dictates the church's reading of the Scriptures which themselves are the divinely inspired source of that gospel.

## Conclusion

Scripture is the locus of God's self-revelation as it details God at work in Christ reconciling the world to himself. The human authors were inspired by the Spirit. The texts they produced were not their own interpretations of the events they saw or encounters they had. Rather than recording events which contained the revelation of God, the texts themselves are God's revelation. By reading them rightly, meditating on them in light of the gospel, and reflecting on them in community, Christians discern the authoritative and reliable revelation of God's being and work.

Scripture is therefore the ultimate authority in Baptist dogmatics, in ways that are distributed distinctly within our own confessional and ecclesial inflections. Theological interpretations, even long-held traditional ways of articulating the Christian faith, exercise authority in the life of the church because those interpretations are derived from and consistent with the message of the Bible. The Nicene Creed, for example, exercises authority in Baptist theology. But one must ask why the creed exercises this authority. Or, better, by whose authority does the Nicene Creed dictate our faith? It is not the authority of the creed itself, as though the internal logic, grammar, or claims are themselves self-evidently truthful and therefore authoritative. It is also not the authority of the authors of the creed. The synod of bishops at Nicaea do not possess universal authority by virtue of their position or theological acumen. The Nicene Creed was not new revelation from the Spirit. Rather, the Nicene Creed is the demonstrable articulation of the biblical gospel. Therefore, the authority by which Baptists teach and confess the Nicene Creed, among others, is the authority of Scripture. The Nicene faith is the Christian faith because its theological logic, grammar, and articulation is derived from the authoritative Scriptures.

This reminds us that Scripture needs interpretation, and dogmatics is the work of engagement with Scripture. The gospel itself, found in summary form in Matt 28:18–20, forms the most basic guide for a "ruled" reading of Scripture. This reading is displayed in the second century rule(s) of faith or canon(s) of truth, which in turn forms the basis of the Nicene Creed and other credal formulations that follow. Baptist dogmatics recognizes the consistent witness to the apostolic faith evident in these canons and creeds as demonstrable summaries and explanations of the self-revelation of God in Scripture. These confessions and creeds of the great tradition play an important role in the task of theologizing in that they carry forward or deliver over the apostolic faith of Jesus Christ according to the Scripture. Baptist confessions of faith likewise recognize both the ultimate authority of Scripture for theology as well as the faithful representation of that authority in the rule(s) of faith. The rules themselves locate dogmatic authority in Scripture while also forming an inviolable guide to how to read the Scripture Christianly.

Baptist dogmatics begins and ends with the confession that Jesus is the Christ, according to the Scriptures. The doctrines which form Christian theology are themselves derived from Scripture, which is the self-revelation of God. The authors wrote under the inspiration of the Holy Spirit for the purpose of revealing God's being and his work to guide human beings into a true knowledge of God. This saving knowledge of God is the goal of Baptist theology.

# CHAPTER 2

# THE DOCTRINE OF GOD

## Ross D. Inman and Stephen O. Presley

## The Consensual Christian Doctrine of God

### *The Revelation of the Triune Name*

God graciously reveals his Holy name to his creatures by way of wide-ranging patterns of biblical discourse across both testaments, the whole counsel of God. These patterns of scriptural discourse regarding God's name serve as textual "pressures" that naturally guide and govern the church's theological reflection and interpretation of God's self-disclosure in Scripture.[1]

God's name is "the mode of revelation that most fully and faithfully indicates the inexhaustible reality of God's *being*. God's name signifies

---

[1] See Kavin Rowe, "Biblical Pressure and Trinitarian Hermeneutics" *Pro Ecclesia* 11: 3 (2002). For a fuller explication of how these textual pressures organically give rise to theological construction and the consensual Christian doctrine of God, see R.B. Jamieson and Tyler R. Wittman, *Biblical Reasoning: Christological and Trinitarian Rules for Exegesis* (Grand Rapids, MI: Baker Academic, 2022).

God's nature."[2] What dim light we have into the fullness of God's being is due mainly to God's unmerited initiative to *name himself* and make himself accessible to his lowly creatures; by naming himself, God thereby addresses and summons us to praise in his holy presence.[3] Even with the gracious self-disclosure of God's Holy name, the fullness and shape of God's inner life remains shrouded in "unapproachable light" (1 Tim 6:15–16 ESV), forever beyond full creaturely ken. Yet when the Holy One of Israel names himself and therein provides a measure of light into God's inner life, the light and mystery contained therein is neither domesticated nor diminished; rather, it is intensified.[4]

God's self-disclosure of his Holy name, then, is the disclosure of his divine being, the very being of "the One who is high and lifted up, who inhabits eternity, whose name is Holy" (Isa 57:15 ESV). The primal revelation of God's name is the Tetragrammaton (YHWH) of Exod 3:14, "I AM WHO I AM". YHWH is the personal, proper name of the God of Israel. God's revelation of his personal name as YHWH to Moses attests to God's utter ontological self-sufficiency and uniqueness ("I AM WHO I AM"), as well as God's intent to put his boundless grace and goodness on display in the unfolding of his sovereign purposes in the life of Israel, a "stiff-necked people" ("I will be gracious to whom I will be gracious, and will show mercy on whom I will show mercy," Exod 33:17–23; 34: 5–9 ESV).

In the guise of a self-initiating and self-sustaining fire, one that in no way draws on the life and resources of another for its existence (Exod 3:1–6, 14), God unveils his being as ontologically replete in its existence, life, glory, goodness, and blessedness. Holy Scripture and the consensual Christian tradition bear witness to the absolute ontological

---

[2] Scott Swain, "Divine Trinity," in *Christian Dogmatics: Reformed Theology for the Church Catholic*, ed. Michael Allen and Scott Swain (Grand Rapids, MI: Baker Academic, 2016), 83.

[3] See Janet Soskice, *Naming God: Addressing the Divine in Philosophy, Theology, and Scripture* (New York: Cambridge University Press, 2023).

[4] R. Kendall Soulen, "The Name of the Holy Trinity: A Triune Name," *Theology Today* 59, no. 2 (2002), 244.

self-sufficiency of God's being (Ps 36:7–9; John 5:26), in sharp contrast to the derivative and dependent nature of creaturely being. God is the primal fount and giver of existence and life to "all things" (Gk., *ta panta*), that is, to absolutely everything that is not one and the same being as God (Rom 11:36; 1 Cor 8:6; Col 1:17; Rev 4:11). "The God who made the world and everything in it," the apostle Paul states in Acts 17:24–28, "he himself gives to all mankind life and breath and everything . . . 'In him we live and move and have our being.'" God's Holy name, his being, is categorically unique and incommensurable with creaturely being.

The uniqueness and singularity of God's being is captured in the definitive proclamation of Israel's liturgical confession, the Shema: "Hear, O Israel: The Lord [YHWH] our God, the Lord [YHWH] is one. You shall love the Lord [YHWH] your God with all your heart and with all your soul and with all your might" (Deut 6:4–5 ESV). The oneness confessed in Israel's Shema denotes first and foremost God's ontological exclusivity, that YHWH alone exists of himself and is the absolute creator of all that is not God; "I am the Lord, and there is no other, besides me there is no God" (Isa 45:5 ESV). This ontological exclusivity of the divine name grounds and norms the doxological and devotional exclusivity due to YHWH alone: "I am the Lord [YHWH] your God . . . You shall have no other gods before me" (Deut 5:6–7), and "For I am God, and there is no other . . . 'To me every knee shall bow, every tongue shall swear allegiance'" (Isa 45:22–23). Precisely because "there is no other," it is right and fitting that Israel should bow the knee to YHWH alone; metaphysics and doxology are inseparably wedded in the liturgical life of the people of God.

Strikingly, the New Testament reveals that the ontological uniqueness and oneness of God's Holy name has a three-fold inflection; that the one divine being, YHWH, is numerically the same divine being as the three, distinct persons of the Father, the Son, and the Holy Spirit. While the divine persons are genuinely distinct (non-identical) from one another, they are nevertheless all equally included in the one, holy name, YHWH. As the divine name is attributed equally to the Father, the Son, and the Holy Spirit, "the Tetragrammaton," Kendal Soulen notes, "is alive and well in the New Testament."[5]

While much could be said about the attribution of YHWH to the three, distinct (non-identical) persons of the Father, the Son, and the Holy Spirit, two representative Scriptural examples will suffice for our purposes here: 1 Cor 8:6 and Matt 28:19.[6]

In 1 Cor 8:6 (ESV), the apostle Paul explicitly *identifies* the one Lord God of Israel's *Shema*, YHWH, with the "one God, the Father, from whom are all things and for whom we exist," and with the "one Lord, Jesus Christ, through whom are all things and through whom we exist." The Father and Jesus Christ are equally included within the divine being; they are numerically the same divine being as YHWH, the uniquely self-sufficient and creative source and end of all creaturely being. As Richard Bauckham has shown, the inclusion of Jesus within the divine being is rightly understood against the backdrop of a Second Temple Jewish understanding of YHWH's oneness and uniqueness as the "the sole Creator of all things and sole Ruler of all things."[7] In a similar manner, the Holy Spirit is also described as one and the same divine being as YHWH, the one Lord God of Israel (Acts 5:3–4; 2 Cor 3:16–17; Eph 4:4).[8]

While the Father, the Son, and the Holy Spirit are each numerically one and the same divine being, YHWH, (and thus each are not "another" being, strictly speaking) Scripture also teaches that they are

---

[5] Soulen, "The Name of the Holy Trinity," 250.

[6] For a nice summary of the Scriptural material here, see Robert M. Bowman Jr. and J. Ed Komoszewski, *Putting Jesus in His Place: The Case for the Deity of Christ* (Grand Rapids, MI: Kregel, 2007).

[7] Richard Bauckham, *Jesus and the God of Israel* (Grand Rapids, MI: Eerdmans, 2009), 9.

[8] Scott R. Swain, *The Trinity* (Wheaton, IL: Crossway, 2020), 31. For a further treatment on 1 Cor 8 and other texts that associate the divine name, YHWH, with the Son and the Spirit, see Jamieson and Wittman, *Biblical Reasoning*, 96–99.

personally distinct (non-identical) in the way they are eternally related to one another; the one, triune name admits of real, personal distinctness and plurality, independent of God's action toward creatures in the economy of salvation.

This is evident in the way that Scripture marks out the distinct personal names of Father, Son, and Spirit by the way they are eternally, yet one-directionally, related to one another. God the Father is uniquely and eternally distinguished from the Son and Spirit in so far as he eternally begets his beloved Son (John 1:14) and, with the Son, eternally breathes forth the Holy Spirit. The Father is the origin from which the eternal Son proceeds (and not vice versa) and is himself unbegotten. The Son is uniquely referred to as the "beloved Son" of the Father (Matt 3:17; 17:5 ESV), the Word of God (John 1:1; Rev 19:13), the wisdom and power of God (Proverbs 8; 1 Cor. 1:24), the "image of the invisible God" (Col 1:15 ESV), and the radiance of the Father's glory (Heb 1:3), and never the other way around. It is the eternal "Son . . . through whom also he [the Father] created the world" (Heb 1:2 ESV). God the Spirit is described in Scripture as both "the Spirit of your Father" (Matt 10:20 ESV; cf., Rom 8:9) and the "the Spirit of Christ" (Rom 8:9 ESV; Gal 4:6), indicating that the personal distinctness of the Spirit is grounded in the Spirit's being eternally from the Father *and* the Son together (John 16:12–15).

Though genuinely distinct, Scripture also attests to the fact that the divine persons act *inseparably* from one another in their works of nature and grace. And this in virtue of the fact that they together *are* the one God. The Son "can do nothing of his own accord, but only what he sees the Father doing. For whatever the Father does, that the Son does likewise" (John 5:19 ESV). While the Son does the very same works as the Father, the Son does them not from himself but from the Father (John 7:17; 14:10). Likewise, the Spirit does the very same works as the Father and the Son, but he does them from both Father and Son (John 14:16–17, 26; 15:26). Precisely because they together are the one Lord God of

Israel, the divine persons act inseparably, even while they do so by way of the proper manner in which they are uniquely and eternally related in the Godhead.[9]

Chief among New Testament texts that capture both the supreme *oneness* of God's revealed name alongside the distinctness yet co-equality of the Father, Son, and Holy Spirit is the baptismal formula of Matt 28:19 (ESV), "Go therefore and make disciples of all nations, baptizing them in the name of the Father and of the Son and of the Holy Spirit." The name into which Christians are to be baptized is *singular*, echoing the Tetragrammaton, the personal proper name of Israel's God by which he discloses his very being.[10] Yet the baptismal formula is equally clear that the one, divine name is distinctively *triune* in that it consists of three, distinct (non-identical) divine persons, each of whom are the one God. As we will see below, the consensual Christian tradition has understood the baptismal formula of Matt 28:19–20 as offering a basic, trinitarian grammar and touchstone for rightly ordered praise and proclamation of the triune name.

### *The Ecclesial Interpretation of the Triune Name*

The church's doctrinal reflection on the nature of the triune God is the humble and Spirit-enabled attempt to "follow the grain" of the above Scriptural pressures regarding the simultaneous *oneness* and *distinctness* of the triune God. "As an interpretation of biblical revelation," Scott Swain writes, "the doctrine of the Trinity is the church's attempt, under Jesus's promise of illumination, to refine its speech and thought about God in light of God's revealed name in order that it may bear truthful witness to the one true God."[11]

---

[9] Here we're indebted to Jamieson and Wittman, *Biblical Reasoning*, 116.

[10] R. Kendal Soulen, *The Divine Name(s) and the Holy Trinity: Distinguishing the Voices* (Louisville, KY: Westminster John Knox, 2011), 176.

[11] Swain, "Divine Trinity," 93–94.

More generally, we define the *consensual Christian doctrine of God* as the church's interpretive judgments regarding the revelation of the triune name in Scripture that have been affirmed by the broad spectrum of Christendom across time. The consensual Christian doctrine of God is expressed most pointedly (but not exclusively) in the ecumenical creeds (The Apostles', the Nicene, and the so-called Athanasian creeds) and the seven ecumenical councils of the undivided church, which provide "the 'canon' of beliefs about God ratified by the whole Church prior to the Great Schism."[12] In addition, the consensual Christian doctrine of God is also codified in the various aspects of the doctrine of God that are jointly affirmed by confessional statements of particular ecclesial bodies, whether Eastern Orthodox, Roman Catholic, and Protestant (Lutheran, Baptist, Reformed, etc.).[13] Consequently, and in line with the *historical* and *ecclesial* signposts, Baptist dogmatic reflection on the triune name is an exercise in judiciously hearing, receiving, and proclaiming the corporate testimony of the one, holy, catholic church; it is an ecclesial exercise carried out *by*, *with*, and *for* the community of the redeemed on earth.

What, then, is the shape of the consensual Christian doctrine of God? Of course, a full treatment of the consensual Christian doctrine of

---

[12] Oliver D. Crisp, *God Incarnate: Explorations in Christology* (New York: T&T Clark International, 2009), 13.

[13] The ecumenical creeds and councils of the one, undivided (catholic) church in particular act, as Crisp puts it, "as a sort of hermeneutical bridge between Scripture and the church." That is, they provide an interpretative script by which the church universal can, with one voice, publicly profess allegiance to the triune God whose gospel alone has the power to save (Rom 1:16). As Kevin Vanhoozer puts it, the decrees of conciliar creeds and councils are "the Spirit-guided embodiment of right biblical understanding." While the authority of conciliar creeds and councils are ultimately normed by Holy Scripture, and thus have a derivative authority, they nevertheless serve as a kind of corporate testimony—a collective, cross-temporal cloud of theological witnesses—concerning which interpretive judgments are apt and successfully carve Scripture at its deepest theological joints, and which do not. The consensual Christian tradition regarding the nature of the triune God acts as an interpretive witness to God's self-disclosure of his triune name, not a judge.

God is well-beyond the scope of a chapter like this. Given the centrality of the baptismal formula of Matt 28:19–20 as a touchstone for rightly ordered trinitarian praise and proclamation throughout the Christian tradition, we want to employ it here as a guide in demonstrating the organic connection that links biblical exegesis with trinitarian dogmatic reflection.[14] In the baptismal formula, the church has recognized the convergence of biblical pressures concerning God's supreme *oneness*, together with the genuine *distinctness* or *non–identity* and co-equality of the divine persons.

Consider the following tenets of the consensual Christian doctrine of God (CT for "consensual tradition") in light of the baptismal formula:

- (CT1) There is exactly one God. ["Baptizing them into the *name . . .*"]
- (CT2) The persons of the Father, the Son, and the Holy Spirit are not identical. [. . . of *the* Father and of *the* Son and of *the* Holy Spirit . . ."]
- (CT3) The persons of the Father, the Son, and the Holy Spirit are consubstantial [". . . of the Father *and* of the Son *and* of the Holy Spirit . . ."]

The church's corporate witness to CT1–CT3 is concisely summarized by the following declaration from Constantinople II (AD 553), the Fifth Ecumenical Council, which "benefits from the long and patient effort of doctrinal reflection undertaken by many Fathers of the Church":[15]

---

[14] For sources on the use of the formula as a touchstone and scriptural warrant for the doctrine of the Trinity, see Johann Gerhard, *On the Nature of God and the On the Most Holy Mystery of the Trinity*, trans. Richard J. Dinda (Saint Louis: Concordia, 2007), 342–57; Francis Turretin, *Institutes of Elenctic Theology* Vol. 1, trans. George Musgrave Giger (New Jersey: P&R, 1992), 267–68; Khaled Anatolios, *Retrieving Nicaea* (Grand Rapids, MI: Baker Academic, 2011), chap. 3.

[15] Gilles Emery, *The Trinity: An Introduction to Catholic Doctrine on the Triune God*, trans. Matthew Levering, (Washington, D.C.: The Catholic University of America Press, 2011), 84.

If anyone will not confess that the Father, Son and Holy Spirit have one nature (*phusis, natura*) or substance (*ousia, substantia*), that they have one power (*dunamis, virtus*) and authority (*exousia, potestas*), that there is a consubstantial (*homoousios, consubstantialis*) Trinity, one Deity to be adored in three hypostases (*hupostaseis, subsistentiae*) or persons (*prosopa, personae*): let him be anathema. For there is only one God and Father, from whom all things come, and one Lord, Jesus Christ, through whom all things are, and one Holy Spirit, in whom all things are.[16]

In this passage, we have the basic metaphysical and theological grammar of CT1–CT3 that constitutes the historic, orthodox doctrine of the trinity confessed and proclaimed by the church catholic. Let's take a closer look at each tenet.[17]

## "Baptizing them into the name" (CT1)

As for CT1, the consensual Christian tradition has affirmed that there is a single divine nature or substance (*ousia*), "one Deity," and numerically

---

[16] Council of Constantinople II, Anathema I in Norman P. Tanner, ed. *Decrees of the Ecumenical Councils, Volume 1* (Washington DC: Georgetown University Press, 1990), 114. Quoted in Gilles Emery, *The Trinity*, 83.

[17] It is important to point out that the church's interpretive task of formulating trinitarian dogma has historically employed a variety of metaphysical concepts, terms, and distinctions—a metaphysical grammar, we might say—such as substance (*ousia/substantia*), nature (*phusis/natura*), person (*hupostaseis/subsistentiae*), and consubstantiality (*homoousios, consubstantialis*)—for the purpose of adequately articulating and preserving the biblical patterns of speech about the *oneness* and the *distinctness* of the triune God as revealed in the baptismal formula. The church's dogmatic employment of metaphysical grammar is to aid right biblical understanding of God's self-disclosure of his triune name in Scripture. As Kavin Rowe has said, "the ontological judgements of the early ecumenical Creeds were the only satisfying and indeed logical outcome of the claims of the New Testament read together with the Old." See Rowe, "Biblical Pressure and Trinitarian Hermeneutics," 308.

one and only one divine power and authority in the Godhead. Regarding CT1, the oneness of the power and authority in the Godhead is grounded and reflected in the oneness of the divine nature itself; the power by which (*principium quo*) the three, distinct persons of the Godhead act is numerically one precisely because it is anchored in numerically one and the same divine nature.[18]

Along these lines, it is noteworthy that later ecumenical material from Constantinople III (sixth ecumenical council, 680–81), a council centered on establishing two wills in Christ, would further crystalize and clarify the above passage from Constantinople II by affirming that the one divine nature "has one natural will, power, operation, domination, majesty, potency, and glory." This indicates that the ecumenical witness of Constantinople II and III is that "the number of activities or operations is to be apprehended with the number of essences or natures, and the number of activities or operations is not to be apprehended with the number of divine *hypostases*."[19] This "canonical logic" ecumenically affirmed at Constantinople II and III—that the number of wills in the Godhead tracks the number of natures (*ousia*) in the Godhead, not the number of persons (Gk., *hypostases)*—is precisely what we find throughout the consensual Christian tradition regarding CT1.[20]

Moreover, CT1 situates the consensual Christian doctrine of God squarely in the camp of monotheism. As the triune name into which believers are to be baptized is singular, there is only one God, YHWH.

---

[18] Gregory of Nyssa, "That There Are Not Three Gods," in William G. Rusch, ed., The *Trinitarian Controversy* (Minneapolis: Fortress Press, 1980), 121–23.

[19] Scott M. Williams, "Discovery of the Sixth Ecumenical Council's Trinitarian Theology: Historical, Ecclesial, and Theological Implications," *Journal of Analytic Theology* 10 (2022): 343.

[20] This credally normed, canonical logic pushes against certain social models of the trinity that entail more than one divine will in the Godhead as out of step with the consensual Christian doctrine of God.

While there is a plurality of distinct divine *persons* (*hupostaseis*) in this one God (CT2), there are not a plurality of divine beings (*ousia*).

Let's press further and ask of CT1: what, according to the consensual Christian tradition, is true of the one, divine nature? The consistent witness of the Christian tradition is that the one divine nature—the one triune name into which believers are baptized—consists of both immanent and relative perfections, perfections pertaining to how God is in himself (*ad intra*) as well as how God is in relation to creatures in the works of nature and grace (*ad extra*). We will focus chiefly on a handful of perfections (both immanent and relative) that have been at the foundation of a consensual Christian doctrine of God and have served an important dogmatic role in trinitarian and Christological reflection historically: *aseity, simplicity, immutability, eternity,* and *impassibility.*

*Divine Aseity.* Following the grain of God's revealed name to Moses in the Tetragammaton of Exod 3:14, the attribute of *divine aseity* ascribes to God both an immanent as well as a relative perfection (although the immanent grounds the relative perfection).[21] In himself (*ad intra*), apart from his relation to creatures, the one God is utterly replete in the "underived fullness"[22] of his triune glory, life, blessedness, and perfection. As we've seen in the first section, Scripture bears witness that God in no way derives any aspect of the plenitude of his being from another. God and God alone is the ontologically sufficient condition for his existence, life, nature and activity; there is nothing behind or in back of God that explains *that* God is, *what* God is, or what God *does.*

In relation to creatures (*ad extra*), God is the absolute creative source of all that is not God (Col 1:15–17; Acts 17:24–27; Rev 4:11). This second, relative dimension to divine aseity is attributed to God in the very first ecumenical council, the Council of Nicaea, in AD 325, and later

---

[21] See John Webster, "Life in and of Himself," in *God Without Measure: Working Papers in Christian Theology,* Vol. 1 (New York: Bloomsbury T&T Clark, 2016), 13.

[22] John Webster, "Life in and of Himself," 13.

reaffirmed at subsequent ecumenical councils such as Constantinople I (381), Ephesus (431), and Chalcedon (451). Absolutely everything that exists, other than God, is brought into existence by God; God is the *sole* uncreated being (*agenētos*).[23] The second century church father Irenaeus put it succinctly when he said, "In all things God has the preeminence, who alone is uncreated, the first of all things, and the primary cause of the existence of all."[24]

*Divine Simplicity*. Traditionally, divine aseity has been at the root of many other divine perfections affirmed by the consensual Christian tradition, including divine simplicity, immutability, eternity, and impassibility. While divine simplicity has taken a variety of forms and varying strengths throughout the Christian tradition, at bottom, divine simplicity has played a key dogmatic role in both demarcating the Creator from the creature as well as providing a metaphysical grammar—anchored in the scriptural witness to divine aseity—to clarify and chasten creaturely reflection and discourse about the triune God.[25] The ubiquity of divine simplicity throughout the Christian tradition is hard to overstate. Richard Muller summarizes this consensus well when he says, "The doctrine of

[23] William Lane Craig, *God Over All: Divine Aseity and the Challenge of Platonism* (New York: Oxford University Press, 2016), chap. 2. See also G. L. Prestige, *God in Patristic Thought* (Eugene, OR: Wipf and Stock Publishers, 2008), chap. 2.

[24] *Against Heresies* 4.38.3. Cited in Craig, 33.

[25] For further reading on these dogmatic roles played by divine simplicity, see Andrew Radde-Gallwitz, *Basil of Caesarea, Gregory of Nyssa, and the Transformation of Divine Simplicity* (New York: Oxford University Press, 2009), Jordan P. Barrett, *Divine Simplicity: A Biblical and Trinitarian Account* (Minneapolis: Fortress, 2017), and Steven J. Duby, *Divine Simplicity: A Dogmatic Account* (New York: T&T Clark, 2016). For a nice overview of different versions of divine simplicity as it pertains to trinitarian doctrine, see Thomas McCall, "Trinity Doctrine, Plain and Simple," in Oliver D. Crisp and Fred Sanders, eds. *Advancing Trinitarian Theology* (Grand Rapids: Zondervan, 2014). For a more in-depth look at the various formulations of divine simplicity throughout the Christian tradition, see Ross D. Inman, *Contemplating Divine Simplicity: Five Views from Theology and Philosophy* (London: Bloomsbury Academic, forthcoming).

divine simplicity is among the normative assumptions of theology from the time of the church fathers, to the age of the great medieval scholastic systems, to the era of Reformation and post-Reformation theology, and indeed, on into the succeeding era of late orthodoxy and rationalism."[26]

In the consensual Christian tradition, simplicity has served as a guardrail against attributing creaturely conditions to the divine being—in this case, ontological complexity or composition.[27] There are a host of different types of ontological composition (substance/attribute; essence/existence; genus/species), and a discussion of each of them would be well outside the scope of our discussion here.[28] At the very least, to say that the divine nature is simple is to say that it lacks all forms of ontological composition. The reason being that, in general, ontological composition is thought to entail *ontological dependence*; what is composed of parts or constituents is in some way dependent on or conditioned by those parts and constituents, either with respect to its existence, its nature, or both. If God is *a se* and is himself the primal font and fullness of being and dependent on and conditioned by no other, then God cannot derive his existence or any aspect of his nature from any entity that is not God, including would be parts or intrinsic accidents (*goodness, wisdom, power*, etc.). Ontological composition, then, is unfitting for a being that exists *a se*.

While this much is consistent with a variety of formulations of divine simplicity in the consensual tradition, many have taken this line of

[26] Richard A. Muller, *Post-Reformation Reformed Dogmatics: The Rise and Development of Reformed Orthodoxy*, vol. 3, *The Divine Essence and Attributes* (Grand Rapids, MI: Baker Academic, 2003), 39.

[27] See Thomas Aquinas, *Summa Theologiae* I.3 in Thomas Aquinas, *Summa Theologiae*, trans. Fr. L. Shapcote, O.P., ed. J. Mortensen and E. Alarcón (Lander, WY: The Aquinas Institute, 2012); *De potentia* q. 7 in Thomas Aquinas, *The Power of God*, trans. Richard J. Regan (New York: Oxford University Press, 2012); Gisbertus Voetius, "God's Single, Absolutely Simple Essence," *Confessional Presbyterian* 15 (2019), trans. R. M. Hurd.

[28] For a helpful overview of these various kinds of ontological complexity and their absence in the divine nature, see Voetius, "God's Single, Absolutely Simple Essence."

reasoning to entail that God is the same as what he has in himself, that the various immanent perfections predicated of the divine nature are one and the same as the divine nature.[29] Hilary of Poitiers (AD 310–367) captures the Creator-creature distinguishing dogmatic function of divine simplicity well, which is received throughout the Christian tradition, when he states, "Unlike human beings, God is not a composite being so that in him there is no difference between what is possessed by him and he who possesses. But all that he is is life, namely a perfect and infinite nature, and not composed of disparate elements, but the same life permeating the whole."[30] Consequently, "a Being really single and absolutely one," must be "identical with goodness rather than possessing it."[31]

Divine simplicity has also provided a metaphysical grammar for rightly ordered speech about the triune God revealed in Scripture. If God is simple, then there are no more fundamental parts or constituents that divide or compound the one, divine nature. Moreover, since the divine nature is "simple, uniform, incomposite"[32] it can in no way

---

[29] This is amply attested in the Christian theological tradition and arguably precedes Aquinas's full-strength formulation of the doctrine of divine simplicity. For a sample, see Gregory of Nyssa, "Gregory of Nyssa against Eunomius" I.19, in *Gregory of Nyssa: Dogmatic Treatises, Etc.*, ed. Philip Schaff and Henry Wace, trans. William Moore et al., vol. 5, A Select Library of the Nicene and Post-Nicene Fathers of the Christian Church, Second Series (New York: Christian Literature Company, 1893); St. Augustine, *The Trinity* bks. 5–7, trans. Stephen McKenna (Washington DC: The Catholic University of America Press, 1963); St. John of Damascus, *On the Orthodox Faith* 9, trans. Norman Russell (New York: St. Vladimir's Seminary Press, 2022), 83; St. Anselm of Canterbury, *Monologion* 15–17 in *Anselm: Basic Writings*, trans. and ed. T. Williams (Indianapolis: Hackett, 2007); Richard of St. Victor, *On the Trinity* bk. 1, in Boyd Taylor Coolman and Dale M. Coulter, eds., *Trinity and Creation* (New York: New City Press, 2011).

[30] Hilary of Poitiers, "On the Trinity" Bk. 8 in *St. Hilary of Poitiers, John of Damascus*, ed. Philip Schaff and Henry Wace, trans. E. W. Watson et al., vol. 9a, A Select Library of the Nicene and Post-Nicene Fathers of the Christian Church, Second Series (New York: Christian Literature Company, 1899), 150.

[31] Gregory of Nyssa, "Gregory of Nyssa against Eunomius," I.19. See references in footnote 28.

[32] Gregory of Nyssa, "Gregory of Nyssa against Eunomius" I.22.

admit of degrees or gradations. Nothing can be *more or less* God on the assumption of divine simplicity. Whatever has the one, simple, undivided divine nature is *wholly* and *fully* God and the bearer of each of the divine perfections. As the divine nature is undivided and "without mixture or conflux of qualities . . . without parts and composition," it follows that "simplicity in the case of the Holy Trinity admits of no degrees."[33]

Additionally, neither can, on divine simplicity, the divine persons be understood as distinct parts or constituents of the one, divine nature.[34] Since each divine person "possesses the whole essence undivided," the "whole fullness of the Godhead dwells in the Father, so in the Son . . . and so in the Spirit, and therefore but one God."[35] Far from undermining the doctrine of the trinity, divine simplicity has traditionally been understood as an indispensable piece of metaphysical grammar that safeguards and preserves it.[36]

*Absolute Immutability.* Absolute divine immutability has been traditionally thought to be a close corollary to divine simplicity. Absolute divine immutability is the perfection in which the divine nature is incapable of undergoing any intrinsic change *whatsoever*—that is, the sort of change that involves an alteration in God's being as he is in himself, apart from any relations he stands in to creatures.[37] As Augustine clearly

---

[33] Gregory of Nyssa, I.19.

[34] John Calvin, *Institutes of the Christian Religion* I.13.2, ed. John T. McNeill, trans. Ford Lewis Battles (Lousville, KY: Westminster John Knox, 2006).

[35] John Gill, A *Complete Body of Doctrinal and Practical Divinity* I.26.4 (Paris, AR: Baptist Standard Bearer, 2007).

[36] As Stephen Holmes puts it, summarizing the consensual tradition on the matter, "From Gregory of Nyssa . . . to Francis Turretin . . . there was an assumption on all sides that to believe in divine simplicity was to be an orthodox trinitarian, and to deny simplicity was to attack the doctrine of the trinity." See Stephen R. Holmes, "The Attributes of God", in John Webster and Kathryn Tanner and Iain Torrance, eds. *The Oxford Handbook of Systematic Theology* (New York: Oxford University Press, 2007), 65. This truth is clearly reflected in the early modern Protestant polemic against Socinianism.

[37] See Anselm *Mon.* 25 for a careful discussion of the kind of relational change and relational "accidents" that are consistent with absolute immutability

noted, if a being is absolutely simple and lacks ontological composition—
including varying characteristics that determine how a being is in itself—
then such a being cannot undergo change in itself (intrinsic change).[38]
Divine immutability in this sense has been part and parcel of the consensual Christian doctrine of God. Immutability is attested at the ecumenical councils of Nicaea I (325) and Ephesus (431), the latter by way of
conciliar documents affirmed therein.[39]

Conciliar attestation of divine immutability is largely limited to
Christological contexts concerning the question of whether the eternal
Word of God, in taking on human flesh (Phil 2), underwent any change
or alteration of nature in doing so. In response, the fathers at Nicaea
explicitly denied of the Son "that he is a creature, or subject to change
or conversion."[40] Cyril of Alexandria, in his third letter to Nestorius,
is instructive on precisely this point, "We do not say that his flesh was
turned into the nature of the godhead or that the unspeakable Word
of God was changed into the nature of the flesh. For he (the Word) is
unalterable and absolutely unchangeable and remains always the same
as the scriptures say."[41] Moreover, Cyril, in his letter to John of Antioch

---

and simplicity. "Absolute" or "unqualified" immutability" here is to be compared
with a modified or "weak immutability," which claims that God is immutable
with respect to his essential nature, character, and/or covenant faithfulness. For
a helpful overview of various construals of divine immutability and historical
background, see Timothy Pawl, "Divine Immutability," *Internet Encyclopedia of
Philosophy*. https://iep.utm.edu/divine-immutability/.

[38] Augustine, *The Trinity* Bk. 5.

[39] In terms of the conciliar material supporting immutability, atempo-
ral eternity, and impassibility, we are indebted to the work of Timothy Pawl,
*In Defense of Conciliar Christology: A Philosophical Essay* (New York: Oxford
University Press, 2016).

[40] Philip Schaff and Henry Wace, eds., "The Nicene Creed," in *The Seven
Ecumenical Councils*, trans. Henry R. Percival, vol. 14, A Select Library of the
Nicene and Post-Nicene Fathers of the Christian Church, Second Series (New
York: Charles Scribner's Sons, 1900), 3.

[41] Tanner, *Decrees*, 51.

(which was affirmed at Ephesus, 431) would later emphatically declare that "he [God] is unchangeable and immutable by nature." Indeed, Cyril goes so far as to say "I think that those are quite mad who suppose that 'a shadow of change' is conceivable in connexion with the divine nature of the Word. For he remains what he is always and never changes, nor could he ever change or be susceptible of it."[42]

*Divine Eternity.* Divine Eternity is also well attested in the consensual Christian teaching concerning the nature of the triune God. The main, scriptural discourse about God's eternity has been interpreted, in light of other revealed divine perfections, along the lines of *divine atemporality*. God's atemporal eternity entails that God's inner life (*ad intra*) lacks temporal beginning or end, succession or division and, in relation to creation (*ad extra*), is in no way constrained, bound, or subject to time. God's eternity, then, is that relative perfection, anchored and explained by the fullness of God's immanent perfection, by which God's triune being transcends the limits and mutability of temporal existence (which is why eternity is often discussed in conjunction with divine infinity and divine immutability).

As with simplicity and immutability, eternity follows on the heels of other divine perfections revealed in Scripture. There can be no temporal succession in the inner life of God (ad intra) "because his essence, with which it is really identified, admits none. This is so both because it is perfectly simple and immutable (and therefore rejects the change of former into latter, of past into present, of present into future, which succession involves), and because it is immeasurable, as being the first and independent."[43]

Divine eternity finds support in the ecumenical tradition, including the so-called Athanasian Creed, "eternal is the Father, eternal the Son, eternal the Holy Spirit; yet they are not three eternal beings but

---

[42] Tanner, *Decrees*, 72
[43] Turretin, *Institutes*, 203.

one eternal. . . ."[44] Moreover, divine eternity, viewed along the lines of atemporality, has indirect ecumenical support by way of the definitive Christological affirmation at both the Council of Ephesus (AD 431) and at Constantinople II (AD 553) that the Father communicates the divine nature to the Son "before all ages" and "outside of time [*achronos; sin tempore*]."[45] This suggest that the church fathers at Ephesus and Second Constantinople thought that the divine nature was in no way conditioned by time nor susceptible to temporal succession, even if Christ's assumed human nature is conditioned and susceptible in this way.

*Divine Impassibility*. Divine impassibility has also been viewed as a close corollary with divine aseity, simplicity, and immutability as perfections of the one, divine nature. In classical thought, roughly, a *passion* (*passio*) is a *received* or *caused* state of being that brings about an intrinsic change in the recipient and causes them to be in a way that they were not before, normally for the worse.[46] If the triune life of God is *a se* and completely self-sufficient in itself, simple and lacking ontological composition, and absolutely immutable, then the idea that God's being in itself can be altered, caused, conditioned, or determined *to be* in any way by anything not God is unbefitting of God's ultimacy. While God lacks passions in this specific sense of the word (one that entails ontological deficiency and dependence on another), this does not entail that God lacks affections, that love, anger, hate, mercy and so on cannot be aptly predicated of him; far from it! Rather, as Richard Muller states, "impassibility, when attributed to God in the Christian tradition and, specifically, in medieval and Protestant scholastic thought, indicates, not a Stoic notion of *apatheia*, but an absence of mutation, distress, or any other sort of negative *passiones*.[47]

---

[44] Jacques Dupuis, ed.,The *Christian Faith in the Doctrinal Documents of the Catholic Church*, Rev. Edition (New York: Alba House, 1998), 12.

[45] See Tanner, *Decrees*, 79, 114.

[46] Thomas Aquinas, *Summa Theologiae* Ia–IIae, 26.2.

[47] Muller, *Post-Reformation Reformed Dogmatics*, 3:310.

Impassibility is strongly attested in the consensual tradition and is affirmed at the fourth ecumenical council of Chalcedon as well as in the conciliar documents explicitly affirmed at Chalcedon (including Cyril of Alexandria's letters to Nestorius and John of Antioch and Leo's Tome to Flavian). The definition of Chalcedon, the definitive ecclesial symbol of an orthodox Christology, explicitly rejects the view that "the divine nature of the Only-begotten is passible."[48] Cyril of Alexandria notes that Christ, while "according to his own nature he was not subject to suffering," yet "suffered for us in the flesh according to the Scriptures, and was in his crucified body, and without himself suffering made his own the sufferings of his own flesh . . ."[49] Here Cyril is tracking the scriptural language that demarcates the manner in which the Word suffered, namely "in the flesh." Christ "suffered once for sins . . . being put to death in the flesh" (1 Pet 3:18; 4:1) according to his assumed human nature and thus, as Leo says in his Tome to Flavian, the "invulnerable nature was united to a nature that could suffer."[50]

Impassibility is an integral aspect of a consensual Christian doctrine of God, in part, due to its organic connection to other well-entrenched divine perfections. Some go so far as to say of divine impassibility that "this venerable doctrine enjoyed near-universal acceptance until the end of the nineteenth century—carefully crafted by the Fathers, systematized by the great medieval schoolmen, and affirmed by the major

---

[48] Tanner, *Decrees*, 84.

[49] Tanner, 53

[50] Tanner, 78. For further reading on the role and prominence of impassibility in the conciliar tradition, see Gilles Emery. "The Immutability of the God of Love and the Problem of Language Concerning the 'Suffering of God,'" in James F. Keating and Joseph White, O.P., eds. *Divine Impassibility and the Mystery of Human Suffering* (Grand Rapids: Eerdmans, 2009). For an excellent treatment of impassibility as it relates to the incarnation, see chapter 7 of Steven J. Duby, *Jesus and the God of Classical Theism: Biblical Christology in Light of the Doctrine of God* (Grand Rapids: Baker Academic, 2022).

Reformed theologians (It even makes it into the first of the Thirty-Nine Articles)."[51]

## Divine Processions and Missions: Eternal Depths Upon a Temporal Shore[52]

*"Baptizing them into the name of* the *Father and of* the *Son and of* the *Holy Spirit" (CT2)*

Let's turn now to our second tenet of the consensual Christian doctrine of God, CT2. While the Father, Son, and Spirit equally share the one divine nature, one power, and one glory (and all of the divine perfections above), they are nevertheless genuinely distinct and thus in no way identical to one another; there are numerically three divine persons that subsist in numerically one divine essence.

But what, exactly, accounts for the numerical distinctness of the three divine persons according to the consensual tradition? When explicating the personal distinctions between the Father, Son, and Spirit within the one simple Godhead, the consensual tradition has been careful not to "turn the union into confusion, nor the distinction into a difference of natures," but to "keep equally aloof from the Sabellian identification and the Arian differentiation—errors diametrically opposed, but equally irreverent."[53] Minimally, to safeguard against "the Sabellian identification" which collapses the genuine distinctions between Father, Son, and

---

[51] Mark S. Smith, "'Only the Non-Suffering God Can Help': Recovering the Glory of Divine Impassibility." *Churchman* 126:2 (2012), 147. As quoted in Pawl, *In Defense of Conciliar Christology*, 185.

[52] We owe this lovely phrase to Scott Swain, *The Trinity*, 114. Swain traces the original source of the phrase back to John Webster.

[53] Gregory Nazianzen, "Select Orations of Saint Gregory Nazianzen," 39.11, in *S. Cyril of Jerusalem, S. Gregory Nazianzen*, ed. Philip Schaff and Henry Wace, trans. Charles Gordon Browne and James Edward Swallow, vol. 7, A Select Library of the Nicene and Post-Nicene Fathers of the Christian Church, Second Series (New York: Christian Literature Company, 1894), 356.

Spirit, the divine persons must be distinct from each other *extra-mentally*, that is, apart from how creatures think about them or name them.[54] At the same time, to safeguard against "the Arian differentiation," the divine persons must not be distinct in such a way that they constitute distinct beings or natures, thereby dividing or composing the divine nature.

Reflecting on this problem, Karl Rahner famously quipped, 'the "economic" Trinity is the "immanent" Trinity and the "immanent" Trinity is the "economic" Trinity."[55] Others after him have struggled to conceptualize this association and hold them in unity, especially among evangelical theologians that want to remain closely tied to the testimony of the Scriptures.[56] On one hand, some question whether the issue of processions is even discussed in the Scriptures. Others see the topic of the Trinity as irrelevant and disconnected to embedded Christian life and practice. These two extremes do not hold in tension the unity of the testimony of Scripture or unity of God taught in the Christian tradition.

Throughout the Christian tradition, it is commonly (though not universally) held that the divine persons differ from one another by way of their distinctive *manner or mode of procession* within the one divine nature.[57] In general, to say that there are eternal processions in the one,

---

[54] As John Gill, *Complete Body of Doctrinal and Practical Divinity,* 141, puts it, "The distinction between them is not merely *nominal*, which is no distinction at all; as when the Sabellians says, God is one Person, having three names, Father, Son, and Spirit; there is no distinction."

[55] Karl Rahner, *The Trinity*, trans. Joseph Donceel (New York: Burns and Oates, 2001), 22.

[56] For a good introduction to this conversation, see Keith S. Whitfield, ed., *Trinitarian Theology: Theological Models and Doctrinal Application* (Nashville: B&H Academic, 2019).

[57] There are important discussions surrounding whether the persons are distinguished by relation or by some absolute, non-relative feature of the divine persons. This discussion finds its head in the high medieval period between the Franciscans (Scotus and Bonaventure) and the Dominicans (especially Aquinas). For the Franciscans, the Father generates because he is Father (not vice versa); for the Dominicans, the Father is Father because he generates (and not *vice versa*). For a clear but accessible introduction to this discussion, see

simple God is to say that each divine person is eternally ordered to or related to another. Following the grain of Scriptural language concerning the eternal relations between the divine persons (as we noted above in the previous section), the consensual tradition has maintained an ordering (*taxis*) to the inner life of the one God. The Father's unique mode of procession is his eternally begetting the Son (*paternity*); the Son's unique mode of procession is his being eternally begotten of the Father (*filiation*); and, among Western theologians, the Spirit's unique mode of procession is his eternally proceeding from both Father and Son.[58] Thus, the Son's *filial* manner or mode of having the one, divine nature—being eternally begotten of the Father—is what distinguishes him from the Father and the Spirit.

The distinct modes of procession of the Father, Son, and Spirit in the one, divine nature have been referred to as "relations of origin" to emphasize that the personal-difference-maker between them is widely thought to be purely *relational*.[59] As each divine person is distinct solely in virtue of being ordered toward or related to another and not *absolutely* distinct, the processions in no way divide or compose the one, simple divine essence.[60] The persons are, to use older terminology widely employed

---

chapter 13 of Carl L. Beckwith, *The Holy Trinity* (Fort Wayne, IN: Luther Academy, 2016). For an excellent more scholarly treatment, see the introduction to Russell L. Friedman, *Intellectual Traditions at the Medieval University*, vol. 1 (Leiden: Brill, 2013).

[58] Orthodox theologians in the East, of course, lament the addition of the Latin phrase *filioque* ("and the Son") to the Niceano-Constantinopolitan creed (AD 381). For a succinct but clear introduction to the *Filioque* controversy between the East and the West, see Stephen L. Holmes, *The Quest for the Trinity* (Downers Grove: InterVarsity Press, 2012), chap. 7.

[59] See Gregory Nazianzen, "Select Orations of Saint Gregory Nazianzen," 29.16; St. Augustine, *The Trinity* 5.5.6; St. Anselm, The *Procession of the Holy Spirit*, 1, in *Complete Philosophical and Theological Treatises of Anselm of Canterbury*, trans. Jasper Hopkins and Herbert Richardson (Minneapolis: Arthur J. Banning Press, 2000).

[60] As Aquinas notes in *Summa Theologiae* Ia 30.2, ad. 3, "The supreme unity and simplicity of God exclude every kind of plurality of absolute things, but

throughout the Christian tradition, distinct "modes of subsistence" of the one, divine nature.[61] The Father, Son, and Spirit "differ from another not in essence, but in the manner of subsisting."[62] The divine processions have wide ecumenical backing as they are explicitly affirmed at Nicaea I (325), Constantinople I (381), Ephesus (431), Constantinople II (553), and Constantinople III (680–81). The processions, together with divine simplicity, have played a vital dogmatic role in the church's interpretation and proclamation of the triune name revealed in the baptismal formula.

As the divine processions are purely relative distinctions in the Godhead, the relation between the one divine essence and any given divine person is not one between "a thing and a thing" (which would divide the divine essence and compromise simplicity and introduce a quaternity) but, rather, between "a thing and a mode of the thing."[63] It is important to note that historically, there is not a strict (Leibnizian) identity relation that obtains between the divine nature and the divine persons, otherwise the divine persons would, given the transitivity of strict

---

not plurality of relations, because relations are predicated relatively; and thus the relations do not import composition in that of which they are predicated, as Boethius teaches in the same book."

[61] See Gregory of Nyssa, "Gregory of Nyssa against Eunomius" IV; John of Damascus, *On the Orthodox Faith* 8, 75; St. Bonaventure, *The Breviloquium* I. 4–6, trans. Jose de Vinck (Paterson, N.J.: St. Anthony Guild Press, 1963); Turretin, *Institutes* 3.1.25, 270; John Owen, *The Works of John Owen*, ed. William H. Goold, vol. 2 (Edinburgh: T&T Clark, n.d.), 407.

[62] Thomas Monck, *A Cure for the Cankering Error of the New Eutychians; saying, that our blessed mediator did not take his flesh of the Virgin Mary, etc.* Few MS. Notes (United Kingdom: n.p, 1673), 68.

[63] Turretin, *Institutes of Elenctic Theology*, 3.1.27. 3–4, 278. For many, though not all by any stretch, in the consensual tradition, there is a modal distinction between the divine nature and the persons, and not a real distinction. Some understandings of a real distinction (two really distinct entities differing in essence) would compromise both strict oneness of the divine nature (simplicity) and the consubstantiality of the divine persons. For more, see Petrus van Mastricht, *Theoretical-Practical Theology: Faith in the Triune God*, Vol. 2, trans. Todd M. Rester, ed. Joel R. Beeke (Grand Rapids, MI: Reformation Heritage Books, 2019), 503 and Turretin, *Institutes of Elenctic Theology*, 3.27.1–11.

identity, be strictly identical to one another, which leads to Sabellianism. The divine nature is one, the persons are three; the divine nature is absolute, the persons are relative; the divine nature is communicable, the persons are incommunicable.[64] While often unnoticed or underemphasized in contemporary trinitarian dogmatics, there is a type of sameness relation at play in classical trinitarian thought between the divine nature and the persons that doesn't itself entail sameness *in every respect* (as strict, Leibnizian identity demands). Along these very lines, Turretin notes, "whatever is in God essential and absolute is God himself (such as are the divine attributes, power wisdom, justice, etc.). But whatever is in God that is personal, relative and modal may not immediately in every way be identified with the divine essence."[65]

These doctrines do not contradict divine simplicity, rather they flow from it. "Just as God is one in essence and distinct in persons," Bavinck argues, "so also the work of creation is one and undivided, while in its unity it is still rich in diversity."[66] And this forms the clear teaching of the Scriptures. First, the consistent use of the titles "Father" and "Son" imply a relation. This relation is not absolute, but relative; it articulates a correspondence between antecedents.[67] Throughout the New Testament, the titles Father and Son are used in relational correspondence, in ways that are mutually informing.[68] The singularity of God does not deny the distinction of the persons but grasps them through the relations of origin. Several attributive terms describe the relation between the Father

---

[64] Turretin, *Institutes of Elenctic Theology*, 3.27.1, 278.

[65] Turretin, 3.27.5, 278–279. For a helpful primer on the variety of sameness and identity relations at play in medieval ontology, see Andrew Arlig, "Identity and Sameness" in the *Routledge Companion to Medieval Philosophy*, ed. Richard Cross and JT Paasch (New York: Routledge, 2021).

[66] Herman Bavinck, *Reformed Dogmatics*, ed. John Bolt, trans. John Vriend, vol. 2 (Grand Rapids: Baker Academic, 2004), 422.

[67] Jamieson and Wittman, *Biblical Reasoning*, 182. Cyril of Alexandria, *Dialogues on the Trinity*, 4.509c-d.

[68] For example: Matt 11:27, Matt 28:19, Luke 9:26, John 1:14, 1 Cor 15:24, 28, 1 Cor 13:14, Heb 1:5 and 1 John 1:3.

and the Son. For example, the Scriptures use personal possessives such as "my" Father (Matt 11:27; Luke 10:22, John 6:40), "his" [the Son's] Father (Matt 16:27) or "his" [the Father's] Son (1 John 1:3), or "my" Son (Heb 1:5, 2 Pet 1:17). Other passages describe the relation with other qualifiers: "the only Son from the Father" (John 1:14 ESV), "whatever the Father does, that the Son does likewise (John 5:19 ESV), or "as the Father has life in himself, so he has granted the Son also to have life in himself" (John 5:26). In other places the Father teaches the Son (John 8:28), the Father is glorified in the Son (John 14:13, John 17:1), the Father sends the Son (1 John 4:14), to confess the Father is to confess the Son (1 John 2:23), and those who abide in the teaching of Christ "has both the Father and the Son" (2 John 9 ESV). Together these passages assume a relation of the Father and the Son that is mutual, sourced, and unique. Indeed, such a derivation is strongly implied by the very words "Father" and "Son," as the church fathers repeatedly emphasized.[69]

Second, the problem of "begotten," is related to this discussion of titles. The debate about this term harks back to the Arian debates of the early church. The language of "only-begotten" found in passages such as John 1:14, "And the Word became flesh and dwelt among us, and we have seen his glory, glory as of the only-begotten (*monogenēs*) from the Father, full of grace and truth." Arians use this to defend Christ's creatureliness, but in the words of the Nicene Creed, the Son of God is "begotten, not made." Today many biblical scholars avoid this debate by interpreting this term to mean "unique" or "only" Son, but recent studies have recovered a more nuanced metaphorical and biological sense of the term.[70] In John 1:14 and others, such as John 1:18, 3:16–18, 1 John 4:9, the *monogenēs* language is only properly understood in a relational sense. The Son is at the Father's side and the Father has made him known (John 1:18) and

---

[69] Kevin Giles, *Eternal Generation of the Son: Maintaining Orthodoxy in Trinitarian Theology* (Downers Grove, IL: IVP Academic, 2012).

[70] Charles Lee Irons, "A Lexical Defense of the Johannine 'Only Begotten,'" in *Retrieving Eternal Generation*, ed. Fred Sanders and Scott R. Swain (Grand Rapids: Zondervan, 2017), 98–116.

the Father sent the Son (John 1:14, John 3:17, 1 John 4:9). John 5:26, "For as the Father has life in himself, so he has granted the Son also to have life in himself," presses the relational sense further into the very "life" of God.[71] Just as the Father has life, and this is the divine eternal life, this life is in the Son and the Son also has the divine eternal life. As Jamieson and Wittman argue, "the same life that belongs to the Father belongs to the Son."[72] The Son cannot have the same life as the Father if he had a beginning or is not eternally generated from the Father.

Finally, Scripture uses various qualifiers to explain the nature of the Son. When taken as a whole, these attributive qualities reinforce the eternal generation of the Son. Passages such as John 1:1 (ESV), "In the beginning was the Word, and the Word was with God, and the Word was God," and John 17:5 (ESV), "Father, glorify me in your own presence with the glory that I had with you before the world existed," describe the preexistence of the Son with the Father. Other passages, such as Col 1:15–16 (ESV), explain that the Son "is the image of the invisible God, the firstborn of all creation" and "by him all things were created." Similar passages include Phil 2:6 (ESV), the Son "was in the form of God," and Heb 1:3, "[the Son] is the radiance of the glory of God and the exact imprint of his nature." Denying the eternal generation of the Son, necessitates that the Son must have a beginning or inception. As Berkhof writes, "It is that eternal and necessary act of the first person in the Trinity, whereby He, within the divine Being is the ground of a second personal subsistence like His own, and puts this second person in possession of the whole divine essence, without any division, alienation, or change."[73]

Alongside the discussion of the Son, the Scriptures use personal and attribute language to describe the relationship of the Spirit with the

---

[71] This passage was important to Augustine's interpretation of the Son. See Keith Johnson, "Augustine, Eternal Generation, and Evangelical Trinitarianism," *Trinity Journal*, 32 (2011), 147–53.

[72] Jamieson and Wittman, *Biblical Reasoning*, 185.

[73] Louis Berkhof, *Systematic Theology* (Grand Rapids: Eerdmans, 1949), 94.

Father and the Son. The Son is eternally begotten of the Father, while the Spirit eternally proceeds from the Father and the Son. As Fairbairn explains, "The relation between the Son and the Father is not identical to the relation between the Spirit and the Father, even though all three persons possess identical characteristics and even though they share in the same relationship of love and fellowship."[74]

Many passages communicate the procession of the Spirit. The Spirit is called the "Spirit of your Father" (Matt 10:20) or the Spirit of God (Matt 12:28). Romans 8:9 teaches that belonging to the Spirit is also belonging to God. The Scriptures also teach that the Spirit belongs to both the Father and the Son, implying a double procession. For example, Gal 4:6 teaches that God has sent "the Spirit of his Son," and in many places the Spirit is referred to as the Spirit of the Son (or Jesus Christ): Acts 16:7, Phil 1:19, and 1 Pet 1:11. Romans 8:9 even equates the Spirit of God and the Spirit of Christ. As the Nicene Creed confesses, "together with the Father and the Son he [the Spirit] is worshipped and glorified."

Like the discussion of the Son, there are many passages that explain the relationship of the Spirit to the Father or the Son in relational proximity. The Spirit is "from" the Father or the Spirit teaches the things of God. First Corinthians 2:11–12 (ESV), for example, teaches that "no one comprehends the thoughts of God except the Spirit of God," and the Christian has received "the Spirit who is from God, that we might understand the things freely given us by God," while Gal 4:6 (ESV) teaches that "God has sent the Spirit of his Son into our hearts" (see also Matt. 10:20). Finally, John 15:26 explains that the "Spirit of truth" is sent from the Father and the Son to bear witness about Christ. In this case the language the Spirit "proceeds" (*ekporeuomai*) from the Father and the Son. In Oration 31:8, Gregory summarizes the Spirit's procession, saying, "Insofar as he proceeds from the Father, he is no creature; inasmuch as he is not begotten, he is not Son, and to the extent that procession is the

---

[74] Donald Fairbairn, *Life in the Trinity: An Introduction to Theology with the Help of the Church Fathers* (Downers Grove: IVP Academic, 2009, 53.

mean between ingeneracy and generacy he is God." While a definitive rational explanation of the Spirit's procession is beyond human capacity, as Gregory adds, the Scriptures provide the theological framework to make sense of the relationship between the Father and the Son.[75] All of these terms point to the procession of the Spirit. Fairbairn summarizes these points, saying, "the Father and the Spirit are not the begotten persons of the Trinity; only the Son is begotten. In other words, he has eternally been in a relation as Son to Father, not brother to brother or something else. In an analogous way, the Father and the Son are not the proceeding persons; only the Spirit proceeds. In other words, he is not in a filial relation to the Father, the way the Son is, but rather he is in a processional relation; he goes out ("proceeds") from the Father to accomplish his will."[76]

Yet the consensual tradition has been quick to add that the precise way in which the Son proceeds from the Father needs to be normed by the various perfections that are true of the divine nature (aseity, simplicity, immutability, eternity, etc.), as well as a healthy dose of epistemic humility in the face of an incomprehensible mystery that, in the end, demands "the tribute of our reverent silence."[77] We must guard against conceiving of the Son's eternally proceeding from the Father along the lines of how a human child proceeds from or is generated from a human progenitor. When chastened by the various God-befitting perfections of the divine nature previously discussed, the divine processions entail neither ontological inferiority or creature-hood (to safeguard CT3), change (immutability), nor temporal succession (eternity). Stripped of all creaturely imperfections, procession in

---

[75] Gregory adds, "let us not go mad the pair of us for prying into God's secrets." See Gregory Nazianzen, "Select Orations of Saint Gregory Nazianzen" 31.8.

[76] Fairbairn, *Life in the Trinity*, 53–54.

[77] Gregory Nazianzen, "Select Orations of Saint Gregory Nazianzen" 29.8, John of Damascus, *On the Orthodox Faith*, 73–74; Thomas Aquinas, *Summa Theologiae*, Ia.27.1

the Godhead denotes the communication of one and the same divine essence to another.

### *"Baptizing them into the name of the Father and of the Son and of the Holy Spirit" (CT3)*

Once chastened by the fullness and perfection of the triune life, the divine processions secure the consubstantiality of each of the divine persons (CT3) and thereby safeguard against ontological subordination in the divine life. Since the Father eternally begets the Son and communicates numerically one and the same divine nature to him, the Son is, as Constantinople I (AD 381) puts it, "Light from Light, true God from true God, begotten, not made, consubstantial (*homoousious*) with the Father. . . ."[78] And since the divine nature is simple and indivisible, its communication from one person to another in the Godhead admits of no degrees, gradations, or divisions. Each divine person—the Father, the Son, and the Spirit—is to be equally adored as the one God as they are consubstantial (*homoousios*) in virtue of the one divine nature in that they share by way of the divine processions (CT3). While the persons are numerically the same divine being, YHWH, it remains the case that "things that are identical on the score of being will not all agree equally in definition of the score of personality, as Gregory of Nyssa put it."[79]

Consequently, as Basil the Great and Augustine helped clarify, the fact that there are (relative) distinctions in the one, simple God requires attention to different kinds of predication when we speak of the inner life of the triune God. We can speak of the one God *ad intra* either *substance-wise* according to what the persons have essentially in common in virtue of the one divine nature (e.g., aseity, simplicity, immutability, and impassibility); or we can speak of the one God *relation-wise*

---

[78] Tanner, *Decrees*, 24
[79] Gregory of Nyssa, "Gregory of Nyssa against Eunomius" I.19.

according to what distinguishes each divine person (*paternity, filiation, spiration*). As Basil puts it, "The divinity is common, whereas father-hood and sonship are distinguishing marks: from the combination of both, that is, of the common and the unique, we arrive at compre-hension of the truth."[80] As Scripture naturally employs both modes of divine predication, rightly ordered speech about the triune God requires facility in both and grave theological errors ensue when one fails to heed this distinction.[81]

God's saving and sanctifying actions toward us in Christ and by the Spirit—what have traditionally been called the visible and invisible mis-sions of the Son (incarnation) and the Spirit (Pentecost, indwelling)—"open a door into the eternal processions within God."[82] Following the grain of Scripture regarding Jesus's origin from the Father and regarding his being sent by the Father (Matt 10:40; Mark 12:6; John 7:27–29; 8:42; 16:48; Gal 4:4–5; Rom 8:3), classical Christian thinkers like Augustine and Aquinas argued that the temporal missions *reveal* the eternal pro-cessions, that "the reason why the Son is said to have been sent by the Father is simply that the one is the Father and the other the Son."[83] The Father's sending of the Son in the incarnation, and the Father and the Son's sending of the Spirit at Pentecost, is in no way arbitrary but is indicative of a deeper, eternal ordering (*taxis*) in the immanent life of the triune God. Just as the Son's being eternally from the Father in no way entails that the Son is ontologically inferior to the Father, so too the

---

[80] Saint Basil of Caesarea, *Against Eunomius* 2.28, trans. Mark Delcogliano and Andrew Radde-Gallwitz (Washington, DC: The Catholic University of America Press, 2011), 174. Cited in Jamieson and Wittman, *Biblical Reasoning*, 104.

[81] See Augustine's interaction with the Eunomians as an example. See St. Augustine, *The Trinity* 5.3, 8.

[82] Jamieson and Wittman, *Biblical Reasoning*, 212. For an excellent fuller treatment of the relation between divine processions and missions, see Jamieson and Wittman, *Biblical Reasoning*, chap. 9.

[83] St. Augustine, *The Trinity* 4.26

Son's being sent in time by the Father in no way entails that the one sent is ontologically inferior to the sender. Consequently, "the divine missions are not some other relation added to the processions, but the processions themselves extended into time, stretched down into creation, where they can scoop us up into their saving embrace."[84]

Missions are closely associated with processions. "A mission," Swain writes, "has an eternal depth (in a divine person's relation of origin) and a temporal shore (in a divine person's coming to dwell among creatures)."[85] Jamieson and Wittman summarize the nature of divine missions as follows: "A divine mission thus consists of two elements: a relation of the person sent to the sender (*terminus a quo*; source), and a relation of the person sent to the goal of their sending (*terminus ad quem*; destination), which includes a created effect."[86] In this sense, missions reside at the intersection between persons and creation, detailing their economic distinctions. "All the works *ad extra*: creation, providence, rule, incarnation, satisfaction (atonement), renewal, sanctification, and so on," Bavinck writes, "are works of the Trinity as a whole."[87] But in an "economic" sense, he continues, "the work of creation is more specifically assigned to the Father, the work of redemption to the Son, the work of sanctification to the Holy Spirit."[88] Daniel Treier underscores the importance of the organic connection between processions and missions as follows: "If the divine missions do not manifest corresponding divine processions, then salvation may be a mere appearance and not the reality of God's triune love."[89] He continues, "For salvation to involve knowing the true God revealed in Jesus Christ, the Father, Son, and Holy Spirit must be proper

---

[84] Jamieson and Wittman, *Biblical Reasoning*, 208.
[85] Swain, *The Trinity*, 114.
[86] Jamieson and Wittman, *Biblical Reasoning*, 185.
[87] Bavinck, *Reformed Dogmatics* 2:230.
[88] Bavinck, *Reformed Dogmatics* 2:230.
[89] Daniel J. Treier, *Introducing Evangelical Theology* (Grand Rapids: Baker Academic, 2019), 80.

names for divine persons, not just alternative masks that the one God wears."[90] Irenaeus uses the image of the Father's "two hands" to capture the economic idea of the Father working through the Son and the Spirit.[91] Several passages communicate this idea of the Father orchestrating activity through the Son and Spirit. Scripture affirms that "all things are made through" the Word of God (John 1:3, Col 1:16, Heb 1:2). Even Christ himself proclaims that "the Son can do nothing of his own accord, but only what he sees the Father doing. For whatever the Father does, that the Son does likewise" (John 5:19 ESV) and that all that he teaches and does is according to the will of God (John 7:16–18). Christ does not speak on his own authority, but, he says, "the Father who dwells in me does his works" (John 14:10 ESV).

Alongside the Son, there are several passages that describe the work of the Spirit. The Father and the Son send the Spirit (John 14:26, 15:26) and the Spirit "will guide you into all the truth" (John 16:13 ESV). Throughout the divine economy, the Father works through the Spirit to communicate his word or commands (2 Sam 23:2, Neh 9:20; Ezek 2:2). The Spirit also empowers, indwells, and inspires (Matt 3:11, Luke 3:16, John 1:33, Acts 1:1–2; 1:8; 2:1–4).

The missions point to the nature of God, but also to the economic activity of God who saves and redeems. While the doctrine of God has broader issues and implications, the discussion of divine processions and missions is essential for thinking carefully about the nature of God and the revelation of Scripture. It is a key feature of the church's faith and, as we will show in the next section, it helps frame some distinctive features of a Baptist dogmatics.

---

[90] Treier, *Introducing Evangelical Theology*, 80.

[91] Irenaeus of Lyons, "Irenaeus against Heresies," 4.20.1, in *The Apostolic Fathers with Justin Martyr and Irenaeus*, ed. Alexander Roberts, James Donaldson, and A. Cleveland Coxe, vol. 1, The Ante-Nicene Fathers (Buffalo, NY: Christian Literature Company, 1885), 487.

# Baptist Reception of the Consensual Christian Doctrine of God

The above tenets of the consensual Christian doctrine of God, CT1–CT3, including aseity, simplicity, absolute immutability, eternity, and impassibility, are foundational to a patristic, medieval, Reformation, and Post-Reformation doctrine of God. In addition to their support in the ecumenical creeds and councils, CT1–CT3 are rooted in the broad creedal and confessional literature of Christendom, both East and West. CT1–CT3 are explicitly mentioned and affirmed by symbols of faith spanning a wide array of ecclesial bodies: *Roman Catholic* (Third Council of Toledo, 589; Fourth Lateran Council, 1215; Council of Basel, 1431–45; First Vatican Council, 1869–70), *Lutheran* (the Solid Declaration of the Formula of Concord; The Augsburg Confession, 1530), *Reformed* (Second Helvetic Confession, 1592; Belgic Confession, 1561; Westminster Confession, 1647), *Anglican* (Thirty-Nine Articles, 1563), and *Methodist* (Articles of Religion, 1784).

Most relevant for a volume like this focused distinctively on Baptist dogmatics, is that CT1–CT3—including the divine perfections of aseity, simplicity, absolute immutability, eternity, and impassibility—are all explicitly affirmed and defended in the early Baptist dogmatic and confessional material. Historically, Baptist dogmatic reflection on the doctrine of God displays strong continuity with the consensual Christian tradition regarding the divine perfections and God's trinitarian being along the lines of CT1–CT3. Historic Baptist confessions of faith show continuity with CT 1–3. The London Confession of 1644, the Second London Confession of 1689, The Orthodox Creed of 1678, and many others retain articles consistent with these points (see appendix at the end of this chapter).[92]

---

[92] See William L. Lumpkin and Bill J. Leonard, eds., *Baptist Confessions of Faith*, 2nd rev. ed. (Valley Forge, PA: Judson, 1959).

While much could be said about the early Baptist appropriation of the consensual Christian doctrine of God, space permits us to provide one notable example of the early Baptist reception of the church's consensual interpretation of the triune name. Thomas Monck, an English farmer, autodidact, and one of the foremost seventeenth-century General Baptist theologians, wrote a polemical work in response to General Baptist Matthew Caffyn's (1628–1714) heterodox doctrines of God and Christ. In particular, Caffyn held that "the divine nature of Christ . . . was made flesh, viz., by turning his divine nature or Godhead into flesh, even as the water was turned into wine."[93] In his 1673 work, *A Cure for the Cankering Error of the New Eutychians*, Monck situates his defense of a classical, Chalcedonian Christology within the larger dogmatic framework of a consensual Christian interpretation of the triune name.

Monck displays an astute knowledge of the church fathers, medieval schoolmen, and Reformed divines, such as Augustine, Gregory of Nazianzus, Thomas Aquinas, Girolamo Zanchi, and Peter Martyr Vermigli.[94] Citing the revelation of the divine name in Exod 3:14, Monck affirms CT1 in that God is supremely one,[95] *a se*,[96] pure act,[97] absolutely simple and immutable,[98] and eternal.[99] Monck employs this consensual understanding of the divine name in his polemic against Caffyn's heterodox view that the divine nature underwent intrinsic change or alteration in the incarnation.

Monck also explicitly defends the consensual trinitarian grammar outlined in CT2–CT3, replete with the classical metaphysical

---

[93] Monck, "The Author to the Reader," *A Cure for the Cankering Error of the New Eutychians*.

[94] Monck, *A Cure*, 27, 44–45, 64, 69.

[95] Monck, 25, 55.

[96] Monck, 25.

[97] Monck, 26, 33.

[98] Monck, 27, 30, 33, 45, 55, 57–58.

[99] Monck, 28.

categories of essence, nature, substance, and person.[100] He echoes the creedal language of the Athanasian Creed[101] and unequivocally affirms the divine processions (eternal generation of the Son),[102] inseparable operations,[103] and the dogmatic function of divine simplicity in safeguarding the numerical oneness of God (CT1) as well as the consubstantiality of the divine persons (CT3), who subsist in the divine nature and are "only distinguished, and not severed; as three men are indeed separated, though they be but one in kind."[104] As Monck was a principal architect of one of the earliest English Baptist Creeds, the General Baptist Orthodox Creed (1678), CT1–CT3 are also explicitly and beautifully articulated throughout the Creed (see the appendix at the end of this chapter).

Importantly, and in view of our original formulation of CT1–CT3 in terms of the baptismal formula of Matt 28:19, Monck employed the baptismal formula both as an exegetical mooring for trinitarian dogmatics,[105] as well as the baptismal act itself as the seal of a saving confession/faith and rightly ordered worship.[106] Monck, following a long interpretive tradition with roots in the church fathers as well as other early English Baptist theologians, finds in the baptismal formula an exegetical mooring for trinitarian dogmatics as per CT1–CT3. In reference to trinitarian patterns in Scripture, Monck underscores that, "further, Matthew 28:19, Baptize all Nations in the Name of the Father, of the Son, and of the Holy Ghost: he saith not Names, but in the [Name] to shew the unity of the three persons,"[107] and, "If we may be baptized in their Name; then are they God by Nature: but we may, yea

---

[100] Monck, 56.
[101] Monck, 39.
[102] Monck, 64.
[103] Monck, 39, 69.
[104] Monck, 63.
[105] Monck, 40.
[106] Monck, 62.
[107] Monck, 62.

ought to be baptized in their Name; therefore God by Nature, Matt 21:19, 20."[108] Here, Monck appeals to the baptismal formula to exegetically anchor the distinctness of the Father, Son, and Spirit (CT2), the unity or oneness of God (CT1), and the co-equality and consubstantiality of the divine persons.

In addition to serving a dogmatic role, Monck conceives of the baptismal formula and baptism more generally—as the seal and sign of a true, saving profession of the triune name. Along these lines, he says, "We cannot worship God aright, without the knowledge of the Trinity. As God the Father, Son, and Holy Ghost, is of the object of Faith; so is he of the object of divine worship. Baptism is an act of Worship, and sign of the Covenant; but we are baptized into the Name of the Father, and of the Son, and of the Holy Ghost (Matt. 28:19)."[109] He also writes, "If we may be baptized in their Name; then are they God by Nature: be we may, yea ought to be baptized in their Name; therefore God by Nature, Matt. 21:19, 20. The reason is plain, because we expect the remission of our sins in his Name, into which we were baptized, as also promise to worship him in Spirit and in Truth."[110] As many in the Christian tradition have previously noted, *which* name we are baptized into determines the efficacy, quality, and stability of life found in that name.[111]

---

[108] Monck, 112.

[109] Monck, 40.

[110] Monck, 112.

[111] See Athanasius, *Letters to Serapion* 1.30.1, in *Works on the Spirit*, trans. Mark DelCogliano, Andrew Radde-Gallwitz, and Lewis Ayres (New York: St. Vladimir's Seminary Press, 2011), 98–99; Gregory of Nyssa, *An Address on Religious Instruction* 38, in *Christology of the Later Fathers*, ed. Edward R. Hardy, trans. Cyril C. Richardson, Library of Christian Classics (Philadelphia: Westminster, 1954), 322. We owe the Nyssa reference to Joseph T. Lienhard, SJ, "The Baptismal Command (Matthew 28:19–20) and the Doctrine of the Trinity," in Khaled Anatolios, ed., *The Holy Trinity in the Life of the Church* (Grand Rapids: Baker Academic, 2014).

## Credobaptism as Our Sacred Initiation into the Triune Name

What might a distinctively Baptist inflection on the consensual Christian doctrine of God look like? How might Baptists uniquely accentuate the trinitarian nature of God, in particular the divine processions and missions, in their confession and practice?

In closing, we'll make two exploratory points on this score. The first, preliminary point concerns the role of the divine name in the gospel of John in disclosing both Jesus's identity as the eternal, name-bearing Son and his mission in the world to hallow and make the divine name known among the nations. We'll look at the tight connection in John's Gospel between *believing in the name of Jesus* (1:12) and *having life in the name of Jesus* (20:31), and the implication that the fullness of life found in the triune name is available to us by means of our abiding profession of the triune name. Building on the first point (a point about the procession and saving mission of the eternal Son), we turn to our second point that baptism marked by trinitarian belief and profession (credobaptism) is the sacred initiation into the fullness of life in the triune name (Matt 28:19).

In John's Gospel, the divine name plays a central role in disclosing Jesus's identity and mission as well as the identity and mission of those who believe in his name.[112] As is well known, John's sevenfold "I am" (Gk., *Egō eimi*) sayings throughout his Gospel identify Jesus with the divine name, YHWH, the Tetragrammaton revealed to Moses in Exod 3:14. By his self-naming at Sinai, God reveals himself to be the all-sufficient one who alone has being, life, and glory in himself and not from another. And, according to John's sevenfold witness in his Gospel, Jesus himself bears this same divine name.

---

[112] We are particularly indebted here and in what follows to Grant Averbeck, "Name Christology, Divine Aseity, and the I Am Sayings in the Fourth Gospel," in *Journal of Theological Interpretation* 12:2 (2018), as well as Charles A. Gieschen, "The Divine Name that the Son Shares with the Father in the Gospel of John" in *Reading the Gospel of John's Christology as Jewish Messianism* (Leiden: Brill, 2008).

Yet Jesus himself makes it clear that this same divine name, YHWH, is *granted* to him by the Father (John 17:11b; 12). Given the rich Old Testament connection between the divine name and the divine glory (Exod 33:17–23; Isa 48:11), it is suggestive that the Son's own glory that was given to him by the Father "before the foundation of the world" is a reference to the eternal communication of the divine name to the Son (John 17:5, 22, 24).[113] "For as the Father has life in himself," Jesus says, "so he has granted the Son also to have life in himself" (John 5:26 ESV). Thus, the eternal fullness of life and self-sufficiency of the divine name revealed at Sinai belongs equally to the Father and the Son yet is eternally given by the Father to the Son, signifying the Son's eternal procession from the Father. Jesus's divine identity as the one who eternally receives the divine name from the Father anchors his temporal mission in the world as the one who is sent in the Father's name (John 5:43), whose works bear the Father's name (John 10:25), that the Father's name would be "hallowed" (Luke 11) once again and made known among the nations (John 17:6).

In John 17:11–12 (ESV) Jesus prays that those to whom he manifests the Father's Holy name—the divine name given to him by the Father—would be kept in that same name. He says, "Holy Father, keep them in your name, which you have given me, that they may be one, even as we are one. While I was with them, I kept them in your name, which you have given me." The use of "name" in Scripture can indicate "power, protection, presence, and character, so that those identified with the name benefit from its nature."[114] Here, Jesus is likely praying that his followers remain "in firm fidelity to the revelation [of the divine name] Jesus himself has mediated to them,"[115] and by so doing benefit

---

[113] We owe this point to Gieschen, "The Divine Name that the Son Shares with the Father in the Gospel of John," 398–99.

[114] G. K. Beale, *Union with the Resurrected Christ* (Grand Rapids: Baker Academic, 2023), 243.

[115] D. A. Carson, *The Gospel according to John*, The Pillar New Testament Commentary (Grand Rapids, MI: Eerdmans, 1991), 562.

from the power, protection, presence, and character of the divine name. The very same divine name, glory, power, and love that the Son has eternally received from the Father is now manifest and opened to those who likewise receive the name of the divine Son whom the Father has sent (John 17:8, 22, 26).

Interestingly, John bookends his Gospel with an emphasis on receiving the Son by "believing in his name" (John 1:12) and "that by believing you may have life in his name" (John 20:31 ESV). Conversely, the one who fails to receive the Son by believing in his name is "condemned already, because he has not believed in the name of the only Son of God" (John 3:18 ESV). Here we have the positive connection between *belief* and *life* in the name of the eternal Son, YHWH. The way that we *receive* the fullness of life in the divine name is by *believing* in the eternal name-bearing Son of the Father; belief in the name of the Son is the instrumental cause of one's entrance into the new-found triune life from above (John 1:12; 3:1–21).

This brings us to our second point, which dovetails closely with the first. As we've seen in the baptismal formula of Matt 28:19–20 (ESV), Christ commands us, "Go therefore and make disciples of all nations, baptizing them in the name of the Father and of the Son and of the Holy Spirit, teaching them to observe all that I have commanded you. And behold, I am with you always, to the end of the age." As Jesus's own baptism bears the imprint of the triune name (Matt 3:13–17; Matt 1:9–11; Luke 3:21–23; John 3:13–17), so too does the baptism of those who believe in his name.

There is, of course, a rich history of dogmatic reflection on the trinitarian shape of the baptismal act, much of it centered on Jesus's command to his disciples in Matt 28:18–20 to baptize his followers into the three-fold name.[116] Some have stressed the procedural importance

---

[116] For an excellent overview of this reflection, see Lienhard, "The Baptismal Command (Matthew 28:19–20) and the Doctrine of the Trinity." See also chapter 7 of Anatolios, *Retrieving Nicaea*.

of the repetition of the three-fold name in baptism.[117] Others have laid emphasis on the participatory nature of the baptismal act, holding that in baptism we are initiated into the very life of the one whose name we confess.[118] Others have emphasized the close association, in some way or other, of the baptismal act with the remission of sins and regeneration. Others still highlighted the inseparability, yet priority, of belief/profession to salvation in the baptismal act, referring to baptism as "faith signed and sealed in the Father and the Son and the Holy Spirit.[119] Along similar lines, Basil the Great, in his *On the Holy Spirit* XII, points out:

> Well, then, if the separation of the Spirit from the Father and the Son in baptism is dangerous for the baptizer and useless for the baptized, how is it safe for us to separate the Spirit from the Father and the Son? Now faith and baptism are two ways of salvation that are naturally united with each other and indivisible. While faith is perfected by baptism, baptism is established by faith, and each is carried out by the same names. For as we believe in the Father, Son, and Holy Spirit, so also we are baptized in the name of the Father, Son, and Holy Spirit. The confession that brings salvation comes first and there follows baptism which seals our assent.[120]

---

[117] *Didache* 7, in *Early Christian Writings: The Apostolic Fathers*, trans. Maxwell Staniforth (Harmondsworth: Penguin, 1968), 194. We owe this reference to Lienhard, "The Baptismal Command."

[118] Gregory of Nyssa, *Address on Religious Instruction*, 38; Athanasius, *Letters to Serapion*, 99.

[119] Tertullian, "On Baptism" 6, in *Latin Christianity: Its Founder, Tertullian*, ed. Alexander Roberts, James Donaldson, and A. Cleveland Coxe, trans. S. Thelwall, vol. 3, The Ante-Nicene Fathers (Buffalo, NY: Christian Literature Company, 1885), 672.

[120] St. Basil the Great, *On the Holy Spirit* 12.28, trans. Stephen Hildebrand (New York: St. Vladimir's Seminary Press, 2011), 59.

In some way or other, then, the church has confessed that in the baptismal act "the character of the trinity is imprinted in that fundamental sacrament."[121]

From their earliest beginnings among English Separatists, Baptists have defended credobaptism.[122] The topic of baptism was the subject of numerous debates and served to distinguish early Baptists from other denominations and traditions. Baptism was always conceived as baptism in the triune name. The Helwys confession of 1611, for example, reads "That every Church is to receive in all their members by Baptism upon the Confession of their faith and sins wrought by the preaching of the Gospel, according to the primitive Institution, (Matthew 28:19) and practice, (Acts 2:41)."[123] The Orthodox Creed (1678) states that baptism ought to be performed "in a solemn manner, in the name of the father, son, and holy ghost."[124] The New Hampshire Confession of 1833 designates that "Christian Baptism is the immersion of a believer in water, in the name of the Father [and] Son, and Spirit, to show forth in a solemn and beautiful emblem, our faith in a crucified, buried, and risen Saviour, with it purifying power."[125] Baptism in this manner is a prerequisite for participation in church life and the benefits of common covenantal fellowship.

---

[121] St. Bonaventure, *Disputed Questions on the Mystery of the Trinity*, in *Works of St. Bonaventure*, vol. 3, trans. Zachary Hayes, OFM (New York: The Franciscan Institute, 2000), 130.

[122] H. Leon McBeth, *The Baptist Heritage: Four Centuries of Baptist Witness* (Nashville: B&H Academic, 1987), 79.

[123] "A Declaration of Faith of English People," in Lumpkin and Leonard, *Baptist Confessions of Faith*, 109.

[124] "The Orthodox Creed," in Lumpkin and Leonard, eds., *Baptist Confessions of Faith*, 326. See also the "Second London Baptist Confession," in *Baptist Confessions of Faith*, 292.

[125] "The New Hampshire Confession," in Lumpkin and Leonard, *Baptist Confessions of Faith*, 382.

In *A Sober Discourse of Right to Church Communion*, a polemical work on the sacrament of the Lord's Supper, seventeenth-century Baptist theologian William Kiffin (1616–1701) portrays baptism into the triune name as "the pledge of our entrance into Covenant with God," "the giving up ourselves unto Him in the solemn bond of religion," and the act whereby we "are dedicated unto the service of the Father, Son, and Holy Ghost."[126] Precisely because we take "the profession of Their Name upon us" in baptism, we are "sacredly initiated and consecrated, or dedicated unto the worship of the Father, Son, and Holy Ghost as that text Matthew 28:19 sheweth we are, and take this upon us in our baptism, and thereby owning the Spirit to be God, equal with the Father, and the Son . . ."[127] By professing and believing in the name of the eternal Son of the Father, who has been given the "name that is above every name" (Phil 2:9), we now bear the triune name and, by grace, partake of the fullness of life in that name. In this way, baptism is "the foundation of all our faith and profession." Importantly, Kiffin explicitly grounds his understanding of baptism as a "sacred initiation" and seal by means of our trinitarian baptismal confession by explicitly appealing to church fathers such as Athanasius and Basil of Caesarea.[128]

---

[126] It is important to note that Kiffin draws heavily and quotes directly from various portions of John Owen's *Discourse on the Holy Spirit*, bk. 1, chap. 3. We owe the insights in this section to Michael Haykin, *Amidst Us Our Beloved Stands: Recovering Sacrament in the Baptist Tradition* (Bellingham, WA: Lexham Press, 2022), 72–73.

[127] William Kiffin, "To the Christian Reader," in *A Sober Discourse of Right to Church Communion* (Paris, AR: Baptist Standard Bearer, 2006), 13.

[128] See Haykin, *Amidst Us Our Beloved Stands*, 73. Gregory of Nyssa also underscores the participatory nature of the baptismal act *in so far as it is tied to proper, believing confession of the triune name*. He says, "For what happens in the sacrament of baptism depends upon the disposition of the heart of him who approaches it. If he confesses that the holy Trinity is uncreated, then he enters on the life which is unchanging. But if, on a false supposition, he sees a created nature in the Trinity and then is baptized into that, he is born once more to a life which is subject to change. For offspring and parents necessarily share the same nature. Which, then, is more advantageous: to enter upon the

Following Kiffin, and by way of explicating the *covenantal* and *confessional* signposts of Baptist dogmatics, respectively, we explore how our baptismal confession of the triune name signals a new *triune identity* (as bearers of the triune name) and generates an accompanying *triune mission* in the world (to hallow and make the triune name known among the nations).

Our confession of the triune name in baptism, then, signals a new *triune identity*; we now, by grace, participate in the fullness of triune life found in Jesus's name (John 1:12–13; 17; 20:31). God places his divine name and seal upon that which belongs to him: the ark of the covenant (2 Sam 6:2), the tabernacle and temple (1 Kgs 8:43; 2 Chr 6:33), the people of Israel and Jerusalem (Dan 9:18–19), and the end-time saints (Rev 3:8–13; 14:1).[129] By way of our believing profession of the triune name in the baptismal act, the triune name is now placed upon us; we belong to YHWH, the triune God. Indeed, "The Lord knows those who are his," namely, "everyone who names the name of the Lord . . ." (2 Tim 2:19 ESV).

As the Spirit descended and remained upon the natural Son in his baptism, so too the Spirit who comes in the name of the Father and Son (John 14:26; 15:26) is poured out upon and dwells within adopted children of God. Upon our believing profession in the name of the Son, the Father seals us with the Spirit of his Son to be conformed to the image of the Son (Rom 8:29; Gal 4:6; Eph 1:13); we receive from the Father "the Spirit of adoption" and thereby a creaturely share in

---

life which is unchanging or to be tossed about once more in a life of instability and fluctuation?" See Gregory of Nyssa, *Address on Religious Instruction* 38, 322. We owe this reference to Joseph Lienhard, "The Baptismal Command (Matthew 28:19–20) and the Doctrine of the Trinity," in *The Holy Trinity in the Life of the Church*, ed. Khaled Anatolios (Grand Rapids: Baker Academic 2014), 3–14.

[129] We owe these insights to Carmen Joy Imes, *Bearing YHWH's Name at Sinai: A Reexamination of the Name Command of the Decalogue* (University Park, PA: Eisenbrauns, 2018). See also Imes, *Bearing God's Name: Why Sinai Still Matters* (Downers Grove, IL: IVP Academic, 2019).

the Son's own eternal Sonship (John 17; Rom 8:15), "by whom we cry, 'Abba! Father!'" (Rom 8:15; Gal 4:6).[130] In this way, baptism is "the seal of eternal life and rebirth unto God, that we may no longer be sons of mortal men, but of the eternal and everlasting God."[131] As the thrice-repeated name of YHWH placed upon the people of Israel resulted in rich, divine blessing (Num 6:24–27), so too the three-fold name of Father, Son, and Spirit placed upon adopted name-bearers results in the rich, overflow of the trinitarian blessings of salvation (Ephesians 1–2). In this way, believing profession in the triune name in baptism signals the "sacred initiation" into participation in the eternal rest and fullness of self-sufficient life that flows from the triune God; indeed, whoever professes and bears this name will never thirst or hunger again (John 6:35). Those adopted, name-bearing children *receive* the fullness of life in the triune name by *believing* in the name granted to and revealed by the eternal name-bearing Son.

Our confession of the triune name in baptism signals not only a new triune identity, but it also generates a new *triune mission* in the world. Jesus, the name-bearing Son by nature, was sent in the Father's name to "hallow" it and to make it known to the nations (Matt 6:9–13). Likewise, those who by believing have life in Jesus's name, name-bearing sons and daughters by grace, have been sent in the triune name to "hallow" it and to make it known to the nations (Luke 11:2) where it has been gravely profaned. We are sealed with the triune name in believer's baptism for the purpose of bearing it well and representing God's holy name to the nations (Ezek 36:16–32).

As YHWH's "treasured possession" (Exod 19:3–6 ESV), in virtue of bearing his holy name, Israel was called to represent him well to the surrounding nations by being holy and set apart. Yet Israel profaned the

[130] Thomas Aquinas, *Commentary on the Gospel of John: Chapters 1–21*, trans. Fabian Larcher and James A. Weisheipl, Vol. 3 (Washington, DC: The Catholic University of America Press, 2010), 87.

[131] Irenaeus, *On the Apostolic Preaching*, trans. John Behr, with introduction (Crestwood, NY: St Vladimir's Seminary Press, 1997), 3.

divine name they carried—they carried it in vain (Exod 20:7)—by collectively closing their ears and hardening their hearts to YHWH and his commands and worshiping other gods.[132] Similarly, those of us who bear the triune name in our baptismal confession are commissioned to carry his holy name to the world and "bring about the obedience of faith for the sake of his name among the nations" (Rom 1:5 ESV; cf., Matt 28:18–20). Like Israel, we can choose to either hallow or profane the triune name we carry among the nations (1 Pet 2:9–12). We profane the triune name by devoting ourselves to rival objects of worship, hardening our hearts and failing to heed his voice (Heb 3:7–12), and walking contrary to his commands. Conversely, we sanctify the holy, triune name we bear by consecrating ourselves and being sanctified in truth (Lev 11:44; John 17:19), keeping our "conduct among the Gentiles honorable, so that . . . they may see your good deeds and glorify God on the day of visitation (1 Pet 2:12 ESV), and therein observe all that God has commanded (Matt 28:20: cf. Lev 22:31–33; Matt 5:48, 1 Pet. 1:15). After being baptized into the triune name (and renouncing all allegiances to other names), Aquinas says, "if one returns to his sins, the name of God has been taken in vain."[133] Consequently, "Let everyone who names the name of the Lord depart from iniquity" (2 Tim 3:19).

From their earliest days, Baptists have been a missional people and committed to the task of the Great Commission.[134] As the Father sent the eternal Son to sanctify and manifest the divine name in the world, we are also sent by the eternal Son, empowered and sealed by the Spirit of the Father and the Son, to sanctify "the name that is above every name"—God's holy triune name—and to make it known among the

---

[132] See Carmen Joy Imes, *Bearing YHWH's Name at Sinai: A Reexamination of the Name Command of the Decalogue* (University Park, PA: Eisenbrauns, 2017).

[133] Thomas Aquinas, *The Ten Commandments of God: Conferences on the Two Precepts of Charity and the Ten Commandments*, trans. Laurence Shapcote (London: Burns, Oates & Washbourne, 1937), article 4. We owe this reference to Imes, *Bearing YHWH's Name at Sinai*, 42.

[134] See Garrett, *Baptist Theology*, 581–660.

nations (John 20:21). And our identity as bearers of the triune name drives our triune mission to hallow and represent the divine name well, to "bring about the obedience of faith" first and foremost in our own lives as those "called to belong to Jesus Christ," and also, "for the sake of his name among the nations" (Rom 1:5–6).

# Appendix: The Consensual Christian Doctrine of God in the Orthodox Creed (1678)[135]

CT1: There is exactly one God ["baptizing them in the *name* . . ."]

| | |
|---|---|
| Oneness | • "We verily believe, that there is but one, only living and true God . . ."<br>• "Therefore but one God, who is indivisible, and not to be divided in nature, or being . . ."<br>• "In this divine, and infinite being, or unity of the Godhead . . . of one Substance, Power, Eternity, and Will." |
| Aseity | • "whose subsistence is in and of himself . . . hath an absolute, independent, unchangeable, and infinite being . . ." |
| Simplicity | • "without matter or form, body, parts, or passions."<br>• "God, who is simplicity, viz. one mere and perfect act, without all composition, and an immense sea of perfections . . ." |
| Absolute Immutability | • "having immutability without any alteration in being, or will . . .<br>• "Therefore, we believe the Godhead was neither turned nor transfused into the manhood, not the manhood into the Godhead, but both; the divine nature keepeth entire all his essential properties to its self . . ." |
| Eternity | • "who is the only eternal being, everlasting without time . . ." |
| Impassibility | • "without matter or form, body, parts, or passions." |

---

[135] "The Orthodox Creed, 1687," in Lumpkin and Leonard, eds., *Baptist Confessions of Faith.*

## CT2:
### The persons of the Father, the Son, and the Holy Spirit are not identical.
["... of *the* Father and of *the* Son and of *the* Holy Spirit ..."]

| CT2: Divine Persons are Distinct (Processions) | • "In this divine, and infinite being, or *Unity* of the Godhead, there are three Persons, or Subsistences, the Father, the Word, or Son, and the Holy Spirit."<br>• "The Father is of none, neither Begotten nor Proceeding; the Son is Eternally Begotten of the Father; the Holy Ghost is of the Father, and the Son, proceeding."<br>• "We confess and believe, that the Son of God, or the Eternal Word, is very and true God, having his Personal Subsistence of the Father *alone*, and yet for ever of himself as *God*, and of the Father as the Son, the *Eternal Son* of an eternal Father; not *later* in Beginning ..." |

CT3:
The persons of the Father, the Son, and the Holy Spirit
are consubstantial
["... of the Father *and* of the Son *and* of the Holy Spirit ..."]

| CT3: Divine Persons are Consubstantial | • ... there are three Persons, or Subsistences, the Father, the Word, or Son, and the Holy Spirit ... each having the whole Divine Essence, yet the Essence undivided."<br>• "There was never any time when he was not, not less in Dignity, not other in Substance, Begotten without diminution of his Father that begat, of one Nature and Substance with the Father; Begotten of the Father, while the Father communicated wholly to the Son, which He retained wholly in himself, because both were Infinite; without inequality of Nature, without division of Essence, neither Made, nor Created, not Adopted, but Begotten before all Time; not a Metaphorical, or subordinate God; not a God by Office, but a God by Nature, Coequal, Coessential, and Coeternal, with the Father, and the Holy Ghost."<br>• "We believe that there is one holy Spirit, the Third Person subsisting in the Sacred Trinity; one with the Father and Son, who is very and true God; of one Substance or Nature, with the Father and Son, Coequal, Coessential, and Coeternal with the Father and Son, to whom with the Father and Son, Three Persons, and but one Eternal and Almighty God, be by all the Hosts of Saints and Angels, ascribed Eternal Glory and Hallelujahs. Amen." |

# CHAPTER 3

# ANTHROPOLOGY

Rhyne R. Putman and Malcolm B. Yarnell III

## Reclaiming the Sacred Dignity of Every Human Being in the Dogma of Anthropology

The secular term, "human dignity," which indicates "the fundamental moral worth or status supposedly belonging to all persons equally," has become a familiar term in Western thought.[1] Documents like the "Universal Declaration of Human Rights" (1948) begin with the presumption that "all human beings are born free and equal in dignity and rights."[2] While human dignity is increasingly recognized as the foundation for human rights, its widespread acceptance has a relatively short history. The popularization of the term may be a recent development, but the idea of the inherent worth of the human person is rooted in Scripture and has a long history in cultural tradition

---

[1] Remy Debes, ed., *Dignity: A History* (New York: Oxford University Press, 2017), 1.

[2] United Nations, "Universal Declaration of Human Rights" (1948), art 1.

influenced by Christian teaching.[3] The robust theological anthropology which includes human dignity, derived from natural philosophy and biblical exegesis, was recognized in Baptist confessions, both personal and communal.

Our primary goal in this essay, due to constraints of space, is to recall the dogmatic relationship between the *imago Dei* (Latin, "image of God") and human dignity, which includes discussions of conscience, covenants, and the divine command to love. We believe that the truths of human dignity and the inherent rights which derive from a person's liberty of conscience to live within human covenants, freely and responsibly, are necessary aspects of an orthodox theological anthropology. To address properly the anthropological dogma of the sacred dignity of every human being, we must first review its biblical basis and then its historic development. After rehearsing its history, we demonstrate the doctrine is part and parcel of Baptist and free church dogma before we issue a call for contemporary Baptists and other free church Christians to reclaim this important and nonnegotiable truth. Without a proper doctrine of human dignity, contemporary Christians may repeat the horrific mistakes of even the recent past, when the precious bearers of God's own image were oppressed under false "Christian" regimes practicing religious persecution, false theologies supporting the depraved institution of human slavery, and other great evils.

## Biblical Considerations

An orthodox theological anthropology requires critical, dogmatic reflection on the biblical teachings about humanity, their reception in the history of the churches, and their applications today. Theological anthropology encompasses a wide variety of topics related to human nature,

---

[3] Larry Siedentop, *Inventing the Individual: The Origins of Western Liberalism* (New York: Allen Lane, 2014); Tom Holland, *Dominion: How the Christian Revolution Remade the World* (New York: Basic Books, 2019).

including the image of God in humanity, the human constitution, human beings as male and female, human unity, human sexuality, and humanity's final destinies. Many theologians place hamartiology, or the doctrine of sin and its effects, under the broader category of theological anthropology. The exploration of human dignity in this article is bound with all these related categories in theological anthropology and hamartiology; however, we will not attempt a full anthropology here.[4] Several recent works may be used advantageously to construct a whole theological anthropology.[5] Rather, our primary concern will be to address human dignity in relation to anthropology.

## *Human Dignity in Creation*

The first chapter of the Bible establishes the grounds for human dignity, linking the inherent value of human beings to the image of God (Gen 1:26–27). Unlike naturalism, which asserts that human beings are merely highly evolved members of the animal kingdom, the Bible paints a picture of human beings as unique creatures endowed with the image of their Creator. Human beings may bear some superficial similarities to other mammals and primates in our physiology, but we are categorically different from these other creatures in our substance, design, and

---

[4] The doctrine of the *imago Dei* intersects with every part of the Christian confessional tradition, from the inseparable Trinitarian loci of theology, Christology, and pneumatology to the inseparable triune works of creation, redemption, and consummation.

[5] Marc Cortez, *Theological Anthropology: A Guide for the Perplexed* (New York: T&T Clark, 2010); David S. Dockery and Lauren McAfee, eds., *Created in the Image of God: Applications and Implications for Our Cultural Confusion* (Nashville: Forefront, 2023); John S. Hammett and Katie J. McCoy, *Humanity* (Brentwood, TN: B&H Academic, 2024); John F. Kilner, *Dignity and Destiny: Humanity in the Image of God* (Grand Rapids: Eerdmans, 2015); Reinhold Niebuhr, *The Nature and Destiny of Man*, 2 vols. (New York: Scribner, 1941–43); Hans Schwarz, *The Human Being: A Theological Anthropology* (Grand Rapids: Eerdmans, 2013).

*telos* (Gk., "purpose" or "end"). The Bible does not describe the process by which other members of the animal kingdom were created, but it does give an account of the special, direct creation of man (Gen 2:4–24). Genesis teaches that because God is worthy of dignity, those who are made in his image are also inherently worthy of it, too.

The claim that God "created them male and female" in his own image affirms the value and dignity of both sexes. The Bible does not provide any grounds for that distorted theological anthropology which exalts one sex over the other, but it does reveal God's purposes in creating two powerful and complementary sexes (Gen 1:27; 2:18, 23–24). Because all human beings derive from the one man with the one woman, humanity is also marked by a foundational unity. Eve is truly "the mother of all the living" (Gen 3:20). In response to attempts to divide and subjugate human beings on the basis of ethnic characteristics, James Leo Garrett Jr. noted the "exegesis of texts in early Genesis in behalf of racism stands as a monumental example of genuine eisegesis."[6] Orthodox Christians must affirm "the unity of humankind despite the diversity of racial characteristics and the impact of racism."[7]

The triune God proclaimed that men and women "will rule the fish of the sea, the birds of the sky, the livestock, the whole earth, and the creatures that crawl on the earth" (Gen 1:26).[8] These human beings, created in the divine image, are creature-kings who reflect the ruling activity of their Creator-King. Man and woman were commanded to "subdue" (*kabash*) the earth and to "rule" or "have dominion" (*radah*) over its creatures (Gen 1:28). The rule granted to humanity is derivative, dependent upon the prior reality of divine sovereignty. Likewise, human intelligence (Gen 11:6), relationality (Gen 1:27c; 3:16b),

---

[6] James Leo Garrett Jr., *Systematic Theology: Biblical, Historical, and Evangelical*, vol. 1, 2nd ed. (North Richland Hills, TX: BIBAL, 2000), 482.

[7] Garrett, *Systematic Theology*, 1:483.

[8] On the necessity of identifying the God of Genesis with the Trinity of the New Testament, see Malcolm B. Yarnell III, *God*, vol. 1, Theology for Every Person (Brentwood, TN: B&H, forthcoming 2024), chap. 5.

creativity (Gen 2:19b; 4:20–22), and freedom (Gen 2:16a; 4:7) are limited creaturely realities. God graciously made provision for all vegetation and animal life on the earth to nourish those made in his image (Gen 1:29–30).

The eighth psalm reiterates the theme of human dominion. The psalmist marvels at the value God gives to humanity in comparison with their smallness in the vast universe he created. God made the human being "ruler over the works of [his] hands" and "everything [is] under his feet" (Ps 8:6). His statement that God "made [the human being] little less than God" (Ps 8:5) prompts our bold claim that humanity is the pinnacle of creation.

While the Old Testament elevated humanity, it was through the incarnation, death, resurrection, and exaltation of the Son of God that the elevation of humanity reached a previously unparalleled height. God placed humanity in Christ upon the divine throne which rules all creation (Heb 2:5–9). The biblical canon, consisting of both the Old Testament and the New Testament, thereby paves the way for a truly dignified humanism. Biblical humanism differs from the secular brand which demotes human beings to evolutionary accidents who play an ultimately inconsequential role in the cosmos.

Secular humanism is a creature of the eighteenth-century Enlightenment, while Christian humanism arose during the fifteenth-century Renaissance. Secular humanism therefore depends upon prior Christian contributions to Western thought. Moreover, on its own, secular humanism lacks the eternal foundation necessary for society's continued respect for human dignity. Only theology, which makes human beings responsible to a higher reality, possesses the metaphysical resource necessary to sustain a truly dignified humanism. According to Christian theology, those creatures made in the image of God are continually and ultimately responsible to the Creator in whose image they were made. By contrast, secular humanism depends entirely upon its self-referential and thus ultimately limited resources for authentication.

## Human Dignity after the Fall

Christian theologians disagree with one another over whether the image of God was at the most lost, or at the least marred, or whether it was entirely unaffected by the fall of Adam.[9] We believe that both the continuance of the image in Adam's son, Seth (Gen 5:3), and the prohibition against harming those created in God's image (Gen 9:6) indicate the divine image, in some sense, remains in the human being after the fall. Moreover, the Bible teaches that while Adam's disobedience afflicted his posterity with a sin nature that leads to actual sin with the consequence of death (Rom 5:12–21), Adam's rebellion did not strip humanity of its God-given dignity. The early chapters of the first book of the biblical canon witness to the maintenance of human dignity after the fall described in Genesis 3.

God still pursued a personal relationship with Adam (Gen 3:8–9). The Lord cursed the serpent who tempted the first human beings (vv. 14–15). He cursed the ground which Adam worked (v. 17). And he warned Eve about the difficulties which lay ahead for her both in her marriage and in her childbearing (v. 16). However, exercising patience toward his creature, God never directly cursed Adam nor Eve. These first human beings retained the dignity of a personal relationship with God originally accorded them as his image bearers. Death came upon them, but God granted the promise of redemption (v. 15). Moreover, he made provision for their temporal needs (v. 22).

God continued to maintain the dignity of human beings after further egregious sins. The history of Cain and Abel in Genesis 4 provides the first account of one human being denying the dignity of another human being, in this case through bodily assault leading to death. Cain resented Abel for the superiority of his religious offering. Internal resentment over

---

[9] For a history and evaluation of this debate, see John F. Kilner, *Dignity and Destiny: Humanity and the Image of God* (Grand Rapids: Eerdmans, 2015), 134–76; cf. Kilner, "Humanity in God's Image: Is the Image Really Damaged?" *Journal of the Evangelical Theological Society* 53, no. 3 (2010): 601–17.

his failure in comparison with Abel led Cain to commit murder. It is notable that only after Cain killed his brother was he considered "cursed" and "alienated" (Gen 4:11). However, although Cain had been alienated from other human beings, God continued to grant Cain dignity through a modicum of a personal relationship with God.

We believe that Genesis 4 describes the development of the human *conscience*. The conscience demonstrates to each human being his or her ultimate responsibility to God alone for his or her actions, external and internal. God engaged with Cain repeatedly during his internal struggle with the temptation to sin and the committal of that sin. First, before he sinned, God activated Cain's conscience by warning him he must overcome sin to avoid judgment (Gen 4:6–7). Second, after he sinned, God reminded Cain of the evil he had done (vv. 9–10). Third, the struggle in Cain's conscience prompted him to pray for preservation of his own life. God showed grace to Cain through his prayer (vv. 14–15). Paul later described such internal human struggle as a movement of the "conscience" (Greek, *syneidesis*), wherein humanity's "competing thoughts either accuse or even excuse them" (Rom 2:15). The conscience witnesses to the eschatological "day when God judges what people have kept secret" (Rom 2:16). The conscience assists human beings in remembering the dignity which belongs to every human being.

Afterwards, the protection of human dignity was also attached by God to the *covenant of human society*. The first direct prohibition against murder appears in the context of the first explicit divine "covenant" (Hebrew, *berith*) with human beings.[10] The covenant made with Noah contains two important provisions for the maintenance of human flourishing. First, God promised to preserve the lives of those who bear his image by never again destroying every creature by flood (Gen 9:1–17; cf. Gen 6:18). Second, God issued a warning that the inherent dignity of

---

[10] Many theologians surmise the covenant which Adam broke was a covenant of works whereby God promised Adam life for obedience (Gen 2:16–17; Hos 6:7).

his image-bearers should be respected: "Whoever sheds human blood, by humans his blood will be shed, for God made humans in his image" (Gen 9:6). Murder is an affront to the God who created human beings because he created humanity in his image. God instructed his image bearers to carry out his justice in the world he created also within their own human society. The covenant with Noah by God created an ongoing need for mutual covenants between human beings to maintain justice between themselves on earth.

## Human Dignity in the Law and the Prophets

Covenantal relations between God and Israel laid the groundwork for Israel's ethical code in the law of Moses. Much of this code is dedicated to preserving the dignity of those made in the image of God. In the Exodus, God rescued the descendants of Abraham from slavery in Egypt. The biblical narrator makes it clear that the Egyptians oppressed the Hebrews, denying them their basic human dignity: "They worked the Israelites ruthlessly and made their lives bitter with difficult labor in brick and mortar and in all kinds of fieldwork. They ruthlessly imposed all this work on them" (Exod 1:13–14). When God liberated the people of Israel through Moses, he made a covenant promising to make them his "own possession out of all the peoples" at Mount Sinai (Exod 19:5–6).

He also gave Israel his Law. One of its key purposes was to prevent his people from violating human dignity the way that their Egyptian oppressors had. While the Decalogue (Exod 20:1–17; Deut 5:6–21) makes no explicit mention of the image of God, it creates a logical relationship between one's treatment of God and one's treatment of neighbor. Although the organizational division between the commandments is not as exact as some interpreters might claim, the first commandments emphasize relationship with God while the latter commandments focus on relationships between human beings. This arrangement of the law into two tables implies that a love for God naturally leads to a love for those who are made in his image.

Even those commandments which focus on the proper worship of God magnify the worth of those who bear his image. The command against idolatry considers the consequences of disobedience for other human beings (Exod 20:5–6; Deut 5:9–10). The fourth commandment not only established a day for worship; it also broke the paradigm of the seven-day workweek in the Ancient Near East. In Israel, a day of rest was required for every member of the community, including slaves and freemen. Although the additional sabbath laws later created by religious men became burdensome regulations, the original intent of the fourth commandment was for the good of the image bearer. Jesus reinforced this point when he said, "The Sabbath was made for man and not man for the Sabbath" (Mark 2:27).

Many regard the fifth commandment as an instruction for small children to obey their parents. Paul certainly reads it this way in Eph 6:1–4. However, the command was originally directed toward adults. The commandment teaches human beings that advanced age does not diminish a person's dignity or worth, even when the elderly can no longer care for themselves. The law treats this commandment so seriously that capital punishment is provided as the maximum sentence for its violation (Deut 21:18–21). Mosaic prohibitions against patricide and matricide (Exod 21:15) still apply in contemporary debates over euthanasia. Jesus thus chided the Pharisees who used their religious traditions to justify neglecting the needs of their elderly parents (Matt 15:3–9; Mark 7:8–13).

The commandments against murder, adultery, theft, false testimony, and coveting all have the inherent dignity of the image bearer in mind. First, the act of murder takes away the life of an image bearer, thereby robbing him of his God-given dignity. Second, adultery violates the covenant of marriage and the dignity of the spouse who was betrayed. The outlines of a *covenant of marriage* were laid in the Lord's description of the relationship between a man and a woman as a "bond" (Hebrew, *dabaq*), wherein a man leaves his parents and the two "become one flesh" (Gen 2:24). Job treats marriage as a sacred "covenant," while

Solomon treats its violation as breaking "covenant" with God (Hebrew, *berith*; Job 31:1; Prov 2:17). Third, false testimony in the courts of Israel slandered innocent image bearers (Deut 19:16–21) and endangered the national covenant by allowing the true perpetrators to roam free (Deut 17:7; Prov 14:25).

The Law also contains extensive instructions for how Israel was to treat the "sojourner" or "resident alien" (Hebrew, *ger*) who lives in the land. "You will regard the alien who resides with you as the native-born among you. You are to love him as yourself, for you were aliens in the land of Egypt; I am the Lord your God" (Lev 19:34). God reminded Israel that they were to treat those living in their territory with more dignity than they received from the Egyptians when they lived among them. Because they were oppressed themselves, they know better than to become oppressors (Exod 22:21; 23:9). While Israel was still called to be set apart from the other nations—to serve a God who is set apart—the instruction given to them about immigrants was a reminder that God's salvation was not exclusive to Israel. Human dignity belongs to image bearers from every tribe, tongue, and nation. As image bearers with like dignity, foreigners may also "join themselves to the LORD" and enter his covenant with Israel (Isa 56:6).

Through the Law, God expressed his clear desire for Israel to flourish and prosper: "See, today I have set before you life and prosperity, death and adversity. For I am commanding you today to love the LORD your God, to walk in his ways, and to keep his commands, statutes, and ordinances, so that you may live and multiply, and the LORD your God may bless you in the land you are entering to possess" (Deut 30:15–16). However, true prosperity depended upon Israel's obedience to the covenant: "Choose life so that you and your descendants may live, love the LORD your God, obey him, and remain faithful to him. For he is your life, and he will prolong your days as you live in the land the Lord swore to give to your ancestors Abraham, Isaac, and Jacob" (Deut 30:19b–20). The law of Moses thus became a template for the good life. Human flourishing flows from obedience to the Creator.

The prophets reinforced the covenant of Moses and declared its promises were conditioned upon how the Israelites respected the human dignity of one another and of outsiders: "Instead, if you really correct your ways and your actions, if you act justly toward one another, if you no longer oppress the resident alien, the fatherless, and the widow and no longer shed innocent blood in this place or follow other gods, bringing harm on yourselves, I will allow you to live in this place, the land I gave to your ancestors long ago and forever" (Jer 7:5–7; cf. Zech 7:9). The prophets required basic human dignity be extended to everyone within Israel, especially to those groups of people who might be too easily ignored or oppressed: sojourners, orphans, and widows.

### Human Dignity in Christ's Command to Love

In the Sermon on the Mount, our Lord Jesus uses the phrase, "You have heard that it was said . . . but I tell you . . ." (Matt 5:21–22, 27–28, 33–34, 38–39, 43–44), to introduce his teaching on the law of Moses. Christ's adversative expression—"but I tell you"—did not change God's law but corrected the way it was misinterpreted and misapplied by religious leaders in his day. Jesus does not reject these laws but magnifies their original spirit and intent. He moved his hearers from focusing on mere external obedience to inculcating internal obedience. Simply put, it is not enough to obey the law in a purely technical sense. For example, even if a person never committed the physical act of murder, Jesus said murderous motivations in the heart result in the same judgment (Matt 5:22). For Jesus, respecting human dignity requires more than merely allowing another person to live. Jesus also commanded the loving pursuit of reconciliation with brothers, sisters, and adversaries (Matt 5:23–26).

Likewise, a person who has never had sexual relations with another man's wife may still be guilty of adultery if he looks lustfully at another woman (Matt 5:28). The clear implication is that women (and men), being made in the image of God, should not be objectified as mere sexual conquests. Jesus also leveled criticism against what many rabbis of his day taught about divorce, the breaking of the marriage covenant, which typically left the weaker partner to suffer. The rabbinic school of Hillel allowed a man to divorce his wife for any reason, including ruining his dinner![11] Knowing their callous view of marriage and divorce diminished human dignity, especially the dignity of women, and violated the sanctity God accorded the marriage covenant, Jesus stated the only legitimate ground for divorce was adultery (Matt 5:31–32). However, unlike many of his contemporaries, Jesus did not require divorce. He did require love.

Jesus extended human dignity to those outside of his cultural group, even among the enemies of Israel. He commanded his followers to "love your enemies and pray for those who persecute you" (Matt 5:44). Just as God extends common grace to the righteous and the unrighteous, all humans participate in human dignity. The dignity of humanity belongs even to those who threaten our mortality and endanger our flourishing. The love which we show to our enemies also provides evidence of our identity as God's children (Matt 5:45). Threats to a national covenant do not diminish the force of God's command to honor every person's dignity.

Jesus used the command to "love your neighbor as yourself" (Lev 19:18) as a summary statement for the second table of the Decalogue (Matt 22:39; Mark 12:31; Luke 10:27). Paul expressed the same judgment when he asserted, "The commandments, Do not commit adultery; do not murder; do not steal; do not covet; and any other commandment, are summed up by this commandment: *Love your neighbor as yourself*" (Rom 13:9, emphasis ours). Jesus corrected the destructive assumption that only some people are neighbors deserving of dignity while others, enemies, do not deserve love or possess human dignity. Subverting the expectations of his audience, the Lord asserted that the command to love neighbors even applies to the way we treat those who hate us and persecute us (Matt 5:44).

---

[11] m. Gittin 9:10; see also Deut 24:1–4; Matt 19:3.

## Human Dignity in Conscience and Covenant

The command to love one's neighbor may never be abrogated by personal fiat; nor may love ever be reduced by social covenants, nor for that matter by marital covenants. Human covenants both require and limit certain behaviors toward other human beings, but covenants exist within the divine framework of love. For example, as seen above, the *covenant of marriage* limits sexual activity, internal and external, to the man and the woman in that marriage. Alongside the covenant of marriage, we must address the common human covenants which guide human beings in their social relationships and in their relationships with other Christians. These covenants should account for human dignity and the human conscience. In the dialectic between the human conscience and human covenants, human dignity must be consistently maintained.

Jesus taught that taxes must be paid to the governments within whose *social covenants* we live. "Give then to Caesar the things that are Caesar's," he said (Matt 22:21b). While Christians must conform to social covenants, he reminded his disciples they were not to treat one another according to society's hierarchical norms (Luke 22:25–26). He also addressed the source and end of social authority. Jesus taught his disciples that all authority belongs to him eternally as the second Person of the Holy Trinity (Matt 28:18–20). He taught Pontius Pilate that all authority ultimately descends "from above" (John 19:11). And he prophesied to the High Priest that he, the Messiah, would visibly rule from the divine throne, bringing judgment upon those who misused their authority (Matt 26:64).

Continuing the Christian discourse about social covenants, the apostles, in word and by example, taught the church to pray for, to obey, and to honor secular rulers (Rom 13:1–7; 1 Tim 2:1–4; 1 Pet 2:13–17). Paul connected obedience to social covenants to the Christian's *conscience*, effectively restricting human covenants under divine authority (Rom 13:5). However, Christian loyalty ultimately remains with Christ alone, and obedience to his commands necessarily shapes the Christian response

to human commands (Acts 4:19–20; 5:29). The church must be careful
to recognize the demonic potential of secular government; certainly, we
ought never sacralize it (Rev 13:1–10). As James Leo Garrett taught,
both Romans 13 and Revelation 13 are canonically normative. Therefore,
Christians must "recognize, accept, and seek to implement the dialectical
obligations of obedience and disobedience" toward the state.[12] Garrett's
warning comes from the tradition of Thomas Helwys, the first pastor of
the first Baptist church in England, who argued for universal liberty of
conscience and the freedom of the church under Christ.[13]

The third major covenant which shapes the ethics of human life for
the believer is the *covenant of the church*. The free church understanding of
the origin of a local church and its authority to function is grounded in
Jesus Christ's promise that he would bring his authoritative presence to the
covenantal gathering of believers in his name (Matt 18:18–20). The individual human "conscience" (Greek, *syneidesis*) makes a covenantal "pledge"
(Greek, *eperotema*) directly to the eternal God through faith in the resurrected Christ. The believer's internal pledge is visibly manifested in the
believer's first act of public confession, water baptism by the church (1 Pet
3:21–22). The local church covenant requires that its members, who have
been baptized upon their personal profession of becoming a disciple of
Christ (Matt 28:19), also disciple one another (Matt 18:15–17). If exclusion becomes necessary, it must be enacted in love with the goal of bringing the apparently lost member to salvation (1 Cor 5:4–5; 2 Cor 2:6–8).

Elsewhere, we characterized the relationship between conscience
and covenant as a "dynamic dialectic."[14] Having described covenant more

---

[12] James Leo Garrett Jr., "The Dialectic of Romans 13:1–7 and Revelation
13 (Part Two)," in Wyman Lewis Richardson, ed., *The Collected Writings of James
Leo Garrett Jr., 1950–2015*, vol. 7 (Eugene, OR: Wipf and Stock, 2023), 161.

[13] For more detail, see the discussion on Hewlys in the section below on
Baptist dogma.

[14] Malcolm B. Yarnell III, "The Free Church Form of Dogmatics: Covenant and Conscience under Christ," *Southeastern Theological Review* 14, no. 2
(2023): 115.

thoroughly there,[15] we must now detail the biblical doctrine of the *conscience*. In the first place, the evil conscience can be purified through faith in Christ's atonement for our sin (Heb 10:22). The purification of the conscience, we may assume, accompanies the individual Christian's initial justification by faith in the Lord. In the progress of the Christian life, the Christian conscience must also be sanctified.

Luke reports that the apostle Paul strived toward having a "good" conscience primarily in his relationship with God but also in his relationships with other people (Acts 23:1; 24:16). The Christian maintains a "good" or "pure" conscience by holding to the Christian faith and loving other people (1 Tim 1:5, 19; 3:9; 2 Tim 1:3; Heb 13:18; 1 Pet 3:16). Paul said his conscience bears witness through the work of the Holy Spirit to his external maintenance of Christian truth (Rom 9:1). As an external witness to the internal work of the conscience, the church has a role in shaping consciences through teaching the faith which can both purify and maintain the goodness of the conscience. Sadly, however, some persons have "defiled" and "seared" their consciences through willful sin (1 Tim 4:2; Titus 1:15).

Maintaining a good conscience amidst a diverse and dynamic Christian community requires careful discernment and constant love. Some early Christians had a "weak" conscience which defiled them if they partook of meat consecrated to idols (1 Cor 8:10). A Christian with a strong conscience unaffected by such considerations will nevertheless sin against both his fellow believer and the Lord if he wounds a weak person's conscience (1 Cor 8:12). For the sake of another's conscience, one should avoid knowingly participating in idol's meat (1 Cor 10:25–28). Yet the "liberty" of the strong believer's conscience must also be respected (1 Cor 10:29 ESV).

To summarize the biblical doctrine of *the human conscience* we note the following truths: First, every human conscience remains directly accountable to God alone. Second, the evil conscience can be purified

---

[15] Yarnell, "The Free Church Form of Dogmatics," 117–29.

through personal faith in the resurrected Christ. Third, receiving external water baptism witnesses to the internal covenant of a good conscience with God. Fourth, the Christian's conscience must seek continual sanctification through recourse to the church's teaching. Fifth, the conscience may be defiled through willful sin. Sixth, Christians must strive to respect one another's consciences in community. Finally, Christians must advocate mutual respect for every human conscience in society.

In conclusion, the biblical doctrine of humanity includes the following basic truths: All human beings are made in God's image. All human beings possess sacred dignity. Humanity has fallen into sin, but God continues to pursue a relationship. The human being is responsible directly to God for his or her conduct through the witness of the conscience. The human being enters human communities through various covenants which demand certain behaviors. Three primary covenants include the covenant of marriage, the covenants of society, and the covenant of the church. These covenants shape our behavior to conform to their norms, but no human covenant may compromise our primary loyalty to God through the conscience. Nor may a covenant abrogate God's command to love our neighbors as ourselves. The covenanted Christian community should disciple us to live out his command to love. We must treat every human being with the dignity they possess as a gift from God.

## Historic Considerations

The winsome practical anthropology which we believe Scripture prescribes has inspired believers to strive toward treating all human image bearers with dignity. However, the problem of sin continues to challenge Christian institutions of that practical anthropology, especially in respecting human dignity. Not every Christian has respected the dignity of other image bearers, nor has every Christian community honored liberty of conscience. Some Christians have misused liberty of conscience, making it an instrument of antinomianism. Other Christians have abused other consciences by imposing slavish social hierarchies and demanding cultlike loyalty and fealty to human institutions. John Dickson reviews the long history wherein self-professing Christians have striven against Christ's commands to love and the apostles' affirmation of human equality and dignity.[16] While realistically recognizing and genuinely lamenting such contradictions, we will focus on the more exemplary developments of Christian history.

## Human Dignity in the Early Church

Many early church fathers rejected cultural practices in the Roman Empire that were an affront to human dignity, even if these practices were not explicitly condemned in the biblical text. For instance, at the end of the first century, Christians began expressing their opposition to human abortion. Their view was consistent both with the command of Jesus to love others and with biblical condemnations of infant exposure (Acts 7:19) and ritual infanticide (Lev 18:21; Deut 12:31).

The early Christian document known as *Didache* (written c. AD 80–120; Gk., "teaching") began with the presumption there are "two ways" by which persons can conduct themselves: "one of life and one of death." The "way of life" involves love of God and love of neighbor, which the author associates with the teaching of Jesus from the Sermon on the Mount.[17] The *Didache* defined the neighbor broadly, even ascribing to unborn children the important status of full humanity. The author strictly prohibited "gross sin." Such wickedness characteristically fails to

---

[16] John Dickson, *Bullies and Saints: An Honest Look at the Good and Evil of Christian History* (Grand Rapids, MI: Zondervan, 2021). For a short historical account about the devastation caused by various misunderstandings of the image of God, see Kilner, *Dignity and Destiny*, 17–37. Please note that we do not necessarily agree with Kilner's position that the image of God was "undamaged." This will be considered in more depth in *God's Word to the World*, the forthcoming second volume of Malcolm Yarnell's systematic theology.

[17] *Didache* 1. Many of the sources under this heading are collected in Ronald J. Sider, ed., *The Early Church on Killing: A Comprehensive Sourcebook on War, Abortion, and Capital Punishment* (Grand Rapids, MI: Baker, 2012).

practice love toward one's neighbor. Gross sin includes, but is not limited to, fornication, the sexual abuse of children (pederasty), and the "murder [of] a child by abortion."[18]

The third-century theologian Cyprian of Carthage (c. 202–258) bemoaned the way gladiatorial games robbed human beings of their dignity for entertainment:

> What can be said more inhuman—what more repulsive? Training is undergone to acquire the power to murder, and the achievement of murder is its glory. What state of things, I pray you, can that be, and what can it be like, in which men, whom none have condemned, offer themselves to the wild beasts—men of ripe age, of sufficiently beautiful person, clad in costly garments? Living men, they are adorned for a voluntary death; wretched men, they boast of their own miseries. They fight with beasts, not for their crime, but for their madness. Fathers look on their own sons; a brother is in the arena, and his sister is hard by; and although a grander display of pomp increases the price of the exhibition, yet, oh shame! Even the mother will pay the increase in order that she may be present at her own miseries. And in looking upon scenes so frightful and so impious and so deadly, they do not seem to be aware that they are parricides with their eyes.[19]

One of the strongest prohibitions against human slavery in the ancient world came from the pen of Gregory of Nyssa (c. AD 335–395). This Cappadocian Father had a view on slavery that was radical compared with his Christian and non-Christian contemporaries, who either viewed the institution as a necessary evil or who enthusiastically supported it. In a homily on Eccl 2:7—"I acquired male and female servants and had slaves who were born in my house"—Gregory explicitly condemned the

---

[18] *Didache* 2.
[19] Cyprian, *Epistle to Donatus* 7.

institution of human slavery.[20] He argued that human beings who are made in God's image belong to God and God alone. The mere possession of a bill of sale for a slave does not constitute ownership: "Has the scrap of paper, and the written contract, and the counting out of obols deceived you into thinking yourself the master of the image of God?"[21] Image-bearers cannot be chattel because both slaves and their masters truly belong to God. Nyssa was a staunch advocate for human dignity.

## Human Dignity in the Medieval West

Several church fathers addressed key issues related to human dignity and the image of God, but that relationship is more difficult to discern in medieval theology. Medieval theologians were more often preoccupied with the metaphysics of the *imago Dei* than its practical consequences for human dignity. Augustine of Hippo (ca. 354–430) was the figure largely responsible for this shift. Augustine never connected the image to universal human worth, and medieval Western theology was shaped by commentary on his voluminous texts.

Matthew Puffer identified three views of the *imago Dei* which appear at various stages in Augustine's thought. In his earliest works (written ca. 386–400), Augustine interpreted the "image" in Gen 1:27–28 to refer specifically to the human nature of the Son. The divine image was not something applicable to all human beings. In his middle period (ca. 401–412), Augustine came to connect the image of God with the human capacity to love God. However, he also contended this image could be lost as well as regained. Finally, in his later writings (ca. 413–430), Augustine viewed the image of God as an internal capacity which all

---

[20] Gregory of Nyssa, *Homily on Ecclesiastes*, 4. Cf. David Bentley Hart, "The 'Whole Humanity': Gregory of Nyssa's Critique of Slavery in Light of His Eschatology," *Scottish Journal of Theology* 54.1 (2001): 51–69.

[21] Gregory of Nyssa, *Homily on Ecclesiastes*, 4.

human beings possess. The gift of reason allows human beings to know and to contemplate God.[22]

Augustine's successors in the West were quite concerned to answer the question of whether the image of God was affected by the fall. Leo the Great (d. AD 461) ascribed dignity to human beings by their nature. But he also believed their dignity was lost during the fall and needed to be reinstated by God's grace in Christ.[23] Peter Lombard (1100–1160) drew upon Augustine to emphasize the rational aspects of the image. Rationality, even in fallen men, sets human beings apart from other animals.[24]

Thomas Aquinas (1225–1274) contended that the image of God could be seen in three ways: the "natural [intellectual] aptitude for knowing and loving God" which is "common to all men," the habitual love of God which only belongs to the just, and the perfect love of God which only belongs to glorified man. Although Thomas distinguished between the image and likeness of God in humans—a common view in patristic and medieval theology—he did assert that the image was common to all people.[25] In a discussion on capital punishment, Aquinas expressed the belief that, by sinning, "man departs from the order of reason and consequently falls away from the dignity of his manhood." This man has become a beast and "it may be good to kill a man who has sinned, even as it is to kill a beast."[26]

While fallen human beings have the image in the rational sense, medieval theologians did not typically equate this image with the

---

[22] Matthew Puffer, "Human Dignity After Augustine's *Imago Dei*: On the Sources and Uses of Two Ethical Terms," *Journal of the Society of Christian Ethics* 37.1 (2017): 68–69.

[23] Bonnie Kent, "In the Image of God: Human Dignity After the Fall," in *Dignity: A History*, 90–92.

[24] Kent, "In the Image of God," 77.

[25] Thomas Aquinas, *Summa Theologica* I. q. 93, a. 4.

[26] Thomas Aquinas, *Summa Theologica* II-II. q. 64, a. 2; cf. Kent, "In the Image of God," 93–95.

universal *dignitas* or worth of all human beings. They ascribed some form of dignity or honor to God, and to various created things such as angels, men, or other powers, but they did not presume the modern connection between the image and human dignity. Bonnie Kent observed, "Very few works expiate on some dignity that all people have just because we are human, or because humans are created in God's image."[27]

## Human Dignity in and after the Reformation

Anthropological discussions about the Protestant Reformation of the sixteenth century typically refer to the courageous performance of Martin Luther at the Diet of Worms. Refusing to recant his writings before the emperor as well as the gathered German nobles and Roman clergy, Luther famously appealed to the authority of the human conscience. His reply to the emperor was simple: "Unless I am convinced by Scripture and plain reason—I do not accept the authority of popes and councils, for they have contradicted each other—my conscience is captive to the Word of God. I cannot and will not recant anything, for to go against conscience is neither right nor safe. God help me. Amen."[28] Luther's sensational resort to conscience, however, did not conclude in a clear and practical affirmation of universal human dignity. Instead, Luther called upon the nobility to crush the peasants when they appealed to their own consciences.[29] Luther muted his previous advocacy for both the priesthood of all believers and some form of ecclesiastical congregationalism.[30]

---

[27] Kent, "In the Image of God," 73.

[28] Roland Bainton, *Here I Stand: A Life of Martin Luther* (New York: Abingdon-Cokesbury Press, 1950), 185.

[29] See, for instance, "The Twelve Articles," which were written by Sebastian Lotzer and Christoph Schappeler and widely disseminated among the peasants. Tom Scott and Bob Scribner, eds., *The German Peasants' War: A History in Documents* (Atlantic Highlands, NJ: Humanities Press, 1991), 252–57.

[30] Malcolm B. Yarnell III, *Royal Priesthood in the English Reformation* (New York: Oxford University Press, 2013), 91–96; Gert Haendler, *Luther on*

Baptist views toward covenants and liberty of conscience, which we describe below, developed out of the Protestant Reformation. The Reformers generally regarded "the three institutions of family, church, and state as fundamental orders of creation, equal before God and each other, and vested with certain natural rights and duties that the other authorities could not trespass."[31] These rights and duties derived from the Decalogue and from natural law. John Witte argues that Protestantism not only broke the unity of Western Christendom but "laid the foundations for the modern constitutional system of confessional pluralism."[32]

Witte believes the major branches of the Reformation—Lutheran, Anglican, Anabaptist, and Calvinist—respectively "territorialized," "nationalized," "communalized," and "congregationalized" the faith.[33] For their part, through their conviction regarding the baptism only of confessing believers, the Anabaptists "gave new emphasis to a voluntaristic understanding of religion." The Free Churches which came after the Anabaptists turned such believers' baptism "into a powerful platform of liberty of conscience, free exercise of religion, and separation of church and state."[34]

Bypassing John Calvin's restriction of rebellion to lower magistrates and advocacy of muted forms of hierarchy,[35] later Calvinists also developed ideas which helped lead toward modern human rights. Theodore Beza argued that every political government originated in a popular covenant and spoke obliquely about universal "equal rights and

---

*Ministerial Office and Congregational Function*, trans. Ruth C. Gritsch, ed. Eric W. Gritsch (Philadelphia: Fortress Press, 1981).

[31] John Witte, Jr., "Introduction," in John Witte Jr. and Frank S. Alexander, eds., *Christianity and Human Rights: An Introduction* (Cambridge: Cambridge University Press, 2010), 27.

[32] Witte, "Introduction," 27.

[33] Witte, "Introduction," 28.

[34] Witte, "Introduction," 29.

[35] John Witte Jr., "Rights and Liberties in Early Modern Protestantism: The Example of Calvinism," in *Christianity and Human Rights*, 135–43.

liberties."[36] Johannes Althusius detailed a "covenantal theory" for political society. Although human beings are "born free, equal, and individual," they inevitably form associations. The modern political idea of "federalism" developed from Althusius's ruminations about the *foedus* (Latin, "covenant").[37] John Milton popularized the ideas that each person is endowed with "freedom of conscience, reason, and will," and that each Christian is called to be "a prophet, priest, and king." "Every person was called by God to discharge both their private Christian vocations and their public social responsibilities in expression of their love of God, neighbor, and self."[38]

As the English, Dutch, and American experiences demonstrate, the movement toward universal respect for human dignity may have its theological roots in Scripture and in various evangelical doctrines about conscience and covenant, but these ideas sometimes coalesced slowly toward the modern consensus. John Locke, the father of English political liberalism, advocated toleration and liberty of conscience. But Locke failed to embrace full religious liberty and failed to apply political freedom to Africans and American Indians.[39] The Dutch Reformed clergy were dragged toward religious toleration despite constantly digging in their heels. And although they originally opposed the slavery of Christians, many became participants in and apologists for the wicked subjugation of whole human populations.[40] Despite calls to repent from British Baptists and northern Baptists, Southern Baptists adopted novel slaveholder theologies in their own vain attempt to justify their subjugation of

---

[36] Witte, 144–45.

[37] Witte, 146–48.

[38] Witte, 151; cf. Theo Hobson, *Milton's Vision: The Birth of Christian Liberty* (New York: T&T Clark, 2008).

[39] Malcolm Yarnell, "The Baptists and John Locke," in Thomas S. Kidd, Paul D. Miller, and Andrew T. Walker, eds., *Baptist Political Theology* (Brentwood, TN: B&H Academic, 2023), 115–18.

[40] James C. Kennedy, *A Concise History of the Netherlands* (New York: Cambridge University Press, 2017), 151–56, 176–78, 212–19.

their African brothers and sisters in Christ. The founder of the Southern
Baptist Theological Seminary proudly described himself as "an ultra pro-
slavery man."[41] Human dignity has sometimes been honored by the heirs
of the Reformation more in vague word than in actual deed.

## Human Dignity as a Baptist/Free Church Dogma

Despite such failures in implementation, at important historic moments
Baptist and other Free Church theologians have spoken clearly and
courageously regarding the truth of human dignity. In the seventeenth
century, the first Baptist pastor in England, Thomas Helwys, was the
first in a long line of Free Church leaders to argue for universal liberty
of conscience. Helwys argued that the apocalyptic prophecy regarding
the "mystery of iniquity" applied to any attempt to usurp the place of
Jesus Christ upon his throne (Dan 9:27; Matt 25:15–16; 2 Thess 2:1–8;
Rev 13:4–7). Since the human conscience is directly and only subject to
the divine throne (Rom 2:15–16; Heb 10:19–22; 1 Pet 3:21–22), it must
be kept inviolate against every form of human coercion. According to
Helwys, biblical proclamation is the "all-sufficient" means for establishing the kingdom of Christ among men. The state must use the physical
sword only for its divinely given civil purpose, while the church must use
the spiritual sword as the only means to attain its distinct spiritual end.[42]

---

[41] John A. Broadus, *Memoir of James Petigru Boyce, D.D., LL.D. Late
President of the Southern Baptist Theological Seminary* (New York: Armstrong and
Son, 1893), 185.

[42] Thomas Helwys, *A Short Declaration of the Mystery of Iniquity* (1612), in
Joe Early Jr., ed., *The Life and Writings of Thomas Helwys* (Macon, GA: Mercer
University Press, 2009), 155–310 (esp. 192–93). A review of the theological exe-
gesis of Helwys's famous work will be found in my preface for the forthcoming
*Every Man's Conscience: Early English Baptists and the Fight for Religious Liberty,
A Primer* by Ryan Burton King. See also Malcolm B. Yarnell III, "'We Believe
with the Heart and with the Mouth Confess': The Engaged Piety of the Early
General Baptists," *Baptist Quarterly* 44 (2011): 36–58.

Two decades later, a former clerk for the Chief Justice of England became a Particular Baptist and issued his own passionate plea for "soul liberty." Roger Williams's writings emphasized this powerful concept, and his charter for Rhode Island enshrined liberty of conscience for the first time in a Western constitution. The American colonies hereby started a movement toward the now general belief that a proper political covenant necessarily includes religious freedom. His legacy led one Jewish commentator to assert that Williams was, conceptually speaking, "the real founder of the new republic."[43] With such a great cloud of witnesses, subsequent Baptist theologians have argued that the first freedom, liberty of conscience or religious liberty, is the freedom through which all other human freedoms derive.[44]

George W. Truett, the most prominent Southern Baptist pastor of the early twentieth century, proclaimed what may properly be called a "high anthropology." His doctrine of humanity was exalted because it was grounded in the biblical doctrine of the image of God. The *imago Dei* in the human being reflects the dignity which *Deus* (Latin, "God") himself possesses and grants. Therefore, Truett wrote in 1907, "Next in importance to a right conception of God, is a right conception of man. To think meanly of human life is to live meanly."[45] Flowing out of this high anthropology came Truett's lifelong concern to promote freedom of conscience and human flourishing as part and parcel of proclaiming the Baptist vision of the gospel of Jesus Christ and its kingdom-establishing purpose.[46]

---

[43] Joseph Martin Dawson, *Baptists and the American Republic* (Nashville: Broadman Press, 1956), 15.

[44] Jason G. Duesing, Thomas White, and Malcolm B. Yarnell III, eds., *First Freedom: The Beginning and End of Religious Liberty*, 2nd ed. (Nashville: B&H Academic, 2016).

[45] George W. Truett, "Why Save Human Life?" *The Baptist Standard* (December 26, 1907), 1.

[46] On Truett's life and theology, see Powhatan W. James, *George W. Truett: A Biography* (New York: Macmillan, 1940); Keith E. Durso, *Thy Will Be Done: A Biography of George W. Truett* (Macon, GA: Mercer University Press, 2009); Malcolm B. Yarnell III, "A Theology for the Church: George W. Truett and the

His high anthropology continually drove Truett's passion for advancing human flourishing through the establishing of churches, hospitals, and universities. It also led him to declaim against "that terrible Trinity of horrors—suicide, lynching, murder" on the front page of the *Baptist Standard*. Alas, however, these horrors, he said, "still mock us, with their awful carnival in every section of our great country."[47] After noting "the priceless value of human life" in "all of its races in classes," Truett continued, "This is the doctrine that needs profoundest emphasis today, the dignity and value of human life."[48]

Truett's thesis remains true, for America not only began with anthropological error,[49] it still struggles with racism and misogyny. In the mid-twentieth century, Thomas Buford Maston, an ethics professor at Southwestern Baptist Theological Seminary, helped lead the effort to overturn the ideology of racism. He wanted to integrate African Americans with Southern Baptists and in church and society. However, his thoughtful efforts created such an uproar in the Southern Baptist Convention that he was forced into early retirement.[50] Advocating human dignity can bring persecution not only from wicked societies but from recalcitrant churches. Alas, since the days of Truett and Maston, America has added legalized abortion and mass murder to its list of "terrible horrors."[51]

---

Southwestern Tradition," *Southwestern Journal of Theology* 63 (2020): 9–32; O. S. Hawkins, *In the Name of God: The Colliding Lives, Legends, and Legacies of J. Frank Norris and George W. Truett* (Nashville: B&H Academic, 2021); Yarnell, "The Gospel, Religious Liberty, and Social Duty: The Holistic Theology of George Washington Truett," *Southwestern Journal of Theology* 64 (2022): 69–84.

[47] Truett, "Why Save Human Life?" 1.

[48] Truett, 1.

[49] For a summary of the Southern Baptist struggle with our "original sin," see Malcolm B. Yarnell III, *The Formation of Christian Doctrine* (Nashville: B&H Academic, 2007), 199–203.

[50] Malcolm B. Yarnell III, "Foreword," in Paul J. Morrison, *Integration: Race, T. B. Maston, and Hope for the Desegregated Church*, Monographs in Baptist History (Eugene, OR: Pickwick, 2022), ix–xii.

[51] Truett's pacific character has been faulted for keeping him from more boldly addressing the "systematic racist culture" of Southern Baptists. The next

More positively, historical theologian Jim Spivey eloquently argues that the Baptist doctrine of human dignity is grounded in the biblical teaching about the image of God and incorporates both liberty of conscience and personal justification by faith. "Being created in God's image, each person possesses infinite dignity and is a rational, moral agent with a conscience capable of responding to him by faith. Faith is a gift from God, not of human origin or institutional fabrication. This faith elicits voluntary obedience from the rational soul: the equal and independent right of every person to choose without coercion."[52] Although Southern Baptists have drawn on such historic Baptist logic and even placed a robust doctrine of human dignity in their official confession, they have applied this doctrine with equivocation, as we have seen above.

## Confession

It will be helpful at this point to consider the themes of confession, conscience, and covenant in their relationship to the Baptist dogma of human dignity. The language of the third and seventeenth articles of the Baptist Faith and Message, on humanity and religious liberty, echoes the sermons and writings of Truett. Truett collaborated with several members of the 1925 committee for decades, including Edgar Young Mullins and Lee Rutland Scarborough, and these themes are also common in their writings. Mullins and Scarborough were respectively the presidents of the two leading Baptist seminaries in the American south.

These leading confessional Southern Baptists interpreted Scripture's doctrine of humanity to mean that human beings were directly

---

pastor of the First Baptist Church of Dallas, Wally Amos Criswell, at first affirmed racism but repented of his rhetoric. Hawkins, "Race and Racism in the Southern Baptist Convention: The Lost Legacies of George W. Truett and W. A. Criswell," *Southwestern Journal of Theology* 63 (2021): 119–26.

[52] Jim Spivey, "Separation No Myth: Religious Liberty's Biblical and Theological Basis," *Southwestern Journal of Theology* 36, no. 3 (1994): 10.

related to God from the moment of their creation. And that direct divine–human relation comprehended every human being, specifically both the male and the female (cf. Gen 1:26–27). They therefore began the third article in this way, "Man is the special creation of God, made in his own image. He created them male and female as the crowning work of his creation."[53]

The Baptist dogma of humanity incorporates hamartiology, for the impact of the Fall upon the image is a major part of the biblical witness, the historic Christian conversation, and Baptist confessions. Baptists affirm that, despite the debilitating impact of the Fall upon human nature, human persons continue to inherit the image and likeness of God through human generation (Gen 5:1–3). Personal freedom is granted to every human being. In consequence, moral agency is demanded of every human being. Decoupling personal guilt from original sin, they wrote, "By his free choice man sinned against God and brought sin into the human race. Through the temptation of Satan man transgressed the command of God and fell from his original innocence whereby his posterity inherit a nature and an environment inclined toward sin. Therefore, as soon as they are capable of moral action, they become transgressors and are under condemnation."[54]

The elevated place of humanity in Baptist dogmatics requires further exploration. Such elevation began at creation and continues in redemption. Human elevation depends upon its connection with Christ. The eternal Christ is the *imago Dei* (Col 1:15; Heb 1:3), in whose image humanity was originally created. Moreover, the church via redemption is the "body of Christ" (Rom 12:5; 1 Cor 12:27). On the basis of such Christology, not only does our denomination's confession describe humanity with exalted language like "special" and "crowning work of creation," it also describes

---

[53] The new article on the family adds, "The husband and wife are of equal worth before God, since both are created in God's image" (Baptist Faith and Message, Article XVIII).

[54] Baptist Faith and Message, Article III.

the human person in near divine terms as "sacred" and explicitly states every human person possesses God-given "dignity." "The sacredness of human personality is evident in that God created man in His own image, and in that Christ died for man; therefore, every person of every race possesses full dignity and is worthy of respect and Christian love."[55]

## Conscience

The seventeenth article of the Baptist Faith and Message takes the previous centuries of Baptist discourse regarding the liberty of conscience—and its implications for human dignity and human relationships in the church and in the state—and codifies it in a dogmatic way. However, it must be understood that the seventeenth article, along with the preamble of the Baptist Faith and Message, make it clear that the Southern Baptist understanding of the dogmatic authority of a confession is quite limited. There is a significant difference between a Baptist dogmatic and the dogmatics of those Christian communions who fostered the confessionalization of the post-Reformation period. Baptists simply do not treat their confessions with the same authority or in the same way as Roman Catholics, Lutherans, Anglicans, or Presbyterians.

Among the historic free churches, the primary locus for the exercise of divine authority is within the human conscience; the secondary locus is within the ecclesiastical community. The conscience of the free church Christian listens first, foremost, and finally to the authoritative voice of God through the Word in the Spirit. The authority of the ecclesiastical community is necessary for the individual Christian's well-being through its pedagogy, but it depends upon the conscience voluntarily submitting to the religious community's covenant. The church has authority over the community's dogma and boundaries, but it has no authority to enforce that dogma beyond terms of membership. Neither the church nor the

---

[55] Baptist Faith and Message, Article III.

state may coerce the conscience. From the Baptist and Free Church perspective, moreover, the state, unlike the church, simply has no dogmatic voice whatsoever.

Note below how Article XVII of the Baptist Faith and Message grounds the Baptist doctrine of religious liberty in the unique and untrammeled Lordship of Jesus Christ. Next, the article proceeds through the liberty of the human conscience to human relationships within the separate institutions of the church and the state. Finally, the church and the state utilize different instrumental means to maintain the integrity required of their respective members. The article rightly begins with the sovereignty of God over the conscience before proceeding to consider the covenantal aspects of the different communities to which human beings belong.

God alone is Lord of the conscience, and He has left it free from the doctrines and commandments of men which are contrary to His Word or not contained in it. Church and state should be separate. The state owes to every church protection and full freedom in the pursuit of its spiritual ends. In providing for such freedom no ecclesiastical group or denomination should be favored by the state more than others. Civil government being ordained of God, it is the duty of Christians to render loyal obedience thereto in all things not contrary to the revealed will of God. The church should not resort to the civil power to carry on its work. The gospel of Christ contemplates spiritual means alone for the pursuit of its ends. The state has no right to impose penalties for religious opinions of any kind. The state has no right to impose taxes for the support of any form of religion. A free church in a free state is the Christian ideal, and this implies the right of free and unhindered access to God on the part of all men, and the right to form and propagate opinions in the sphere of religion without interference by the civil power.

## *Covenant*

The conscience of the human person made in the image of God provides the basis for Christian ethics. However, "the essentially socially interactive nature of human constitution and the emergence of personhood" must also be recognized.[56] Therefore, while Baptists believe that God holds each person accountable to himself through personal conscience, they also believe God holds human beings stringently accountable for our treatment of other human beings. After all, each person is created in his image and likeness (Gen 9:6). He holds each person accountable for their rule of the earth on his behalf (Gen 1:26–28; 2:16–17). We believe that recovering both the conscience and covenantal aspects of Baptist dogmatics, which we surveyed above, can contribute to the melioration of modern anthropological error against human dignity. Abusive power relationships challenge individual human dignity in every human covenantal community, whether it is a family, a church, or a state.

While metaphysical covenantal theologies have largely determined Reformed dogmatics,[57] practical covenantal ecclesiology deeply influences free church dogmatics.[58] The covenantal relations formed in families, churches, and societies must be developed into maturity. It is in the *covenant of marriage* between two image-bearers that the dignified relations which respect both the individual accountability of the conscience before God and the corporate responsibility of the marriage partners for

---

[56] Christian Smith, *What Is a Person? Rethinking Humanity, Social Life, and the Moral Good from the Person Up* (Chicago: The University of Chicago Press, 2010), 16.

[57] Guy Prentiss Waters, J. Nicholas Reid, and John R. Muether, eds., *Covenant Theology: Biblical, Theological, and Historical Perspectives* (Wheaton, IL: Crossway, 2020), 327–445.

[58] Paul Fiddes identifies the entire movement of free church ecclesiology during the early modern period as "the Fourth Strand of the Reformation." Paul Fiddes, ed., *The Fourth Strand of the Reformation: The Covenant Ecclesiology of Anabaptists, English Separatists, and Early General Baptists* (Oxford: Centre for Baptist History and Heritage, 2018).

one another and children and other dependents can be framed. It is in the *covenant of a church* that the dignified relations which respect the sole Lordship of Jesus Christ over each human being's soul and the proper functioning of the household of God should be framed. And it is in the *covenants or constitutions which govern society* that the dignified relations between the consciences of all human beings and every human being of every race, gender, and creed should be framed.

## Recent Views of the Southern Baptist Convention on Human Dignity

In the nearly 180-year history of the Southern Baptist Convention, numerous resolutions have been passed from the convention floor which have reflected our developing views on human dignity and worth. While SBC resolutions do not necessarily bind or govern our churches and institutions, they do mirror the views of the convention at particular moments throughout our history. They express biblical and theological emphases on the social concerns of their day. These convention-approved documents give a window into the ecclesial signpost of Baptist dogmatics, i.e., how Southern Baptist churches have developed their theological views in their distinctive historical circumstances.

The history of the SBC demonstrates that Southern Baptists have changed their minds on race relations issues over time as they grew in their understanding of the image of God and human dignity. Although a pro-slavery stance played an undeniable role in the formation of the convention, Southern Baptists have always had a missional concern for all persons made in the image of God. At the first annual meeting in 1845, the convention resolved to provide religious instruction to Native and African Americans for "their spiritual benefit."[59]

---

[59] The Southern Baptist Convention, "Resolution on Indians" (1845); "Resolution on Negros" (1845). Similar resolutions were made in 1849, 1886, 1884, 1886.

The first half of the twentieth century saw several resolutions that condemned lynching, mob violence, and various forms of racism.[60] Other resolutions in the mid-twentieth century gave support to the ministerial education of African American pastors (even if such support was given with an implicit affirmation of segregation and segregated churches and universities).[61] In 1995, 150 years after the first convention, the SBC passed a resolution on racial reconciliation that bemoaned the role slavery and racism played in the history of the SBC.[62]

While the relationship between the image of God and human dignity is common in convention documents today—over seventy resolutions have referred to the image of God and human dignity since 1988—it took some time for the SBC to frame human dignity in this way. The relationship between human dignity and the image of God was not made explicit in convention documents until the 1963 Baptist Faith and Message, which stated, "The sacredness of human personality is evident in that God created man in His own image, and in that Christ died for man; therefore every man possesses dignity and is worthy of respect and Christian love." The first convention resolution to make mention of the "image of God" was a 1971 resolution on prejudice. The use of this terminology remained sparse, as the next resolution to invoke this language came six years later.

The issue of abortion is another area where Southern Baptists have developed in their conception of human dignity and the image of God. A year and a half before the *Roe v. Wade* decision, the convention passed a resolution that allowed for abortion "under such conditions as rape,

---

[60] The Southern Baptist Convention, "Resolution on Lynching" (1934); "Hillyer Resolutions" (1906); "Resolution on Lynching" (1935); "Resolution on Lynching and Mob Violence" (1937); "Resolution Concerning Lynching and Race Relations" (1939); "Resolution Concerning Race Relations" (1941).

[61] The Southern Baptist Convention, "Resolution on Race" (1944); "Resolution on Ministerial Education for Negro Baptists" (1944).

[62] The Southern Baptist Convention, "Resolution on Racial Reconciliation on the 150th Anniversary of the Southern Baptist Convention" (1995).

incest, clear evidence of severe fetal deformity, and carefully ascertained evidence of the likelihood of damage to the *emotional, mental*, and *physical health* of the mother."[63] This broad acceptance of abortion practices is no different from the view of contemporary pro-choice advocates. A 1974 resolution sought "a middle ground between the extreme of abortion on demand and the opposite extreme of all abortion as murder."[64] A 1979 resolution both decried abortion as a "serious moral and spiritual problem" and called for "the limited role of government in dealing with matters related to abortion."[65]

Compare those explicitly pro-choice and moderately pro-choice resolutions with a 1980 resolution for a "constitutional amendment prohibiting abortion except to save the life of the mother."[66] Over nine years, the views expressed about abortion in convention resolutions changed dramatically. No doubt, these developments reflected broader changes in the SBC associated with the Conservative Resurgence, the Moral Majority, and the Reagan Revolution. But this development was more than an ecclesiological or political shift; it was also a theological shift. A 1982 resolution making the same claim directly tied the "sanctity and worth of all human life" to "being created in the image of God."[67] For the first time on public record, Southern Baptists had affirmed the dignity of unborn children made in the image of God.

The 2018 resolution "On Reaffirming the Full Dignity of Every Human Being" emphasized the impact of the image of God in shaping our view of human dignity. That 2018 resolution was prompted by concerns about the treatment of victims of clerical sexual abuse. But it plainly

---

[63] The Southern Baptist Convention, "Resolution on Abortion" (1971), emphasis ours.

[64] The Southern Baptist Convention, "Resolution on Abortion and Sanctity of Human Life" (1974).

[65] The Southern Baptist Convention, "Resolution on Abortion" (1979).

[66] The Southern Baptist Convention, "Resolution on Abortion" (1980).

[67] The Southern Baptist Convention, "Resolution on Abortion and Infanticide" (1982); cf. "Resolution on Abortion" (1984).

listed numerous threats to the dignity of the human being, including "the heinous murder of the unborn child in the womb, the enforced withdrawal of life-sustaining medical care from the ill or infirm, the prejudices and discriminations of racism and ethnocentrism, various abuses of other human persons, the denigration of opposing political groups, and persecutions of religious minorities."[68]

# Conclusion

The dignity of every human, simply because each has been created in God's image, requires widespread reclamation, as a glance at the secular news any day you read this essay will verify. Moreover, the histories of Southern Baptists and other free church Christians, indeed the repeated conduct of Christians throughout church history, demonstrate our need to advocate for human dignity as irreducible dogma. As stated at the beginning of this essay, we believe that the truths of human dignity and the inherent rights which derive from a person's liberty of conscience to live within human covenants, freely and responsibly, are necessary aspects of an orthodox theological anthropology. We are more convinced than ever that reclaiming and implementing orthodox anthropology has been the greatest challenge for Southern Baptists. Theological anthropology remains the most underdeveloped aspect of Baptist dogmatic reflection, so we invite others to join us in the effort to proclaim the truth about the sacred dignity of those who have been made in the image of God.

---

[68] The Southern Baptist Convention, "On Reaffirming the Full Dignity of Every Human Being" (2018).

# CHRISTOLOGY

### R. Lucas Stamps and Tyler R. Wittman

*And Mary said, My soul doth magnify the Lord,*
*And my spirit hath rejoiced in God my Saviour.*
*For he hath regarded the low estate of his handmaiden: for, behold, from*
*henceforth all generations shall call me blessed.*
*For he that is mighty hath done to me great things; and holy is his name.*
*And his mercy is on them that fear him from generation to generation.*
*He hath shewed strength with his arm; he hath scattered the proud in the*
*imagination of their hearts.*
*He hath put down the mighty from their seats, and exalted them of low degree.*
*He hath filled the hungry with good things; and the rich he hath sent empty away.*
*He hath helped his servant Israel, in remembrance of his mercy;*
*As he spake to our fathers, to Abraham, and to his seed for ever*
*(Luke 1:46–55 KJV).*

## Introduction: Magnifying the Lordship of Christ

With these words, the mother of our Lord extols the changing tides
that ebb within her virgin womb. Mary's beatitude is grounded in the

beatitude of the divine person to whom she will give birth. The Holy One of Israel (Luke 1:49) has done great things by conceiving within her a Holy Son by the Holy Spirit (Luke 1:35). This new mercy brings to remembrance the promises made to Israel, Abraham, and Eve.

Theological reflection on Christology does well to begin with Mary's *Magnificat* for at least two reasons. First, Mary's significance in the divine economy has often been diminished or downplayed by Protestant theologians, perhaps in response to Roman Catholic excess. But here, as elsewhere, *abusus non tollit usum* (abuse does not negate use). Second, and more to our present purposes, Mary's *Magnificat* provides a portrait for the way that Baptist theology should respond to Christ in its confession of his person and work. Mary of course teaches us many things, not least of which is her model of servanthood that devoutly receives the word of the Lord (Luke 1:38). But Mary's song also honors the Lord for the power and might of his goodness, filling the hungry and remembering his mercy for generations. Against this backdrop, earthly powers do not disappear but are necessarily relativized: since she will give birth to the Lord whose kingdom will have no end, then the mighty will be taken from their thrones and the humble exalted (Luke 1:33, 52). Implicit in Mary's song is the ontological foundation of so many Baptist distinctives: the irreplaceable Lordship of Christ. This Lordship entails the believer's freedom and the civil authority's toleration of that freedom.[1] All passing temporal authorities—whether civil or ecclesiastical—must respect Christ as the Lord of the conscience and King over each local assembly of new covenant believers.

This chapter sketches the main contours of Christology for Baptist theology, specifically focusing on Christ's person. Special attention is given to the biblical teaching on the Virgin Birth and its dogmatic significance, drawing from, among others, several important Baptist theologians for support. Baptists do not have a unique Christology—something

---

[1] See Stephen R. Holmes, *Baptist Theology* (London: T&T Clark, 2012), 119–39.

the present chapter stresses—yet Baptists do employ that Christology in distinctive ways. We therefore conclude with some reflections on a distinctively Baptist inflection of Christology, built upon the sole Lordship of Christ and his royal presence in his church.

## Christ's Preexistent Fullness

Christology is "a distributed doctrine," requiring patient consideration of the incarnation's eternal ground in the Son's relation to the Father and the Spirit, as well as God's will to rescue sinners in the Son's temporal mission, the constitution of Christ's person, the relation and ordering of his two natures, and the entirety of his mediatorial work in its objective and subjective aspects.[2] For our purposes, we may survey many of these elements through a twofold consideration, focusing on Christ's preexistence and pro-existence. After some initial remarks about this distinction, we will consider each aspect of Christ in turn.

### *Theology and Economy*

The distinction between preexistence and pro-existence is propaedeutic and heuristic. It simply mirrors what Christian tradition calls theology (*theologia*) and economy (*oikonomia*), God's divine nature and his works, respectively.[3] The *preexistence* of the Son is not sequential, so his temporal mission is not another episode in a timeline that stretches "backwards"

---

[2] On this distribution, see John Webster, "Christology, Theology, Economy: The Place of Christology in Systematic Theology," in *God Without Measure*, vol. 1, *God and the Works of God* (London: Bloomsbury, 2016), 43–58 (47). Space prevents us from extending our reflection into Christ's mediatorial work.

[3] See, e.g., Amandus Polanus, *Syntagma theologiae christianae* (Hanoviae, 1615), for whom Christology consists of a twofold consideration: first, it considers the Son "incompositely" (*asunthetos*) as existing in the divine nature, begotten of the Father; second, it considers the Son "compositely" (*sunthetos*), that is, as incarnate, with two natures hypostatically united.

into eternity analogous to how today is preceded by yesterday. Part of registering the Son's preexistence requires us to see that his eternality is an ontological rather than temporal reality, the indivisible and permanent vitality—transcending all temporal division—of the one who is Life (John 11:25). Hence, Christ's preexistence concerns the Son's divine *pre*eminence. In this respect, Christ is both "before" and "above" all things (John 1:15; 3:31; cf. Rom 9:5). Likewise, Christ's *pro*-existence concerns the temporal *economy* of his flesh, which has its deep background in God's decree to rescue sinful creatures from their corruption and alienation from God. The "pro" echoes the *pro nobis* ("for us") of the Constantinopolitan Creed: the Son was incarnate *propter nos homines et propter nostrum salutem* (for us and for our salvation), and was crucified under Pontius Pilate *pro nobis*.[4] Everything the Son undertakes in his temporal mission is struck through with pronobeity, "for-us-ness." After all, "the Son of Man came not to be served but to serve, and to give his life as a ransom for many" (Mark 10:45 ESV).

Preexistence and pro-existence are distinct, but not separate. Theology and economy illuminate one another, though they are asymmetrical in important respects. Christ's mission gathers its vitality and sufficiency from the fact that "in him the whole fullness of deity dwells bodily" (Col 2:9 ESV). Because he is full in and of himself, he fills all things (Eph 2:23); because he is blessed and full of joy, he can promise and deliver that beatitude and joy to us (John 15:11; Titus 2:13); because the Son is Life in himself he can become and be the Way to life for us.[5] Theology therefore supports economy, the Son's pro-existence is good news because Jesus is goodness itself in his preexistent fullness (Mark 10:18). Dogmatics seeks to coordinate theology and economy, preexistent fullness and pro-existent filling in due proportions.

---

[4] Heinrich Denzinger, *Compendium of Creeds, Definitions, and Declarations on Matters of Faith and Morals*, 43rd ed., ed. Peter Hünermann (San Francisco: Ignatius, 2012), 159. Henceforth *DH*.

[5] Augustine, *City of God* 9.15 (*Works of St. Augustine* I/6:293–95, hereinafter WSA).

A characteristic feature of many trinitarian and Christological heresies is confusing or collapsing preexistence with pro-existence. Where the soteriological "for us" is located in Christology matters a great deal to the doctrine's overall coherence.[6] Theologians who locate the "for us" at the beginning of the Son's being ultimately confuse the Father's eternal generation of the Son with God's purpose to create or redeem. The Son's personal distinction from the Father is thereby a means to an end. Effectively, God's decree subsumes eternal generation. Subordinationism results, for the Father's relation to the Son is thereby misunderstood as voluntary rather than natural.[7] Historically, this has also resulted in a distorted portrait of Christ's humanity.[8] If the Son's incarnation merely extends a quasi-divinity that the Father creates for him "at the beginning of his work" (Prov 8:22), then his humanity is easily exalted beyond any creaturely recognizability. From the premise of a God who can change into a man it is a small step to a portrait of man who can change into God.[9]

The soteriological "for us" must be located in the economy of Christ's flesh, beginning with God's eternal counsel, and executed in the Son's temporal mission. However, this can be mishandled. An abstractly philosophical account of divinity could create problems for the unity of Christ,

---

[6] Khaled Anatolios, *Retrieving Nicaea: The Development and Meaning of Trinitarian Doctrine* (Grand Rapids: Baker Academic, 2011), 42–79 (discussion of Arius, Asterius, Eusebius, and Eunomius), 93–95.

[7] Along these same lines, conflating Christ's pro-existence and his preexistence entirely at the historical level can result in adoptionism. Thus, John Owen criticizes the Socinians for believing that Christ, "being only a man . . . was made a god for his own sake." Owen, *Meditations and Discourses Concerning the Glory of Christ* iv in *The Works of John Owen* (Edinburgh: T&T Clark, 1962), 1:326.

[8] Anatolios, *Retrieving Nicaea*, 94–97.

[9] For similar reasons, Reformed theologians have resisted Hegel's idealist apotheosis of the human and the historical, not without mentioning its affinity with the Lutheran *genus majestaticum*. For instance, with due nuance, Bavinck, *Reformed Dogmatics* 3:265–76, 303; and, more directly, Karl Barth, *Unterricht in der christlichen Religion*, vol. 3 (Zürich: Theologischer Verlag, 1985), §28 (56–57). Steven J. Duby, *Jesus and the God of Classical Theism* (Grand Rapids: Baker Academic, 2022), 180–82, offers a mature, balanced approach to these matters.

if divinity were mistakenly thought to be at odds with what Jesus is and does. That is, an inadequate understanding of Christ's preexistent fullness generates problems where divinity and humanity are related competitively within Christ (even if only possibly so).[10] A portrait of two persons easily results, as does the temptation to set aside true divinity or true humanity. The modern versions of these errors are typically varieties of kenoticism and historicism.[11] These views might secure a Christology that is easier to understand, but at the cost of obscuring Christ's pro-existence—the

---

[10] Christopher A. Beeley, "Christological Non-Competition and the Return to Chalcedon: A Response to Rowan Williams and Ian McFarland," *Modern Theology* 38.3 (2022): 592–617, argues that the much-used idea of "non-competitiveness" between divinity and humanity can do too much work for Christology if it effectively sidelines the divine nature in an account of Christ's humanity, as it appears to do in some (but not all) of the instances he criticizes. The danger is real, with wider applicability than just Christology. Like any philosophical aid, the grammar of non-competition cannot bear too much material freight. As Beeley remarks, "God and humanity are non-competitive in a minimal ontological sense, though of course not in every sense, if we think of sin and evil" (612–13). Curiously, however, Beeley's concerns seem to extend to the Christological *extra carnem* (610). Yet surely the ontological non-competitiveness of divinity and humanity asserts itself here, for the strict unity of Christ's person is compatible with his divinity's immeasurability. The Logos is *extra humanitatem* not by any separation, but in the minimal sense of "non-circumscription" or *non inclusionem* (Francis Turretin, *Institutes of Elenctic Theology*, 13.8.xxviii). So also Damascene, *On the Orthodox Faith* §51 (Popular Patristics Series, 62:177, hereinafter PPS): "without abandoning the bosom of the Father (because he exists in an uncircumscribed manner) the Word came to dwell in the womb of the holy Virgin" (cf. §13). Hence, Christ can be both removed physically and nevertheless with his church always (Matt 26:11; 28:20). Christ's physical absence coheres with his royal presence.

[11] See the magisterial treatment of such themes in Duby, *Jesus*, 141–91. On the several varieties of kenoticism, and a response, see Stephen J. Wellum, *God the Son Incarnate: The Doctrine of Christ* (Wheaton, IL: Crossway, 2016), 355–419; from a sympathetic voice, Bruce L. McCormack, "Kenoticism in Modern Christology," in *The Oxford Handbook of Christology*, ed. Francesca Aran Murphy (Oxford: Oxford University Press, 2015), 444–57. It arrived too late for us to use, but readers looking for more will also want to consult Daniel J. Treier, *Lord Jesus Christ*, New Studies in Dogmatics (Grand Rapids: Zondervan, 2023).

significance of Christology for disciples.[12] The fundamental mistake is to bracket or lose either of Christ's natures in a consideration of his person. Coordinating pre- and pro-existence therefore begins with careful attention to Christ's divinity.

## Christ's Divinity

The following survey of Christ's divinity proceeds in two broad strokes. First, we must consider Christ's eternal relation to the Father and, second, the way that his fullness supports and shapes his pro-existence. Brief consideration of each point will prepare a lengthier analysis of the Son's temporal mission.

Repeatedly in his ministry, Jesus justifies and illuminates his own works by pointing his audience to their antecedent grounds in his relation to his Father. This eternal relation belongs to his preeminence over all things. Scripture describes it with a variety of metaphors: "For as the Father has life in himself, so he has granted the Son also to have life in himself" (John 5:26 ESV); "He is the image of the invisible God" (Col 1:15 ESV); "He is the radiance of the glory of God and the exact imprint of his nature" (Heb 1:3 ESV). In addition to naming the Son as the "Word," John tells us the Son is divine because he is the "only-begotten" Son of the Father (John 1:14).[13] And because he is the eternal, natural Son, he can create adopted children by grace: "to all who did receive him, who believed in his name, he gave the right to become children of God, who were born, not of blood nor of the will of the flesh nor the will of man, but of God" (John 1:12–13 ESV). His disciples' new birth echoes Christ's own miraculous birth from a mother without a father. Yet the virgin birth itself testifies to the Son's eternal begetting, or "birth," from

---

[12] Kathryn Tanner, *Jesus, Humanity and the Trinity: A Brief Systematic Theology* (Minneapolis: Fortress, 2001), 10.

[13] Charles Lee Irons, "A Lexical Defense of the Johannine 'Only Begotten,'" in *Retrieving Eternal Generation*, ed. Fred Sanders and Scott R. Swain (Grand Rapids: Zondervan, 2017).

the Father without a mother.[14] This antecedent relation consists in the Son's eternal generation from the Father.[15]

The relation between the Father and the Son is therefore analogous to the biological relation between human fathers and sons, since both are instances of "begetting." However, on account of God's infinitude and simplicity, this relation is qualitatively different from all biological procreation. It is an anthropomorphism that must be understood in a manner befitting God's nature.[16] John Damascene states the basic rule: "just as a human being and God do not make in the same way . . . similarly, neither do God and a human being beget in the same way."[17] Indeed, "fatherhood" and "sonship" are applied to humans secondarily, since their source is found in God (Eph 3:14–15).[18] What "begetting" means within God's life is unique. A series of negations registers this uniqueness: the begetting is timeless, without beginning, without passion or change, and without separation. Yet, like human generation, the begotten bears the begetter's likeness and is a distinct person. Damascene shows how the biblical imagery implies these several points: "Thus the Word is also called the radiance through his being begotten of the Father without copulation, impassibly, timelessly, intransiently, and inseparably; he is called Son and imprint of the Father's hypostasis through his being perfect and enhypostatic and in every respect like the Father except for the Father's unbegottenness; and he is called

---

[14] Hence, the angel tells Mary that her child "shall be called" the Son of God, not "shall be" the Son of God (Luke 1:35); Turretin, *Institutes of Elenctic Theology*, 3.29.27 (1:301).

[15] This overview is too brief and inadequate to do the doctrine justice. See Fred Sanders and Scott R. Swain, eds., *Retrieving Eternal Generation* (Grand Rapids: Zondervan, 2017); John Webster, "Eternal Generation," *God without Measure* 1:29–41; Duby, *Jesus and the God of Classical Theism*, 51–96.

[16] Turretin, *Institutes of Elenctic Theology*, 3.29.5 (1:293). On the idea of God-befittingness, see Jamieson and Wittman, *Biblical Reasoning: Christological and Trinitarian Rules for Exegesis* (Grand Rapids: Baker Academic, 2022), 63–90.

[17] John of Damascus, *On the Orthodox Faith* §8 (PPS 62:73–74).

[18] John of Damascus, §8 (PPS 62:76).

only-begotten because he has been begotten uniquely and alone from the only Father."[19]

For all these reasons, eternal generation is incomprehensible—infinitely unlike what we know about "begetting." According to the wisdom of Gregory Nazianzen, it must be honored with silence.[20] What Christian tradition says here is quite reserved: begetting is necessary and natural, not contingent and voluntary; eternal, not temporal; intrinsic, not extrinsic to God's life. The union of Father and Son is thus ontological rather than moral or adventitious. They possess the same being (*homoousios*), having all things in common except for what distinguishes them as persons: the Father communicates everything he is to the Son, except for "fatherhood." The Son is therefore the supreme likeness of the Father, and therefore the one in whose human face we also see the Father (John 1:18; 14:9). He is not a secondary or subordinate divinity, nor does he supply the Trinity with some capacity the Father or the Spirit do not have. The three divine persons are equally invisible, incomprehensible, sovereign, and blessed; the only thing that distinguishes them are the relations of origin in which they face one another.[21] As the Son's mode of existence is from the Father, so too is his mode of acting from the Father. Consequently, Jesus acts as the divine Son, *ex Patre.* Jesus can do nothing "from himself" because his being and his acting are *from the Father* (John 5:30).[22] The Son's eternal generation from the Father therefore shapes his human life from beginning to end, for the incarnate Word is and remains the eternal *Son of God.*

The Son's preeminent fullness as God is the backdrop for understanding his incarnation. Paul thus argues from Christ's existence in the "form of God," in which he enjoys "equality with God," to his assumption of the "form of a servant," in which he came to be in our

---

[19] John of Damascus, §8 (PPS 62:75).

[20] Nazianzus, *Or.* 29.8.

[21] Scholastic theology designates these as relations of "opposition."

[22] Aquinas, *In Ioan.* 5.5.797–798.

likeness (Phil 2:6–7 ESV). Jesus did not consider his divinity something to be "exploited" for his own advantage (Phil 2:6). And how could he? Enjoying the fullness of goodness together with the Father and Spirit, the Son is blessed and self-sufficient. His divine existence is beyond need, want, or augmentation, so naturally he does not consider it something to be used to get something he does not already have. Rather, his fullness means he stands ready to *fill* others. From the infinite communication of the divine goodness from Father to Son, and from Father and Son to Spirit, God is poised to communicate himself *ad extra*. God does not need this further communication, but it is consistent with his divine fullness. Christ's preexistence grounds the economy of his flesh, which is entirely *pro nobis*. The Son's beatitude authors our beatitude; his self-sufficiency becomes sufficient also *for us*; his incorruptibility bursts the cords of death and overflows to our frame (Rom 1:23; 1 Cor 15:42). He condescends to assume our flesh, to humble himself in obedience unto death on a cross, not because he needs to nor because we deserve it. Rather, it pleases him in mercy and grace to rescue lost sheep. The economy therefore rests upon God's philanthropy.[23] The incarnation and everything that follows is rooted in God's eternal purpose to save sinners (Eph 1:3–14), out of his good-pleasure alone. Hence, the outworking of that purpose is the Son's pro-existent movement towards his people, to fill them with his fullness (Eph. 1:15–23).

## Christ's Pro-Existent Filling

Christ's humanity acquires importance against the backdrop of his divinity, for it is the instrument by which he communicates his divine

---

[23] Gregory of Nyssa, *Catechetical Discourse* 15.2 (PPS 60:96); John of Damascus, *On the Orthodox Faith* §45 (PPS 62:163); Turretin, *Institutes of Elenctic Theology* 13.3.6 (2:300). Cyril of Alexandria, *On the Unity of Christ* (PPS 13:79), is representative: "It was not impossible to God, in his loving-kindness, to make himself capable of bearing the limitations of the manhood."

blessedness to miserable sinners.[24] His humanity is therefore the hinge of our salvation (*caro salutis est cardo*).[25] This truth requires that he is "truly God and truly man," else he is not our Savior.[26] A full account of Christ's pro-existent mission cannot be limited to his person, but encompasses his full mediatorial office in its prophetic, priestly, and royal duties, which come to a highpoint in his cross and resurrection. Since the present account is partial, however, we will focus on the Mediator in the unity of his person. This may be summarized in terms of the hypostatic union and the effects of that union.[27] Consideration of each of these points will finish laying the groundwork to give an account of the significance of the Virgin Mary.

## *The Hypostatic Union*

The divine *Word* became flesh (John 1:14) by being "born of a woman" (Gal 4:4) and descending "from David according to the flesh" (Rom 1:3). He therefore "partook of the same things" as us, such as flesh and blood (Heb 2:14 ESV). The consequence of this "becoming" flesh is a personal

---

[24] See, again, Augustine's argument in *City of God* 9 (WSA I/6:277–302).

[25] Tertullian, *De resurrectione carnis* 8.2, ed. and trans. Ernest Evans (London: SPCK, 1960), 24.

[26] *Definitio* of Chalcedon (*DH* 301). On the necessity of the Savior being both God and man, see Turretin, *Institutes of Elenctic Theology*, 13.3 (2:299–304); Owen, *Christologia* xvi–xvii (*Works* 1:178–223).

[27] Christian tradition has also often articulated Christ's pro-existence through an analysis of the Son's many names—Christ, Immanuel, Jesus, Lamb of God, Way, Door, High Priest, etc. For example, Gregory Nazianzen, *Oration* 30.20–21 (PPS 23:109–112); Cyril of Alexandria, *Scholia on the Incarnation of the Only Begotten* §§1–3, in McGuckin, *Saint Cyril of Alexandria and the Christological Controversy* (Crestwood, New York: St. Vladimir's Seminary Press, 2011), 294–97. Theologians have not always understood all of these titles as strictly "economic" names (e.g., "Christ"). Nevertheless, when these names are considered economically, with a view to Christ's saving economy, their meaning illuminates Christ's movement *pro nobis*. Limitations of space dictate we must set this approach aside.

union between the divine Son's two natures, his divinity and his human-ity.[28] There are many things this unity is not: not a *unity of essence*, as exists among the persons of the Trinity; not a *relational unity*, as one could find among people who share a common purpose; not a mystical union, as exists between Christ and the church; nor a union of roles, persons, or of dignity, or anything else for which we have some example else-where.[29] This union is *sui generis*: "there has not been, nor will there ever be, another Christ out of divinity and humanity, the same being perfect God and perfect man in divinity and humanity."[30] The union is *hypostatic* or *personal* because the Logos communicates his personal existence to his humanity in the same operation whereby it is conceived by the Holy Spirit. He assumes the human flesh conceived in Mary's womb as his "own," into his person. His humanity has no personality from itself since its only personhood is *his* personhood. On its own, it *would be* anhypo-static; in the Word it *is* enhypostatic.[31] According to the Chalcedonian definition, Jesus therefore exists "in two natures, without confusion or change, without division or separation."[32] In Christ there are not two persons, but one person; not one nature, but two. Distinction and identity

---

[28] The following overview is necessarily too brief. Fuller, helpful accounts may be found in Thomas Joseph White, *The Incarnate Lord: A Thomistic Study in Christology* (Washington, D.C.: Catholic University of America Press, 2015), chap. 1; Duby, *Jesus and the God of Classical Theism*, chap. 4.

[29] See Damascene, *On the Orthodox Faith* §47 (PPS 62:169); Owen, *Christologia* xviii (*Works* 1:228–232); Turretin, *Institutes of Elenctic Theology* 13.6.3 (2:311).

[30] Damascene, *On the Orthodox Faith* §47 (PPS 62:167).

[31] Note well the difference; cf. Damascene, *On the Orthodox Faith* §53 (PPS 62:182). On the concept of "enhypostasis," see Benjamin Gleede, *The Development of the Term* ἐνυπόστατος *from Origen to John of Damascus* (Leiden: Brill, 2012).

[32] *Definitio* of Chalcedon (DH 302). Damascene states the essential point with brevity: "although Christ's natures are united, they are united without confusion, and although they interpenetrate each other, they do not change or mutate into each other, for each nature preserves its own natural property unaltered." *On the Orthodox Faith* §49 (PPS 62:173).

work together: since his natures remain distinct, then Christ is *identical* with God and with us; since the hypostasis of both natures is identical, then Christ "differs from the Father and the Spirit, and from his mother and us."[33] We may consider this truth more carefully by looking at (a) the person assuming and (b) the nature assumed.

## A. The Person Assuming

The hypostatic union is predicated upon a divine act of assumption of which it is the result.[34] No creature by any agency or merit of its own can be ingrafted into the divine life, so God must condescend and take the initiative in the incarnation. It is in this sense the "grace of union" (*gratia unionis*).[35] Paul describes this divine act of assumption as the Son emptying himself "by taking" our common human nature, rather than by divesting himself of or transforming his divinity into something it was not (Phil 2:7 ESV).[36] The assumption of flesh reminds us that the incarnation was not the result of natural or moral processes. It was an act of divine mercy, Mary says (Luke 1:54), on account of which the Father *sent* the Son and the Son *came* and "dwelt among us" (John 1:14; 8:42).

Already we can see how assumption involves the whole Trinity. It is the Son alone who assumes human nature, but he does not *act* without the Father and the Spirit. This assumption is an "external" divine work and therefore undertaken indivisibly by all three persons of the Trinity (*opera trinitatis ad extra indivisa sunt*). While the work is common to the

---

[33] Cf. Damascene, *On the Orthodox Faith* §47 (PPS 62:170).

[34] On the differences between union and assumption, see Aquinas, *Summa Theologica* III.2.8, hereinafter *STh*.

[35] Aquinas, *STh* III.2.10–12; Owen, *Christologia* xviii (Works 1:225); Turretin, *Institutes of Elenctic Theology* 13.12.1 (2:347).

[36] Cyril of Alexandria, *Second Letter to Succensus* 2–3 (The Cambridge Edition of Early Christian Writings 3:742–44, hereinafter CEECW). Athanasius, *Ep.* 59.4 (CEECW 3:283), recognized that if the Son transformed his divinity into humanity, and he is *homoousios* with the Father, then the Father's nature would have been transformed into human nature.

Father, Son, and Holy Spirit, nevertheless the result is proper to the Son alone.[37] That is to say, since the Son assumes human nature by the power of his divinity, then he does so together with the Father and the Spirit. Yet since only the Son assumes human nature into his own personal existence, then this work is consummated in the Son alone.[38] The Father sends and the Spirit conceives in the virgin's womb, but neither Father nor Spirit were incarnate.

Among the important truths this point secures, three are salient for our purposes. First, the assumption really involves the unity of Christ's human flesh with his divinity. The Son is the divine nature in his distinct filial mode of subsistence. Hence, the hypostatic union does not negate the fact that divinity is indeed incarnate: "in him all the fullness of God was pleased to dwell" (Col 1:19 ESV). However, it was divinity as it subsists in the Son that was thus incarnate.[39] Chalcedon's affirmation of the two natures existing in Christ "without division or separation" depends on this point. Second, and following from this, it is the divine Son who assumes flesh and who thus appears in the flesh: "we have seen his glory, glory as of the only-begotten from the Father" (John 1:14). The whole incarnation is shot through with the revelation of the Trinity because the incarnate Son lives out in our flesh his eternal relations from the Father and to the Spirit. Finally, therefore, the Son's incarnate relationship to the

---

[37] Thus, the Sixth Synod of Toledo (638): "Though the entire Trinity cooperated in the formation of his assumed humanity—since the works of the Trinity are inseparable—yet he alone, in the singularity of Person, not in the unity of the divine nature, became man; in this is something proper to the Son, not something common to the Trinity" (DH 491, rev.). For an exemplary exposition of this point, see Dominic Legge, *The Trinitarian Christology of St. Thomas Aquinas* (Oxford: Oxford University Press, 2017), chap. 4.

[38] Aquinas, *STh* III.3.1–2, among many others, thus distinguishes the divine nature as the principle and the divine person (of the Son) as the terminus of the assumption.

[39] The technical way of stating this affirms that the divine nature was united mediately, whereas the Son was united immediately with human flesh. See, e.g., Bavinck, *Reformed Dogmatics* 3:275–76.

Spirit exhibits their eternal relations and order: the Son acts through the Spirit and the Spirit acts from the Son, both acting by the same power. Christ's relation to the Spirit is as unique and *sui generis* as he is, since there is no other God-man; his humanity is an example for us, even in his relation to the Spirit—an example we nevertheless follow by registering the *difference* between Jesus and us. The "Spirit through whom [Jesus] performed the divine signs is his very own," who proceeds through him from the Father.[40] No other possesses the Spirit as his or her own.

## B. The Nature Assumed

The assumption of human flesh sits within the covenant history between God and Israel, as God prepares his people for the fulfilment of his promises to Eve, Abraham, Isaac, and Jacob, as well as David. If the Son is the promised seed (Gen 3:15), the one in whom all the nations are glad (Ps 67:3–4), the dwelling place of God and the restoration of Israel (John 1:51; 2:19–20), the one who establishes David's throne forever (2 Sam 7:16), then he must be human. More to the point, he must be crucified and resurrected because the humanity in question is under the curse of death: "the same nature had to be taken on as needed to be set free."[41] Since the whole of our nature was corrupted and subject to death on account of sin, then Christ had to assume everything we are to redeem us—except for sin (Heb 4:15).

Theology must show the compatibility of Christ's humanity with the salvation he works and the worship he receives. Gregory Nazianzen famously voices the necessity of Christ's full humanity for our salvation: "what is not assumed is not healed, but what is united to God is saved. If half of Adam had fallen, then that's the half that would have

---

[40] Cyril of Alexandria, *Third Letter to Nestorius*, ninth anathema (CEECW 3:635); cf. *Against Theodoret* (Fathers of the Church Series 129:117).

[41] Augustine, *True Religion* 16.31 (WSA I/8:48); cf. *Faith and the Creed* 8 (WSA I/8:161).

been assumed and saved. But if the whole [Adam], then he was united as a whole to the Begotten and wholly saved."[42] Whatever sin touches in humanity needed the physician's remedy (Mark 2:17). The integrity of Christ's humanity corresponds to the extent of death's reign, which encompasses all that we are, body and soul. The soteriological necessity of Christ's whole and enhypostatic humanity safeguards any retreat into Pelagianism, for there is no domain of human nature that does not need to be saved, nor is it capable of salvation apart from the Logos (Rom 8:29). Christ was born under the law to fulfill it, so he needed all that Adam had, including the intellective and volitional powers of human nature. Hence, his two natures are "without confusion or change" and thus retain their proper characteristics—and it is proper to human nature to be something substantial and real. On the other hand, Christ's humanity is not an impediment to the worship he receives and is due (Matt 17:6; 28:9; Rev 1:17; 5:8, 14). No worship may be given to a mere creature (Matt 4:10). And so with Jesus: Christ's humanity "as such" is not worshipped for it does not exist anhypostatically, but enhypostatically. Worship is rendered to divine persons, so worship is piously rendered to "God incarnate" because he is God.[43] With this affirmation, we arrive at the consideration of the hypostatic union's effects.

---

[42] Nazianzen, *Letter* 101.32–33 (CEECW 3:392). Gregory means that all of "Adam" is being saved. On the controverted question of whether Christ assumed "fallen" human nature, see Michael Allen, "Christ," in *T&T Clark Companion to the Doctrine of Sin*, ed. Keith L. Johnson and David Lauber (London: Bloomsbury, 2016), 451–465. For the current state of the question, see Jerome Van Kuiken, "Torrance and Christ's Assumption of Fallen Human Nature: Toward Clarification and Closure," in *Thomas F. Torrance and Evangelical Theology: A Critical Analysis*, ed. Myk Habets and R. Lucas Stamps, Studies in Historical and Systematic Theology (Bellingham, WA: Lexham, 2023), 204–20.

[43] Damascene, *On the Orthodox Faith* §76 (PPS 62:230). Scholastics like Owen will stress that the "formal object" or the respect under which worship is due to Christ, is the divine nature he shares with the Father and the Spirit (*Works* 1:131). However, he observes that in Rev 5:9–12, Christ's incarnate, mediatorial work provides the "motive" for our adoration of Christ (*Works* 1:109). These

## *The Effects of the Union*

The hypostatic union's "effects" consist of a threefold communication between the Son's divinity and his humanity, some unilateral and others mutual.[44] This communication is between Creator and creature, so nothing happens here that blurs that distinction. Each nature has communion with the other in their union, which is hypostatic. Hence, the communications are "mediate," through the person, rather than "immediate," from nature to nature. These communications are threefold, concerning (a) grace, (b) idioms, and (c) operations. Consideration of each will suffice to conclude our overview of dogmatic Christology.

### A. The Communication of Graces

The communication of graces (*communicatio gratiarum*) is twofold. And as is the case with all divine grace, this movement is unilateral: from God to the creature. First, as we have seen when discussing the hypostatic union, the grace of union (*gratia unionis*) consists in the Lord communicating his personal existence to his human nature such that humanity is one with God in the most intimate possible manner.[45] This is an infinite grace, because the divine person communicated to the humanity is infinite. Distinct from this is the habitual grace (*gratia habitualis*) that the Trinity bestows upon Christ's humanity in the womb. These graces are all the finite "spiritual and excellent gifts" that come to Christ's humanity by the Spirit, who rests upon Christ "without measure" and makes him "holy" (John 3:34; cf. Isa 11:2; Luke 1:35). Gifts such as wisdom, righteousness, holiness, and faithfulness equip him for his threefold office as the Mediator. While Christ

---

points cohere because only God can save, and he does so through the economy of Christ's flesh.

[44] Johan Heinrich Heidegger, *The Concise Marrow of Christian Theology*, xvii.vii, trans. Casey Carmichael (Grand Rapids: Reformation Heritage Books, 2019), 119.

[45] Aquinas, *STh* III.6.6.*resp.*

has them more eminently compared to his brothers and sisters (Ps 45:7), these are the same gifts the saints have from Christ (Eph 4:7–8).[46] Since grace does not destroy—but rather perfects—nature, then habitual grace perfects the integrity of Christ's humanity. From both communications follow Christ's impeccability, his inability to sin (*non posse peccare*). His divine holiness and his human holiness are distinct, but related. While the nature he assumed would have had the capacity to sin on its own, it is not its own, but *his* own. And since his humanity is united to the divine Son in the grace of union, the Son's own Spirit anoints his human flesh with every habitual grace he needs to destroy the works of the devil (1 John 3:8).[47]

## B. The Communication of Idioms

The communication of idioms consists in the mutual communication of the natures' distinct properties (*idiomata*) to the person in whom they are united.[48] A Christology disciplined by Scripture will discern the communication of idioms from Scripture's own usage. Scripture speaks of God's "own blood" (Acts 20:28), of sinners who "crucified the Lord of glory" (1 Cor 2:8) and "killed the Author of life" (Acts 3:15 ESV). Cyril, observing such paradoxical things we must say about Jesus to say what Scripture says, concludes that they apply to Jesus "in one manner and another manner."[49] The predicates are true of Jesus in different respects, on account of his distinct natures: the eternally begotten (from the Father) is born of a woman in the fullness of time (from Mary); he is worshipped (as God) and he worships (as man); the impassible (God)

---

[46] Further: Michael Allen, *Sanctification*, 246–55; Duby, *Jesus and the God of Classical Theism*, 229–41.

[47] See here Bavinck, *Reformed Dogmatics* 3:313–16.

[48] This category of communications has occasioned the most debate, historically. See Bavinck, *Reformed Dogmatics* 3:308–13; Duby, *Jesus and the God of Classical Theism*, 165–91, for some brief analyses. For an exegetical argument, see Jamieson and Wittman, *Biblical Reasoning*, chap. 7.

[49] Cyril of Alexandria, *Scholia on the Incarnation* 34 (McGuckin, 329ff).

suffers (humanly); the immortal (God) dies (a human death); he raises the dead (with the Father and the Spirit, as God) and he is raised (as a man); and so on. This is not a mere grammatical feature of the texts, but it is predicated upon the ontology of the hypostatic union. What truly belongs to each nature distinctly belongs to Christ indistinctly, because both natures belong to him. Because Christ's person embraces both natures, then whatever belongs to them really belongs to him. Yet, the properties of one nature are not thereby the properties of the other nature, because there is no immediate union between them, and the "distinction between the natures was never abolished by their union but rather the character proper to each of the two natures was preserved."[50] Therefore, "Christ is God not verbally but really; the same is man not verbally but really."[51] And he is really both without confusion or change because the communication is mediated by his hypostasis.

## C. The Communication of Operations

The third and final communication is that whereby Christ accomplishes our redemption by the mutual operation of his two natures: "each form does what is peculiar to it in communion with the other."[52] Jesus accomplishes what only God can do, salvation (Ps 3:8; Isa 43:11; 45:21; Hos 13:4), by his human obedience unto death on a cross (Phil 2:8). He cannot be our mediator without being God and man, and neither can he accomplish our salvation without divine and human actions. What he does involves the activity of both his natures, and activity springs both from the power and will resident in each nature. Hence, the Third Council of Constantinople (681) confesses that in Christ there are "two natural volitions or wills and two natural actions, without division, without change, without separation, without confusion. The two natural wills are not—by

---

[50] *Definitio* of Chalcedon (DH 302).
[51] Amandus Polanus, *Syntagma theologiae Christianae* 6.16 (378c).
[52] Leo of Rome, *Tome to Flavian of Constantinople* 4 (CEECW 4:43).

any means—opposed to each other as the impious heretics assert; but his human will is compliant; it does not resist or oppose but rather submits to his divine and almighty will."[53] The doctrine of the communication of operations (*communicatio operationem*) spells this out.

Here we must once more draw upon our discussions of the Son's eternal generation and the Trinity's inseparable operation of assumption that terminates on the Son alone. Combined, these points entail that the divine Son acts distinctly and properly in our flesh. On the one hand, Jesus enacts his subsistent relation to the Father and Spirit by working *from the Father* and *through the Spirit*, which is to say that he acts in accordance with his filial mode of subsisting in the divine nature. On the other hand, when Jesus performs actions, the human operations are proper to him alone since he alone assumes humanity into his own person. Every incarnate act of the Son proceeds from the indivisible Trinity considered as a primary cause, but only the Son acts as secondary cause.[54] In the hypostatic confluence of these two forms of causality we find something unprecedented and new, grounding the "new song" (Rev 5:9) of the heavenly liturgy: a "new theandric energy."[55]

With the organ of his humanity, the Savior plays the new song of his incarnate economy.[56] Some have worried that the idea of Christ's

---

[53] Heinrich Denzinger, *Compendium of Creeds, Definitions, and Declarations on Matters of Faith and Morals*, 43rd ed., ed. Peter Hünermann (San Francisco: Ignatius), 174.

[54] So too Ian A. McFarland, *The Word Made Flesh: A Theology of the Incarnation* (Louisville, KY: Westminster John Knox Press, 2019), 104n10; cf. Aquinas, *STh* III.19.1.*ad*1.

[55] Pseudo-Dionysius the Areopagite, *Letter* 4. "Theandric" means "divine-human."

[56] Cyril of Alexandria, *Scholia on the Incarnation of the Only Begotten* §25 (McGuckin, 320): "the body was made his very own through a true union and thus served the function of an instrument, in order to fulfil those things which it customarily does, sin alone excepted." Thus, also Damascene, *On the Orthodox Faith* §63 (PPS 62:217). Further, readers should consult J. David Moser, "The Flesh of the Logos, *Instrumentum divinitatis*: Retrieving an Ancient Christological Doctrine," *International Journal of Systematic Theology* 23.3 (2021): 313–32.

humanity as an organ or "instrument" diminishes his human agency, but this worry forgets momentarily the uniqueness of the incarnation. As it is joined to the Word, his human nature is not an ordinary, lifeless instrument—a mere tool. Rather, the Word's humanity is an "animate instrument"—here we feel the analogy's breaking point—because it has its own motion, though one that is moved by the person to whom it belongs.[57] As an animate instrument, Christ's humanity has everything necessary for action issuing from intrinsic powers: it possesses body and soul, as well as power and will. From the *communicatio gratiarum*, this instrument is joined to the Word (*gratia unionis*) and tuned as a fit instrument for the symphony he plays (*gratia habitualis*). His human willing is still *human* and so it wills human things, like the preservation of life, but since it is attuned to the divine will, then it wills things greater still: "Whoever seeks to preserve his life will lose it, but whoever loses his life will keep it" (Luke 17:33 ESV); "not my will, but yours, be done" (Luke 22:42). Henceforth, the song that the Word plays "for us and for our salvation" is therefore played in the communion of both his divine and human operations. As Maximus the Confessor instructs us: "Being God He worked wonders in a human way, for they were accomplished through naturally passible flesh. Being man, He experienced the sufferings of human nature, but in a divine way, for they unfolded at the command of His sovereign will. Or rather, both were done in a theandric way, since He is God and man at the same time."[58]

Christ does divine things humanly and human things divinely. Their communion means that each nature's operation "is contemplated along with the other."[59] We cannot neatly parcel out which of Christ's actions are "divine" and which are "human," precisely because he is neither "mere man" nor "naked God."[60] This does not negate the difference

---

[57] Aquinas, *STh* III.7.1.*ad*3.
[58] Maximus the Confessor, *Ambiguum* 5.26 ed. and trans. Nicholas Constas (Cambridge, MA: Harvard University Press, 2014), 1:57.
[59] Damascene, *On the Orthodox Faith* §63 (PPS 62:217).
[60] Damascene, *On the Orthodox Faith* §63 (PPS 62:216).

between the natures: the operations of the human nature are finite, as is the human nature; the divine operations are likewise infinite. It is therefore true that, consequent upon the hypostatic union, "there is no human *activity* of Jesus that is not also divine."[61] Typical examples include Christ's healing by means of human touch or walking upon water with a human body. However, it remains the case that Christ's divine operations transcend his human operations.[62] Everything that the Word does involves both his natures, but the involvement is asymmetrical. For example, the only contribution his human nature makes to his sustaining the universe by his power (Heb 1:3)—clearly an act of infinite, divine power—is his human will's agreement: "your will be done on earth as it is in heaven" (Matt 6:10). And from this radical harmony of his human and divine wills, what he humanly wills is effected divinely in a way infinitely transcending the capacities of his human nature in itself.[63] This point registers the fact that Christ's person exercises a hegemonic control over his humanity; he is the one who acts (*principium quod*) and his humanity is that by which and as which he acts (*principium quo*), but the one who acts is irreducibly "our great God and Savior" (Titus 2:13).

The communication of operations is important not only for what it affirms about Christ's full human integrity and agency, but also for

---

[61] McFarland, *The Word Made Flesh*, 90.

[62] Cf. Maximus the Confessor, *Ambiguum* 5.15 (Constas, 47).

[63] Thus, *pace* McFarland, *The Word Made Flesh*, 90–91n48, the doctrine of Christ's "new theandric energy" is compatible with the traditional affirmation of the so-called *extra Calvinisticum* (which McFarland mostly affirms, 87–88). In the way suggested here, one should say with Maximus that "neither of the natural energies was displaced in the union, neither functioned independently after the union, and neither was divided from that to which it had been conjoined and with which it coexisted" (*Ambiguum* 5.25 [Constas, 57]). Jesus's sustaining the universe by his divine power, for instance, does not work "independently" of his human assent to do what he can only do as God since Jesus is the person who wills and acts: *actiones et passiones sunt suppositorum* ("actions and passions belong to supposits," of which persons are an instance).

the way in which it exhibits the saving efficacy of Christ's work. Every work of the Mediator is "theandric" or divine-human, proceeding from his human nature and his divine person. This point must be maintained as Christology proceeds to discuss Christ's two states and his three offices. At every point, the theologian must resist the temptation to assign certain actions of Christ purely to his divine nature and others purely to his human nature. The communion of both natures in Christ's person means that even those acts most characteristically human, such as obedience and suffering death by crucifixion, are radically characterized by the Son's divine mode of subsistence and therefore by his divine nature.[64] Just so, all Christ's acts are therefore suffused with infinite worth. Christ's active and passive obedience are sufficient for all because they are infinitely meritorious; they are infinitely meritorious because they are theandric. In this way, dogmatic Christology grounds what we confess about Christ's saving work in the mysterious ontology of the hypostatic union and its effects. Dogmatics thus supports the church's conviction that "we preach Christ crucified" (1 Cor 1:23) and seek to "listen to him" (Matt 17:5) in the testimony of the prophets and apostles. The theandric mystery of Christ is inexhaustibly rich and "great indeed" (1 Tim 3:16).

The foregoing sketch emphasizes Christ's pronobeity and irreplaceability on account of his infinite perfection, fully united to our humanity in his person. His theandric mediation is so plentitudinous that we must confess just as "there is one God," so "there is one mediator between God and men, the man Christ Jesus" (1 Tim 2:5 ESV). Here below, this one mediator gifts offices to his church "for building up the body of Christ" (Eph 4:12 ESV) without abdicating his royal presence or mediatorship. In this way, Baptists stammer to confess with Mary God's sovereign mercy.

---

[64] None of this prevents "partitive exegesis" (cf. Jamieson and Wittman, *Biblical Reasoning*, chap. 8), but it reminds us of what we are *not* doing under that banner: parceling out actions belonging exclusively to one nature.

# The Dogmatic Significance of the Virgin Birth within Christology

Having considered the main contours of the doctrine of the incarnation, we now turn our attention to the significance of the virgin birth. The hypostatic union commences in what is at once a most unlikely place (for God) and the most likely of places (for man): the womb. And herein lies the depths of divine humility expressed and embodied in the incarnation. As the ancient hymn *Te Deum* renders it, "When thou tookest upon thee to deliver man, thou didst not abhor the Virgin's womb." Or, as Joseph Ratzinger would remind us, "God is so great that he can become small."[65] As with all the mysteries of the gospel, we acknowledge that we are treading on holy ground when considering the virgin birth.[66] It is an event that takes place within our history but whose origin and cause lies beyond

---

[65] Joseph Ratzinger, *God and the World: A Conversation with Peter Seewald* (San Francisco: Ignatius, 2000), 31.

[66] The phrase "virgin birth" can admit of some nuanced differences. Presumably Christ's *birth* took place like any other human birth. So Turretin: "This parturition [giving birth] although it was miraculous because of a virgin, still may be called natural because she labored in a manner usual with mothers." Turretin, *Institutes of Elenctic Theology*, 2:343–44. But not all have agreed. The Orthodox and Roman Catholic traditions insist that Mary's "perpetual virginity" remained intact not only *after* the birth of Jesus but also *in* the birth of Jesus. In the premodern mind, the opening of the womb would violate a woman's virginity (marked by the penetration of the hymen). So, in this view, the birth of Christ was attended by the miracle of his (somehow) passing through a closed womb. Some have even speculated that Christ was delivered by a kind of miraculous and bloodless C-section. In any event, the birth of Jesus, on this view, left the virginity of Mary's womb intact—like passing "through the gate without breaking its seals," as John of Damascus put it. John of Damascus, *On the Orthodox Faith*, 4.14. On a related front, some expressions of popular piety seem to present the nativity of Jesus as somehow immune from the ordinary trauma of human birth: "the little Lord Jesus, no crying he makes," as one Christmas carol puts it. In our judgment, this premodern view of Mary's virginity *in* the birth of Jesus is warranted neither from Scripture nor from a proper understanding of female anatomy (the absence of the hymen does not negate virginity). Nor is this latter, quasi-docetic understanding of the birth as entirely tranquil. We leave open the

historical investigation. Far less is it open to our scientific observation and analysis. Francis Turretin speaks of this divine mystery as "secret and incomprehensible, which can neither be tracked by reason, nor expressed in words."[67] And yet "we cannot but speak the things which we have seen and heard" (Acts 4:20 KJV). Faith compels us to speak of this mystery, but only in the mode of reverent confession. The virgin birth is an article of faith, so central to the Christian religion that it finds expression in the ancient creeds of the church: "conceived by the Holy Spirit, born of the Virgin Mary." It is a most fitting opening scene to the dramatic revelation of divine condescension we encounter in the incarnation of God. In this section, we will survey the biblical material on the virgin birth, explore its theological significance, drawing on some Baptist sources along the way.

## *The Biblical Accounts of the Virgin Birth*

Only two of the Gospel accounts, Matthew and Luke, record a narrative of the virgin birth. But if we take a more panoramic view of the biblical story, references to Christ's assumption of humanity in Mary's womb are more frequent. Figural readings of certain Old Testament texts insinuate aspects of the virgin birth. Consider, for example, the promised "seed" of the woman (Gen 3:15 KJV) or the great Passion Psalm, which speaks of the Messiah taken from "the womb" and made to trust at his "mother's breasts" (Ps 22:9–10). And, of course, Matthew's virgin birth narrative positions itself explicitly as a fulfillment of Isaiah's prophecy that a "virgin shall conceive and bear a son" (Isa 7:14 ESV). Even outside the infancy narratives of Matthew and Luke, the virgin birth is sometimes alluded to in the New Testament. Luke speaks of Jesus as "the son (as was supposed) of Joseph" (Luke 3:23 ESV). Paul writes of Christ as one "born of a woman, born under the law" (Gal 4:4). John's Gospel may even hint at the

---

question of the virginity of Mary *after* the birth of Christ, which even some of the Reformers and their heirs held as true or at least probable.

[67] Turretin, *Institutes of Elenctic Theology*, 2:342.

virgin birth in the accusation of the Jewish religious leaders against Jesus: "We were not born of sexual immorality" (John 8:41 ESV), which would have been the understandable, alternative explanation for the seemingly illegitimate circumstances of Jesus' conception (which was before Mary and Joseph "came together," Matt 1:18).

Still, the most extensive biblical teaching on the virgin birth comes in the two infancy narratives of the first and third Gospels. Matthew's version tells the story from Joseph's perspective, to whom the angel appeared after Mary "was found to be with child from the Holy Spirit" (Matt 1:18 ESV). Naturally, Joseph's first thought was to end the betrothal, thinking that Mary had been unfaithful (though, "being a just man," he determined to do so "quietly," Matt 1:19 ESV). The angel forestalls Joseph's plan by revealing the remarkable event that has taken place. In Luke's account, the angel Gabriel appears to Mary herself and explains the stunning miracle that will take place in her: "The Holy Spirit will come upon you, and the power of the Most High will overshadow you; therefore the child to be born will be called holy—the Son of God" (Luke 1:35 ESV). The same creative power that hovered over the face of the primordial deep (Gen 1:2), the same protective presence that fluttered over Israel like a mother eagle (Deut 32:11), will come over Mary and produce a child in her womb.[68] Matthew interprets this unprecedented event as a fulfillment of Isaiah's prophecy. Much has been written about the context of the virgin birth prophecy and Matthew's use of it, but those details need not detain us. Whether one takes Isaiah's text as a straightforward prediction of the virgin birth or in a more figural or typological manner, its inclusion in the Gospel narrative indicates that the birth of Jesus is the fulfillment of God's promises made long ago. In Jesus' miraculous birth, the prophecies of old are being fulfilled.

There are several *dramatis personae* in this climactic biblical scene. The creed highlights two in particular: the Holy Spirit and the Virgin

---

[68] Sinclair B. Ferguson, *The Holy Spirit*, Counters of Christian Theology (Downers Grove, IL: InterVarsity, 1996), 19–20, 33.

Mary. But the angel and Joseph also play supporting roles, the one in Annunciation, the other in absence (as regards his biological contribution, not as regards his fatherly love as the Lord's caretaker). Then, of course, there is the Son of God himself, who assumes humanity, in its earliest and most vulnerable state, into personal union with himself.[69] But it is the Spirit and the virgin who take center stage and stand on opposite sides of this divine condescension. Respectively, the two serve as the active and passive principles of the virginal conception.

As the active principle, the Holy Spirit is the divine person to whom the miracle is appropriated, highlighting his unique personhood as the perfecting terminus of the Holy Trinity's external works. But given the doctrine of inseparable operations, the Father and Son also concur in this work. It is the Father who has "prepared" a body for the Messiah, through which he will render voluntary and vicarious obedience (Heb 10:5; cf. Ps 40:6–8). And the Son himself willingly "partook" of flesh and blood to accomplish his death-destroying work (Heb 2:14 ESV).[70] But it is especially appropriate to highlight the Holy Spirit's agency in the virginal conception inasmuch as it draws attention to the "consummation" and "fecundation" (fruitfulness) that is proper to the Spirit within the Trinity's indivisible work.[71] Appropriating the virgin conception to the Holy Spirit reiterates the Spirit's work of creation, as the one hovering over the waters, and anticipates the Spirit's work of regeneration, as the one who brings about the new birth in God's people (John 3:5–8; cf. John 1:12–13, which speaks of God's adopted sons too as those born not "of the will of man"). In this work, the Spirit is the efficient, not the material, cause of the Son's miraculous conception. The Son is taken from the substance of Mary, but not from the

---

[69] For a treatment of Christ's assumption in utero and its implications for the treatment of human embryos, see Oliver D. Crisp, *God Incarnate: Explorations in Christology* (London: T&T Clark, 2009), 103–21.

[70] For a treatment of the roles of the Son and Spirit in the Son's incarnate life, see Duby, *Jesus and the God of Classical Theism*, chap. 5.

[71] Turretin, *Institutes of Elenctic Theology*, 2:340.

substance of the Spirit. In other words, the Holy Spirit is not another father to the Son; he is the not the "origin of substance but . . . the original cause of this conception."[72]

As the passive principle of the virgin conception, we may consider Mary's indispensable role in two respects: her willing consent and serving as the "material cause" of the incarnation. As for the first, Mary's faithful response to the annunciation is an exemplar of faith without sight. After querying the angel about how she, a virgin, could conceive and hearing his unprecedented reply, she simply responds, "Behold the handmaid of the Lord; be it unto me according to thy word." As such, Mary is presented in Luke's Gospel as the first and paradigmatic believer. Her "yes" becomes the occasion by which God saves the world. Martin Luther follows Bernard of Clairvaux in enumerating three miracles in this story: (1) "that God and man should be joined in this child," (2) "that a mother should remain a virgin," and (3) "that Mary should have such faith as to believe that this mystery would be accomplished in her." The last, Luther adds, is "not the least of the three."[73] Protestants rightly object to the Roman Catholic doctrines of Mary's immaculate conception and sinlessness, but they need not swing the pendulum in the other direction by downplaying or even denigrating Mary's role in this dramatic scene. Unlike Zechariah earlier in Luke's narrative (1:19–20), Mary is not chastised for her question to the angel. Elizabeth's words at the visitation, in Luke 1:42-45 (ESV), clearly express the perspective of the evangelist as well: "Blessed are you among women, and blessed is the fruit of your womb! And why is this granted to me that the mother of my Lord should come to me? For behold, when the sound of your greeting came to my ears, the baby in my womb leaped for joy. And blessed is she who believed that there would be a fulfillment of what was spoken to her from the Lord."

---

[72] Wilhelmus à Brakel, *The Christian's Reasonable Service* (n.p.: Reformation Heritage, 2012), 1:501.

[73] Martin Luther, *Martin Luther's Christmas Book*, ed. Roland Bainton (Minneapolis: Augsburg, 1948), 15.

Protestants should feel no compunction about honoring Mary as uniquely sanctified for this blessed role. They should confess (and must not deny) that she is the *theotokos*, the bearer of God. This title is primarily a confession of the unity of Christ's personhood: the person of the divine Son, the second person of the Trinity, is the only person in Mary's womb.[74] But it is also, secondarily, an acknowledgement of Mary's uniqueness. The twentieth-century Southern Baptist theologian, A. T. Robertson, objected to the Catholic Marian dogmas, but he also lamented that Mary suffers such "cold neglect" from Protestants. Robertson suggests that Protestants need to recover Mary's "glory," as the mother of the Lord (he explicitly affirms the *theotokos*), the "chief mother of the race."[75]

Mary's second indispensable role in this miracle concerns the humanity that she shares with her Son. Historically, certain heretical and heterodox groups denied that the Son partook of Mary's humanity. Various gnostic groups (such as the Manichaeans and Marcionites) made this mistake as did certain Anabaptist theologians such as Menno Simons.[76] Maintaining that the Son brings his humanity with him from heaven (his so-called "celestial flesh"), such views suggest that Mary serves only as a conduit or channel through which Christ passed rather than his biological and genetic mother. The church has always rightly recognized this position as a fatal error. If Christ did not partake of Mary's humanity— our common humanity in Adam—then he cannot serve an adequate

---

[74] See Cyril, *On the Unity of Christ*, trans. John Anthony McGuckin, Popular Patristics Series (Crestwood, NY: St. Vladimir's Seminary Press, 1995). The *theotokos* doctrine was affirmed at the Council of Ephesus and the Council of Chalcedon. Later, when the remaining Nestorian texts were condemned at the Second Council of Constantinople, the church affirmed that "one of the Trinity" was incarnate and died.

[75] A. T. Robertson, *The Mother of Jesus: Her Problems and Her Glory* (Grand Rapids: Baker, 1963). Robertson's work seems unique among Baptists: a positive and constructive treatment of Mary and her place in the biblical story.

[76] For a discussion and evaluation of Anabaptist Christology, see Stephen R. Holmes, "Evaluating a Neglected Tradition of (Ana)Baptist Christology," *Scottish Journal of Theology* (2023): 1–18.

representative and substitute for fallen humanity.[77] His miraculous conception apart from a human father marks a break with the sinful line of Adam, but his consecrated humanity taken from Mary ensures that his work is truly vicarious for Adam's posterity. Even without a human father, Mary suffices as the material cause of his humanity, ensuring that he is the seed of the woman (Gen 3:15), the seed of Abraham (Gen 12:3; Gal 3:16), and the seed and son of David (2 Sam 7:12; Rom 1:3). The General Baptists of the seventeenth century faced a revival of the "celestial flesh" view in their own ranks. The Baptist divine, Thomas Monck, forcefully rejected this view as a "new Eutychianism," which threatened to swallow up the true humanity of the Mediator. "Even so it is written, Christ was made of a Woman, Gal. 4:4., for he did not pass through her as Water through a Pipe, but took part of her substance."[78] Christ is "took the flesh of the Virgin Mary" and is thus "flesh of our flesh."[79]

## The Fittingness of the Virgin Birth

The theological significance of the virgin birth further resides in its fittingness: this mode of conception and birth fits with the nature of the God who here acts, the needs which his acts redress, and the economy of salvation he procures, and so much more. One might consider hypothetical questions about whether the virgin birth was the only way the incarnation could have happened, but reflecting on its fittingness is a more modest consideration of how this miracle branches out and connects to

---

[77] Several modern theologians (including Edward Irving, Karl Barth, and Thomas F. Torrance) have defended the thesis that Christ not only assumed a *full* human nature (body and soul) but also a *fallen* human nature and yet remained without sin. See above, n. 42.

[78] Thomas Monck, *A Cure for the Cankering Error of the New Eutychians* (1673). Monck's work is an excellent example of Baptist catholicity; in addition to copious biblical citaitons, he quotes liberally from the church fathers, the ancient creeds, the medieval scholastics, and the Reformers.

[79] Monck, *Cure*, 51.

various other elements of the Christian confession. For our purposes, we consider eight such connections.

First, the virgin birth was a fitting fulfillment of prophecy. This reason is, of course, a function of God's having given such prophecies as would require the virgin birth to fulfill them. Again, perhaps the virgin birth was not strictly necessary. Perhaps it was within God's power absolutely considered (*potentia absoluta*) to bring about the incarnation some other way. But having ordained the virgin birth and promised it through his prophet, it became necessary for God to bring it about in just this way (*potentia ordinata*). As the fulfillment of Isaiah's prophecy, the virgin birth marks out the miraculous and special purpose of Jesus' birth as the culmination of God's redemptive plan.

Second and related, the virgin birth was fitting as a miraculous sign that accompanied the beginning of the Incarnation. Isaiah's virgin birth prophecy is explicitly referred to as a "sign" (Isa 7:11). It was a miracle intended to direct particular attention to the astonishing reality that was taking place. The sign was initially privatized—one of the remarkable events Mary kept and pondered in her heart along with her closest kin. But now it is taken up into the inspired Gospel accounts and given expression in the symbols of Christian tradition. If the infinite, eternal God were to take on frail human flesh, one might expect a concomitantly miraculous conception of his human nature. As Turretin puts it, "An extraordinary person demanded an extraordinary birth."[80]

Third, the virgin birth fittingly preserves the uniqueness of the Son's relation to his eternal Father. As Thomas Aquinas put it, the Son's virginal conception maintains "the dignity of the Father who sent him."[81] The Son has but one Father, from whom he is eternally begotten. A natural human father would introduce confusion to this filial identity and transfer the dignity of fatherhood to someone other than the divine Father. As the Son is eternally begotten from the Father "virginally"

---

[80] Turretin, *Institutes of Elenctic Theology*, 2:344.
[81] Aquinas, *STh* 3.28.1.

(there is no theogony or sexual principle in eternal generation), so the Son is temporally begotten from Mary virginally.

Fourth, the virgin birth was the fitting means by which Christ's human nature was sanctified and preserved from original sin. Some have mistakenly argued that original sin is transmitted only through the father, such that the absence of a father alone explains Christ's sinless conception. But Mary was as capable of passing on corruption as Joseph. The Roman Catholic doctrine of Mary's own immaculate conception in the womb of her mother, Anna, is nowhere taught in Scripture. Nor is it a particularly useful dogmatically. It simply pushes the problem back a step. If God was capable of preserving Mary from the corruption of her parents, then surely God can do the same for the human nature he uniquely creates from Mary's womb. Christ's *body* is specially formed in such a way that he is taken from Adam's stock but not Adam's natural posterity. Thus, on either view of the transmission of the human *soul*— traducianism and creationism—the soul of Christ would not be liable to original guilt. According to traducianism, the soul he receives from Mary in conjunction with his body would be inviolate along with that sanctified body. And according to creationism, not being the natural posterity of Adam, Adam's sin would not be imputed to him.

Fifth, the virgin birth was befitting to the legal requirements of Christ's vicarious obedience. In Jesus, there is both continuity and discontinuity with the humanity that stood in need of redemption. Insofar as he partook of Mary's humanity, he was the seed of the woman, the seed of Abraham, and the seed of David. But insofar as he did not have a human father, he could mark a genuine break and a new beginning, serving not just as the offspring of Adam but as a new, Last Adam. As the priests of old were to be chosen from among the Israelites, so also the Savior must be truly identified with his people. "Since therefore the children share in flesh and blood, he himself likewise partook of the same things . . . Therefore, he had to be made like his brothers in every respect, so that he can become a merciful and faithful high priest in the service of God, to make propitiation for the sins of the people" (Heb 2:14, 17 ESV).

Sixth, the virgin birth was fitting as the fulfillment and completion of previous patterns of divine activity. The virgin birth is the culmination of a long line of miraculous births recorded in Scripture. Think of Sarah, Hannah, and Elizabeth, especially. But the virgin birth narrative also takes us back to the very beginning. As early as Irenaeus in the second century, Christian interpreters have seen Edenic overtones in the narrative of the virgin birth. Irenaeus writes:

> And just as through a disobedient virgin man was stricken down and fell into death, so through the Virgin who was obedient to the Word of God man was reanimated and received life. For the Lord came to seek again the sheep that was lost; and man it was that was lost: and for this cause there was not made some other formation, but in that same which had its descent from Adam He preserved the likeness of the (first) formation. For it was necessary that Adam should be summed up in Christ, that mortality might be swallowed up and overwhelmed by immortality; and Eve summed up in Mary, that a virgin should be a virgin's intercessor, and by a virgin's obedience undo and put away the disobedience of a virgin.[82]

There are a few different typologies at work here. Christ descends from Adam and so rightly recapitulates and represents Adam's race. But since he is conceived of a virgin, he can serve as another Adam, the head of a new race. Elsewhere, Irenaeus draws the Adam-Christ parallel even tighter, suggesting that as Adam was taken from "virgin soil" so also the Last Adam was taken from a virgin womb.[83] But Irenaeus is also interested in an evocative Eve-Mary typology as well. A certain tradition of interpretation maintains that Eve was still a virgin at the time of the fall, only consummating her marriage to Adam afterwards. Thus, just

---

[82] Irenaeus of Lyons, *On the Apostolic Preaching*, trans. John Behr, PPS (Crestwood, NY: St. Vladimir's Seminary Press, 1997), 33.

[83] Irenaeus, *On the Apostolic Preaching*, 32 (p. 61).

as death entered the world through a virgin's disobedience, so also life and immortality are brought about through a virgin's obedience. Irenaeus even highlights Mary's role as Eve's intercessor. It would be anachronistic to read a later, more developed Mariology back into this second-century text. Still, it represents an early expression of the unique role Mary's obedience plays in salvation history.

Seventh, the virgin birth was a fitting display of God's power and wisdom to create humanity in a fourth and final way. Bonaventure and others make this case.[84] Heretofore, God had created in three distinct ways; from neither man nor woman (Adam), from a man without a woman (Eve, taken from Adam's side), and from both man and woman (all ordinary human births). The fourth and final means of human creation is from a woman without a man. The virgin birth completes the cycle, so to speak. Some have even read Jer 31:22 in this way: "For the LORD has created a new thing on the earth: a woman encircles a man."

Eighth, the virgin birth was a fitting picture of certain aspects of salvation. Christ's miraculous conception by the Holy Spirit serves as the pattern for the believer's own regeneration by the Spirit. The *gratia habitualis* bestowed upon Christ in the virgin's womb serves as a pattern for the graces that adorn all those united to Christ. The Son's twofold nativity—his generation from the Father in eternity and his birth from Mary in time—are antecedent to the believer's new birth. What Christ is by nature (the only Son from the Father), we become by grace and adoption. But equally true: what Christ is by grace intrinsically (the bearer of the Holy Spirit), we become by grace derivatively. In its active principle (the Holy Spirit), the virgin birth is, therefore, fitted to our regeneration: like Jesus, we are born not "by the will of man." Additionally, in its passive principle (the blessed virgin Mary), it corresponds to our conversion. Like

---

[84] Bonaventure, *Breviloquium*, trans. Dominic Monti, O.F.M., Works of St. Bonaventure, vol. 9 (St. Bonaventure, NY: Franciscan Insitute, 2005), 4.3.5.

Mary, we too are called to give our consent—our own "be it unto me"—
to the offer of divine grace. Certain strands of Christian spirituality have
drawn attention to the ethical application of this doctrine: in a sense,
we too become a *theotokos*—a God-bearer—when Christ dwells in our
hearts by faith (Eph 3:17).[85]

## Conclusion: Jesus Christ, the Mediator of the New and Everlasting Covenant

The doctrine of Christ is not a Baptist distinctive. Far from it! A careful examination of the seminal Baptist confessions of faith and other
works of the seventeenth century indicates that the earliest Baptists
were eager to demonstrate their allegiance to catholic Christianity on
this central dogma. Monck's *Cure* stands out as an exemplar of this tendency. The Orthodox Creed and the two great London confessions of
the Particular Baptists also hew closely to the conciliar and consensus
doctrine. The doctrine of Christ in the Baptist confessional tradition
is noticeably orthodox. The Second London Confession, for example,
affirms that "two whole, perfect, and distinct natures were inseparably
joined together in one person, without conversion, composition, or confusion; which person is very God and very man, yet one Christ, the only
mediator between God and man." The First London Confession had
already spoken of the communication of gifts given to Christ in his
humanity: "anointed most fully and abundantly with all gifts necessary,
God having without measure poured out His Spirit upon Him." Where
the Mennonites and even some in their own ranks had parted ways with
the tradition and reverted to the older docetic view of Christ's relation to
Mary, the vast majority of Baptists insisted that Christ partook of Mary's
humanity as the seed of the woman and the Son of David. So, the story

---

[85] Isaac of Nineveh, *On Ascetical Life*, trans. Mary Hansbury, PPS (Crestwood,
NY: St. Vladimir's Seminary Press, 1989), n.p.

of the Baptist doctrine of Christ is a story of *historic*, even creedal, orthodoxy (the *historical* signpost).

But Baptists have refracted this classical view of Christ in some
unique ways. Stephen Holmes has suggested that while Baptists are only
distinctive in our ecclesiology, nonetheless "our different ecclesiology is
surprisingly generative of radical positions."[86] This observation holds true
in Christology, as much as anywhere. For Baptists, the doctrine of Christ
has telling *ecclesial* implications (the *ecclesial* signpost). Christ alone is
Lord of the conscience and Christ alone is the prophet, priest, and king
of the new covenant church. No civil authority can compel, much less
coerce, true saving faith. One implication is that the civil magistrate has
no authority to overstep his bounds by inserting himself into religious
matters. The First London Confession asserts that the office of mediator
and the *munus triplex* (threefold office) it entails "is so proper to Christ,
that neither in whole, or any part thereof, . . . [can it be] transferred
from Him to any other" (Article XIII).[87] Later, in rejecting the government's right to regulate worship, the confession adds, "And concerning
the worship of God; there is but one lawgiver, which is able to save and
destroy, James 4:12; which is Jesus Christ, who hath given laws and rules
sufficient in His word for His worship" (see note on Article XLVIII).
Christology is upstream from all of the Baptist distinctives.

Christ calls individuals to a personal relationship with him, irrespec-
tive of their parents' faith. Christ enjoins only those who believe to pledge
allegiance to him in Christian baptism and so to be joined to local assemblies of visible saints. Since Christ alone is Lord of the conscience, no

---

[86] Stephen R. Holmes, "Toward a Typology of Baptist Theology," *Pacific
Journal of Theological Research* 14, no. 2 (November 2019): 8.

[87] Note well: Baptists do not maintain any sort of metaphysical necessity at
play here, as if there were a *de iure* competition between divine and human mediation. Instead, Baptists maintain that Christ has in fact and fittingly reserved
this office to himself alone. The question is not whether God *could* employ the
mediation of merely human priests (and saints) within his new covenant community, but whether God *in fact* does.

human government can compel faith; religious liberty is thus grounded not only in the freedom and dignity of the individual but also in a particular understanding of Christ's sole mediatorship of the new covenant—a covenant not governed by external laws and human kings, entered into by birth, but a covenant governed by Christ alone and his gospel, entered into by the new birth and by the grace of conversion (the covenantal signpost).

To return to our introductory remarks, Christology is the church's faithful response to the revelation that Mary's Son is none other than the eternal Son of the Father. Nations and kings must finally bow to his supreme regal lordship. Christology is the church's discourse about its Lord in worship and witness. Historically, Baptists have been marked by an insistence upon an "experimental" faith, that is, a faith lived out in personal and congregational *experience*, in obedience, holiness, and worship. This response to the revelation of Christ recognizes that the Risen Lord Jesus remains the sole king of his church. By virtue of his continuing royal presence within his church, the Lord Jesus Christ remains our contemporary. We continue to hear his voice in his Word as we read and hear it together in the body of Christ, the borders of which expand as the church obediently heeds the Lord's command to make his glories known among the nations (the *confessional* signpost).

Once again, all these Baptist distinctives—personal conversion, a believers' church, believers' baptism, religious liberty—are downstream from our doctrine of Christ. Christ, the king of the church, is "the Son of God, the brightness of His glory." In its own distinctive way, the Baptist vision focuses singular attention on this Royal Christ, who "was made the mediator of a new and everlasting covenant of grace between God and man, ever to be perfectly and fully the prophet, priest, and king of the Church of God for evermore" (First London Confession, Articles IX and X).

CHAPTER 5

# SOTERIOLOGY

## John D. Laing and Stefana Dan Laing

## Introduction

While it is true that all doctrines are interconnected, at least in a consistent biblical theology, it is no overstatement to claim that the doctrine of salvation sits at the heart of Christianity. In at least one sense, salvation is the primary focus of the Scriptures, and it also serves as the central focus of the Christian's experience of God. Soteriology reveals the nature, character and being of God, from his holiness to his love, from his wrath to his mercy, from his forgiveness to his justice, from his power to his knowledge, to his triune nature. It speaks to the plan of God in creating and to his purpose in redemption. Similarly, it points to the unique status of humanity as made in the image of God, of our propensity for sin, and of our ability to be faithful. It serves as the foundation for the establishment of the church as the people of God, and to God's purpose to bring all things to their rightful end.

Although the doctrine of salvation is central to the biblical story, the Bible does not present a sustained, systematic soteriology. Rather, it offers praxis for worship that highlights various aspects of salvation and presents images that depict some of what takes place in God's saving work. Of course, no image can fully encapsulate the work of God, and there is always a measure of tentativeness in the use of analogy and imagery. Still, taken together, they form a picture of God's work that is revelatory and requires a proper response of worship and awe.

Early on, the church recognized these facts, and as it sought to present a more formalized explication of the gospel, various explanations or theories of atonement emerged. The theories were often developed in conversation and/or opposition to one another, but they are probably best understood as highlighting various facets of salvation, and therefore complementary rather than conflicting ideas. As E. Y. Mullins correctly notes, the various historical theories of atonement point to the multifaceted truth of how Christ's death secures salvation for humanity, with the biblical view containing "the true elements in all theories."[1]

Throughout this chapter, we will lay out the doctrine of salvation, drawing upon Scripture and Christian theological tradition, including both the great tradition and historic Baptist thought. While much contained here will be familiar, we will emphasize three particular points that can strengthen Baptist soteriology and aid the church in its work. *First*, both Scripture and tradition emphasize that salvation is a thoroughly trinitarian work, although Baptists tend to speak of it as the work of Christ, or as a transaction between the Father and the Son; as a result, the Holy Spirit's role in salvation has often been overlooked or relegated merely to sanctification. Baptists ought to view salvation as the fully gracious work of all divine persons of the triune God. *Second*, and relatedly, Baptists should resist the tendency to partition too rigidly the various images and aspects of salvation. When they are too sharply separated, some of the richness of God's saving work is missed, specifically in our understanding of the Holy Spirit's work, and the

---

[1] E. Y. Mullins, *The Christian Religion in its Doctrinal Expression* (Nashville: Baptist Sunday School Board, 1928), 305.

inextricable link between justification and sanctification. Losing sight of this link is detrimental to Christian spiritual practices of addressing God in prayer and worship, preaching the gospel of redemption, and engaging in ongoing discipleship. *Third*, we want to affirm historic Baptist contributions to religious liberty and encourage continued involvement in supporting disestablishment. Baptist activism in promoting religious liberty for all has had a massive impact in America, and its effects are enshrined in the United States Constitution's First Amendment. Activism on this issue did not originate in political ideologies, but rather directly flowed out of a Baptist understanding of personal conversion, which affirms a free faith response, and freedom of worship for all people, uncoerced by the state.

## Biblical/Theological Exposition of Soteriology, Focused through John 3:16

Salvation serves as the foundation for who we are as Christians and, therefore, also as Baptists. Somewhat ironically, then, it is arguably the doctrine with the greatest variance of understanding among Baptists. Despite these differences, Torbet rightly observes that Baptists fall squarely within the Reformed Protestant tradition.[2] There is thus no distinctively *Baptist soteriology*, but it is fair to say that Baptists emphasize certain aspects of salvation more than others. These include the love of God, the giving of the Son, the requirement of a personal faith response, and the universal availability of rescue from death unto eternal life. Each of these aspects of salvation is clearly seen in the passage most closely associated with Baptist proclamation of the gospel, John 3:16. In laying out the doctrine of salvation, the text of John 3:16 may function as a lens or paradigm through which to focus our understanding, and we will consider this text in four phrases.

---

[2] Robert G. Torbet, *A History of the Baptists* (Valley Forge: Judson Press, 1963), 22.

## *"For God so loved the world"*

The first phrase, "For God so loved the world," asserts that salvation begins with the infinite, holy, gracious love of God, most clearly revealed in Christ, a love which serves as the basis of God's creative and intercessory work. From this assertion, three truths follow. First, salvific love stands as the basis of creation; second, the salvation of humanity is an ideal expression of sovereign love; and third, God takes the initiative in salvation.

### 1. Salvific Love Stands as the Basis of Creation

Jesus' wording in this first phrase of John 3:16 is intentional, as he states that God's love for the world drives His saving work. In the Greek text, the verbal form of "love" is placed at the front of the clause—"for thus *loved* God the world"—and God's love is thereby emphasized as the primary driver of divine action. To be sure, there is a valid debate over the referent of "the world," and all agree that it primarily refers to persons (either all humanity or the elect), but Jesus' use of "world" (Gk. *kosmos*) here, rather than (for instance) "humanity" (Gk. *anthropos*), may have been intended to suggest divine love as the basis for creating, with the salvation of human beings as the crowning revelation. As Paul makes clear in Rom 8:19–22, the redemption of the created order is intimately tied to the redemption of humanity. Most importantly, God provides salvation because he *loves* humanity, because he views humanity (and the whole created order) as valuable (1 John 3:1, 16).

A number of scholars have explored the implications of trinitarian theology for a doctrine of creation and have argued that a specific Christian theology is needed to make sense of creation *ex nihilo*. First, the Bible declares that the being of God *is* love (1 John 4:17), yet such an understanding makes no sense in a purely monolithic understanding of divine personhood. Since God is self-sufficient (doctrine of aseity), he has no need of anything else, but apart from a triune understanding

of God, there is no object for his love. That is, a God who is not triune will have no expression of love apart from creating, and therefore
would *need* to create to have an object of his love. He would therefore
be dependent upon the creation to realize his potential. By contrast,
the Christian doctrine of God allows the claim that he is essentially
love because that love is realized in the interrelatedness of Father,
Son, and Holy Spirit. Drawing upon the work of the fourth century,
Cappadocian fathers (Gregory of Nazianzus, Basil of Caesarea, and
Gregory of Nyssa), theologian Colin Gunton writes, "Overall, the relations of the three are summarized in the concept of love, which involves
a dynamic of both giving and receiving. The persons are what they are
by virtue of what they give to and receive from each other. As such, they
constitute the being of God . . . God's being is a being in relation."[3]
So, the Son's begetting and the Spirit's procession are ways of speaking
about the love of God within Godself. The Father loves the Son, the
Son loves the Father, the Spirit is the Spirit of love (or in Augustinian
thought the bond of love between the Father and Son),[4] and these relations of love persist in the one triune God, whether he creates or not.
The triune God does not need an object (outside himself) to love for
him to express himself as love, precisely because he exists as Father,
Son, and Holy Spirit. Again, Gunton explains, "Because God is, 'before'
creation took place, already a being-in-relation, there is no need for him
to create what is other than himself. He does not need to create, because
he is already a *taxis*, an order of loving relations . . . Yet it does not follow that for God to enter into relation with the world he must need it
in some way."[5]

Yet God's creative work is an expression of his being: it is an expression of his aesthetic, artistic nature in its beauty, and an expression of his

---

[3] Colin E. Gunton, *The Promise of Trinitarian Theology* (Edinburgh: T&T
Clark, 1991), 148.

[4] Paraphrased from Augustine, *De Trinitate* [*On the Trinity*] XV.17.31.

[5] Gunton, *The Promise of Trinitarian Theology*, 147.

rationality in its orderliness; but it is primarily an expression of his love and relationality, and this is evident beginning with the creation narrative. As the story of creation proceeds, the text calls God's work "good" (Gen 1:4, 10, 12, 18, 21, 25); but once he created human beings—male and female—in his image, with a capacity and a need for relationship, the text calls the creation "very good" (Gen 1:31). Humans were created for relationship with God and with one another, and through their relationships they glorify God. So, while it is sometimes popular to say that God created to glorify himself, the basis and purpose of creation is to express divine love—that unconditional and infinite love (Gk. *agape*) that reflects God's nature—and the result of that expression of holy love is the glorification of God.

## 2. The Salvation of Humanity is an Ideal Expression of Sovereign Love

Just as God's love serves as the basis of his creative activity, creating humans as relational beings to love him—and, as an outflow, to love one another—God's love is best expressed through his salvation of humanity through Christ. This was his plan from the very beginning, which means that God's love is a purposive love that drives his sovereign plan for the ages.

Several passages indicate that before the fall, even before the creation, God purposed for Christ to die in the place of sinners to save from the power of sin and death, and to reconcile humans to God. The apostle Peter writes, in the context of addressing Jesus's death on the cross (1 Pet 1:20), that Christ was "foreknown" (Gk. *proginosko*) before the foundation of the universe (Gk. *kosmos*). He notes that Christ redeems us not by earthly wealth or religious tradition (vv. 18–19), but by his blood, and in v. 21 Peter refers to Christ's resurrection, making clear that his sacrificial death was planned/purposed before God created. Revelation 13 tells of the Book of Life held by the Lamb that was slain "from the foundation of the world" (13:8). The wording is almost identical to 1 Peter 1, so it is likely that this text also points to the pre-creative plan of God to save humanity through the death of Christ. This idea also accords well with Peter's Pentecost sermon in which he states that Jesus was crucified and killed by lawless men according to "God's determined plan and foreknowledge" (Acts 2:23). The reference to foreknowledge indicates that the plan to save was not purely reactionary, but instead was predetermined by God as part of his larger plan to save humanity through his covenant relationship with Israel.

In an alternate context, mentioning God's pre-creative plan, Jesus refers to intra-trinitarian relations existing before the foundation of the world (Gk. *kosmos*), and prays that his disciples would experience the kind of unity in love that the persons of the Trinity share (John 17). Taken together with the passages above, this suggests that divine love drove God's sovereign decision to save humanity and divine love also purposed for the Son to die as an expression of that love before there was a *need* for his sacrificial death. One way to more fully understand these ideas is through Hugo Grotius's governmental theory of atonement. Grotius (1583–1645) was a Dutch Reformed humanist, theologian, statesman, and jurist, whose theory explains that before God created, he sovereignly chose to create beings with a God-given capacity to love and relate to him. God knew that human finitude would preclude their full grasp of the "length and width, height and depth of God's love," a love that "surpasses knowledge" (Eph 3:18–19); and that humans would need a mediated expression of love to understand something of holy *agape*. The greatest love, as Jesus said, is self-sacrificial love (John 15:13), and so, as Paul noted, God demonstrated his love in this way: while we were still enemies of God, Christ died for us (Rom 5:8). God's plan included a fall, a need for redemption, and provision by God himself in the person of Jesus Christ, so that he could reveal his nature as love so that humans might respond in kind with worship, glorifying him supremely.

## 3. Divine Initiative in Salvation

Third, the phrase, "God so loved the world," indicates divine initiative in salvation. When considering how salvation *works*, it is best to think in terms of divine initiative and human response. Christians (and Baptists) may disagree over the specifics of how those two elements work, but all agree that God is the initiator in salvation by calling persons to relationship with him; that there is an operation of sovereign election (predestination); and that those who respond in faith are saved and are the elect. So not only did God sovereignly plan to save humanity by means of an incarnation, sacrificial death and defeat of death through the resurrection of God the Son, but his decision also included several sovereign choices: calling Abraham, establishing a separate people, anointing a descendant of David, and saving those who respond to the gospel call.[6] We do not know all the details of those choices, or why and how they are made, but the Scripture is clear that God's love drives those gracious decisions.

The love of God as the impetus of both his creation and salvation of fallen creatures is clearly seen in the writing and preaching of early church fathers like Athanasius (d. AD 373), who stated that the "savior . . . being by nature bodiless and existing as the Word, by the *love* for humankind (Gk. *philanthropian*) and goodness of his own Father he appeared to us

---

[6] The doctrine of election includes God's election of Israel (Deut 7:6–8; Isa 41:8–9; Rom 11:2, 25–36), election of Christ (Ps 89:3–4; Isa 42:1, 5–9; Matt 12:18–19; Luke 9:35, 23:35; 1 Pet 2:4–6), and election of a new humanity in Christ (Rom 8–11; Eph 1:3–14; 1 Thess 1:2–10; 2 Thess 2:13–14; 2 Tim 1:9–10). Election extends to individual believers and is expressed throughout the biblical narrative in terms of covenant relationship between God and select people: Adamic covenant (Gen 2:15–17), Noahic covenant (Gen 6:18, 9:9–17), Abrahamic covenant (Gen 12:1–7, 15:1–12, 17, 1–17, 22:15–19), Mosaic covenant (Exodus 20; Deuteronomy 5; Leviticus 26), Davidic covenant (2 Sam 7:1–29; 1 Chr 17:1–27), and ultimately new covenant (Deut 10:16–18; Jer 31:33; Ezek 16:62–63, 37:1–23; Matt 26:28; Mark 14:24; Luke 22:20; 1 Cor 11:25; 2 Cor 3:6; Heb 8:1–13). These successive covenants largely represent a narrowing of God's relational focus and are a progressive unveiling of his ultimate plan for humanity.

in a human body for our salvation."[7] After taking on human nature, he delivered himself over to death as an offering to the Father, "doing this in his *love* for human beings," setting them free from condemnation under the law of corruption and death, and turning them to incorruptibility "to give them life from death . . . making the body his own and . . . banishing death from them as straw from fire."[8]

## "That He Gave His Only Begotten Son"

The salvation of humanity is provided in the sacrifice of God the Son, and this giving of the Son reveals God's nature and purpose: his love, holiness, justice, mercy, power, wisdom, grace, transcendence and immanence, and his triune nature are revealed in the cross. Thus, the doctrine of salvation depends upon Christology; the incarnation of the Son reveals both God's triune nature and also his gracious saving purpose (John 1:18). In sending the Son, the Father expresses his love in a manner that best communicates that love by meeting humanity's greatest need, thereby evoking a love response (1 John 4:10). Thus, very early in the church's history, the meaning of the incarnation was closely associated with salvation, such that the incarnation was seen as necessary for redemption. Later theologians noted the utility of the incarnation for the Christian life and saw the *telos* (or goal) of the incarnation in the faith and love response it elicits among humans.

### 1. Necessity of the Incarnation

Irenaeus of Lyon (ca., AD 140–202) is often credited with articulating the first atonement theory, the recapitulation theory. It is so-called because Christ re-worked those aspects in the creation story that led to humanity's

---

[7] Athanasius, *On the Incarnation*, trans. John Behr (Yonkers, NY: St Vladimir's Seminary Press, 2011), 52–53.

[8] Athanasius, 66–67.

fall and subsequent enslavement to sin and death; the first Adam brought death, while the second Adam brought life (Rom 5:12–21; 1 Cor 15:20–23). Although Jesus lived a sinless life in contradistinction to Adam, for Irenaeus, God's assumption of flesh ultimately secured salvation. This principle—that which is assumed is saved—became determinative for the Christological controversies of the fourth and fifth centuries. Thus, a full and true incarnation was necessary to redeem humanity, and ultimately, the created order:

> For unless man had overcome the enemy of man, the enemy would not have been legitimately vanquished. And again: unless it had been God who had freely given salvation, we could never have possessed it securely. And unless man had been joined to God, he could never have become a partaker of incorruptibility. For it was incumbent upon the Mediator between God and men, by His relationship to both, to bring both to friendship and concord, and present man to God, while He revealed God to man.[9]

This argument was further developed in the medieval period by Anselm, archbishop of Canterbury, in his classic work, *Cur Deus Homo*. Anselm begins by suggesting that the root of sin is failing to give God the glory and honor he is due. This failure of humanity (in the person of Adam) resulted in an infinite debt to, or offense, against God because his infinite holiness requires infinite glory and honor. God's justice and holiness require that satisfaction be made to restore his offended honor, and that the satisfaction be made by the one who committed the offense (i.e., a human). This, of course, is problematic on many levels. First, all have sinned and have thereby taken some glory and honor away from God (Rom 3:23); second, God, by his very nature, is due all honor and glory, so any given him after the fall will only meet the standard

---

[9] Irenaeus, *Against Heresies*, 3.18.7. trans. Alexander Roberts in *Ante-Nicene Fathers*, vol. 1., ed. Alexander Roberts, James Donaldson, and A. Cleveland Coxe (Buffalo, NY: Christian Literature Publishing, 1885), 448.

requirement without actually restoring any removed by the offense; and third, no mere human, because of his finitude, can give God infinite honor. As a further related problem, the created order became subject to sin and death with the fall of humanity, and so the satisfaction required to restore it must be greater than the whole created order. Thus, a human must make infinite satisfaction, but no mere human can do so; only an infinite being (i.e., God) could meet the requirement for satisfaction. So, Anselm concludes, there must be an incarnation whereby a God-man makes satisfaction, redeeming humanity and enabling the realization of God's plan in creating. In Anselm's words, "because the aforesaid satisfaction [must] be made, which none but God can make and none but man ought to make, it is necessary for the God-man to make it."[10]

## 2. Utility of the Incarnation

For the salvation of humanity, the incarnation is not only necessary but also vitally helpful for Christians seeking to live in faith. By taking on flesh and becoming fully human in the person of Jesus Christ, God the Son offered us an example of how to live for God in complete faith and obedience (1 Pet 2:21) and for others in loving, self-sacrificial service (John 13:15). Jesus consistently told his disciples that he only does what he see the Father doing (John 5:19; compare to John 5:30; 6:38; 7:16–18; 8:28–29; 12:49; 14:10) and that his actions were meant to glorify the Father (John 10:25), just as our actions should glorify God (Matt 5:16). Paul encourages his readers to follow the example of the Christ they see in him (1 Cor 11:1) and to imitate Christ's self-sacrifice (Eph 5:12) and forgiveness (Col 3:13). John echoes these sentiments, exhorting his audience to live like Christ (1 John 2:6), even to the point of martyrdom (1 John 3:15–16).

---

[10] Anselm, *Cur Deus Homo* 2.6, in *St. Anselm: Basic Writings*, trans. S. N. Deane, 2nd ed. (La Salle, IL: Open Court, 1962), 259.

Unsurprisingly, then, the earliest writings following the age of the apostles focused largely on moral teaching and exhortation. Tertullian (ca. AD 155–225) encouraged his readers to reflect on the crucifixion to motivate them to repentance, charity, and love for neighbor, and suggested these actions can be compensatory to God, but he did not mean to suggest works-salvation. Rather, Tertullian's words reflect the early church's emphasis upon faithfulness in the face of persecution. Pointing to the cross (and prominent martyrologies) was a common way of encouraging perseverance amid suffering.

Example theories of atonement have historically held to defective Christologies, either psilanthropism/Ebionitism (Jesus was merely a man) or Arianism (Jesus was divine/godlike, but not deity); but there is no necessary connection between a heretical view of Christ and recognizing the importance of Jesus' example for Christians. Quite the contrary: diminishing the importance of Jesus's example means diminishing his humanity and opening the door to heresies that so prioritize his deity as to make his humanity superfluous! As the writer of Hebrews makes clear, both his deity *and* his humanity inspire faith. Even though Christ is superior to the angels, to Moses, to Torah, and to the Levitical priesthood, he was still fully human, tempted in every way humans are tempted. He is a high priest who has gone through the heavens, and who has identified with us in weakness, yet without sin; therefore, we may approach his throne with confidence that we will receive mercy and grace in our time of need (Heb 4:14–16). His humanity makes him approachable and relatable, and his deity makes him worthy of worship and adoration.[11]

---

[11] Mental health professionals have recently affirmed through their research what early philosophers and teachers have always thought, namely that positive role models not only serve to instruct, but also to motivate their students. See T. Morgenroth, M. K. Ryan, and K. Peters, "The Motivational Theory of Role Modeling: How Role Models Influence Role Aspirants' Goals," *Review of General Psychology*, 19:4 (2015): 465–83. Available at https://doi.org/10.1037/gpr0000059.

## 3. *Telos* of the Incarnation

More than simply providing an example to follow, inspiring courage in the face of persecution, and rousing confidence in approaching God, the incarnation requires and even empowers a loving faith response. In his moral influence theory of atonement, Peter Abelard was most concerned with understanding the impact of the incarnation upon faith. He argues that the demonstration of divine love in the humiliation of the incarnation—most fully expressed in the humiliation of the cross—not only offers an example of pure, holy love, but is also transformative in itself because it confronts us with our sinfulness, our frailty, and the lengths to which God will go to save us, thus calling us to faith.

In Philippians 2, Paul points to the mystery and humility of the incarnation to exhort the church to unity. In the Christ hymn, he calls his readers to have attitudes (lit. "minds") like Christ's, who humbled himself by taking on flesh and dying on the cross. However, while Paul encourages reflection on Christ's example of humility, it is no mere call to emulate how Jesus lived. Rather, it is a considered theological reflection upon the magnitude of Christ's humiliation. Although he was God, he emptied himself and became human. In obedience to the Father's will and in service to humanity, he died an excruciating and humiliating death on the cross, and in this condescension, the Father exalted him. As Christians reflect upon the depth of God's love demonstrated in the incarnation and sacrificial death, the Holy Spirit—who unites them *in Christ* (Phil 2:2)—will supernaturally enable them to have one mind, to perceive the gospel truth, and to comprehend the meaning of the incarnation and their status as God's children (Phil 2:14). This divine enablement should result in loving obedience and faith, as it is God at work in them throughout this meditative, spiritual process (Phil 2:12–13). This is how they are to work out their own salvation with fear and trembling; it is an awe-filled love response that results in obedience and unity in Christ.

Thus, as we meditate upon Christ's sinless life and sacrificial death, we open ourselves to the work of the Holy Spirit, who moves us to faith. As Abelard writes, "Dispelling our shadows with light, he showed us, both by his words and example, the fullness of all virtues, and repaired our nature."[12] Paul Fiddes explains that Abelard's move from "showed" to "repaired" is an attempt "to express his insight that the love disclosed is at the same time the love which recreates."[13] Abelard adds that God's self-sacrificial, pure, and holy love, demonstrated in Christ's incarnation and substitutionary death, creates in us a faith response by the work of the Holy Spirit: "Wherefore, our redemption through Christ's suffering is that deeper affection in us which not only frees us from slavery to sin, but also wins for us the true liberty of sons of God, so that we do all things out of love rather than fear—love to him who has shown us such grace that no greater can be found, as he himself asserts, saying, 'Greater love than this no man hath, that a man lay down his life for his friends.'"[14]

### "That Whosoever Believes in Him . . ."

Salvation, as noted, is best conceived in terms of divine initiative and human response. It begins with God's sovereign love, proceeds by God's work in the life of the believer, and culminates in eternal life. The gospel is good news precisely because salvation is freely given by God (Rom 6:23), depends upon his gracious love and not human works (Gal 2:16; Eph 2:8–9), and is secured by his word (1 Pet 1:23), power (Rom 3:19), and even his being (i.e., the Holy Spirit as a down payment, 2 Cor 1:22; 5:5; Eph 1:14).

---

[12] Peter Abelard, *Sermons 3*, J. P. Migne, *Bibliotheca Patrum Latina* (Paris: 1855), 396b.

[13] Paul S. Fiddes, *Past Event and Present Salvation: The Christian Idea of Atonement* (Louisville: Westminster/John Knox, 1989), 145.

[14] Peter Abelard, *Exposition of the Epistle to the Romans*, trans. Gerald E. Moffat, *A Scholastic Miscellany: Anselm to Ockham*, ed. Eugene R. Fairweather (Philadelphia: Westminster, 1956), 283–84.

## 1. Personal Conversion

The Reformers recognized the deeply personal aspect of salvation, even while they acknowledged the importance of the church for the Christian life. Martin Luther stood firm on his personal convictions regarding the meaning of the Bible, arguing his need to be convinced in his own conscience that his teachings were false before recanting; appeals to authority, whether traditional or papal, were insufficient. His emphasis on the right and responsibility of the individual to read and interpret the Scripture for himself—a part of the doctrine eventually known as the priesthood of the believer—was particularly formative for early Anabaptist and, later, for separatist Congregational and Baptist understandings of salvation. God grants salvation based on an individual's personal faith response, which includes both repentance and obedience to God's commands. As John Calvin put it, "It is God that calls us, and offers to us salvation; it is our part to embrace by faith what he gives, and by obedience act suitably to his calling; but we have neither from ourselves."[15]

The individualistic language Jesus uses here, often translated, "whosoever," highlights the personal nature of saving faith and the universal offer of God's grace to believers. As noted earlier, Baptists disagree over the nature and basis of election and predestination, even while we agree on the fact of God's sovereignty in salvation. Similarly, Baptists disagree over the so-called extent of the atonement—that is, the identity of those for whom Jesus died. Proponents of limited atonement claim that Jesus died only for the elect, according to the logic that God's foreknowledge and sovereignty over salvation preclude his dying for those not elected to salvation. Proponents of unlimited/general atonement argue that Christ died for all persons because salvation is available to all who believe. This universal provision is merciful, loving, and just. If Christ were to die only for the elect and not all persons, then it would appear that God is not fair

---

[15] John Calvin, *Commentary on the Epistle of Paul to the Philippians*, II.13, trans. John Pringle, in *Calvin's Commentaries*, vol 21, *Galatians-Philemon* (Grand Rapids: Baker, 2005), 69.

or perhaps, not omnibenevolent. As Vines puts it, "It is the design of the sovereign God to make salvation of all people possible and to secure the salvation of all who believe. What kind of God would not make salvation possible for all?"[16]

Despite disagreements over the identity of those for whom Jesus died, all agree that Jesus' death (and resurrection) was necessary to make salvation available, sufficient to save all persons, efficient to secure salvation for the elect, and that his death—or more properly, the salvific benefits of his death—are applied to all who believe. This agreement allows Baptists to disagree over what most see as a theological concern of *secondary* importance so they can partner in an ecclesial concern of *primary* importance: missions and evangelism. Baptists of all kinds have seen the missional mandate in the requirement of personal conviction for sin, personal penitence, and personal faith, suggested in Jesus' proclamation here that all who believe will be saved (cf. Joel 2:32; Acts 2:21; Rom 10:13).

Southern Baptist theologian E. Y. Mullins wrote extensively of the importance of Christian experience in conversion/salvation and in the life of the believer. In fact, true religious experience—Christian experience—grounds much of his theological and apologetic work. Mullins correctly notes that we first sense a need for salvation in personal experience. Our experience of our own lostness—like that of the Philippian jailer, where we cry out, "What must I do to be saved?"—leads us to seek forgiveness of sins, reconciliation with God, lasting peace, abundant life, and, ultimately, redemption (Acts 16:30; cf. Acts 2:37). This can only be found in personal faith in Christ, effected through a personal encounter with Christ mediated by the Holy Spirit through God's Word (i.e., the Bible). The experience of Christ is real and confirms our salvation, but it can also have apologetic value. A critical but fair examination of the historical evidence for Christ, along with the evidence for the power of salvation

---

[16] Jerry Vines, "Sermon on John 3:16," in David L. Allen and Steve W. Lemke, eds. *Whosoever Will: A Biblical-Theological Critique of Five-Point Calvinism* (Nashville: B&H, 2010), 24.

seen in the changed lives of diverse peoples throughout Christian history, will lead the objective examiner to the only conclusion: Jesus is Lord and Savior.[17]

## 2. Personal Faith and Repentance

Many form critics argue that the earliest *kerygma* (preaching/message) of the church was the coming of the kingdom of God, but there is good reason to think that the message was a warning about the coming kingdom, with a concomitant call to repent and trust in Christ. John the Baptist testified to Christ so that persons would believe (John 1:6–7), but his was a message and baptism of repentance (Matt 1:11; Mark 1:4) *because* of the coming kingdom of heaven (Matt 1:2). Jesus's earliest preaching proclaimed the imminence of God's kingdom, but it was *primarily* a call to "repent and believe the gospel" (Mark 1:15), pointing to the relationship between faith and repentance. As Erickson notes, they are "two distinguishable but inseparable aspects" of conversion.[18] The close relationship between repentance and faith mirrors the close relationship between love and obedience, and all four are intimately related (John 16:27; 1 John 5:1–5). Jesus frequently taught that obedience to his commands is a direct reflection of love for him, a theme particularly evident in John's writings (John 14:15, 21, 23; 15:10; 1 John 2:3–6; 3:6, 18, 22; 5:3; 2 John 6) and in Deuteronomy (i.e., love for God; Deut 7:9; 10:12–13; 11:1, 22; 19:9; 30:6, 15–16, 20), but is also found elsewhere in both testaments (e.g., Ps 111:10; Rom 13:8, 10; 1 Tim 1:5; Titus 1:16; Jas 2:18–26). It is

---

[17] E. Y. Mullins, *The Christian Religion in its Doctrinal Expression* (Nashville: Baptist Sunday School Board, 1928), 21–22. See also Mullins, chap. 16, "The Data of Christian Experience," where Mullins catalogs a diverse group of conversion stories to note their striking similarities, in *Why Is Christianity True? Christian Evidences* (Philadelphia: American Baptist Publication Society, 1905), 291.

[18] Millard J. Erickson, *Christian Theology*, 3rd ed. (Grand Rapids: Baker, 2013), 805.

summarized in Jesus' teaching on the greatest commandment and love of God and neighbor as encapsulating the Torah (Matt 22:36–40) and in his claim to fulfill Torah in his loving mission (Matt 5:17–20).

Biblical, saving faith is at its core (1) volitional, (2) intellectual, and (3) emotional. Contrary to some existentialist philosophies, biblical faith is not opposed to knowledge, but instead depends on the apprehension of key doctrinal and biblical truths to have an appropriate object (i.e., the trinitarian God). It is an informed and reflective faith, but not mere intellectual assent to discrete propositions (e.g., that Jesus is God the Son). As James notes, even the demons believe that there is one God (Jas 2:19), and the Gospels report that demons acknowledged the identity, power, and authority of Jesus (Matt 8:29; Mark 1:23–24). Knowledge, then, is not enough, for faith is also emotive. It not only accepts the truth of proper theological claims, but it is personally invested in those claims. It acknowledges their claim upon the individual, moving him or her to desire reconciliation with God and to experience godly penitence. The last component is perhaps best described as volitional, indicating a trust response in God's saving grace. Somewhat paradoxically, then, faith can be understood as both active and purposeful on the one hand, and passive and receptive on the other hand. It is active insofar as the individual accepts Christ as Lord, and responds to God's call to divine relationship, but passive insofar as it adopts a posture of surrender and contrition. It involves taking up one's cross, dying to self and living for Christ (Matt 16:24–26; John 11:25; Phil 1:21).

Similarly, repentance includes intellectual, affective/emotional, and volitional/active components. The intellectual component may be seen as the appropriate response when confronted with the vast disparity between oneself and God, as Isaiah responded upon seeing the exalted Lord. He cried out in both anguish and awe: "Woe is me for I am ruined because I am a man of unclean lips . . . and because my eyes have seen the King, the Lord of Armies" (Isa 6:5). This worship-filled response includes an acknowledgment of both moral standards and one's personal violation of those standards, an admission of guilt. More than mere admission, though, true repentance must also include a feeling of guilt or shame, something akin to a broken heart over sin against a holy, loving, righteous God, as David demonstrates: "For I am conscious of my rebellion, and my sin is always before me. Against you—you alone—have I sinned and done what is evil in your sight" (Ps 51:3–4). Although David had clearly sinned against Uriah, Bathsheba, Michal, Abigail, Ahinoam, Joab, Israel's armies, and the whole nation, it was his offense against God's righteous law, character, and holiness that was particularly grievous. Repentance also includes a volitional/active component that requires a willful decision to turn from sin and active steps to shun sinning in the future. Only when God's people "turn from their evil ways" does the Lord hear their prayers and heal their land (2 Chr 7:14). The biblical language of repentance connotes active turning, emotional regret, and (literally) change of mind (Hb. *naham, anna, shubh*; Gk. *metanoia, metanoeo*), even a change of disposition away from sinful activity and thought. It results in godly actions because it includes a change of heart and a change of attitude, so that the penitent views the world as God does, with the mind of Christ (Phil 2:5). This change of mind about God from doubt to trust, this change of affection toward God from enmity to love, and this change of allegiance from self to the Lord, is termed *conversion* and encompasses the proper human responses to God's salvific work.

In a classic sermon, "Conversions Desired," Charles Spurgeon exposited the inner and outer dynamics of conversion: "We desire, dear hearers, that faith in the Lord Jesus may lead you to give up the objects of your idolatrous love, yourselves, your money, your pleasures, the world, the flesh, the devil."[19] Such saving faith results in total conversion of action, heart, and soul: "He who looks sinward has his back to God—he who looks Godward has his back to sin . . . With weeping and supplication do men so turn, confessing their wrongdoing, lamenting their transgressions,

---

[19] Charles Spurgeon, "Conversions Desired," March 5, 1876. *Metropolitan Tabernacle Pulpit*, vol. 22. Accessed at https://www.spurgeon.org/resource -library/sermons/conversions-desired/#flipbook/12.

abhorring their evil lustings, desiring pardon, and hoping for renewal of their nature."[20]

All these responses—repentance, faith, love, and obedience—are human responses to God's saving work, but not *mere* human responses, as all are *divinely-empowered* human responses requiring a work of God upon the mind, heart, and soul of the person (Deut 6:4–5; Matt 22:37; Mark 12:30; Luke 10:27). They are variously described as works of God (John 6:29, 44, 65; Acts 11:18; Rom 12:3; 15:13; 2 Cor 4:6; 2 Tim 2:25), works of Christ (Mark 9:24; Luke 17:5; Heb 12:2), effects of grace and/ or gifts (Acts 3:16; Phil 1:29; 2 Pet 1:1; possibly Eph 2:8–9), and products of the Holy Spirit (John 14:26; 16:13; 1 Cor 12:9). Throughout Jesus' farewell discourse, the interplay between loving Jesus and obeying his commands includes a promise of the coming Holy Spirit. Jesus tells his followers that they will do greater works than he *because* he is going to the Father (John 14:15), an allusion to his sending of the Spirit (Compare John 14:23, "[W]e will . . . make our home with him [i.e., with the believer]," with John 16:7, "[I]f I don't go away, the Counselor [Gk., *paraclete*] will not come").

So, these responses to God's work—his call, his demonstration of love, his grace—are human responses empowered by God, though the nature of that empowerment is not clear. Bible-believing Baptists disagree over the nature and extent of that divine enablement. Some believe that, to believe with saving faith, one must be born again and given a new nature. They reason that, since unregenerate persons are dead in their trespasses and sin, they are unable to respond positively until they are made alive in Christ (Eph 2:1,4–6). The new nature imparted in regeneration makes the individual love God and, in this way, engenders a faith response. Others believe that the only requirement for faith is a gracious divine enablement that overcomes the negative effects of the fall upon the individual's disposition so that he/she may favorably respond to God's call. In this model, regeneration is thought to be granted as a result

---

[20] Spurgeon, "Conversions Desired."

of one's faith, viewing Paul's use of Abraham's justification as evidence: "Abram believed the Lord, and he credited it to him as righteousness" (Gen 15:6; cf., Rom 4:13, 16, 20–25; Gal 3:6–7). Despite these disagreements, all agree that salvation is by grace through faith, that faith is a result of God's empowering, and that faith is a human response accompanied by repentance characterized by a change of mind, heart, and actions concerning God.

## 3. Personal Union with Christ

Two important features of salvation are referenced in the words, "in him" (John 3:16). First, *Christ* is the object of faith. While faith in God generally is biblical, it is faith in the triune God that is salvific, since the concrete revelation of God in space and time for our salvation is the incarnation of God the Son in the person of Jesus Christ. When we trust in God's salvific work, our primary focus is upon the work realized in the sinless life, sacrificial death and victorious resurrection of Christ. Because of this work, he received a name above all other names (Phil 2:9–11), a name by which salvation is secured (Acts 4:12), and because of this work, we are saved when we confess, "Jesus is Lord" (Rom 10:9).

Second, it is *in Christ* that salvation is found. Upon rebirth—the focus of Jesus' teaching to Nicodemus throughout John 3—we are united with Christ in death and new life (Eph 2:10, 22). Union with Christ may be seen as an overarching category for understanding the whole of salvation and the Christian life. We are regenerated *in Christ* (2 Cor 5:17), justified *in Christ* (Rom 8:1), adopted *in Christ* (Eph 1:5), sanctified *in Christ* (1 Cor 1:2), are *in Christ* in death (1 Thess 4:14, 16; Rev 14:13), will be resurrected *in Christ* (1 Cor 15:22), and will be glorified with him at the eschaton (Rom 8:17; 1 Cor 15:48–49; 1 John 2:28; 3:2). While it is not entirely clear what it means to be *in Christ*—apart from living in a state of spiritual surrender and trust in Christ—it is clear that the New Testament authors regarded it as vital to our salvation. Ken Keathley suggests that it has both positional and experiential features: "First, *positionally* God looks upon Jesus Christ as our representative, and all his accomplishments are considered by God to be our accomplishments, too. Second, *experientially* we begin to undergo the transforming benefits of our union with him when at conversion the Holy Spirit comes to dwell within us."[21] Jesus's use of the vine and branches metaphor confirms this two-feature interpretation of what it means to abide in Christ (John 15), as does the image of the church as Christ's body (Eph 5; 1 Cor 12).

### "Shall not perish, but have eternal life"

Salvation is both an immediate reality and a promise for the future. It is a redemption of God's creative purposes, primarily for individuals, but also for humanity, and through humanity, the entire creation (Rom 8:29–31). It was earlier noted that salvation refers to a rescue from some ill fate. Here, Jesus identifies that fate as death and exclusion from the kingdom of God (John 3:3, 5). Elsewhere, such exclusion is depicted as suffering in outer darkness (Matt 8:12) and in unquenchable fire (Mark 9:43–48), clear references to hell (cf., lake of fire, Rev. 20:15). Thus, the everlasting life promised in salvation is participation in God's glorious kingdom in a resurrected, perfected, spiritual body (1 Cor 15:35–55).

### 1. Salvation as Rescue from Evil and Death

Our salvation is secured by the Father's infinite love and power, by the resurrection of the Son, and by the seal of the Spirit. By dying and being resurrected, Jesus conquered the power of death, which held sway over all (Rom 6:9; 1 Cor 15:21–22, 26, 54–55; cf. John 2:19–21; 10:10, 17–18). Yet the New Testament also says that God (the Father) raised Jesus from the dead (Acts 2:24, 32; 3:15, 26; 4:10; 5:30; 10:40; 13:30–37; Rom 4:24; 6:4; 10:9; 1 Cor 6:14; Gal 1:1; Col 2:12) in the power of the Holy Spirit

---

[21] Kenneth Keathley, "The Work of God: Salvation," in *A Theology for the Church*, ed., Daniel L. Akin (Nashville: B&H, 2014), 548.

(Rom 8:11) to vindicate his person/identity and ministry (Rom 1:4). Thus, all three persons of the Godhead act in overcoming death. Not only was death conquered in Jesus' death and resurrection, but so also was the power of sin, which enslaved humanity (John 8:30–36; Rom 6:16–18; 1 Cor 15:17). By God's grace we were freed from sin and the tyranny of the law. The economic imagery of redemption and purchase speaks to this release from slavery—we were purchased with Christ's blood (1 Cor 6:20; 7:23; 1 Pet 1:9)—and its corollary is our adoption as children of God (Rom 8:15; Gal 4:7).

The early church tended to emphasize these motifs in its thought on atonement. Christ's victory over death, sin, and evil; Christ's payment of a ransom (Matt 20:28; Mark 10:45); and our release from destructive powers are all themes found in the early church referencing how Jesus saves us. These were not developed, systematized models of atonement, however, but rather were foci of sermons and exegetical works. It was not until Gregory of Nyssa's ransom to Satan theory that one may speak of an atonement model. Gregory argued that humanity was enslaved to Satan and purchased in exchange for Jesus. However, Satan was unable to contain the resurrected Christ, and therefore, lost both humanity and Christ. Later theologians rejected this model, largely because it was unflattering to God; it suggests God owed Satan something and that God is a dishonest broker. While Gregory's model represents advancement in atonement thought, it faltered in its basic premise: it takes the economic language too literally. Rather than seeing the language of enslavement and ransom as cultural imagery that reveals a facet of salvation, Gregory sought a literal, personal recipient of the ransom. It is doubtful, however, that the ransom is paid to anyone. Instead, it is best to see the enslavement and ransom language as one way of speaking about a spiritual, heavenly reality using physical, earthly imagery. In saying this, we do not mean to minimize the way that sin has a grip on the lost, for the language of slavery captures the futility of trying to overcome sinful attitudes, thoughts, and actions in one's own strength. To proclaim that Jesus conquered the power of sin and death, that he conquered the grave, that he set us free from the law and from sin, though, is not to explain *how* his death has done this. To do this, legal and sacrificial imagery is needed.

## 2. Salvation as Acquittal from Judgment and Wrath

Perhaps the most popular model of the atonement—due to its focus on the mechanics of salvation—is penal substitution, which incorporates both legal and sacrificial images. Briefly, it is the claim that, in dying on the cross, innocent Jesus served as a legal and sacrificial substitute for guilty humanity. All (save Jesus) have sinned (Rom 3:23) and deserve death and condemnation (Rom 6:23). Jesus's righteous and sinless life (2 Cor 5:29; Heb 4:15) was an acceptable and blameless substitute for those condemned (Rom 5:8; 1 Pet 3:18). By faith, believers are united with Christ in death and resurrection, thereby securing forgiveness of sins and averting the wrath of God; Jesus is the propitiation for our sins (1 John 2:2). Since sin not only makes persons guilty, but also makes them cere-monially unclean and unable to approach God (Isa 64:6), all must be cleansed and reconciled to God. Jesus, as God the Son, was sinless and infinitely holy, and could therefore serve as a spotless, perfect sacrifice on behalf of unclean humanity (1 Pet 1:19). He simultaneously served as a guilt or sin offering (Rom 8:3; Heb 9:26–28; 10:12; 13:10–12) and as a peace and thanksgiving offering (John 14:27; Col 1:20; Eph 2:14; 1 John 1:3, 7), thus eradicating the need for the Israelite sacrificial system, which was never capable of ultimately cleansing and reconciling humanity to God (Heb 10:1–3, 11). His death on Passover (John 19:14) tied him to the notion of the Passover lamb (1 Cor 5:7; Isa 53:7; compare John 19:33, 36 with Exod 12:46; Num 9:12), whose blood on the doorposts signaled people of faith inside so that the angel of death would bypass the house, allowing the firstborn to live. In dying on the cross, he took on sin and *became* sin, thus indicating his replacement for sinful humanity (Deut 21:22–23; Acts 5:30; 10:39; Gal 3:13; 2 Cor 5:21; 1 Pet 2:24). His blood thus is seen as analogous to that of sacrificial animals for atone-ment, whose blood was sprinkled on the altar to cover and remove sin

(Lev 16:10, 14–15, 18–19; 1 Pet 1:2, Ps 51:2; 1 John 1:7–9; Rev 7:14). As John the Baptist proclaimed, "the Lamb of God, who takes away the sin of the world!" (John 1:29). By his shed blood, Christ mediates the new covenant (Matt 26:28; 1 Cor 11:25; Heb 9:15; 13:20) that is rooted in personal accountability and divine grace and that is characterized by the indwelling of God's Spirit in those who believe (Isa 59:19–21; Jer 31:31–34; Heb 8:6–7).

## 3. Salvation as Forgiveness and Renewal

Two other ways of speaking of salvation using legal imagery are justification and adoption. Baptists have typically followed the Reformed Protestant understanding of justification as forensic and punctiliar, as a declaration of "not guilty" by God the Father. This justification is often seen as a two-step process whereby the sins of humanity are transferred to Christ (2 Cor 5:18–21; 1 Pet 2:24) and the righteousness of Christ is imputed or credited to those who believe (Isa 53:11–12; Rom 4:5–8; 5:19; 1 Cor 1:30; 2 Cor 5:21) at the moment of faith. The distinction between imputation and infusion is key: believers are *declared* "not guilty" and *considered* righteous because of the transaction, but are not actually *made* righteous in justification. It is positional in nature. Similarly, adoption is another legal image used to speak to one's position before God. Paul uses it to contrast the state of believers in Christ with their state before salvation. They are no longer slaves, but free, and are made children of God and heirs with Christ (Rom 8:15; Gal 4:5; Eph 1:5). While by nature they are children of wrath (Eph 2:3), by grace they have become members of God's household (Eph 2:19).

Medical language is also used to speak of salvation, and it is this language of regeneration that forms the context for Jesus' teaching to Nicodemus in John 3. Jesus tells Nicodemus that one cannot enter the kingdom of God unless he is born again, of water and the Spirit (John 3:3–12). This rebirth occurs at the moment of faith/justification with the indwelling of the Holy Spirit and results in washing and renewal

(Titus 3:5; 1 Pet 1:23). The language of renewal is especially relevant. Paul speaks of putting "on the new self" (Col 3:10), of becoming a new creation (2 Cor 5:17; Gal 6:15), of becoming children of light rather than of darkness (Eph 5:8; Col 1:13; 1 Thess 5:5; cf., John 12:36). John also uses this language of change and renewal (1 John 2:29–3:3, 9–10; 5:1–5). All of these images—rescue, cleansing, forgiveness, renewal, and acquittal highlight change that occurs when we place our faith in Christ. The proper response to this new reality is worship in humility, gratitude, and awe.

## Baptist Distinctives and Theological Trajectories

We want to suggest two ways for Baptists to consider a somewhat different approach to soteriology from those traditionally followed in systematic theologies. *First*, we suggest that an approach to soteriology in terms of a primary divine actor fails to fully capture the Christian revelation of God's salvific work. Rather than seeing the work of salvation as primarily that of God the Son, we ought to view salvation as the gracious work of all divine persons of the triune God. The Holy Spirit's role in salvation has often been overlooked or relegated to merely sanctification and deserves greater attention. We affirm that the Holy Spirit plays a vital and integral role in salvation from beginning to end. *Second*, we suggest that Baptists should resist the tendency to partition too rigidly the various images and aspects of salvation. This doctrinal partitioning detracts from a biblical understanding of soteriology and from our practice of the Christian life. Alongside these theological trajectories, and issuing forth from our soteriological principles, we want to affirm Baptists' continued lobbying for disestablishment, which is consistent with our historical legacy and insures religious liberty for all faiths.

### 1. Trinitarian Salvation

No Christian theologian would purposely suggest that salvation is *not* the work of the triune God. However, the way doctrines are typically categorized and discussed can leave the impression that God's major works are the purview of particular persons of the Trinity and not of God as triune. For example, the doctrine of creation and its attendant doctrines (providence, angelology, theological anthropology, hamartiology) are often examined after theology proper (the doctrine of God), suggesting that God the Father is the focus of that work. Similarly, soteriology follows Christology, and the doctrine of the church follows pneumatology, suggesting salvation belongs exclusively to Christ, and the church is the purview of the Holy Spirit. While a case can be made for these loci of operations, it can lead to the false impression that all three persons are not intimately involved in all works of God.

We want to affirm a thoroughly trinitarian soteriology that still recognizes the unique work of each person and the unique ways we relate to each. On the one hand, the distinctions of persons within the trinitarian economy are real and matter. As a result, certain operations or actions are proper to particular persons of the Trinity. For example, the Son properly serves as the mediator between God and the creation so that it was the Son who had to take on flesh, live a sinless life, die on the cross for humanity's sins, and rise from the dead to conquer the power of the grave. It is not proper to speak of just any of the persons dying on the cross for our sins; the Father did not die on the cross. Such a view of the interchangeability of persons is the heresy of modalism, what the early church eventually termed patripassianism.[22] On the other hand, the work of God is properly conceived in terms of the trinitarian economy such that God's saving work is understood to be that of Father, Son and Holy Spirit, and that we may speak of certain aspects of that salvific work as interchangeably that of the different persons of the Trinity. While most Baptist theologians have followed the standard Western approach to organizing the study of theology outlined above, two of the most prominent point us in a trinitarian direction: John L. Dagg and Edgar Young Mullins.

---

[22] See Tertullian, *Against Praxeas*, chap. 1.

## J. L. Dagg

J. L. Dagg's 1857 *Manual of Theology*—the first Baptist systematic theology written in the United States—offers a unique approach to soteriology. He organizes his discussion around the theme of divine grace, following Christology and pneumatology, and just before eschatology (there is no separate section on ecclesiology). In an unusual move, Dagg discusses the Trinity under the doctrine of divine grace (salvation), rather than as a subset of theology proper. He begins by noting that all are obliged to thank God for the blessings he has bestowed upon them, most notably the blessing of salvation, because it flows from and reveals the love of the triune God, the Father (John 3:16), the Son (Eph 3:18–19), and the Spirit (Rom 15:30). Dagg claims that the doctrine of the Trinity most clearly appears in salvation, hence he includes it here: "In the work of salvation, the divine persons co-operate in different offices; and these are so clearly revealed, as to render the personal distinction in the Godhead more manifest, than it is in any other of God's works."[23]

The Son and the Spirit are subordinate to the Father in office, not nature, and they voluntarily consent to that subordination, but each brings to his office the fullness of the Godhead so that the work of each—indwelling of the Spirit and humiliation of Christ—is the work of God. In salvation, the work of God begins with the Father, proceeds through the agency of the Son, and is completed by the Spirit, who bestows the blessings of grace upon believers. However, human response to God proceeds in the reverse order: the Holy Spirit prompts humans to acts of faith and supplication, aiding them in those acts (even with words for prayer), which are mediated through Christ to the Father, who is the ultimate object of worship. While maintaining these distinctions of office, Dagg correctly notes that in some works of the divine persons, the whole Godhead is represented and thus, the work of one may be ascribed to another. For example, the work of the Holy Spirit drawing

---

[23] John L. Dagg, *Manual of Theology* (Harrisburg, VA: Gano Books, 1980), 254.

persons to Christ may be ascribed to the Father (John 6:44), just as the work of Christ in reconciliation may be ascribed to God [the Father] (2 Cor 5:19). The consequence of this identification is that in worship, believers may direct their adoration to any of the persons of the Trinity, or to God generally: "With equal freedom from distraction we may worship the Infinite One, whether we approach him as the Holy Spirit, operating on the heart; or as the Son, the Mediator between God and men; or as the Father, representing the full authority and majesty of the Godhead. We worship God, and God alone, whether our devotions are directed to the Father, the Son, or the Holy Spirit; for the divine essence, undivided and indivisible, belongs to each of the three persons."[24]

While Dagg's placement of the doctrine of the Trinity within soteriology points to the fact that salvation is the work of the triune God, emphasizing that all persons within the divine economy act in salvation, he nonetheless separates their functions and roles in some unhelpful ways. Thus, while Dagg points us in the right direction, his discussion of the works of Father, Son, and Spirit, respectively, falls short of a fully trinitarian soteriology.

## E. Y. Mullins

E. Y. Mullins more closely approaches a fully trinitarian theology. His theology is firmly rooted in Christ (as seen in its ordering), but he departs from the traditional systematic categories and order. Beginning with the doctrine of revelation, as is typical in evangelical theologies, Mullins grounds revelation in Jesus Christ, whom he considers God's supreme revelation. Thus, his doctrine of revelation—five chapters long—is thoroughly Christological. He proceeds to discuss the Holy Spirit, the Trinity, and theology proper before moving to the works of God: creation, providence and fall of humanity, salvation, the Christian life and eschatology.

---

[24] Dagg, 257.

This theological ordering suggests that all work of God is that of the trinitarian God who acts as one; all three persons are active in all works of God. However, Mullins's intense focus on Christology and personal experience can lead to such a prioritization of Christ that the other members of the Trinity appear secondary.

We have attempted throughout this chapter to highlight the saving work of all three persons of the Trinity because properly Christian theology *is* triune. Thus, we hope to inspire Baptists to theologize "trinitarianly." One way to accomplish this is to begin with revelation (Scripture) and then move to the doctrine of the Trinity before considering Theology Proper, Christology, and pneumatology. This ordering grounds our reflection upon God's works (in creation, salvation, the church, and last things), so we may rightly handle the word of truth (2 Tim 2:15).

## 2. Interrelatedness of aspects of salvation

A second idea we wish to present is the interrelated nature of aspects of salvation. Traditionally, Baptists have followed the Reformed approach to justification, explained as a legal transaction involving only the Father and the Son. With Luther and Calvin, Baptists have seen justification as a declaration by the Father of "not guilty" because of the Son's work, and have eschewed talk of being *made holy* in justification for fear of conflating justification with sanctification, as in traditional Catholic sacramental theology. This Reformed approach downplays the Holy Spirit's work in justification.

James P. Boyce (1827–1888) represents this approach. He considers it "obvious" that justification, properly speaking, is only a judicial act and does not include an infusion of holiness for several reasons. First, Scripture opposes justification to condemnation, not sinfulness, and therefore pertains to release from guilt. Second, those justified are not made free of sin or holy, at least not in a way that is realized in one's present lived experience. Third, the biblical language used in connection with justification shows it to be a forensic act arguing that the Greek

New Testament's *dikaiou*-language "means everywhere 'to declare righteous' and not 'to make righteous' in the sense of conferring personal righteousness."[25] Fourth, the change of nature in salvation is a consequence of regeneration, which "differs essentially from justification" and is the work of the Holy Spirit, while justification is an act of the Father. At this point, Boyce expresses his primary concern with connecting one's justification with his or her righteousness: it leads to a confusion of justification and sanctification. He states, "If justification includes an infused righteousness as the opposite of sinfulness, then it includes sanctification, and there is no ground for the scriptural distinction between them."[26] But it need not be seen this way.

In his discussion of the beginnings of salvation, Boyce carefully distinguishes justification, regeneration, and adoption. He particularly emphasizes the gracious character of adoption, maintaining that it is a gift of God (Eph 1:5) bestowed upon the believer at the moment of faith (like justification) due to his good pleasure. For Boyce, this means that adoption does not "arise from any new image or likeness of God, which has come through regeneration."[27] It is an everlasting sonship, dependent upon what Christ has done, "not upon what they [believers] do, *and are*."[28]

Boyce has here too strictly separated adoption and regeneration, and in doing so, has diminished the role of the Holy Spirit in salvation. His concern to maintain the gracious character of salvation is admirable, but he makes unwarranted logical connections and ignores the soteriological importance of regeneration. One may maintain that regeneration imparts a new nature that God considers in his legal assessment of individual believers, and still consistently assert that salvation is by grace alone, through faith alone, in Christ alone, for God's glory alone.

---

[25] James P. Boyce, *Abstract of Systematic Theology* (Hanford, CA: den Dulk Christian Foundation, 1887), 397.
[26] Boyce, 396.
[27] Boyce, 405.
[28] Boyce, 406 (emphasis added).

We can affirm with Boyce that Christ's righteousness is imputed to us and that this transaction serves as part of the basis of our being considered not guilty by God. However, we can also affirm that we are *made righteous* in Christ without compromising the forensic nature of justification by tying that status to regeneration and adoption. Paul seems to view the indwelling of the Spirit in regeneration as the basis of adoption. In Romans 8, the Holy Spirit who leads us is the Spirit of adoption by which we call God "Abba," and the same Holy Spirit who bears witness with our spirits that we are God's children and joint-heirs with Christ (Rom 8:14–17; Gal 4:4–7).

This closer association between the various aspects of salvation can also be seen in their timing. It is common to speak of the already/not-yet aspect of salvation, with the "already" referring to justification, and the "not-yet" referring to sanctification and glorification. The contingent component of salvation is most often referenced under the rubric of sanctification, because we have all experienced the very real post-conversion struggle with sin, and we find comfort in Paul's own very-relatable frustration (Romans 7). Yet there is a sense in which the "already/not yet" distinction applies to all aspects of salvation.

Justification is already complete in that we have been declared "not guilty" at the moment of faith in Christ, and our legal standing is one of righteousness because of Christ's imputed righteousness. Yet justification is "not yet" in that we will still stand before the judge and be officially declared "not guilty" and allowed to enter God's rest at that time (Rev 20:11–15). Adoption, which is closely associated with regeneration, is presented as a current reality for believers, and as one way of speaking of our hope in redemption. Adoption is closely tied to the indwelling of the Holy Spirit, to our familial relationship to the Father, and enables us to be joint heirs with Jesus (Rom 8:14–17; Gal 4:5–6). Adoption, though, is also referenced in terms of a future hope, tied to the redemption of our bodies at the end (Rom 8:23). Thus, we are currently children of God—the Holy Spirit testifies to this fact—even though we are not fully what we will be (1 John 3:1–3).

Sanctification is "not yet" in that we all struggle with sin, even after we accept Christ and are regenerated (Romans 7). Yet sanctification is "already" in that we have been given a new nature in regeneration, made new creatures, and have not only gone from death to life, but have been transformed from children of the night and of darkness to children of the day and of light (John 12:36; Eph 5:8; 1 Thess 5:5), from children of wrath to children of mercy (Eph 2:3–4), and from children of the devil to children of God (1 John 3:10). Glorification is "not yet" in that we are still subject to pain, sickness, death and decay. We await the redemption of our bodies, just as the creation groans for its own redemption that will take place at the revealing of the children of God (Rom 8:19–23). Yet glorification is "already" in some sense, since in regeneration we have been made new, a prefiguring of what we will be.

Thus, we maintain that justification should not be divorced from regeneration and adoption. Such an artificial division fails to appreciate intimate connections among various aspects of salvation. Baptists, like their other Reformed brethren, often seem to view sanctification as something that will never be achieved and therefore place greater emphasis upon the initial conversion experience and future eschatological perfection. By contrast, W. T. Conner (1877–1952), a student of Mullins, rightly argued that reception of Christ for justification and reception of the Holy Spirit for sanctification are not separate transactions but occur simultaneously at the moment of saving faith. In fact, Conner notes, they are so close in the biblical witness that they are sometimes treated together: "As to sanctification, Paul's main use of this term is not something subsequent to justification. Paul uses sanctification in the main as another way of describing what takes place when one becomes a Christian. In Paul's usage, all Christians are saints or sanctified persons."[29]

---

[29] W. T. Conner, *The Work of the Holy Spirit* (Nashville: Broadman Press, 1940), 99.

Augustine argued similarly, that in justification, the image of God is renewed in human beings as they are transformed in regeneration. McGrath explains, "Augustine's understanding of adoptive filiation is such that the believer does not merely receive the *status* of sonhood, but *becomes* a son of God. A real change in man's *being*, and not merely his *status*, is envisaged in his justification, so that he *becomes* righteous and a son of God, and is not merely *treated as if he were* righteous and a son of God."[30] Thus, justification has two complementary meanings: in one sense, we are declared not guilty because our sins have been reckoned to Christ and his righteousness imputed to us. This transaction is biblically referenced by several images: removal, cleansing, covering, expungement, transfer, etc. In another sense, we are made holy because we have been born again through our union with God (Eph 3:16–19). The Bible references rebirth by several images: born of the Spirit, new self, new creation, adoption, children of light, children of God, "in Christ," and so on.

### 3. Baptists and Religious Liberty: Continuing Support of Disestablishment

The biblical teaching of personal conversion and personal relationship with God serves as the theological basis for several Baptist distinctives, both ecclesial and missional. There are at least three Baptist ecclesial distinctives directly related to the doctrine of personal responsibility for faith: 1) believers' baptism, 2) regenerate church membership, and 3) congregational church polity. Since baptism is a physical portrayal of one's union with Christ (by faith) in his death and resurrection (Rom 6:3–11), and since it is meant to be both proclamation and celebration of that union within the context of the gathering of believers, it is only properly applied to born again believers. Since the church is the body of Christ, and persons are only united with Christ by personal

---

[30] Alister E. McGrath, *Iustitia Dei: A History of the Christian Doctrine of Justification*. 2nd ed. (Cambridge: Cambridge University Press, 1998), 32.

faith in regeneration, church membership is restricted to born again believers. Since individuals are responsible before God for their own faith responses, and since the church is a composite of individual believers, united in Christ by the Spirit, every church member is responsible to God and accountable before God for the health and ministries of the local church, and therefore a congregational structure is proper for church governance.

There are also several missional Baptist distinctives directly related to the doctrine of personal repentance and faith, the most obvious being the requirement to engage in missions, emphasizing personal evangelism, producing converts ("soul winning"), and making disciples. While missionary work is not uniquely Baptist, Baptists have characteristically been a missions-oriented people. The primary relationships among disparate Baptist congregations have been missions focused. A second related group of missional Baptist emphases (though not technically distinctives) are related, partnering endeavors like social ministries, theological education, and cultural engagement. However, the most distinctively Baptist missional concern directly related to the doctrine of personal faith has perhaps been the historic Baptist commitment to religious liberty.

Nicholas Miller demonstrates that it was largely theological concerns—in particular, respect for the integrity of private biblical interpretation as most clearly articulated in the writing and preaching of colonial Baptists and other Congregationalist dissenters—that led to the disestablishment of religion in the American colonies and ultimately, to the Establishment Clause of the United States Constitution.[31] He writes, "While the right of private judgment played a role in both Enlightenment and Protestant thought, it originated in the West as a Protestant religious idea that was only later borrowed and modified

---

[31] Some have claimed that it is a uniquely Baptist contribution to American democracy. See, for example, J. M. Dawson, *Baptists and the American Republic* (Nashville: Broadman, 1956).

by Enlightenment thinkers."[32] Specifically, it relied upon *sola Scriptura*, the perspicuity of Scripture, and the interpretation of Scripture by the individual believer.

Baptist and other dissenting thinkers drew and expanded upon Luther's emphasis upon two kingdoms of authority. In addressing the question of the authority of earthly government over religious affairs, Thomas Helwys argued that there is a category mistake in play. Government is not qualified to rule on matters of religion and faith because Christ is the proper sovereign over the church; for the king to rule on issues of the church would be a supplanting of Christ's position as king over the kingdom of God. Writing to King James, he said, "Does the king not know that the God of Gods and Lord of Lords has under him made our lord the king an earthly king and given him all earthly power, and that he has reserved to himself a heavenly kingdom, . . . and that with this kingdom our lord the king has nothing to do (by his kingly power) but as a subject himself; and that Christ is King alone."[33] Isaac Backus expressed the same sentiment in opposing favorable tax laws for pedo-baptists: "Now who can hear Christ declare that his kingdom is not of this world, and yet believe that this blending of church and state together can be pleasing to him?"[34] In addition, though, he made the concern more concrete: the government might use its power to pervert or abuse true religion, as it is not in a proper position to adjudicate spiritual matters: "Religious matters are to be separated from the jurisdiction of the state, not because they are beneath the interests of the state but, quite to the

---

[32] Nicholas P. Miller, *The Religious Roots of the First Amendment: Dissenting Protestants and the Separation of Church and State* (New York: Oxford, 2012), 92.

[33] Thomas Helwys, "The Mystery of Iniquity," quoted in Joseph Early Jr., ed., *Readings in Baptist History* (Nashville: B&H, 2008), 15–16; See also Leon McBeth, ed., *A Sourcebook for Baptist Heritage* (Nashville: Broadman, 1990), 72. The letter resulted in Helwys' arrest and imprisonment, where he died sometime before 1616.

[34] Isaac Backus, "An Appeal to the Public for Religious Liberty," quoted in Joseph Early Jr., ed., *Readings in Baptist History* (Nashville: B&H, 2008), 50.

contrary, because they are too high and holy and thus are beyond the competence of the state."[35]

The "Great Baptists" petition to Patrick Henry's Virginia statute prescribing taxes to support the Anglican church referred to disestablishment as a gospel principle, seeing the bill as "contrary to the spirit of the Gospel" as well as to the Bill of Rights.[36] They argued that the early church flourished without state support and that its legalization under Constantine opened the door to "error, superstition, and immorality."[37] This petition was instrumental in Virginia's adoption of a religious freedom statute that formed the framework for the Establishment Clause of the United States Constitution's First Amendment.

Baptists should continue to support a theologically responsible understanding of disestablishment, opposing efforts to undermine the Establishment Clause for at least three theological reasons. First, our belief in total depravity should make us wary of the designs of any secular government. Although good Christians serve in government, they are rarely in the majority, and the need to compromise within a representative system also makes standing firm for the truth exceedingly difficult and often unpopular. Additionally, those in power wield it in self-interested or evil ways. In a culture increasingly hostile to God's Word, we should expect governmental policies and regulations to be at odds with biblical values. Put simply, we should not want a secular government to make judgments regarding theological truth and/or religious practice.

Second, our belief that salvation requires an individual and free faith response commits us to support the free exchange of ideas, and

---

[35] Isaac Backus, cited in James E. Wood, Jr., "Theological and Historical Foundations of Religious Liberty," *Journal of Church and State* 15:2 (1973): 253. Although these words reflect the scope of Backus's efforts and ideals, it is unclear if Backus actually said or penned these words.

[36] "Petition of the Inhabitants of the County of Westmoreland, Nov. 2, 1784," in Daniel Dreisbach and Mark David Hall, eds., *The Sacred Rights of Conscience* (Indianapolis: Liberty Fund, 2009), 307–8.

[37] "Petition of the Inhabitants of the County of Westmoreland," 308.

our missionary mandate should commit us to freedom of religion. Thus, we should support the rights of individuals to hold competing religious views. We cannot force persons to faith, and legislative action against false religions could produce unintended effects; it could cause adherents to hold to their false beliefs more strongly or cause them to feel affirmed in their faith as a state-persecuted minority. Freedom of religion is based in a biblical theology of missions and evangelism.

Third, in a post–"Moral Majority" world, we should carefully balance supporting religious liberty and lobbying for laws based upon biblical morality and values. Government exists to protect God-given rights and to promote the good while restraining and punishing evil (Rom 13:4), but there is a fine line between enacting laws that are based upon biblical moral principles and supporting legislation that, in effect, forces biblical faith upon the citizenry. Similarly, we must be "as wise as serpents and as innocent as doves" in our advocacy for ethical issues in the public square and should offer secular arguments in favor of any proposed legislation addressing those topics, even though we may have biblical passages that undergird our concerns. Secular governments require secular arguments; offering up biblical arguments for legislation challenges disestablishment and ultimately undermines evangelism and missions.

CHAPTER 6

# THE CHRISTIAN LIFE

NATHAN A. FINN AND KEITH S. WHITFIELD

## Introduction

In his letter to Titus, the apostle Paul identifies himself as a servant of
God and his people, laboring for their faith and knowledge of the truth
(Titus 1:1). Building up the faith and knowledge of the triune God and
his work is a theological task, which Paul says leads to godliness (Titus
1:1). In this sense, theology, the knowledge of God in Christ according to
Scripture, communicates how we are to walk in Christ, whom we received
in faith, and are instructed to continue in faith as we are being established
in him (Col 2:6–7). Christ is the wisdom of God, and as such, is the way
of wisdom for the people of God (Col 2:3). Reflecting this biblical vision,
Kevin Vanhoozer and Daniel Treier suggest the main responsibility of
theology is "to say, on the basis of Scripture, what God is doing *in* Christ,
and then to indicate how to live it out."[1] Puritan theologian William
Ames, using different terms, projects the same goal in his classic definition

---

[1] Kevin J. Vanhoozer and Daniel J. Treier, *Theology and the Mirror of Scripture:
A Mere Evangelical Account* (Downers Grove, IL: IVP Academic, 2015), 45.

of theology. He writes, "[theology is] the doctrine or teaching of living to God."[2] However, theology has not always retained its ministerial purpose of forming God's people into the image of his Son. In *By the Renewing of the Mind*, Ellen Charry argues that conceiving of theology as a discipline that cultivates Christian wisdom and godliness became foreign to modern theological studies in the wake of the Enlightenment, because the way of knowing and way of being in the modern world surrendered theological realism.[3] As she aptly summarizes, "Theology came to be thought of as the intellectual justification of the faith, apart from the practice of the Christian life."[4]

In recent years, many modern evangelical theologians, following J. I. Packer's classic work *Knowing God*, have highlighted the function of doctrine in cultivating Christian maturity.[5] This includes academic theologians such as Simon Chan, Keith Johnson, Beth Felker Jones,

---

[2] William Ames, *The Marrow of Theology*, trans. John D. Eusden (Grand Rapids: Baker, 1968), 77.

[3] Theological realism asserts that God and His actions are knowable, emphasizing that knowledge is not an abstract concept but a deeply personal one. This perspective posits that God exists inherently, independent of human beliefs, and can be genuinely comprehended and communicated with through human language. The realist stance leans heavily on the credibility and core essence of Christian doctrines, viewing them as genuine and faithful representations of the Christian faith.

[4] Ellen Charry, *By the Renewing of Your Minds: The Pastoral Function of Christian Doctrine* (New York: Oxford, 1997), 5.

[5] J. I. Packer, *Knowing God* (Downers Grove: IVP, 1973). IVP published the volume in a new format in 2021 with a foreword by Kevin J. Vanhoozer. In it, Vanhoozer says, "Knowing Packer means coming to grips with the Puritan conviction that all theology is also spirituality. Modern evangelicals who put a premium on having spiritual experiences must learn from seventeenth-century Puritans who put a premium on becoming spiritually mature, which involves forming godly disciplines—habits of life conducive to the formation of godliness. Packer advises people not to read the Puritans unless they were interested in spiritual growth. My advice is similar: you shouldn't read Packer unless you're serious about spiritual transformation. The knowledge of God does not sit idly in the mind, but is living and active, and insists on a personal response" (7).

Ronni Kurtz and Kevin J. Vanhoozer, as well as ecclesial theologians such as R.C. Sproul, Jen Wilkin and J. T. English.[6] Sound doctrine that inflects a theological realism does help form mature disciples as they seek to live faithfully *coram Deo*—before the face of God. Theological realism brings the knower in relationship with the known, rather than the known being merely an object of the knower's enquiry. John Webster defines and identifies the necessity for such theological realism when he says Christian theology is about a name. He says:

> Christian theology speaks about mercy by speaking about Jesus Christ: in order to speak of a virtue, theology is required to speak a name. What it has to say about both the mercies of God and creaturely mercy retains Christian specificity only in the closest proximity to this name and to the sphere of reality which this name indicates, and, further, only in such proximity can theology be genuinely helpful and interesting to its neighbors in the human community.[7]

Such realism fills the pages of Scripture. Paul's instructions to Titus are based on the conviction that the knower is in relationship with the known (Titus 2:11–14). He explains the knowledge that manifests godliness is nurtured through the ministry of the local church: the appointing

---

[6] See Simon Chan, *Spiritual Theology: A Systematic Study of the Christian Life* (Downers Grove: IVP, 1998); Keith L. Johnson, *Theology as Discipleship* (Downers Grove, IL: IVP Academic, 2015); Beth Felker Jones, *Practicing Christian Doctrine: An Introduction to Thinking and Living Theologically*, 2nd ed. (Grand Rapids: Baker Academic, 2023); Ronni Kurtz, *Fruitful Theology: How the Life of the Mind Leads to the Life of the Soul* (Nashville: B&H, 2022); R. C. Sproul, *Everyone's a Theologian: An Introduction to Systematic Theology* (Sanford, FL: Ligonier, 2014); Kevin J. Vanhoozer, *Hearers and Doers: A Pastor's Guide to Making Disciples Through Scripture and Doctrine* (Bellingham, WA: Lexham, 2019); and Jen Wilkin and J.T. English, *You Are a Theologian: An Invitation to Know and Love God Well* (Nashville: B&H, 2023).

[7] John Webster, "Mercy," in *God Without Measure: Working Papers in Christian Theology*, vol. 2, *Virtue and Intellect* (New York: Bloomsbury T&T Clark, 2016), 49.

of elders (Titus 1:5–9), silencing empty talkers (Titus 1:10–16), mentoring young men and women (Titus 2:1–10), and remembering the gospel (Titus 3:3–8). It is through the church that that those who believe in God learn to put on Christ and display the good faith by practicing good works. Again, Vanhoozer and Treier describe the formative purpose of theology as to "make communities of disciples . . . people who become 'little Christs' and thus fulfill their vocation to live as images of God."[8]

The Baptist tradition models a particular form of ecclesial understanding and practice of what we have in Christ and his gospel. Baptists profess the lordship of Christ in a particular way that is reflected in our baptismal practice, which celebrates a theological reality for every person who confesses Christ and is baptized. Through baptism, one's new covenant identity is articulated to the church as his or her identity with Christ and his people are displayed.

While doctrine in general should play an important role in the Christian life, this essay is more narrowly focused on a dogmatic account of the latter, to provide an account for how God sanctifies his people and how the believing church works out the sanctifying grace that God works in them (Phil 2:12–13). Our goal in this chapter is in Charry's words, to articulate theology "as a sanctifying practice of the Christian life, one that integrates understanding with love for practical wisdom,"[9] that is, what it means to live the new life in communion with Christ and his body.

We will begin with an overview of the doctrine of sanctification primarily as an exposition of Romans 5–8. Our principal dialog partner will be the prolific and noted Baptist theologian John Gill (1697–1771), who wrote a theological commentary of Romans.[10] Next, we will focus atten-

---

[8] Vanhoozer and Treier, *Theology and the Mirror of Scripture*, 45.

[9] Ellen Charry, "Theology," in *Sanctified by Grace: A Theology of the Christian Life*, ed. Kent Eilers and Kyle C. Strobel (New York: Bloomsbury, 2014), 203–4.

[10] John Gill, *An Exposition of the Epistle of Paul the Apostle to the Romans*, The Newport Commentary Series (Springfield, MO: Particular Baptist Press, 2002); hereinafter, *Romans*.

tion on union with Christ, a central aspect of the Christian life. This doctrine is the power for and pattern of the transformed life. We will then offer our perspective on how Baptist followers of Christ understand what it means *to live for God*. Our emphasis will be on the dynamic synthesis of the individual's confession of Jesus's Lordship and the congregational commitment to walk together in corporate faithfulness, exemplified in classic Baptist distinctives and our tradition of covenantal membership. These features of a believer's church ecclesiology are frequently represented in the various Baptist church covenants, which articulate the responsibility of those in Christ to remain in the faith and to practice good works.

## Overview of the Doctrine of the Christian Life

Because of Baptists' commitment to the lordship of Christ over every person, his Word and its authority holds a central position in our knowledge of God and communicating our knowledge of him. Scripture is particularly principal to our understanding of sanctification, for in God's Word the people of God dwell with the One who sanctifies (John 17:16–19). We believe, by the Bible, the peace of Christ rules our hearts and the Word of Christ dwells richly in us (Col 3:15–16) and through it we are directed toward a life of obedience and conformity to Christ's character.

The doctrine of the Christian life, in short, is about the life of the redeemed, because God "rescued us from the domain of darkness and transferred us into the kingdom of the Son he loves" (Col 1:13). This doctrine explains the grace of God that rescues from sin and death (Rom 5:18–21), describes and guides the divinely enabled life given to God's people that they walk in it (2 Pet 1:3), and reminds God's children that they are to be holy as he, himself, is holy (1 Pet 1:16). We understand the Christian life to be an ongoing journey of holiness that is characterized by love for God and neighbor, a commitment to the body of Christ with emphasis on local congregations, the desire to mortify sin and cultivate godly virtues and the fruit of the Spirit, and obedience to the cultural commission to be fruitful and multiply, and the Great Commission to make disciples of all peoples.

Paul's epistle to the Romans explores the Christian life extensively and serves as a guide for Christian holy living, offering instructions, principles, and examples for the church to follow. Central to his exposition of the Christian identity and call to new life is the transformational truth that, in Christ, the reign of death has been defeated for Christians, and they live under the reign of life (Rom 5:12–21). Romans 12:1–2 functions as a hinge in the epistle, pivoting from the theological basis for the Christian life to practical instruction for living this life in one's contexts within the community of faith. These two verses emphasize the calling of Christians to present themselves wholly to the Lord and to his will as an act of worship, offering themselves as living sacrifices by the renewing of their minds.[11] Paul's instructions that follow these two verses focus on the way Christians live their new lives, contributing to the building up of the church (Rom 12:3–8) and reflecting the character of the redeemed (Rom 12:9–15:7) for the purpose of extending the mission of Christ (Rom 15:8–21). John Gill captures the function and the theological force of Rom 12:1–2 when he writes:

> The illative particle *therefore*, shows that the following exhortations are so many conclusions, consequences, and inferences, deduced from what had been said in the latter part of the preceding chapter; that since all things are of God, and by him and to him, then the saints ought to present their bodies to him, and to know, approve, and do his will and since they have nothing but

---

[11] Indeed, Gill describes the act of presenting as wholistic commitment to God. He explains, "themselves, their whole soul and bodies, all the powers and faculties of their souls, and members of their bodies; and the presenting of them, designs a devoting of them, with all readiness and willingness, to the service of God for his honor and glory, without putting any confidence in, or planning any dependence upon them." Gill, *Romans*, 457.

what they have received from him, they ought not to think too highly of, or glory in their attainments.[12]

What we find in the preceding passages, particularly Romans 5–8, that this exhortation is divinely enabled by the very life Christians have in Christ and through the transformative work of the Holy Spirit, enabling them to discern and follow God's will.[13]

## Divinely Enabled New Life

Paul provided a concise theological basis for the Rom 12:1–2 instruction in Rom 8:9–11. In these verses, he encapsulates all that God does within and through believers to enable them to live a new life in Christ. He accomplishes his divine purpose in them through life-giving grace, saying, "You, however, are not in the flesh, but in the Spirit, if indeed the Spirit of God lives in you" (Rom 8:9a). The Spirit's dwelling within believers allows them to partake in his life, experience his grace, and belong to him. John Gill captures the essence of this life: "to be possessed of him as one's own; to have communion with him, and to have him dwelling in us."[14] Paul reasons that the promise of this life is guaranteed by Jesus's resurrection (Rom 8:11). Romans 8:9 offers a commentary of sorts on Paul's words in Rom 5:5, where he assures that the believer's hope is a blessed hope because the Giver of life has been given to them. The life-giving Spirit guarantees this new reality for believers, as it is through the Spirit that we receive the life he imparts.

---

[12] Gill, 456.

[13] This is the mind renovation work that Paul exhorts the Ephesians Christians to engage in also, saying "be renewed in the spirit of your minds" (Eph 4:23). He excavates what this renewal looks like when he exhorts the church to put off the old self (which "is corrupted by deceitful desires," Eph 4:22) and to put on the new self (which is "created according to God's likeness in righteousness and purity of the truth," Eph 4:24). Compare to Rom 8:5–8.

[14] Gill, *Romans*, 255.

It is through the Spirit that Christ dwells in believers, even as he reigns in heaven at the right-hand of God the Father. Christ, having ascended to the right hand of the Father and representing believers there, dwells by his Spirit in those who were created slightly lower than the angels (Ps 8:5) that he might conform them to his own image (cf. Heb 2:5–10). Gill reflects on this mystery, "[It is] through the work of the Holy Spirit in regeneration, Christ enters and takes possession of believers' hearts, manifesting himself to them, communicating his grace, and granting them communion with him."[15] The gift of the Spirit is fitting, he reasons, "to our Lord's ascension and intercession, and to the love and grace of the Father; and this proves a man to be a regenerate man, to be in the Spirit, and not in the flesh; for the Spirit of God is never in this sense in an unregenerate man."[16]

The indwelling of the Spirit serves as a distinguishing characteristic of a regenerated person. He also fulfills his roles as a Comforter (John 14:26), a Spirit of adoption (Rom 8:15), and an intercessor (Rom 8:26–27), and he is present as a guarantee of the consummation of "the hope of the glory of God" (Rom 5:2; cf. v. 5). The Spirit illuminates (John 16:13–16), sanctifies (2 Cor 3:18), and empowers faith (1 Cor 12:3). The Spirit is personal, active, and effectual in the lives of believers. These divine works are appropriated to the Spirit, but he acts inseparable with the Father and the Son. Gill explains, "[The] inhabitation is personal; is not peculiar to him to the exclusion of the Father and of the Son; is expressive of property and dominion; is not confined to the souls of men, for he also dwells in their bodies; it is operative, powerful, and perpetual; it is the security of the saints' perseverance, and the pledge of their resurrection and future glory."[17]

When the Spirit dwells, he does so with his divine power and favor, and his presence is the seal of God's work in his people. "The Spirit," Gill

---

[15] Gill, 255.
[16] Gill, 254.
[17] Gill, 254.

writes, "is the grand evidence of relation to God, of an interest in Christ and union to him, and of a man's state and condition God-ward."[18]

The Spirit is the sign of the new covenant and the promise of eternal life, which is the hope and glory of humanity. While the body is subject to death due to sin, the Spirit provides life through righteousness (Rom 8:10). Gill interprets the reference to "spirit" in Rom 8:10 to be referring to the soul of humanity, as opposed to the physical body. He writes, "the soul of man is here meant, in opposition to the body, which is of a spiritual nature, immaterial and immortal . . . it lives a life of holiness from Christ, a life of faith upon Him, and a life of justification by Him, and we live eternally," and he stresses with this text, the wonderful transforming hope that the human soul does not perish with the body at physical death.[19] Alternatively, others interpret the reference in verse 10 to be the Holy Spirit. This understanding seems to be a stronger reading given the use of *pneuma* in Romans 8 refers to the Holy Spirit in every other instance, and Paul is declaring that the power of life results from the Holy Spirit.[20] Regardless of where one stakes their interpretive claim, the life that humanity possesses based on Jesus' righteousness is a gift from the Holy Spirit, and it no doubt has eschatological implications for the believer. It is also worth noting that Gill's interpretation limits the significance of the life promised in Rom 8:10 to an eschatological hope. In our view, the phrase "the Spirit is life" (Rom 8:6) offers hope in this life and in the life to come, for it empowers us to "put to death the deeds of the body" (Rom 8:13; cf. 1 Tim 4:8–9) and not "to fall back into fear" under the reign of death (Rom 8:15; cf. Rom 8:13, Heb 2:14–15).

---

[18] Gill, 254.

[19] Gill, 256–57.

[20] Douglas Moo, *The Epistle to the Romans*, The New International Commentary of the New Testament (Grand Rapids: Eerdmans, 1996), 491–92; Thomas R. Schreiner, *Romans*, Baker Exegetical Commentary of the New Testament (Grand Rapids: Baker, 1998), 415–16; and Leon Morris, *The Epistle to the Romans*, The Pillar New Testament Commentary (Grand Rapids: Eerdmans, 1997), 309.

Christians receive this life in regeneration, which ensures the ongoing work of the Spirit in our sanctification and culminates in our redemption through a glorified body after the resurrection of the saints. The divine mercies bestowed upon Christians through redemption in Jesus Christ do not grant permission for a life surrendered to the sinful nature (Rom 6:1–4). Rather, they call for a renewal of the mind, resulting in a departure from the patterns of the flesh (Rom 12:1–2; cf. 6:6–23; 8:5–11). The redemptive relationship between the new birth (Rom 8:1–4, 11), the eternal hope of glory (Rom 8:15–18), and a life consecrated for ongoing transformation (Rom 8:22–30) establishes how the people of God are set apart by him and for him (Rom 8:31–39). Through the process of sanctification, believers are progressively conformed to the likeness of Christ, growing in holiness and being transformed (2 Cor 3:18).

Paul establishes that God's ultimate purpose for humanity is Christocentric (Rom 8:28–30). God ordained that his people be conformed to the image of his Son. Gill's exposition of Rom 8:29 is worth quoting at length:

> God's elect indeed are chosen to be holy, and through the Sanctification of the Spirit, but are never said to be conformed, made like to the Spirit, nor is the Spirit ever called the image of Christ; but this designs either likeness to Christ as the Son, or conformity to him in his human nature. There is indeed a great disparity between the Sonship of Christ, and of the saints; he is the eternal and natural Son of God, he is the one and only begotten son, they are adopted ones, yet in some things there is a likeness; as he is the Son of God, so are they the sons of God, though not in the same sense; as he is a beloved son, so are they; as he is the firstborn with respect to them, they are the firstborn with respect to the angels; as he is an inheritance, so have they; moreover, he has a very great concern in their sonship; the predestination of them to it is by him; the blessing itself is founded on union to him, on their conjugal relation to him,

and his assumption of their nature; it comes to them through his redemption, and is actually bestowed on them by him; and this conformity to Christ as sons, will more fully appear hereafter, when they shall be like him, and see him as he is. Or this may be understood of the saints' conformity to Christ in his human nature, both here and hereafter. Here in holiness; the image of God was in man, in his first creation, this is defaced by sin; and in regeneration, the image of Christ is stamped, his grace is wrought in them, his spirit is put into them, to enable them to walk in him, and after him. This will be complete hereafter, and will consist in perfect holiness, being freed from the very being, as well as the power and guilt of sin; in perfect knowledge of everything that will tend to their happiness; and in glory like to Christ, both in soul and body.[21]

Gill reflects on the profound mystery that human beings may be conformed to the only begotten, eternal Son of God. He unearths in this passage the transforming role of the Spirit in the sanctification of the people of God, conforming them to the likeness of the Son, and he also shows how this reality is both an eternal one and a present one. He muses how, in Christ, the redeemed share in sonship with the eternal Son, become God's cherished people, regain their honor over all creation, and are heirs of God's divine blessings. While this is a work of Spirit, Gill emphasizes primarily the Christocentric nature of it. He says that the Son secures their election, that the transforming work is joined to the Son because he assumed human nature, and that redemption is his work for God's people. On this basis, Gill says in the present age, the redeemed should pursue conformity to the human nature of Christ by the Spirit—*walking in and after him.*

Speaking in a more pastoral manner, the great nineteenth-century Baptist pastor Charles Spurgeon argued that conformity to Christ's

---

[21] Gill, *Romans*, 289.

image entails at least six realities. First, our nature is conformed to Christ through regeneration. Just as our physical birth unites us with Adam, so our new birth unites us with Christ. Second, our actions are conformed to Christ when we obey his commands to do good, provide for those in need, care for one another, and proclaim the gospel to the spiritually lost. Third, our experience is conformed to Christ as we long more for personal holiness and grow increasingly uncomfortable with the world, the flesh, and the devil. Fourth, our character is conformed to Christ as our loves and our priorities increasingly reflect those of our Lord. Fifth, we are conformed to Christ in our inheritance, receiving by grace all the eternal blessings that belong to him by right. Finally, we are conformed to Christ in glory when our journey of holiness is complete.[22]

The idea of being conformed to Christ's image is common in contemporary discussions of sanctification and spiritual formation, sometimes serving as an organizing principle.[23] As we have seen in Rom 8:28–29, it has an important place in Paul's thought. Baptist biblical scholar Tom Schreiner notes the close connection in Paul's theology between Adam being created in God's image and Christ as the image of God (Rom 5:12–21). Those who were once united only with Adam by nature are restored to the fullness of God's image when, by grace and through faith, they are united with Christ. Our ongoing conformity to the image of Christ via sanctification fulfills God's intention for his human creatures and has been predestined for believers from before the foundation of the world (Rom 6:1–11, 22; 8:29).[24] The doctrine of sanctification reflects an

---

[22] Charles Spurgeon, "Glorious Predestination," a sermon on Rom 8:29 (March 24, 1872), in *The Metropolitan Tabernacle Pulpit*, vol. 18.

[23] For recent examples, see Ken Boa, *Conformed to His Image: Biblical, Practical Approaches to Spiritual Formation*, rev. ed. (Grand Rapids: Zondervan, 2020); Coleman M. Ford, *Formed in His Image: A Guide for Christian Formation* (Nashville: B&H, 2023); and Brian G. Hedges, *Christ Formed in You: The Power of the Gospel for Personal Change* (Wapwallopen, PA: Shepherd, 2010).

[24] Thomas R. Schreiner, *Paul: Apostle of God's Glory in Christ: A Pauline Theology*, 2nd ed. (Grand Rapids: Baker Academic, 2020), 161.

ongoing process of growth in holiness, made possible only by God's grace and the indwelling presence of the Holy Spirit.

## Be Holy as God is Holy

A justified sinner is not free to live her life in whatever manner she chooses. Justification through faith in Christ results in reconciliation with God and a life dedicated to his purposes. The divine act of justification brings with it the testimony of God's love in the giving of the Spirit of life (Rom 5:5) and transformation (2 Cor 3:18). The assurance of this hope is grounded in the guarantee that God's faithful love is displayed in the giving of Christ to die for sinners (Rom 5:8). These redemptive dynamics are predicated on being "justified by faith," having "peace with God" through the Lord Jesus Christ (v. 1). Justification is God's declaration that an individual's sins have been forgiven based on the righteousness of Christ and it is the basis for their relationship with God to be restored through faith in Christ. Through the justifying work of Christ, the people of God receive a position of grace before him (v. 2) and are reconciled to him (vv. 10–11). Paul explains in Rom 5:15–17 that the gift of grace is not like the inheritance of the sinful nature and its corruption. The gift of grace leads to justification (v. 16), as well as the rule and power of a new life in Christ (v. 17), which is the effect of regeneration (Rom 6:4, 11, 23). Thus, we find that the reality of justification in Romans 5 leads to the practice of Christian living.

This is the case because our sanctification lies in God's redemptive act to justify those who believe in the Lord Jesus Christ. This is the reason that Paul concludes Christ is our sanctification (1 Cor 1:30). This line of thinking is consistent throughout Paul's letters. One example may be found in the common indicative/imperative framework in his letters where God's soteriological gifts are explained and are then followed by ethical instructions, which are grounded in God's work of redemption (e.g. Romans 1–11 then Romans 12–15; Ephesians 1–3 then Ephesians 4–6; Col 1–2:5 then Col 2:6–4; cf. Rom 6:12–14, 18–19; 1 Cor 5:7;

Gal 5:16–24; Phil 2:1–18). Paul's letter to the church in Galatia carries the same argument. He establishes that those who are justified by the grace of the Lord Jesus Christ through faith are enabled and expected to walk according to the Spirit, because by being justified, they have participated in new life in the Spirit. Jarvis Williams has summarized the force of Paul's argument. He writes:

> Since God has acted to deliver in Christ the justified ones in Galatia from the present evil age and from the curse of the law so that they would have the Spirit (Gal 1:4; 3:13–14; 4:5–6), the Galatians much conduct their everyday rhythms of life in step with the way of the Spirit in order to inherit the kingdom of God (Gal 5:16–6:10; esp. 5:21), for they received life by the Spirit when they crucified the flesh with its passion and desires at the moment of participating in God's saving action in Christ by faith (Gal 5:24–25; cf. 2:19–21).[25]

The possibility of the Christian life arises from God's love and mercy, who through the grace of the Lord Jesus Christ, shared his life with his redeemed children. The grace of God is indistinguishable from Jesus (Rom 5:15; Titus 2:11) and his redeeming work (Rom 5:16–17). This grace regenerates and gives new life (Rom 7:6). The life is given by the Spirit and through union with Christ (Rom 6:4; 7:4). This is the wonder of the gospel, that the children of God can live the resurrected life of Christ in the present, because he has hidden them in his own body through the Spirit to apply his life, death, resurrection and even ascension in the lives of his people (Col 1:27; 2:11–15; 3:1–4).[26]

Paul argues in Romans 3–5 that regardless of one's religious or ethnic background, all individuals are under the power of sin and stand

---

[25] Jarvis J. Williams, *The Spirit, Ethics, and Eternal Life: Paul's Vision for the Christian Life in Galatians* (Downers Grove, IL: IVP Academic, 2023), 173.

[26] For extensive development of these themes, see G. K. Beale, *Union with the Resurrected Christ: Eschatological New Creation and New Testament Biblical Theology* (Grand Rapids: Baker Academic, 2023).

condemned before God. He emphasizes that no human can attain righteousness through personal efforts or obedience to religious laws, as these laws reveal humanity's fallen nature and inclination to sin. He stresses that religious practices or personal works cannot bring about this justification; it can only be achieved through faith in Jesus Christ. The Law was not provided as a basis for justification (Rom 3:20). Yes, Paul says in Rom 2:13 that those who obey the Law will be justified, but the point of his argument in that passage was to establish that God does not favor Jewish people over the Gentiles merely because they had received the Law of God given through Moses (cf. Rom 3:9). Indeed, the working assumption in the passage is that the Jewish people are transgressors of the Law and not perfect keepers of it. Paul then goes on to clarify that the Law was given to highlight humanity's need for a Savior (Rom 3:19), to increase awareness of sin (Rom 7:7), and to guide people toward faith in Christ (Rom 3:27–31; cf. 4:13–16, 7:21–25). He proclaims that where sin abounds, God's grace abounds even more, showcasing the overwhelming power and sufficiency of God's grace in overcoming sin and providing justification for believers, because righteousness is obtained "through faith in Jesus Christ for all who believe" (Rom 3:22), independent of adherence to the Law.

Justification, therefore, is available to all individuals, regardless of their religious or ethnic background. As Paul declares, "Yes, [God] of Gentiles also, since God is one—who will justify the circumcised by faith and the uncircumcised through faith" (Rom 3:29–20). To illustrate the reality of saving faith, Paul references the example of Abraham in chapter 4, underscoring how Abraham's belief in God's promises resulted in his justification. In this, Abraham's faith serves as a model for all believers, highlighting the importance of trusting in God's redemptive plan for people from all nations. Justification leads to reconciliation with God, peace, and eternal life (Romans 5).

In Rom 6:1, Paul anticipates that some may conclude that it is advisable to continue sinning so that they may continue to receive grace in abundance (cf. Rom 5:20–21). Paul established in these verses the triumph of life in Christ over the reign of death from Adam. He says the grace of God increases even more when sin increases. His response to such a potential inference was an unequivocal *no*. The basis for this clear answer is that the forgiveness of sin is received in union with Christ, and being united with him means one shares in his death to sin and resurrection to new life, raised to new life with the Father (Rom 6:8–10). Thus, the people of God should *"be holy, for I the Lord your God am holy"* (Lev 19:2, 20:7, 20:26, 21:8; 1 Pet 1:16; cf. Exod 19:6, 1 Thess 4:7).

As we have already seen from our survey of Romans 8, the role of the Holy Spirit in sanctification is foundational. The Holy Spirit regenerates, granting life-giving grace, and he acts within believers to produce holiness and conform them to the image of Christ. The Spirit uses various means, such as the Word of God, prayer, and the sacraments, to sanctify believers and enable them to live a life that is pleasing to God. Thus, Gill concludes, "believers should be desirous of, and pray for, and make use of, those means which the Spirit of God owns for this purpose, attending to the spiritual exercises of religion, as reading, meditation, prayer, conference, and the ministration of the Word and ordinances, which is the reverse of conformity to the world."[27] Prayer and dependence on the Holy Spirit are vital components in the Baptist understanding of sanctification. Through prayer, believers seek the power and guidance of the Holy Spirit, who enables them to live godly lives and grow in holiness, for as Prov 16:9 warns, "A person's heart plans his way." We are enticed to follow what is in our minds according to the flesh (Rom 8:5–8; cf. 1 John 2:15–17). For this reason, Christians are exhorted to no longer be conformed to the ways of the world and be transformed by renewing our mind in the Spirit (Rom 12:1–2; cf. 8:6, Eph 4:20–24). These practices may be pursued because we have received new hearts, no longer living under reign of death and the law and living under the reign of life and grace in Christ and with his mind (Phil 2:5–11). The

---

[27] Gill, *Romans*, 459.

Spirit uses the Scriptures to help us see who Jesus is (Eph 5:18–21; Col 3:14–17). The Holy Spirit illuminates believers' hearts and minds, allowing us to know and love Christ more deeply (Eph 3:14–21). This knowledge and love manifest in obedience to God's will and the transformation of our character, as we actively seek to put on the mind of Christ (Phil 1:9–11; 2:1–13).

Paul states in Rom 8:13 that those who live according to the flesh will die, but by the Spirit, believers put to death the misdeeds of the body and live. Believers depend on the Spirit's empowerment to overcome the deeds of the flesh. Consequently, those who are in the flesh are unable to please God (v. 8). Genuine pleasing of God occurs through the new life believers have received from being in union with Christ by the Spirit. Being "in the Spirit" signifies being in a realm of grace that gives life, no longer under the dominion of sin leading to death (see Rom 5:2, 12–21). Without this life in the Spirit, religious activities such as prayer, worship, giving, obedience to God's commands, and following his instructions do not please him, because they were not performed by the favor of divine grace, power of divine strength, wisdom gained by Christ dwelling in one's heart by faith (Eph 3:17), and right ends that endure with hope in glory that outshines any fleeting, temporary afflictions we may face in this life (Rom 8:18).

Sanctification is ultimately the work of God from the beginning to the end (2 Cor 3:18; Phil 1:6; 1 Pet 1:3–21). People of God, however, are also held responsible for their sanctification (1 Pet 1:22–2:3). In his letter to the church in Philippi, Paul emphasized the need for believers to participate actively with the Holy Spirit's work in their lives (Phil 2:12). In Rom 8:13, he says something similar: "if by the Spirit you put to death the deeds of the body, you will live." This involves the believer's ongoing pursuit of holiness, obedience to God's commands, and the cultivation of spiritual disciplines. Gill writes, "in the mortification here spoken of the saints are active, under the influence of the Spirit of God; besides, regeneration is done at once, and does not admit of degrees; and in and by that, sin, as to its being and principle, is so far from being destroyed, that it seems rather to revive in the sense and apprehension of regenerated person."[28]

Believers must view themselves from two perspectives: what they once were *apart from* the life of Christ and who they are now *in* Christ. Under the reign of death, in Adam, we are under condemnation (Rom 6:23) and unable to do anything to please God (Rom 7:18). However, in Christ, we live a new life under the reign of grace and empowered by His Spirit. This life is marked by forgiveness of sin and justification, freedom from being enslaved to sin and sanctification, and hope of eternity from groaning to glorification. In the ultimate state of glory, believers will be finally conformed to the image of Christ. Even then, we remain aware of who we became through his grace and who we would have been without it. But, until then, in Gill's words, we must live, "subduing and weakening the vigor and power of sin in the lives and conversations of the saints, to which the grace and assistance of the Spirit are absolutely necessary; and such who are enabled to do so, shall live comfortably; they shall have communion with Christ here, and shall live a life of glory with him hereafter."[29]

The Holy Spirit's transformative influence is indispensable in the believer's journey, enabling them to mirror Christ's character. This process of sanctification encompasses both internal and external aspects, involving a renewal of the mind and leading to righteous actions.[30] On an internal level, sanctification involves our patterns of thinking, affections, and wills, resulting in a profound transformation of their desires and motives. This inward process is initiated by the redeeming work of Jesus Christ and facilitated by the indwelling presence of the Holy Spirit. Through the sanctifying work of the Holy Spirit, believers are empowered to increasingly align their thoughts, emotions, and choices

---

[28] Gill, 260.

[29] Gill, 261.

[30] See Andrew M. Davis, *An Infinite Journey: Growing Toward Christlikeness* (Greenville, SC: Ambassador International, 2013).

with God's truth and will. The internal aspect of sanctification entails a lifelong journey of growth and maturation, as believers continually submit their minds and hearts to the transformative power of God's Word and Spirit.

The believer's sanctification also finds expression in outward actions and behaviors. The transformed heart and mind of a believer should naturally lead to righteous conduct and obedience to God's moral commands. This external aspect of sanctification involves living a life that reflects the character of Christ and seeks to honor God in all areas of life. This transformation extends to every aspect of believers' lives, including our thoughts, attitudes, desires, and actions. It is a continuous journey of surrender and dependence on God's grace, as believers cooperate with the Holy Spirit's work in our lives. We pursue sanctifying work by responding to God's purpose to set his people apart for himself and participate in the ongoing work of transformation that he accomplishes in their lives (Phil 2:12–13).

By imparting his Spirit to us, God invites us to partake in his divine life and power through the resurrected life we live (John 8:51–52; 11:25–26; Eph 1:19–20; Col 3:1–4).[31] In his second epistle, Peter picks up the themes "divine power" and "partakers of the divine life" to exhort the pursuit of a godly life (2 Pet 1:3). His insights resonate with Paul's insights in Romans 5 and 8. Both proclaim that God has done for us everything that's needed for us to live for him, and both provide instruction for us "to work out our salvation" (Phil 2:12). Second Peter 1:5–7 sets forth an ongoing and deepening pattern of Christian formation that trains us to live the new life through the power of the Spirit: faith enriched with virtue, virtue enriched with knowledge, knowledge enriched with discipline, discipline enriched with faithfulness, faithfulness enriched with godliness, godliness enriched with affection for one another, and affection enriched with abiding love. This pattern of formation must be practiced in the context of the believing community. How else is affection and love

---

[31] See Beale, *Union with the Resurrected Christ.*

for one another enriched and increased? Further, this instruction is provided to help the members of the church to endure together in the face of false teachers (cf. 2 Pet. 2:1–3; 3:1–3).

Paul also describes the dynamic of Christian formation that is reminiscent of 2 Peter 1. He says the Christian pattern is to "rejoice" in the distresses of life because of confidence in God's transformative work to establish in his people the hope of glory (Rom 5:2) that is secured by his divine love. The fruit of hope emerges from the endurance required to face suffering and character that emerges through long suffering (Rom 5:3–4).

The exhortation to renew one's mind calls the people of God to participate in God's sanctifying work in their lives (Rom 12:1; Eph 4:23). The possibility of transformation in the lives of God's people is a testimony to the new covenant promise that the Law will be written on the heart and the people of God will be able, with unveiled faces, to see the glory of God in Christ and be transformed by the Spirit (2 Cor 3:18; cf. Jer 31:31–34). Thus, the "righteous requirement of the Law" (Rom 8:3) can be fulfilled for those who have put on Christ in their baptism, for they have been freed from sin and death to fulfill the Law in love (Rom 13:8–10; cf. Gal 5:6b–15).

## Union with Christ and Sanctification

The doctrine of union with Christ is central to the Christian life. Union with Christ signifies the spiritual reality brought about by the indwelling of the Holy Spirit, wherein the people of God reside within Christ. In Romans 6, Paul establishes there is no life apart from Christ, stating, "For the wages of sin is death, but the gift of God is eternal life in Christ Jesus our Lord" (Rom 6:23). To partake in the benefits of Christ's sacrifice, he must become ours and dwell within us. John Calvin elucidates the crucial nature of this truth, asserting that as long as Christ remains external to us, and we are separated from him, his redemptive work is ineffectual.[32] Grounded in this truth, believers are joined to the Son of God, making what is true of him equally true of them. In Christ, believers are chosen, called, regenerated, justified, sanctified, redeemed, and share in every spiritual blessing (Eph 1:4, 7; Rom 6:5; 8:1; 2 Cor 5:17; Eph 1:3). Union with Christ is a soteriological reality that transcends space and time, forming our identity and relationship with God in Christ. Paul proclaims that Christians have died with Christ (Rom 6:1–11; Gal 2:20), been resurrected with him (Eph 2:5–6; Col 3:1), and have ascended with him in his heavenly reign (Rom 5:17; Eph 2:6). Furthermore, Christians will share in Christ's glory when he returns (Phil 3:20ff; 1 John 3:2).

Romans 6 follows Paul's contrasting exposition, where he vividly depicts the effects of humanity's existence either "in Adam" under the dominion of death or "in Christ" under the reign of life and grace. The overarching narrative underscores how the harmonious life that Adam once shared with God in the Garden of Eden disintegrated into death due to sin. This state of death and sin extended from Adam to all humanity, ensnaring them as instruments of sin's power (Rom 6:13) and compelling them into servitude to sin (Rom 6:14, 17, 20). But through one man, Jesus, the rule of death is undone, because his life defeated it for those who place their faith in Him. Paul summarizes Christ's overcoming work in Rom 8:2–4:

> The law of the Spirit of life in Christ Jesus has set you free from the law of sin and death. For what the law could not do since it was weakened by the flesh, God did. He condemned sin in the flesh by sending his own Son in the likeness of sinful flesh as a sin offering, in order that the law's requirement would be fulfilled in us who do not walk according to the flesh but according to the Spirit.

---

[32] John Calvin, *The Institutes of the Christian Religion*, ed. John T. McNeill and trans. Ford Lewis Battles, Library of Christian Classics, vols. 20–21 (Philadelphia: Westminster Press, 1960), III.I.1.

In Romans 6, he explains that the victory of life comes through the life of Christ, and we possess his life by being united to him by grace through faith. Through union with him, we have forgiveness of sin and are justified. Paul appeals to the sign of the new covenant, baptism, to explain the spiritual reality of our union with Christ. Describing the union through the ordinances of baptism, Gill says it resembles "Christ in his suffering and death, by being immersed in water"; moreover, through baptism, believers "declare their faith in the death of Christ, and also share in the benefits of his death—such as peace, pardon, righteousness, and atonement."[33] To be baptized into Christ demonstrates "affection for him, and subjection to Him, without any stress of dependence on it for salvation."[34] The act of baptism is not an act by which we depend upon it for salvation, for "such who are thus baptized, are baptized into his death." Through his death, those who are baptized as a sign of their faith in Christ "are justified from sin; but by the death of Christ, their old man is crucified, and the body of sin destroyed; besides, believers in baptism profess themselves to be dead to sin and the world, and their baptism is an obligation upon them to live unto righteousness."[35]

Baptism represents the believer's identification with Christ's death, burial, and resurrection. Paul's illusion to this practice emphasizes that through identifying with Christ in this way, churches declare the mystery of Christ dwelling in his people. On the basis of this union, followers of Christ experience the transformative power of his resurrection, resulting in a new life characterized by sanctification. The crucified and risen Savior, Jesus Christ, becomes the focal point of the believer's union with him, as evidenced in Rom 6:8–10. Christ's crucifixion signifies his triumph over sin, while his resurrection represents the defeat of sin and death, granting him dominion over both. It is in the Last Adam, Jesus Christ (Rom 5:12–21), that life is restored, where death reigned

---

[33] Gill, *Romans*, 169.
[34] Gill, 169.
[35] Gill, 169.

in Adam. Thus, we recalled our baptismal confession as a covenantal symbol whereby we appealed "for a good conscience, through the resurrection of Jesus Christ, who has gone into heaven and is at the right of God, with angels, authorities, and powers having been subjected to him" (1 Pet 3:21–22 ESV).

For Baptists, it is by the Spirit *alone* through his regenerating and redeeming work that one becomes identified *in any sense* with the body of Christ, which is manifested in our identification (through baptism) and participation (through communion) with a local, visible gathering of the church. The believing community comprises the people of God who, through the grace of "God, the Giver of life," are united with Christ and form a sacred congregation. The "one, holy, catholic, apostolic" nature of the church reflects the intimate connection between God's people and God Himself.[36] The life bestowed upon us by the Spirit is not an isolated or abstract gift; rather, it is the very life of the Father, Son, and Holy Spirit. In this union, God selflessly gives himself to his people, offering through his own life regeneration, forgiveness of sins, and transformation. Through the illuminating work of the Spirit, we come to comprehend the depth of God's love (Rom 5:5) as he reveals to us the glory of God in Christ (2 Cor 4:4, 3:18, cf. John 15:26), and we come to understand our calling to live for God (Rom 6:22–23). Baptism establishes and orients the Christian life, teaching the regenerate the pattern of their new life. "Regenerate life in Christ," Webster explains, "is not simply a received and completed condition, but a summons actively to reiterate the death of the old nature and to perform the new, to die and rise again not only one for all but also continually."[37]

Paul declares that the old self is put to death with Christ, enabling the believer to overcome the body of sin and its enslavement. Consequently,

---

[36] "One, holy, catholic, apostolic" is from the Nicene Creed.

[37] John Webster, "Mortification and Vivification," in *God Without Measure: Working Papers in Christian Theology*, vol. 2, *Virtue and Intellect* (New York: Bloomsbury T&T Clark, 2016), 104.

the believer is no longer a slave to sin since dying with Christ also entails being resurrected and living with Him. Paul's reasoning in Romans 6 is plain, highlighting the redemptive reality and the transformative power of the gospel. The claim of liberation from sin and its power is firmly established in the indicative mood, as he affirms that "a person who has died is freed from sin" (Rom 6:7). Christ's submission to death also entails subjecting himself to the reign of sin. By dying to sin, Christ transcended its dominion over him. It is crucial to bear in mind that Paul perceives Christ's resurrection as His deliverance, vindication, and justification from the reign of sin in death (1 Tim 3:16), further illuminating his line of thought.

Paul's primary aim is to demonstrate that the reign of grace in Romans 5 signifies the end of sin's power and authority over those who have put on Christ in their baptism, granting freedom to live in righteousness under the Lordship of Christ (Rom 6:18). Through our union with him, believers are liberated from the dominion and guilt of sin and are empowered to resist its practice. Paul adamantly declares, "Sin shall not rule over you" (Rom 6:14). The concept of "death to sin" not only signifies deliverance from sin's dominion but also serves as a fundamental and universal principle of sanctification for every Christian. This truth is so integral to the Christian experience that it practically defines what it means to be a Christian. Believers are called to live as those who are under grace because they are in the union with Christ; "For the wages of sin is death, but the gift of God is eternal life in Christ Jesus *our Lord*" (Rom 6:23, italics added).

This does not mean that we are incapable of committing sin (cf. Rom 6:12–23; 1 John 1:8–10). Indeed, we continue to sin, and we can even become accustomed to sinning again, as personal experience tends in such a bewildering way to eclipse our awareness of the new reality in Christ that we possess, under the reign of grace. Gill describes this twisted dynamic, "after conversion [sin] is still in them, and has great power oftentimes to hinder that which is good, and to effect that which is evil; it entices and ensnares, and brings into captivity, and seems as though it would regain its dominion, and reign again."[38]

Sanctification is rooted in what God has done in Christ. In light of God's grace in Christ, Paul calls us to obedience and imitation of Christ (Rom 6:11–14). His logic follows that because the believer is in Christ, everything that belongs to him belongs to them and everything that he has done to accomplish redemption is for them. Thus, conformity to Christ's image should be the animating desire of our lives, which is why Paul stresses how crucial it is to know one's new status in Christ (Rom 6:3, 6, and 9). Based on this awareness, he instructs believers to consider themselves to be dead to sin and to be alive to God in Christ Jesus (Rom 6:11). Indeed, Paul calls believers to come to terms with the reality that "sin is dethroned; Christ enters as Lord, and . . . saints are in another kingdom, the kingdom of Christ and grace."[39] Sin is not too strong for those in Christ. Gill says, "the apostles declare it as a promise of grace, that sin shall not have the dominion . . . giving this as a reason, because such as are justified and sanctified, are not under the law, as a covenant of works, but under the covenant of grace, of which this promise is part."[40]

The essence of holiness is that we would possess the transforming love that fulfills the first and second great commandments (Matt 22:37–40), for God is love (1 John 4:8). In Romans 8, Paul declares there is no condemnation for those who are in union with Christ (Rom 8:1), because he took on humanity and defeated the enemies that reign over those who are in the flesh—sin and death (Rom 8:2–3). This work, he accomplished so that the "righteous requirements of the law might be fulfilled" in those who walk in the Spirit that brings children of God into communion with the Son of God (Rom 8:4 ESV). The righteous requirement of the law is the law of love (Rom 13:8–10). Thus, we are

---

[38] Gill, *Romans*, 181.
[39] Gill, 181.
[40] Gill, 181.

called to "put on the Lord Jesus Christ, and make no provision for the flesh to gratify its desires" (Rom 13:14). Paul prays in Eph 3:19 that we would walk in this new life by knowing the love of Christ and, by it, "be filled with all the fullness of God."

The eternal love between the Father and his beloved Son becomes known to us as the Spirit opens our eyes, regenerates our hearts, and fills us with love for God, leading us to obedience (1 Pet 1:2, 8; cf. Eph 3:16–17). Our love for the Son echoes the Father's love for the Son. Through the enlightenment of the Spirit, we not only come to know and love Christ, but we are also guided and empowered to have the mind of the One with whom we are in union—the Lord Jesus Christ (Phil 2:5)—to know him and become more like him. In Christ, we find encouragement, comfort, and the privilege of participating in the Spirit (Phil 2:1), and, through Christ, we are to take on His mind, doing "nothing out of selfish ambition or conceit, but in humility consider[ing] others as more important than yourselves" (Phil 2:3).

## Baptists and Sanctification

Most of what Baptists believe about the Christian life is shaped by the great tradition and refined through the Reformation. Contemporary Baptists have also inherited the evangelical emphases that brought significant renewal to the Baptist movement in the eighteenth century. There are no uniquely Baptist understandings of justification, union with Christ, the indwelling of the Holy Spirit, or even the progressive nature of sanctification. However, the Baptist "voice" on these doctrines is shaped by our unique Baptistic experiences. What characterizes a Baptist view of the Christian life is linked to the doctrine of the believer's church. By that, we mean a distinct emphasis on both the individual believer as a follower of King Jesus and the community of disciples who walk together under his Lordship. For Baptists, the personal confession that Jesus is Lord, demonstrated publicly through baptism, is lived out within the local church, formed by covenant with God and one another.

The London Baptist Confession of 1644 defined the believer's church in terms of a two-fold covenant: "a company of visible saints . . . joyned [sic] to the Lord and each other by mutual agreement."[41] We live in the reality of the new covenant as the fulfillment of the old covenant promises, and because of that, we live in covenant fellowship with God and one another.[42] As the Congregationalist theologian P. T. Forsyth observed, *"the same act which set us in Christ sets us also in the society of Christ."*[43] The London Confession 1644 describes this society as those who live under the covenant blessing of God and live out those blessings with one another.

> To this Church he hath made his promises, and given the signes [*sic*] of his Covenant, presence, love, blessing, and protection:

---

[41] The London Confession, article 33, in William L. Lumpkin, *Baptist Confession of Faith*, rev. ed. (Valley Forge, PA: Judson, 1969), 165. The confession follows John Smyth's earlier definition of the church. He wrote, "A visible communion of saints is two, three, or more saints joined together by covenant with God and themselves, freely to use all the holy things of God, according to the Word, for their mutual edification and God's glory." See John Smyth, "Principles and Inferences concerning the Visible Church," in *The Works of John Smyth*, ed. by W. T. Whitley (Cambridge: Cambridge University Press, 1915), 252. On the basis of this covenantal reality of the believer's church, Malcolm Yarnell argues it provides the basis for a free church dogmatics. He writes, "free church dogmatics is characterized by a dynamic dialectic between communal covenant and liberty of conscience where Christ is present to his people with blessings." See Malcolm Yarnell, "The Free Church Form of Dogmatics: Covenant and Conscience Under Christ," *STR* 14/1 (2023), 115–29.

[42] Gregg R. Allison rightly distinguishes this new covenant reality with a foundational theological and a necessary ecclesiological referent from a covenantal conception with the term "conversionistic covenantalism." See Gregg R. Allison, *Sojourners and Strangers: The Doctrine of the Church* (Wheaton, IL: Crossway, 2012), 128.

[43] P. T. Forsyth, *The Church, the Gospel, and Society* (London: Independent Press, 1962), 61 (emphasis original).

here are the fountain and springs of his heavenly grace continually flowing forth; thither ought all men to come, of all estates,
that acknowledge him to be their Prophet, Priest, and King, to
be inrolled [sic] amongst his household servants, to be under
his heavenly conduct and government, to lead their lives in his
walled sheepfold and watered garden, to have communion here
with the Saints, that they may be made to be partakers of their
inheritance in the Kingdome [sic] of God.[44]

And all his servants are called thither, to present their bodies
and soules, [sic] and to bring their gifts God hath given them;
so being come, they are here by himself bestowed in their several order, peculiar place, due use, be fittingly compact and knit
together, according to the effectuall [sic] working of every part,
to the edification of it selfe [sic] in love.[45]

The ongoing process of sanctification entails an increasing knowledge of God's love and a deeper participation in his divine life. It is a lifelong journey of faith and maturity, wherein believers actively cooperate
with the work of the Holy Spirit within their covenant community. The
articles in the London Confession 1644 move from acknowledging the
spiritual battle of all Christians to remain steadfast, confessing assurance
in Christ's kingly power to enable his children to endure (article 32), to
explaining the role of the church in Christ's sanctifying and preserving
grace for his people (articles 33–46). This body is joined to Christ as
its head and operates under his Lordship, for this body is comprised of
members who are united to him in Baptism (article 40).

Several doctrines inform the Baptist dynamic of the individual-in-
community. These so-called Baptist distinctives include the supreme
authority of Scripture, liberty of conscience, believer-only baptism,

---

[44] The London Confession, article 34, in Lumpkin, *Baptist Confession of Faith*, 166.
[45] The London Confession, article 35, in Lumpkin, 166.

regenerate church membership, congregational polity, local church autonomy, and the priority of Christian mission.[46] Each of these distinctives captures the dynamic interplay between the disciple as a personal follower of Jesus and his or her place in a community of disciples that is committed to following Jesus corporately. Taken together, these distinctives evidence a covenantal ecclesiology that has characterized the Baptist movement from its earliest days.[47]

Because of this covenant ecclesiology, Baptists emphasize the communal nature of the Christian life, highlighting the essence of the church as a believing community and the covenantal dimensions of sanctification. Baptists believe Jesus is Lord of every disciple and, just as important, every local congregation, which is a community of disciples. Within the context of a Christian community, believers find a place for growth, encouragement, and the practice of spiritual disciplines that provides the locus for the working out of one's faith and the process of sanctification. Baptist spirituality is marked by a decidedly ecclesial character.[48] This characteristic of the Baptist way for Christian living was set forth in

---

[46] For more on the Baptist distinctives, see John A. Broadus, *The Duty of Baptists to Teach Their Distinctive Views* (Philadelphia: American Baptist Publication Society, 1881); Charles W. DeWeese, *Defining Baptist Convictions: Guidelines for the Twenty-First Century* (Nashville: Providence House, 1996); R. Stanton Norman, *The Baptist Way: Distinctives of a Baptist Church* (Nashville: B&H Academic, 2005); Stephen R. Holmes, *Baptist Theology* (London: T&T Clark, 2012); Anthony L. Chute, Nathan A. Finn, and Michael A.G. Haykin, *The Baptist Story: From English Sect to Global Movement* (Nashville: B&H Academic, 2012), 325–45.

[47] For more on Baptist covenantal ecclesiology, see Paul S. Fiddes, *Tracks and Traces: Baptist Identity in Church and Theology, Studies in Baptist History and Thought* (Milton Keynes, UK: Paternoster, 2003), 21–47; Nigel G. Wright, *Free Church, Free State: The Positive Baptist Vision* (Milton Keynes, UK: Paternoster, 2005), 49–69; Jason K. Lee, "Baptism and Covenant," in *Restoring Integrity in Baptist Churches*, eds. Thomas White, Jason G. Duesing, and Malcolm B. Yarnell III (Grand Rapids: Kregel Academic, 2008), 119–36; Hammett, *Biblical Foundations for Baptist Churches*, 125–29.

[48] Nathan A. Finn, "Contours of a Healthy Baptist Spirituality," *Criswell Theological Review* 12.1 (Fall 2014): 18.

early Baptist covenants. The covenant that Benjamin Keach and his son, Elias, drafted called church members to commit to one another "in a holy union and fellowship."[49]

Regenerate church membership has been called "the Baptist mark of the church" because of the central role it plays in Baptist identity.[50] By definition, a regenerate church emphasizes the transformative work of the Holy Spirit in the lives of believers. Through the teaching of Scripture, prayer, dependence on the Holy Spirit, and the Christian community, Baptists practice sanctification as a lifelong journey of faith, obedience, and conformity to the image of Christ. Understanding and engaging with the Baptist perspective on sanctification provides valuable insights into the implications of this doctrine for all baptistic Christians committed to the believers' church.[51]

For Baptists, doctrine is known and experienced in the context of a particular community—a community that shares the one Lord, faith, and baptism of the church universal, but engages and holds forth the confession to one Lord as a regenerate body, as the epistemological ground of knowledge over and above even his eternal and covenantal promises. We know the one Lord and the one faith through the personal and decisive experience of conversion sealed by a baptism that signals one's union with the king, Jesus Christ, by grace and through faith. This reality shapes the identity of the believer's church, as exiles who walk together, testifying as

---

[49] Charles Deweese, *Baptist Church Covenants* (Nashville: Broadman, 1990), 120–21.

[50] John S. Hammett, *Biblical Foundations for Baptist Churches: A Contemporary Ecclesiology*, 2nd ed. (Grand Rapids: Kregel Academic, 2019), 91–116.

[51] James Leo Garrett and James Wm. McClendon have been especially influential in advancing the belief that a believers' church is central to a wider baptistic tradition that extends beyond self-confessed Baptists. See Paul Basden and David S. Dockery, eds., *The People of God: Essays on the Believers' Church* (Nashville: Broadman, 1991), which is a *festschrift* for Garrett; and Ryan Andrew Newson and Andrew C. Wright, eds., *The Collected Works of James Wm. McClendon*, 3 vols. (Waco, TX: Baylor University Press, 2014–2016), especially volumes 1 and 3.

people of grace, remembering their baptism and appealing to God with a clean conscious on the basis of the promise he made to them in the new covenant (1 Pet 3:21–22).

We receive, through the testimony of the church, the steadfast confession of faith that Jesus entrusted to the apostles, and which they, in turn, proclaimed to the Spirit-filled body of believers who confess, and continue to confess, Jesus according to the Scriptures. This deposit of faith now resides within the church as the "pillar and foundation of the truth" (1 Tim 3:15), expressed through the church's teachings, practices, and covenantal fellowship among its members. As a result, the local church is properly the ground and the goal of Baptist dogmatic reflection. It is the body of Christ, composed of Christ's people, who experience union with Christ, under the rule of Christ, advancing God's mission in obedience to Christ, empowered by the Spirit of Christ. For Baptists, local churches are expressions of the one universal church, established according to the faith and practices outlined in the New Testament, serving as embassies of Christ's kingdom.[52]

Within the context of the community, the believer grows in godliness through the means of grace commanded by Christ in Scripture or consistent with those commands. These means of grace, also known as spiritual disciplines, can be practiced individually or collectively, or both. The Holy Spirit employs personal disciplines to shape believers into the likeness of Christ, progressively revealing God's covenantal grace. Likewise, the Holy Spirit employs corporate disciplines to shape communities of disciples, guiding them toward Christ-like character and advancing the expression of this grace. The personal and corporate aspects of discipleship have a dialectical relationship, mutually reinforcing one another. The mortification of sin, pursuit of holiness, cultivation of virtue as evidenced by the fruit of the Spirit, and obedience to

---

[52] For more on the theme of local churches as kingdom embassies, see Jonathan Leeman, *Political Church: The Local Assembly as Embassy of Christ's Rule* (Downers Grove, IL: IVP Academic, 2016).

the Great Commission form an ongoing rhythm in the life of believers within the community.[53]

The salvation of the believer is grounded in God's eternal covenant of grace, based on the high priest with "an indestructible life" (Heb 7:15–22). The local church represents a communal expression of this same covenantal grace. Thus, our High Priest prayed that his people may be one even as he is one with his Father (John 17:21). For Baptists, particular churches are covenantal communities wherein members pledge their allegiance to Christ through baptism and to one another through membership. In the Lord's Supper, as we commemorate the death of Christ (1 Cor 11:24) and acknowledge his real presence in the church (Matt 18:20), these commitments are reaffirmed (1 Cor 11:29). Thus, particular churches become sanctified communities in which the Spirit enables growth in godliness and faithfulness in mission.

Baptists emphasize the presence of Christ within both individuals and the community, known through Scripture and experienced in the Spirit. The church affirms Christ's presence within its body, confessing this truth to one another and to the world, empowered by the Holy Spirit and in alignment with the Father's good purposes. This confession of hope, directed both internally and externally, purifies the church. Among ourselves, as we walk in the light as he is in the light (1 John 1:7), we confess the eschatological hope that the One within us is greater than the one in the world (1 John 4:4), believing that he will return for his Bride, and we will finally be transformed to be like him (1 John 3:2). In this communal confession, we strive together to keep his Word, and in doing so, we experience the transformative effect of God's love among us (1 John 2:5).

---

[53] While many within the wider spiritual formation movement note the distinction between personal and corporate disciplines, two works that exemplify the importance of the latter are Donald S. Whitney, *Spiritual Disciplines within the Church: Participating Fully in the Body of Christ* (Chicago: Moody, 1996), and James C. Wilhoit, *Spiritual Formation as if the Church Mattered: Growing in Christ through Community*, 2nd ed. (Grand Rapids: Baker Academic, 2022).

When we confess Christ to the world, we do so because we hold him as holy in our hearts, and are emboldened by the secure promises of the blessed hope we have in him (1 Pet 3:15). As a kingdom of priests, we engage in this confession, inviting people to test our testimony by giving an account of our faith in love and kindness, while observing our manner of life (1 Pet 2:13; 3:16). We encourage them to witness how we live among them and how we interact with one another. Through the consecration of our lives, we provide a defense for our proclamation of the gospel. The One we confess and follow, who redeemed us into the New Covenant by his blood, instructed his initial disciples that the love we demonstrate for one another (John 13:34–35) and our commitment to fellowship with one another (John 17:21–23) will reveal to the world that we are followers of the One who embodies Love (1 John 4:15–16) and who was sent in love (John 3:16).

For four centuries countless Baptist churches have published church covenants to guide both individual believers and local churches in the journey of sanctification.[54] These covenants define the expectations of church members, and together with the practice of corrective church discipline, covenants help to safeguard the principle of regenerate church membership. We close with a brief exposition of the most popular Baptist church covenant in the United States, drafted by the pastor J. Newton Brown (1803–1868) in 1853 and included, along with the New Hampshire Confession of Faith (1833), in his widely read *Church Manual*.[55] Brown's covenant continues to be used as a foundational membership document in thousands of churches: "Having been led, as we believe, by the Spirit of God to receive the Lord Jesus Christ as our Savior; and, on the profession of our faith, having been baptized in the name of the Father, and of the

---

[54] For the most thorough collection of Baptist church covenants, see Charles W. DeWeese, *Baptist Church Covenants* (Nashville: Broadman, 1990).

[55] J. Newton Brown, *The Baptist Church Manual* (Philadelphia: B.R. Loxley, 1853). Eventually, the American Baptist Publication Society (ABPS) acquired the rights to The Baptist Church Manual. The book remains in print with Judson Press, the successor to the ABPS.

Son, and of the Holy Ghost, we do now, in the presence of God, angels, and this assembly, most solemnly and joyfully enter into covenant with one another, as one body in Christ."

The covenant begins with an affirmation of the priority of God's grace. It is the Holy Spirit who draws individuals to faith in Christ. Following the apostolic pattern, this faith is professed publicly through water baptism in the name of the triune God. Just as baptism is a public display of a disciple's personal faith, so the covenant is a public display of a group of disciples' corporate decision to join with one another to form a local church. The seriousness of the covenant is brought home by the witnesses who are invoked: God, angels, and the disciples themselves. The church's covenant can only be understood in light of the new covenant that has been inaugurated in Jesus Christ. Each of these covenanting disciples knows the Lord (Jer 31:34), as signified by their individual faith in Christ and reception of believer's baptism.

> We engage, therefore, by the aid of the Holy Spirit, to walk together in Christian love; to strive for the advancement of this church, in knowledge, holiness, and comfort; to promote its prosperity and spirituality; to sustain its worship, ordinances, discipline, and doctrines; to contribute cheerfully and regularly to the support of the ministry, the expenses of the church, the relief of the poor, and the spread of the gospel through all nations.[56]

The covenanters call upon the Holy Spirit to aid them in their communal journey of sanctification. They commit to walk together in Christian love, evidencing the unity that is found in Christ. This love is made manifest by laboring together to advance the church's knowledge of God, obedience to his moral commands, and faith in his promises. Such labors promote the church's numerical growth and spiritual well-being. The church's flourishing is dependent upon the disciples' commitment to

---

[56] "The Church Covenant," in Joe T. Odle, *Church Member's Handbook*, rev. ed. (Nashville: Broadman, 1962), 9.

public worship, the faithful practice of baptism and the Lord's Supper, the maintenance of a regenerate membership through corrective discipline, and the defense of sound doctrine. This commitment is evidenced in part through financial contributions, offered joyfully, which support ministry priorities, benevolence, and gospel advance. Orthodoxy and orthopraxy are intimately related, as are maturation and mission.

> We also engage to maintain family and secret devotion; to religiously educate our children; to seek the salvation of our kindred and acquaintances; to walk circumspectly in the world; to be just in our dealings, faithful in our engagements, and exemplary in our deportment; to avoid all tattling, backbiting, and excessive anger; to abstain from the sale and use of intoxicating drinks as a beverage, and to be zealous in our efforts to advance the kingdom of our Saviour.[57]

The covenant calls upon members to practice personal and familial piety, including the spiritual nurture of children raised in members' households. Piety is not insular, however, for covenanters are also to share the gospel with unbelieving family members and others whose paths they cross. Piety is also evidenced in ethics, which includes wise decision-making, just interactions with others, a track record of godly behavior, kind words and a cool head, sobriety, and a kingdom-mindedness. The internal and external aspects of the Christian life are intricately connected, with spirituality and mission reinforcing one another.[58]

> We further engage to watch over one another in brotherly love; to remember each other in prayer; to aid each other in sickness and distress; to cultivate Christian sympathy in feeling and courtesy in speech; to be slow to take offense, but

---

[57] "The Church Covenant", in Odle, 9.

[58] See Nathan A. Finn and Keith S. Whitfield, eds., *Spirituality for the Sent: Casting a New Vision for the Missional Church* (Downers Grove, IL: IVP Academic, 2017).

always ready for reconciliation, and mindful of the rules of our Saviour, to secure it without delay.

We moreover engage, that when we remove from this place, we will as soon as possible unite with some other church, where we can carry out the spirit of this covenant, and the principles of God's Word.[59]

Disciples covenant to take loving responsibility for the maturation of other members. They support one another in intercessory prayer and look after one another in times of illness and suffering. They demonstrate godly sympathy for other disciples and practice civility in how they speak of and to others. They are not quick to be offended, but rather are quick to seek reconciliation when offense has occurred, always careful to follow the teaching of Christ concerning accountability and church discipline. If God should providentially lead a member to leave the church, the disciple should find another church of like faith and practice where the same covenantal commitments are embodied.

The church covenant makes clear that, in the Baptist vision, discipleship is not intended to be a solitary endeavor. Individual believers follow king Jesus together, within the context of a local church which submits to his kingship. The Christian life is one of the individual-in-community, the regenerated in covenant with both the regenerator and the regenerate. For Baptists, sanctification is a community project as members spur one another on to love and good deeds (Heb 10:24–25) and together obey the Great Commandment (Matt 22:36–40) and the Great Commission (Matt 28:18–20).

---

[59] "The Church Covenant," in Odle, *Church Member's Handbook*, 9.

CHAPTER 7

# ECCLESIOLOGY

BENJAMIN T. QUINN AND JASON K. LEE

## Introduction

The present chapter takes up the doctrine of the church (*ecclesiology*) and offers a vision for Baptist churches in three parts. Part one offers an overview of the doctrine utilizing the imagery of Christ our head and the church as family. Part two considers the communal essence of Baptist churches. Part three reflects on the confessional and covenantal nature of Baptist churches.

A standard treatment on *ecclesiology* will necessarily prioritize discussion about the systems and structures, nuts and bolts of the church and its operations. Indeed, such contributions are important and helpful for clarifying the nature, function, and practice of Baptist churches. This chapter, however, assumes commitments to Baptist congregationalism, the two offices of pastors/elders and deacons, and regenerate church membership, while offering a distinctly Baptist vision of our union with God through Christ our head, and our participation in God's plan of redemption as his confessing and covenant family.[1] Further, this chapter will engage with the ordinances of baptism and the Lord's Supper at various points, but will leave more in-depth consideration of these important church practices for chapter 8.

# Part One

In an effort to offer a succinct overview of the doctrine of the Church, we will organize part one under two unifying themes—Christ our head (vertical relationship) and church as family (horizontal relationship).[2] The first addresses the source, nature, and marks of the church in relation to Christ, the head. This theme also accents the vertical relationship of the church to God through Christ Jesus. The second considers the often and widely used family language to describe the church.

### *The Lordship of Christ, Our Head*

In the great Christ-hymn of Col 1:15–20, Paul spotlights the preeminence of the Lord Jesus Christ in all things.[3] Interestingly, Paul

---

[1] For more on the doctrine of the Church see Benjamin L. Merkle, *40 Questions about Elders and Deacons* (Grand Rapids: Kregel Academic, 2007); Mark Dever, *The Church: The Gospel Made Visible* (Nashville: B&H Academic, 2012); John S. Hammett, *Biblical Foundations for Baptist Churches: A Contemporary Ecclesiology* (Grand Rapids: Kregel Academic, 2019); Thomas White, Jason G. Duesing, and Malcolm B. Yarnell, eds., *Restoring Integrity in Baptist Churches* (Grand Rapids: Kregel, 2007); Jonathan Leeman, *Political Church: The Local Assembly as Embassy of Christ's Rule* (Downers Grove, IL: IVP Academic, 2016).

[2] These two themes as starting points are to address a perceived lack of attention to the church's Christological ontology, as noted by Malcolm Yarnell's comment, "Anthropological, functional, and structural concerns, therefore, dominated American Baptist discussions of the church," in Malcolm B. Yarnell, "From Reformation London to Contemporary Nashville: Changing Baptist Views of the Church," *Southeastern Theological Review* 8.2 (Fall 2017): 62.

[3] Paul does so first by arguing that Jesus is the "image of the invisible God"— the ultimate expression of the *imago Dei*—then by listing the many ways in which

includes the church in his list. With respect to the body (*somatos*), that is the church, Christ is the head. Elsewhere, Paul metaphorically refers to the church as a body, a single unit with multiple parts that cooperate for the health and purpose of the whole. And Jesus, Paul insists, is the head of that great body just as he is "first" in creation, resurrection, and "all things."

Christ's headship over the church illumines its nature in at least two major areas: the presence of the triune God and a community of *koinonia*. The church is where the presence and power of the triune God is found. New Testament authors employ multiple metaphors to describe the nature of the church and its relation to God. Peter called the saints "living stones, a spiritual house . . . being built to be a priesthood" (1 Pet 2:5). This imagery builds upon the words of Isa 28:16 and Ps 118:22, which were read by the apostles as referring to Jesus, the "living stone—rejected by people but chosen and honored by God" (1 Pet 2:4). And like Jesus, Peter teaches that God's people "as living stones, a spiritual house, are being built to be a holy priesthood to offer spiritual sacrifices acceptable to God through Jesus Christ" (1 Pet 2:5). By virtue of the church's nature, it is thus formed to be a spiritual house, a holy priesthood that offers spiritual sacrifices to the Lord. As a building is formed by a collection of individual stones, so too the people of God are a collection of individuals, living stones like Christ, who form a spiritual house that practices the very presence of God in Christ by the Spirit. Whereas a temple made with human hands prepared the place of God's presence in the Mosaic covenant, the people of God are themselves the place of God's presence in the new covenant.

---

Jesus is first in every way. This list includes that He is the firstborn (*prototokos*) of all creation, that He is "before all things" (*pro panton*), He is the head of the body that is the church, He is the beginning (*arche*), and firstborn (*prototokos*) from the dead, that He might be preeminent (*proteuon*). The Greek prefix, *pro*, stands out boldly in the original language, appearing no less than four times alongside *arche* and *kephale*, words that also signify "firstness" and "head," respectively. In other words, Jesus is number one in every way from beginning to end.

Additionally, Paul described the church both as a "body" with many members (1 Corinthians 12) and a "bride" (Ephesians 5, Revelation 19) awaiting the bridegroom. Alongside Peter's "living stones" and "priesthood" imagery we recognize the church's nature as promoting a unity with diversity, as well as a people of anticipation awaiting the arrival of the bridegroom. Until that time, God's people are formed in fellowship ("discipled") by the ministries of the Word, prayer, and sacraments toward love and unity until Christ's return. And all of this with Christ as the groom preparing for the bride, and the head of the body, the church. Whether bride, body, or building, the New Testament authors always understand the church in relation to Christ who unites God's people to the Father and to his work in the world.

The church is also a community of *koinonia*, a divine communion forged in the faith of Christ.[4] The church is active as a people who love God and one another and whose relationship with the church serves as the highest communal connection in their lives, deeper than biological DNA such that Jesus dared to assert that "The one who loves a father or mother more than me is not worthy of me" (Matt 10:37). This community promotes the truth in love with a covenant commitment to provoke one another to love and good deeds in Christ.

While we will discuss the communion of the church in depth below, for now, suffice it to say that the church is fundamentally plural—a community, indeed a family, invited to approach the living God as Father through the work of Christ our brother and in the power of the Holy Spirit. The church is understood both in a universal and local sense with respect to space and time (1 Cor 1:2). In the universal sense, the church is decidedly catholic, referring to all believers, in all times and places, including those who believed and obeyed God before the birth of Jesus.[5]

---

[4] The authors recognize some redundancy in the phrase "community of *koinonia*" but the prefer the phrase as a point of emphasis.

[5] The faith of the Old Testament "saints" is Christological, and therefore saving, because they hoped in the coming Messiah, the son of Abraham. They are a part of the textual community that hopes in the Messiah. See 1 Pet 1:10–12

The more common use of the term, however, applies to the *local* church—local and particular expressions of the body of Christ who belong alike to the "one Lord, one faith, one baptism, one God and Father of all, who is above all and through all and in all" (Eph 4:5–6). For such a community, baptism serves as the proper and normative public means of entrance into the local assembly, and as Baptists we further affirm that the practice of believers' baptism (administering baptism within the local believing community and after an individual's public confession of faith) is the proper and normative practice of the New Testament.[6]

Following their great head, the communion (*koinonia*) of God's people is rooted and grounded in love (Eph 3:17) for God and neighbor. This practice of "loving" is anchored in Jesus' command to love God and neighbor (Matt 22:34-30) and is directed both internally and externally. Internally, God's people seek to align themselves wholly toward God while living in unity with one another, bearing one another's burdens, and tending to those in need. Externally, the church attends to community needs, the poor, widows, orphans, social injustices, and anything further that opposes the gospel. Despite various opinions about precisely how and who from the church should be engaged in ministry in society, it is the nature of the church to act upon love for neighbor, both internally and externally, as a necessary outworking of its love for God. Some expressions of this fraternal love

---

and Heb 11:39–40. In this sense they participate with the universal church in the worship of Christ the Lord.

[6] This Baptist expression agrees with historic, orthodox teaching (i.e., Apostles' Creed, Nicene Creed, Chalcedonian Definition of Christ, Athanasian Creed), but our practice of believer's baptism (credobaptism), rooted in a congregational polity, distinguishes us from other pedobaptist traditions. As such, the remainder of our reflections on the church will be viewed especially through the lens of baptism, the post-conversion practice that signals our union with God in Christ and our union with the people of God both universal and local.

are focused on other members within a local body, but they are also grounded in the general expectation of love for other humans.[7]

The Lord instructs this fellowship to gather and live in both orderly and organic ways—[8] orderly in accord with the offices of pastor (or elder) and deacon, as instructed by the apostles (1 Timothy 3, Titus 1–2), and organically in accord with the giftings supplied by the Holy Spirit through new birth (Romans 12, 1 Corinthians 12). Moreover, God's people are called to holiness, manifesting the fruit of the Spirit (in contrast to the flesh) in all times and places (Gal 5:16–26). For by the Spirit through our new birth, we are freed from sin and enabled to walk by the Spirit. As Herman Bavinck insists, "The office does not suppress the gifts but organizes them and keeps them on track, and the gifts do not cancel out the office but vitalize it and make it fruitful. . . . Both offices and gifts—in conjunction—have been given by Christ to his church for the perfection of the saints and the upbuilding of his body (Rom. 12:5–8; 1 Cor. 12:25, 28; Eph. 4:11–12)."[9]

We can summarize the nature of the church under the headship of Christ by locating the Baptist distinctives within the Nicene and Reformation traditions. The fourth-century Nicene Creed marked the Church as "one, holy, catholic, apostolic" speaking of its unity, purity, universality, and connection to the apostolic faith. Baptists agree to these essential marks of the church. Further, the Reformed tradition, while affirming the language of Nicaea, added that the church is: (1) Where the gospel is rightly preached, (2) Where the sacraments are rightly administered, and (3) Where discipline is practiced.[10] We Baptists understand ourselves within this stream of Christian tradition, as well. The

---

[7] Sometimes the specific expectations for expressed love within a body of believers are referred to as the "one anothers" of the New Testament. This chapter notes some of these love expressions in connection with church offices, administering sacraments, and church discipline.

[8] For a full treatment, see Herman Bavinck's explanation in *Reformed Dogmatics*, vol. 4, part II (Grand Rapids, MI: Baker Academic, 2008), 6.

[9] Bavinck, 332.

[10] Cf. Article 29 of the Belgic Confession.

Baptist tradition builds upon the Nicene and Reformed commitments by recovering the New Testament teaching on believer's baptism and regenerate church membership—each member and each communion organically connected to Christ, our head. Further, under our head, we are held together by the cartilage of congregationalism. The commitment of regenerate membership creates an essential cohesion in the covenant commitment of membership toward unity and mission, the reasonable assumption of the Spirit's work in the lives of the members, and the accountability of church discipline when necessary.[11]

# Part Two

## *The Church's Communal Essence*

Vertically, the church relates to Christ as head, from which we receive the entirety of our nature. Horizontally, the church relates as both family and communion—united to each other in Christ. As we zoom in on the communal essence of the church, we will explain its significance as a critical component of a Baptist ecclesiology. To do so, we will treat the church as a family and church as communion each in turn.

## *The Church as Family*

The family dimension is arguably the most common and developed metaphor to describe God's people across both Old and New Testaments. From the first family to Noah's family to the family of Abraham that

---

[11] It is also worth noting the influential work of 9Marks ministries in recent decades. From among our own Baptist tradition, 9Marks has popularized their nine marks of healthy churches, including expository preaching, biblical theology, the gospel, conversion, evangelism, membership, discipline, discipleship, and leadership. Their work has served as a timely stimulus to churches across the denominational spectrum to reconsider the importance, especially, of the institutional roles and responsibilities of the church.

establishes God's people thereafter, even into the new covenant, where people of every nation, tribe, and tongue join the household of God through Abraham-like faith, family relations are the web that connects the people of God across the ages.

The church therefore is recognized as a family, the household (*oikos*) of God (Eph 2:19), united not by flesh but by faith, joined to the Father through Christ Jesus our brother, with the church as our mother, adopted into the family through new birth by the Spirit, living now as the bride of Christ and exercising faith, hope, and love as a confessing and eucharistic community until the return of the One who is both bridegroom and king. The familial vision of the church is both informed by Scripture and is significant for Baptist expressions of the church.

The family of God begins with God, our Father. This confession is among the most endearing truths of the Christian story. God is Father in at least two ways that demand reflection here. First, God is Father in that he is the *fount* or *source* of all things. Stanley Grenz writes, "The Father fulfills the primary role in the act of creation. He constitutes the ground of all that exists."[12] Secondly, he is Father in that he has a Son. In the fullness of time this Son, the eternal *logos* of God, took on flesh and dwelt among us (John 1:14) in the person of Jesus. But the eternal Son did not *begin* in Bethlehem. He is eternally *begotten* from the Father. Thus, God has always existed as Father, and the Son has always existed as Son. While the Father's relationship to the Son is not the same as earthly father-son relations, the beautiful mystery of family has persisted from eternity past within the Godhead, and in God's providence, he chose to reflect something of that mystery both in natural families and in the church as family.

Further, through union with Christ, he is our brother. By virtue of new birth in the Spirit, believers are joined to the Father by faith in the work of Christ and are made part of the household of God (Eph 2:19).

---

[12] Stanley J. Grenz, *Theology for the Community of God* (Grand Rapids, MI: Eerdmans, 2000), 102.

Paul argues therefore that we are "heirs of God and coheirs with Christ" (Rom 8:17). As such, Christ has become both Savior and brother to those of the household of God. The eternal Son—who became a man, died in the flesh, and rose again in the flesh as the first fruits of the resurrection—serves as the lead heir, the eldest brother ("the firstborn") in the family of God, who secured the birthright of all who confess and believe in him.

Some Christians throughout history have understood the church as the mother of all Christians. This is particularly familiar to the Roman Catholic tradition in their doctrine of the *mater ecclesiae*, though our emphasis here is something different. Herman Bavinck urged that the church be understood not merely institutionally (offices), but also communally with faith and life (organism), and as such the church serves as the *mater fidelium*, the mother of all believers. He writes, "As in the natural world, every human being is a product of communion, and the individual believer is born from the womb of the believing community."[13] The great British Baptist preacher, Charles H. Spurgeon, was also fond of emphasizing the church as a nurturing and training mother, an emphasis we believe Baptists (and evangelicals more broadly) would do well to reclaim.[14] The apostle Paul asserts that he exercised his apostolic

---

[13] Herman Bavinck, *Reformed Dogmatics: Abridged in One Volume*, ed. John Bolt (Grand Rapids: Baker Academic, 2011), 608.

[14] "Those who are brought to Christ need nurture, instruction, example, edification. 'Feed my sheep,' saith he, and yet again, 'Feed my lambs.' The preacher should try to do this, suiting his discourse to the weakest and feeblest lamb, but since he is but one and takes not upon himself the responsibility of others, the whole church should try to be a nursing mother unto those who are born unto her." C. H. Spurgeon "A Sabbath-School Sermon," in *Metropolitan Tabernacle Pulpit: Sermons Preached and Revised by C. H. Spurgeon*, vol. 23 (Pasadena, TX: Pilgrim Publications, 1970–2006), 609.

Credit goes to Brady Glaser for alerting us to this important point, especially in his paper "The Church Our Mother: Maternal Imagery Within Spurgeon's Ecclesiology", Dec. 2019, written for IND 9400, Southeastern Baptist Theological Seminary. Glaser also stresses with Joseph Plumpe, "The notion of the maternity of the Church is wholly neglected in Protestant manuals

ministry with the gentleness of a nursing mother caring for her own children (1 Thess 2:7).

As Christians are born again, we are children of God in the family of God. In John 3, Jesus explains to Nicodemus that one must be born of water (natural birth) and of the Spirit, for "whatever is born of the flesh is flesh, and whatever is born of the Spirit is spirit" (John 3:6). Just as natural birth welcomes one into an earthly family, new birth in the Spirit welcomes one into the family of God. To be truly a member of the family of God, a person must be born again by the Spirit, making the church a believing family. Such glorious truths of becoming children of God lead the Apostle John to doxology in 1 John 3:1–2 when he declares, "See what great love the Father has given us that we should be called God's children—and we are! . . . Dear friends, we are God's children now, and what we will be has not yet been revealed."

Finally, the church is the bride of Christ. In Paul's well-known passage in Eph 5:22–33, he exhorts husbands to love their wives "just as Christ loved the church and gave himself up for her" (Eph 5:25). Augustine connected Christ as bridegroom to Christ as head, writing, "The head [Christ] is the bridegroom, the body is the bride; and they speak as one."[15] Moreover, Millard Erickson recognizes "bride of Christ" language as a call to unity, writing, "The image of the church as the bride of Christ likewise argues for unity among believers. If the church is the bride of Christ, it must be one entity, not many."[16]

As a family, the church practices three unique traditions—baptism, the eucharist (Lord's Supper), and the preaching of the Word. The church family practices baptism as the welcoming of new children into

---

of dogmatic theology." See Joseph C. Plumpe, *Mater Ecclesia: An Inquiry into the Concept of the Church as Mother in Early Christianity* (Washington, DC: The Catholic University of America Press, 1943), viii.

[15] St. Augustine, "Exposition of Psalm 74," in *Expositions of the Psalms*, 73–98, III/18 (Hyde Park, NY: New City Press, 2002), 42.

[16] Millard Erickson, *Christian Theology*, 3rd ed. (Grand Rapids, MI: Baker Academic, 2013), 1009.

the family through new birth. In keeping with the call to new birth by the Spirit which is accompanied by confession and faith (John 3:1–21, Acts 16:31, Rom 10:9–10), Baptists maintain that the normative practice of baptism is reserved for those who have sincerely and consciously repented of sin and confessed Jesus as Lord. Upon such a profession, baptism is administered to the born-again follower of Jesus. Among other things, this serves as a public recognition of the believer's adoption into the family of God, and as a first step toward membership into the local body of Christ for congregational churches.

The Supper also welcomes new family-members to the table of the Lord where the fullness of family fellowship is experienced through remembering, participating in, and proclaiming Christ's death until his return—our brother, bridegroom, and king.[17] This family celebration, along with the corporate practices of preaching and baptism, give the church a "family resemblance" through time and across cultures. The family traditions celebrate the church's communion with Christ (the head) and with one another (the believing family).

### *The Church as Believing Communion*

The church as family explains the relational nature of the church. The communion of the church, as mentioned above, is slightly different. The church is a believing community in communion with Christ as Lord and bound in covenant to the community for corporate confession. The believers' church has a communal essence. While we briefly introduced the concept of the church as communion in the previous section, here we unpack it to unveil the significance of communion for a distinctly Baptist ecclesiology.

In *A Christian Catechism*, Balthasar Hubmaier describes the nature of the church, noting its universal and local expressions. He writes:

---

[17] Further discussion of these "family traditions" follows in the section "Baptist Confessionalism Is Congregational."

The church is sometimes understood to include all the people who are gathered and united in one God, one Lord, one faith, and one baptism, and have confessed this faith with their mouths, wherever they may be on earth. This, then, is the universal Christian corporeal church and fellowship of the saints, assembled only in the Spirit of God, as we confess in the ninth article of our creed. At other times the church is understood to mean each separate and outward meeting assembly or parish membership that is under one shepherd or bishop and assembles bodily for instruction, for baptism and the Lord's Supper.[18]

Notable in Hubmaier's distinction between the universal church and the local church is how the latter's ontology is seen as an extension of the former. This connection does not dissolve the distinction between the universal and the local, but it does provide an impenetrable bond between the two occurrences of the "church." The distinction is not ontological but functional, in how and where the assembly occurs and for what purpose. The universal church is "assembled only in the Spirit of God" and therefore enhances the mystical union between God and his people. The "fellowship of the saints" is both vertical and horizontal. It is the divine presence of the Spirit among this universal body that enables life-giving fellowship with the triune God and faith-stirring fellowship with saints around the world and throughout time.[19] The local church is an "outward meeting assembly" gathered under one pastor for the sake of teaching and the ordinances. There is no separate ontological quality for these local gatherings. What marks off the local church is geography

---

[18] Balthasar Hubmaier, "A Christian Catechism," in *Balthasar Hubmaier: Theologian of Anabaptism*, ed. H. Wayne Pipkin and John H. Yoder (Scottdale, PA: Herald Press, 1989), 351–52. When Hubmaier refers to the "ninth article of our creed," he is referring to the Apostles' Creed and the phrase, the "communion/ fellowship of the saints."

[19] See how Heb 12:1 concludes Hebrews 11 and highlights the connection of faith across time and space among the faithful assisting them in enduring in faith.

("parish membership") and submission to a particular pastor or bishop. In Hubmaier's description this local gathering carries on the central practices in the church of teaching, baptism, and communion.

Foundational for a Baptist ecclesiology, especially in considering the church's ontology, is the apostle Paul's discussion in Ephesians 3 and 4 of how individual believers are baptized into one body by the Spirit.[20] As Paul recounts the glories of the gospel in Ephesians 1–3, he concludes with a list of the main areas of prayer that he uses to intercede on behalf of the church. This ecclesial prayer list is grounded in the gospel that he has proclaimed as "the eternal purpose accomplished in Christ Jesus our Lord" (Eph 3:11) Paul prays that the believers would be strengthened by the Holy Spirit who dwells in their "inner being" (Eph 3:16) while they also experience union with Christ through faith (Eph 3:17). The gospel foundation along with the indwelling Spirit are indications that Paul has in mind a believers' church (ontologically). Furthermore, Paul prays that the church would be grounded in love for each other as a reflection of God's love (Eph 3:17–18) for his saints. The horizontal love shared among believers (pictured in Ephesians 4–6) is the tangible expression of the mysterious love God has for his church. Having entered the church through the gospel and being united in the Spirit, believers can now gather into local bodies to reflect the outward characteristics of a church.

Paul concludes his prayer list with a remarkable petition. He prays that God would receive glory eternally in his church and in Christ Jesus (Eph 3:21). While the themes of Paul's prayers are consistent with typical Pauline descriptions of God's purposes in the gospel, his connection between "the church" and "Christ Jesus" is striking. Paul's petition is that God would receive glory in the church as well as in Christ. That God would receive glory due to his saving work accomplished in Christ also appears earlier in the Ephesian epistle. In Eph 1:11–12, Paul describes the eternal purposes of the gospel that would result in elected believers hoping in Christ to "bring praise to his glory." Paul revisits God's glory

---

[20] See the allusions to this text in the Hubmaier quotation.

three more times in the first chapter as he recounts the gospel of Christ, even referring to God as "the God of our Lord Jesus Christ, the glorious Father." Likewise, the Holy Spirit, which is a "down payment" of God's final salvation, assures the elect "to the praise of his glory" (Eph 1:14). Having well-established the glory of the triune God before his prayer list in chapter 3, Paul concludes the list by saying that God's glory will be displayed in the church also. Paul's tendency to reserve "glory" to the triune God makes his inclusion of the church in the glorious display, especially in verbal symmetry with Christ ("to him be glory in the church and in Christ Jesus to all generations, forever and ever," Eph 3:21), even more illuminating.

How is it that the church will serve as a display of God's glory forever? Paul will address this question in the rest of the letter, especially in Ephesians 4. In brief, the church as the "one body" indwelt by the "one Spirit" has a communal essence that reflects God's glory. Put in other terms, the glory of God is not shown in the church and in Christ as two separate venues of glory. The glory of God is on display in the church as the result of the work of Christ. The identity of the church as the people of God is a goal of the gospel and is central to God's glorious purposes. Stanley Grenz reflects on the gospel culminating in the church as the community of God's redeemed people. Grenz writes:

> From the narratives of the primordial garden which open the curtain on the biblical story to the vision of the white-robed multitudes inhabiting the new earth with which it concludes, the drama of the Scriptures speaks of community. Taken as a whole the Bible asserts that God's program is directed to the bringing into being of community in the highest sense—a reconciled people, living within a renewed creation, and enjoying the presence of their Redeemer.[21]

---

[21] Grenz, *Theology for the Community of God*, 24.

The glorious purposes of God result in a community where his glory pervades because God is "above all and through all and in all" (Eph 4:6). This community is formed by God's Spirit, who then serves as the bond of this peace-filled body. Grenz explains the crucial role the Spirit has in the constitution of the church as God's covenanted people who are now one community under Christ. He writes, "The church as Christ's institution confronts us as a historical reality. The Spirit's constitution of the church as a community, however, involves us. He brings us together to be the contemporary expression of the one church of Jesus Christ."[22] The church constituted as such in Christ by the Spirit is now a living community made up of regenerated believers bearing the image of their creator, Christ (Col 3:10). This community finds concrete expression or "historical reality" in a particular space or culture. Local congregations are to be the visible version of this community, reflecting the particularities of the surrounding historical and cultural moment.

The universal nature of the church now melds with the multicultural local expressions of gathered congregations. Each local church is to find its life in Christ by his Spirit and is to reflect the new creation work of the gospel, which is the foundation of the church. Grenz explains, "At the same time, Jesus is the trailblazer of the new human community. He is the new human, the head of a new humanity. Hence, he shares true community with all who are his disciples. As our trailblazer, he is the one who mediates to us the fellowship of the new humanity, which he shares with all who are united in him through the Holy Spirit."[23]

This new humanity, now formed into a loving community by the Spirit, submits to Jesus as Lord.

This commitment to the "one Lord" is marked by an ordained symbol, "one baptism." Grenz summarizes:

---

[22] Grenz, 481.
[23] Grenz, 305.

Above all, however, baptism is oriented toward our participation in community. As an act of commitment, it marks our initiation into the shared practices of the believing community which is defined and ruled by the story of Christ's life, death, and resurrection . . . The church, therefore, rightly sees in baptism the symbol of the new birth. Our spiritual birth mediates to us the new identity that all initiates into the church enjoy. Baptism represents the change of context that has resulted in the believer now belonging to the family of God. No longer do we define our lives in accordance with the categories of the old community.[24]

Baptism is the mark of this Christ-defined community, unified by the Spirit. This believing community is called (individually) by the word of Christ and is gathered in Christ as his people. This fellowship in Christ is how God's glory will be displayed in the church forever, just as it is in Christ. Paul writes in Eph 1:22–23 that Christ has been given as head over "the church, which is his body, the fullness of the one who fills all things in every way." The church as Christ's body "embodies" his fullness, the fullness of God's own glory. As F. F. Bruce notes, "The fullness of deity resides in him, and out of that fullness his church is being constantly supplied."[25] Furthermore, Bruce explains, "the church may be viewed as that which is filled by Christ with his life, attributes, and powers . . . what is here stated as a fact becomes part of a prayer in Eph. 3:19."[26] As Bruce is commenting on the ontology or "organic relation" of the church from Eph 1:23 he makes an implication for local churches. Bruce writes, "The organic relation between head and body suggests the vital union between Christ and the church, sharers of a common life, which is his own risen

---

[24] Grenz, 523.

[25] F. F. Bruce, *The Epistle to the Colossians, to Philemon, and to the Ephesians,* in the New International Commentary on the New Testament (Grand Rapids: Eerdmans, 1984), 277.

[26] Bruce, 276.

life communicated to his people. The church is here the complete or universal church—manifested visibly, no doubt, in local congregations."[27]

For Baptist dogmatics, the crucial question then becomes, "How does this ontology of the church guide the formation of local congregations?" Defining the church as a community called together by God through the gospel, unified by the Spirit into a body, under Christ as the head, affects what is the most fitting local church expression. Paul Fiddes asserts, "When Baptists speak of a 'gathered church' they certainly mean that believers have agreed to gather together, but this is only in response to the Christ who *has gathered* them. *They* do not themselves make the church, but Christ invites them each one individually to become part of it."[28]

Twentieth-century Baptist Robert Walton asserts the same emphasis of the divine voice in the calling of the church as a community of faith:

What kind of community do we, as Baptists, desire to create? Our first and major emphasis must be upon the fact that we are not members of a human society, but of a divine creation, led by the Holy Spirit, working under the guidance of God and disciplined by His judgments. As John Smyth said, "It is by virtue of the covenant God maketh with us' that our churches stand. To enter the fellowship of a Baptist church involves an act of personal decision, personal faith and self-surrender, but a church is called into existence and its life is maintained, not by the decision of men, but the will of God."[29]

---

[27] Bruce, 275. Bruce adds a parenthetical comment, "although local congregations scarcely come into the picture in Ephesians, as they do in all the other Pauline writings."

[28] Italics original to the author; Fiddes, 233.

[29] Robert Walton, "The Gathered Community," *Baptist Roots*, ed. Curtis Freeman, James McClendon Jr., and C. Rosalee Velloso da Silva (Valley Forge, PA: Judson, 1999), 332–33.

James McClendon raises a series of questions about whether a communal essence can be developed so that an authentic church (in a "gathering" expression) exists and thrives. McClendon asks, "How is such a community formation to work for us? In what sense are we to 'belong to one another' (Rom. 12:5) in Christ?"[30] McClendon then suggests that we apply the "long continuities of Christian teaching," which he summarizes as "God's rule, Christ's centrality, the Spirit's *koinonic* presence. From the rule of God—a consent-seeking, creative, salvific rule—comes membership that consents to that rule. In baptist parlance, that has meant receiving the Spirit, obeying the gospel, receiving Christ, and taking up discipleship. It implies a disciple church, shaped by its distinctive conversion-baptism."[31] These core confessions recognize that the church's communal essence has direct implications on its form and function. Baptist churches are visible expressions of this communal essence as confessional and covenantal bodies.

## Part Three

### *Baptist Churches as Confessional, Covenantal Bodies*

The nature of Baptist churches leads to particular language to describe Baptist churches and to prescribe the core elements of these local bodies. The "describe" and "prescribe" efforts often result in one of two (or both) types of written expressions: confessions and covenants.[32] Baptist confessions and covenants affect the forms and functions of Baptist ecclesial practices and mission. Baptist confessions and covenants provide the path for Baptist churches to submit all things to the lordship of Christ, as the church grows into maturity in him. Baptist confessions and covenants

---

[30] James W. McClendon, Jr., *Doctrine: Systematic Theology*, vol. 2 (Nashville: Abingdon, 1994), 367.

[31] McClendon, 367.

[32] Two of the signposts of Baptist dogmatics are particularly central to the ontology of Baptist churches: confessional and covenantal.

guide the community life of the believing church. While these two types of documents have some shared traits, they also serve different functions. Baptist confessions are often produced and affirmed at a level beyond the local church. As such, they can have the function of providing the theological basis for an association of Baptist churches.[33] The content of these Baptist confessions is comprehensive in that they often include statements on Trinity, Christology, and humanity even if they intend to highlight particular doctrines like soteriology and ecclesiology. These theological statements often serve the function of unifying a variety of local churches around common dogma. The confessions "describe" the theological positions of these congregations, while they also "prescribe" the confessional commitments of this communion of Baptists. The required confessional posture makes this communion exclusive even if its theological stances are not entirely unique. As will been seen in the rest of this chapter, Baptist dogmatics recognizes the interrelated aspects of the communal, congregational, and covenantal qualities to this confession. A community believers made so by its common confession will gather (congregation) together by means of a covenant for the paired purposes of ministry and mission.

### Baptist Confessionalism Is Communal

As noted in a previous section, Baptists (as individual believers and as local gathered bodies) unite under the common confession of Jesus as Lord. This confessing body is an uncommon community due to this confession.

*Confessions.* Creedal orthodoxy is something that Baptists share with other Christian traditions. The ancient creeds and the varied expressions of the rule of faith that preceded the creeds provide essential beliefs to be a faith-family, a church. Baptist confessions have

---

[33] See the editor's introduction to "The Faith and Practice of Thirty Congregations," in *Baptist Confessions of Faith*, ed. William Lumpkin (Valley Forge, PA: Judson, 1959), 171–73.

historically recognized the unified church as holy, catholic, and apostolic.[34] Orthodoxy expressed in the ancient creeds and the shaping of the church by an authoritative biblical canon are at the core of Baptist confessions. After affirming the "authority of the holy scripture," The Orthodox Creed states, "The three creeds, namely the Nicene Creed, Athanasian Creed, and the Apostles' Creed, as they are commonly called, ought thoroughly to be received, and believed. For we believe, they may be proved, by most undoubted authority of holy Scripture, and are necessary to be understood of all Christians, and to be instructed in the knowledge of them."[35]

In addition to vast areas of agreement with confessions from other traditions, Baptist confessions do differ from other confessions, especially in the area of ecclesiology. As Baptist churches are distinguishable from churches in other traditions, so Baptist confessions are distinguishable from other confessional traditions. These confessions have an "identifying" function for a particular local church, or most often, a group of churches to be labeled "Baptist."[36] The confessions also have a "unifying" function to create a community (of believers or churches).[37]

*Lived Text.* Baptist confessionalism is not just expressed through written confessions of faith. Baptist confessionalism is notable as local

---

[34] See Articles 28–30 of "The Orthodox Creed," in Lumpkin, 318–19.

[35] Article 38 of "The Orthodox Creed," in Lumpkin, 324, 326.

[36] See the word to "The Judicious and Impartial Reader" in the *Second London Confession* (1689) in Lumpkin, 244–45. In this preface to the readers, the confession's framers intentionally connect their churches (and the present confession) with the *First London Confession* (1644). The later framers conclude that they "embrace the same truth which is owned therein," even to the point of "making use of the very same words with them" in the "very many" places where the confession of the earlier London Baptists agrees with theirs.

[37] See the editor's introduction to "The Faith and Practice of Thirty Congregations," in Lumpkin, 171–73. Lumpkin states, "The Baptist confessions of faith which appeared during the period of the Commonwealth (1650–1659) were closely connected with the association movement, and they often served as its unifying instruments."

bodies confess Christ as Lord and believe that God has raised him from the dead (Rom 10:9). Drawing on Romans 10 and Matthew 16–18, Balthasar Hubmaier describes the necessity of a public confession of faith. He says that the church is built on "the oral confession of faith that Jesus is the Christ, the Son of the living God. This outward confession is what makes a church, and not faith alone; for the church that has the power to bind and to loose is outward and corporeal, not theoretical, and faith is inward."[38] This confession means that a Baptist church is a believing and submitting community where the lordship of Christ is preeminent. The lordship of Christ functions through Baptist churches returning constantly to Scripture for their very being and even well-being (as a habitus). In relation to this, for Baptist confessionalism, to be a submitted disciple of Jesus is to be a faithful reader of the Scriptures, in covenant with other faithful readers.[39] Faithful readers of the Scripture live the text as they interpret their daily life, their understanding of the way the world works, and the nature of their relationship with God through the lens of God's written revelation.

Historically, Baptists are committed to seeking the Spirit's help in biblical interpretation. This concept of illumination by the Spirit has often led Baptists to emphasize the role of every individual believer to "search the Scriptures."[40] Another implication of the Spirit's presence is that the life-giving Spirit connects readers to the subject matter of the text (God himself) and draws individual believers into the textual community as a faith-filled reader, not necessarily as an autonomous interpreter. The Spirit-filled believer is a faithful Bible reader who recognizes Christ's authority in the biblical literature and is a member of a textual community that is shaped by that authority. Curtis Freeman explains the value of reading the Scripture within a covenant community committed to the text. Freeman calls this interpretive practice the "plain sense in the

---

[38] Hubmaier, *A Christian Catechism*, 352.

[39] See Matt 13:52. See also 2 Pet 3:1–2.

[40] See John 5:39–47 for the concept of reading texts to find life in Christ.

baptist vision." He adds, "Such reading in covenant community demands an 'active, diverse and ongoing engagement with the biblical texts.'"[41]

The biblical texts embody the authority of Christ and the message intended by the Spirit (via human authors). This text-community identity should guide Baptist churches to be shaped by a textual hermeneutic that pays close attention to the biblical author's compositional efforts.[42] The Spirit that guided the biblical authors also helps biblical readers live the text as an ongoing authoritative Word. The illuminating work of the Spirit that enables living by the biblical text is in keeping with the role of Baptist pastors as public ministers of the Word. Baptist pastor John Gill writes in his *Body of Practical Divinity*:

> [Pastors] must be studious in the scriptures, and have a competent knowledge of things contained in them; whereby the man of God, the minister of Christ, may be perfect, thoroughly furnished unto all good works, and particularly unto the work of the ministry, 2 Tim. 3:16–17. They should make the Bible their chief study, and attend to the diligent and constant reading of it, and meditate upon the things in it; and give themselves wholly to them, that their profiting in the knowledge of the mystery of Christ might be manifest; for as they are to feed the churches with knowledge and understanding.[43]

Bible-fed churches have the necessary guidance to live out biblical wisdom ("meditate upon the things in it") in whatever context they are in.

---

[41] Curtis W. Freeman, *Contesting Catholicity: Theology for Other Baptists* (Waco, TX: Baylor University Press, 2014), 289. Freeman utilizes wording from Sean Winter's *More Light and Truth? Biblical Interpretation in Covenantal Perspective* (Oxford: Whitley Publications, 2007).

[42] This hermeneutic is also confessional in that the church reads these canonical texts as a community under the texts' authority and as the direct addressees of their revelation (meaning/theological truth).

[43] John Gill, *A Body of Practical Divinity*, new ed. (Paris, AR: Baptist Standard Bearer, 2000), 928.

*Effected Lives.* Not only does the living community of the church allow the Bible to have a life in culture, but the Bible also gives the church life from her head, Christ. Baptist confessionalism encourages life in the Spirit, a life of maturity. As Paul notes in Colossians 1, he labored for the sake of Christ's "body, that is, the church" (Col 1:24), and his ministry included "teaching everyone with all wisdom, so that we may present everyone mature in Christ" (Col 1:28). This body that Paul is teaching is the community of faith, which is now living by the power of the Spirit. Confessionalism describes and prescribes the life of faith for the believing community. In Ephesians 4, Paul notes some of the marks of this living community of faith. They are pressing on to "the unity of the faith" and "of the knowledge of the Son of God", indicating the doctrinal content that is necessary for "growing into maturity." This growth leads not only to maturity but is "in every way into him who is the head—Christ." These new believers are new creatures who live this new life as "members of one another," intending "to build up the body of Christ" as believers in a living community, the church.

## Baptist Confessionalism Is Congregational

Baptists have often pointed to a related set of theological commitments that distinguish Baptist beliefs about the nature and practices of the church. Believers' baptism as an act of dying and rising with Christ and as an act of covenanting with other believers as a church is a stalwart in Baptist communities. These ecclesial practices lead to a pairing that lies at the heart of Baptist ecclesiological identity: regenerate church membership and congregationalism.[44] These two emphases capture two of the key biblical metaphors for the church. A body (1 Corinthians 12, Ephesians 4) made up of various members pictures a congregational

---

[44] At some level, the "Baptist" part of the Baptist Dogmatics Project is a consideration of how these blended commitments produces a uniquely Baptist dogmatic.

whole, with individual (i.e., members) parts of equal value. A building (1 Pet 2) made of living stones (i.e., individual believers) built on the foundation stone (i.e., Christ) pictures a regenerate church membership. The defining ecclesial commitment to regenerate church membership often sets Baptists apart from other traditions. As a logical follow-up to regenerate church membership, congregationalism affirms the participation of each member in the body life of the church, including the church's theological task, congregational practices, and corporate ministry.

E. Y. Mullins recognizes that since a local church is most properly a believers' church in mutual agreement (i.e., local church covenant) a paradox is created between redeemed, autonomous believers and the mutual submission necessary within a local church. He writes, "Because the individual deals directly with his Lord and is immediately responsible to him, the spiritual society must needs be a democracy."[45] The democracy anticipated by Mullins is not based on a political model or expediency, but on a covenant soteriology that provides individuals with direct relationship with God, "the absolute monarch," and a covenant ecclesiology where believers bind themselves together for mission. Therefore, Mullins asserts, "The church is a community of autonomous individuals under the immediate lordship of Christ, held together by a social bond of common interest due to a common faith and inspired by common tasks and ends, all of which are assigned to him by the common Lord. The church, therefore, is the expression of the paradoxical conception of the union of absolute monarchy and pure democracy."[46] Mullins is not emphasizing personal autonomy as much as he is trying to describe the voluntary association at the heart of the church as a community. One might quibble that Mullins could strengthen his language about the church being "held together by a social bond of common interest." However, since he

---

[45] E. Y. Mullins, *The Axioms of Religion*, 117.

[46] Mullins, 117–18. Notice the relationship of Mullins' terms of "absolute monarch and pure democracy" with the "Christ as head" and "church as family" imagery earlier in this essay.

says this bond is stimulated by their "common faith" and "common tasks" under their "common Lord," Mullins has in mind a believing community with a common confession (and perhaps bound by covenant). This gathering of confessing believers who are bound together are most fittingly self-governed as a congregational whole submitted to Christ as the head of the body. Governed by Christ and bound by covenant and confession, congregationalism is not theological individualism, but a submitted body in common confession.

*Leadership and Ministry.* The self-governed body of believers that are under the headship of Christ have been granted authority to the whole body from the head. Though the authority of Christ extends to the whole congregation, the believing church orders itself under chosen ("called") leaders for the sake of focused ministry. This orderly ministry is a ministry of the Word for the sake of making disciples, a ministry of reconciliation through the gospel.

The apostle Paul is unequivocal that all who are new in Christ are part of the ministry of Christ. In 2 Cor 5:18, for example, Paul writes, "Everything is from God, who has reconciled us to himself through Christ and has given us the *ministry of reconciliation.*" He continues in 2 Cor 5:20, associating this ministry with that of an ambassador urging, "Therefore, we are ambassadors for Christ, since God is making his appeal through us. We plead on Christ's behalf, 'Be reconciled to God.'" Further, in Ephesians 4:11, amid his exhortation concerning unity and diversity in the church, Paul writes that Christ gave some to be "apostles, some prophets, some evangelists, some pastors and teachers." And the reason for such gifting is "to equip the saints for the work of the ministry, to build up the body of Christ . . ." (4:12). This is an "every-member ministry,"[47] wherein all the Saints understand themselves as part of the ministering body equipped for service to the church and the world, beginning with the plea, "Be reconciled to God" (2 Cor 5:20).

---

[47] John R. W. Stott, *God's New Society: The Message of Ephesians*, The Bible Speaks Today (Downers Grove, IL: IVP, 1979), 167.

More specifically to the local church, in accord with Paul's language in 1 Tim 3:1–13 and Titus 1:5–9, Baptist churches have recognized pastor/elder/bishop and deacons as the two offices assigned with the tasks of the ministry of Word and prayer (pastors or elders) and leading in service and administration of church matters (deacons) under the oversight of the pastors.[48] Baptist theologian Chris Morgan summarizes these two offices and their roles:

> The term "pastor" denotes care and nurture with the Word (1 Pet 5:1–4), "elder denotes maturity and wisdom (Titus 1:5–9), and "bishop" or "overseer" denotes leadership and administrative abilities (1 Tim 3:1–7). A qualified pastor is a Christian of sound character who leads his family well, has a good reputation in the community, is able to teach the church (1 Tim 3:1–7; Titus 1:5–9), and is marked by wisdom, love for others, humility, and self-control (Jas 3:1–18). Pastors/elders shepherd the church (1 Pet 5:2), lead the church (1 Tim 3:5), teach the Word (1 Tim 3:2), oppose error (Titus 1:9), pray for the church's members (Jas 5:13–15), and set an example for the others to follow (1 Pet 5:3). The second office is that of *deacon* (Phil 1:1). Deacons' main responsibilities concern service to the church. The qualifications for deacons (1 Tim 3:8–13) are similar to those for pastors, without the requirement to be able to teach.[49]

The leadership provided in these two offices enables ministry by the whole congregation as a body of confessing believers.

---

[48] The gifts listed in Eph 4:11 are best understood as four gifts with the final being a combined, or hyphenated, role of the "pastor-teacher." It is difficult and unnecessary to map the apostle, prophet, and evangelist giftings directly onto the offices of the local church. Rather, we understand the pastor-teacher gifting aligning with the office of the pastor or elder, thereby evaluated according to the character and gifting criteria of 1 Timothy 3 and Titus 1.

[49] Christopher W. Morgan with Robert A. Peterson, *Christian Theology: The Biblical Story and Our Faith* (Nashville: B&H Academic, 2020), 484.

*Preaching.* Baptists share a commitment with the rest of the Christian tradition to the doxological character of theology—that is, its posture and its aim are the proper worship of the triune God. The Second London Confession (1689) affirms, "Religious worship is to be given to God the Father, Son and Holy Spirit, and to him alone." Furthermore, as this confession describes the congregational elements of public worship, it lists the "reading of the Scriptures, preaching, and hearing the word of God, teaching and admonishing one another in psalms, hymns and spiritual songs, sing[ing] with grace in our hearts to the Lord; as also the administration of baptism, and the Lord's Supper are all parts of religious worship of God."[50] Notice the congregational duty of "hearing the word of God" is paired with "preaching," the latter being the primary duty of pastor and the former being associated with many other aspects of the whole congregation's role in worship.

John Gill addresses many of these same congregational elements in Baptist worship gatherings. He also notes the congregational role in the "public hearing of the Word." Gill describes the experience of the congregation as they hear the preached (and read) Word. He says that they

> feel the power of it, enlightening their minds in the knowledge of divine things, attracting their affections to Christ, bowing their wills to him; it works effectually in them; when they taste the sweetness of it, and eat, and it is the joy and rejoicing of their hearts; and they esteem the words of Christ's mouth more than their necessary food; when they hear it so as to believe it, not with a bare temporary faith, but with a spiritual saving faith in God and Christ reveled in it, John 5:24, and when they hear so as to receive the word into their hearts, and it becomes the ingrafted word, and springs up, and brings forth fruit in heart and life.[51]

---

[50] Lumpkin, 280–81. The two editions of this confession were developed in 1677 and 1688 before the broader publication and affirmation of the confession in 1689.

[51] Gill, *Body of Practical Divinity*, 933.

Baptist churches benefit from being more self-aware of their identity as a community that has been founded by and formed by the reading and teaching of the biblical text. Baptist preaching is Christological and textual and asserts that "Christ's rule over theology" comes through his Word as rightly preached, interpreted, understood, and applied in the local church. The Scriptures preached, interpreted, understood, and applied are key elements of a Baptist confessionalism. The "Word as rightly preached, (etc.)" prompts an "embodied theology" within the life of the church. This embodied theology in church life is at the heart of a Baptist congregation.

*Prayer and Singing.* Baptist churches living the confessional life of the Scriptures engage in congregational practices related to their theology and mission. Two common congregational practices in Baptist churches to confess corporate faith are prayer and singing. Both of these practices have an individual capacity but are also central to congregational life. In his discussion of "public prayer," John Gill describes prayer as "the breath of a regenerate soul" and as "the speech of the soul to God."[52] He also says that public prayer "is performed in bodies and communities of men; who meet in public, unite and join together in divine worship . . . for prayer always was made a part of public worship."[53] Baptist churches have engaged in public prayer, utilizing the Lord's Prayer or other written prayers. They have prayed extemporaneous prayers for healing, the conversion of unbelievers, and the church's mission in a congregational setting.

Another aspect of the congregation's participation in the theological task is congregational singing. The embodied theology of songs, hymns, and spiritual songs allows all the members to proclaim scriptural truths and reflect on the testimonial of other believers striving for life in submission to Christ. The musical reflections often hinge around other central communal practices, such as baptism, communion, and the preached

---

[52] Gill, 939.
[53] Gill, 940.

Word. John Gill discusses these various elements of congregational worship (i.e., confession) and provides specific guidance on the songs of the congregation to be "agreeable to the sacred writings, and to the analogy of faith, and are expressed as much as may be in scripture language."[54] The telos of these communal theological recitations is the sanctification of believers, formation into the image of Christ, and the word of Christ dwelling richly in the corporate life of the church.[55]

*Baptism and Communion.* Believers' baptism is a means and a sign of the communal essence of a believers' church. Balthasar Hubmaier explains that the communal essence of the church prompts brotherly admonition but requires the confession of baptism to legitimize the authority of the admonition. He writes that a congregational admonition comes from the baptismal confession or the "baptismal pledge, in which one has made himself subject to the church and all her members, according to the Word of Christ."[56] The congregational habit of baptism celebrates the confession of an individual's personal faith in Christ and also marks that individual's inclusion into the universal church. Furthermore, the person's baptismal confession before a particular gathered church unites them into that congregational life.

The local church body also confesses Christ together through congregational participation in communion. This local body has been united together by the broken (and scattered) body of Christ and in the washing of his blood. Congregational community is renewed and confessed through the elements of the Lord's Supper. Baptists have emphasized not only the act of confessing faith in these two congregational acts, but also the content of that faith (Christ's death and resurrection; Jesus is Lord) and the context of that faith (a new covenant community).[57] Curtis Freeman says of baptism and the Supper, "Without them, the churches

---

[54] Gill, 961.

[55] Col 3:16.

[56] Hubmaier, *A Christian Catechism*, 353.

[57] The next chapter will develop key elements of these ordinances/sacraments in Baptist life more fully.

cannot be the church. Through them, but not without them, persons are made Christians and are sustained in faith and union with Christ and his body. Baptism and the Lord's Supper enact the covenant between God and the people of God."[58] Baptists have regularly confessed that a profession of faith in the Father, Son, and Spirit in baptism and other aspects of public worship leads to a contextualized ministry of making disciples of all nations.

## Baptist Confessionalism Is Commissioned

The reading of the Scriptures shapes the essential (ontological) life of the text community, the church, as well as the shape and content of its confession. The church becomes a worshipping community that engages its current culture (mission) in accordance with the script of the biblical text as an embodied theology. The disposition required for this vision is a high view of Scripture's authority and a commitment to reading it with trained eyes and softened hearts. It also produces a localized community (a local church) that is as aware of its "covenant moment" (biblical covenants) as of its "cultural moment."

*Missions.* In a Baptist theological community ("church"), the preceding confessional commitments lead to a missional purpose. The local churches are on mission, guided by their theology and connected with their theological community.[59] Historically, Baptists have provided a leading voice in the missionary impulse provided in Christ's commission in Matt 28:19–20. This command to "make disciples" among all the nations is linked with the baptism of these new converts and the church effort to disciple them through teaching them Christ's words (found in the Scriptures). Being tethered to the biblical text enhances the church's

---

[58] Freeman, *Contesting Catholicity*, 246.

[59] See D. Scott Hildreth, *Together on God's Mission* (Nashville: B&H Academic, 2018) for more on the historical and theological support for cooperative missions among Baptists.

missional purpose by viewing the contemporary church as a text community that enables the Bible to have a "life" or vibrancy in a contemporary culture. It also means that the commission requires a sacrificial response from local churches. In his *Enquiry*, William Carey wrote, "This commission was as extensive as possible and laid them under obligation to disperse themselves into every country of the habitable globe, and preach to all the inhabitants, without exception, or limitation. They accordingly went forth in obedience to the command, and the power of God evidently wrought with them."[60]

## Suffering

Baptists confess Christ in society and among the nations, resulting in suffering. To confess Christ invites the suffering that comes from persecution (hostile resistance), rejection (active resistance), and indifference (passive resistance) to the message of Christ. The framers of the First London Confession petitioned for mercy from magistrates as they confessed Christ openly. They recognized that the mercy might not be granted, and so they add:

> But if God withholds the magistrates allowance and furtherance herein: yet we must notwithstanding proceed together in Christian communion, not daring to give place to suspend our practice, but to walk in obedience to Christ in the profession and holding forth this faith before mentioned, even in the midst of all trials and afflictions, not accounting our goods . . . our own lives dear unto us . . . we ought to obey God rather than men and grounding upon the commandment, commission, and promise of . . . Christ.[61]

---

[60] William Carey, *An Enquiry into the Obligations of Christians to Use Means for the Conversion of the Heathens* (Leicester: Ann Ireland, 1792), 7.

[61] Lumpkin, *Baptist Confessions of Faith*, 170.

Baptists have long understood that the Great Commission requires a confession of Christ in culture. It is this very confession that means the ontology of the believing church always includes suffering.

## Baptist Confessionalism Is Covenantal

Baptist confessionalism typically unites Baptist churches with other like-minded churches for the sake of mission and witness. Occasionally, this confessional impulse results in a written confession that can unify multiple local congregations. Similarly, another typical written expression of Baptist ideals is a local church covenant. This document is less of a bridge between Baptist churches and more of a glue that holds a local church together as a body. Like Baptist confessions, Baptist covenants can unify, typically around a local church's understanding of body life. Baptist covenants may keep the descriptive statements about the church brief, but they usually prescribe ministry activity and communal care for the body's well-being.

*Believers' church as covenant agreement.* Baptist churches are covenanted bodies made up of individuals saved by God's covenant love and integrated into God's covenantal plan for all people. The concept and practice of covenant affects the confessionalism of Baptists as believers' churches. Stanley Grenz asserts that the unifying work of the Spirit is a covenant dynamic that forms the believing community. Grenz writes, "Viewed theologically, the Holy Spirit is the facilitator of the covenant that forms the foundation of Christ's community. He is the one who brings us to confess Jesus' lordship, which confession lies at the foundation of the covenant we share (1 Cor. 12:3). He is likewise the bond which links us as one unified people. As Paul indicated, among us is a oneness which is nothing less than a unity produced by the Spirit himself (Eph. 4:3)."[62]

---

[62] Grenz, *Theology for the Community of God*, 481.

Historically, the earliest covenantal shape of Baptist confessionalism has accounted for two facets of covenant. John Smyth, the first Baptist theologian and first pastor of the first Baptist church, identified them as "1. respecting God and the faithful. 2. respecting the faithful mutually. . . . The first part of the covenant respecting God is either from God to the faithful, or from the faithful to God. . . . The second part of the covenant respecting the faithful mutually conteyneth all the duties of love whatsoever."[63] Paul Fiddes accordingly refers to these two parts as the "vertical" and the "horizontal" dimensions of the covenant.[64] The two parts of the covenant also go by the names of the eternal "covenant of grace" and the earthly "local church covenant," or even as "covenant theology" and "covenant ecclesiology."

But what is the bond between these two? Robert Browne, the separatist, was one of the first English Reformers to develop the local church covenant idea, but the eternal covenant was expressly connected to the local church covenant in Browne's writings. John Smyth was the first to "fuse together" the eternal covenant with ecclesiology by the making of a covenant in time. Thomas Helwys, the first pastor of the first Baptist church on English soil, clearly united the practice of believers' baptism with the making of the covenant.[65] The shape of the covenant, therefore, requires a connection between the doctrine of the eternal covenant (covenant theology) and the doctrine of the local church covenant (covenant

---

[63] John Smyth, *Principles and Inferences*, 1:254; cited in Jason K. Lee, "Baptism and Covenant," in *Restoring Integrity in Baptist Churches*, ed. Thomas White, Jason G. Duesing, and Malcolm B. Yarnell III (Grand Rapids: Kregel, 2008), 127.

[64] Paul S. Fiddes, *Tracks and Traces: Baptist Identity in Church and Theology*, Studies in Baptist History and Thought (Carlisle, UK: Paternoster, 2003), 22.

[65] Paul Fiddes, "Covenant and the Inheritance of Separatism," in Paul Fiddes, ed., *The Fourth Strand of the Reformation: The Covenant Ecclesiology of Anabaptists, English Separatists, and Early General Baptists* (Oxford: Centre for Baptist History and Heritage, 2018), 78. Fiddes follows B. R. White in the assertion about Browne developing the idea of the local church covenant for English Separatism.

ecclesiology). This linkage is located internally with personal conversion (covenant soteriology) and externally in water baptism.

Baptist covenant ecclesiology is based on the biblical revelation of God's covenant love (covenant theology) and the personal relationship made possible by God's covenant offer (covenant soteriology). Baptist ecclesiology is not based on a person's good will toward another person, but in God's good will toward us. The mutual love for one another displayed in a local church body's covenant expression starts with God's revelation of his covenantal action toward his creation. This covenantal work finds an individual experience when someone hears the promise of the gospel (God's covenant to save those who believe in Christ) and submits to Christ as Lord. Baptized by the Spirit, the new believer is in union with Christ and has been united with other believers into one body. The local church covenant is then the external confession of this "unity of the Spirit in the bond of peace" that binds individual believers to a particular faith family just as water baptism is the external confession of the internal baptism of the Spirit.

*Believers' church as covenant intersection.* The nexus of three interrelated concepts of covenant among Baptists provide the core contours of the churches' theology: covenant theology, covenant soteriology and covenant ecclesiology.[66] Understanding the entire biblical revelation with a theological covenantal framework then allows Baptist dogmatics to pivot to a personal, saving covenantal relationship for each believer. This *covenant soteriology* emphasizes that God has promised to save those who believe in Christ and adopt them as his children. The imagery of the covenant of adoption pictures the change of status and of relationship that occurs in the covenant of salvation. Covenant soteriology also requires a Christological core for Baptist dogmatics and implies the new life (through the Spirit) that the disciple will live in relationship to Christ

---

[66] The term "covenant theology" should not be confused with the "covenant theology" or "federal theology" system of thinking of Johannes Cocceius in Reformed thought or William Ames in English Puritanism.

as Lord. The water baptism of a believer visualizes the hidden baptism of the Spirit that creates this new life.

The two-testament revelation of God (*covenant theology*) which is proclaimed in summary form in the preached gospel brings the offer of relationship (*covenant soteriology*) with the triune God. Believers are called to live this new life in unified relationships with other believers as a church (*covenant ecclesiology*). The covenant to live the new life of the gospel is paired with a covenant to live in reconciled relationships with other believers in the church. For example, the Baptist church in Horse Fair, Stony Stratford, Buckinghamshire, England (1790), declared that they embraced "the Word of God as our only guide in matters of religion, and acknowledge no other authority whatever as binding upon the conscience." They continued by stating, "On looking into the sacred Scripture, we find it was common in the first ages of Christianity for such as professed repentance towards God and faith in our Lord Jesus Christ, voluntarily to unite together in Christian societies called in the New Testament, churches."[67] The Christological emphasis of covenant theology and covenant soteriology is now extended in the body life of the local church (*covenant ecclesiology*) where Christ is the head. The mutual submission of believers to one another is a result of their submission to Christ as Lord.[68]

*Believers' church as covenant confession.* Seen within this covenantal framework, Baptist confessionalism fuels the discipleship initiative of the covenant life of Baptist churches. Moreover, Baptist confessionalism is participatory because it draws on the covenanted congregation's shared faith. The unity of the Spirit in the bond of peace (Ephesians 4) is made evident in the church's covenantal life. For example, the Christian practice of forgiveness of others portrays the covenant theme of forgiveness in Christ (Eph 4:32). The display of God's gracious purposes (*covenant theology*) in Christ made available to individual believers (*covenant*

---

[67] Timothy George and Denise George, eds., *Baptist Confessions, Covenants, and Catechisms* (Nashville: B&H, 1996), 187.

[68] Eph 4:15–16 and 1 Corinthians 12.

*soteriology*) now prompts reconciled relationships (*covenant ecclesiology*). Forgiving each other is a manifestation of our theology of Christ's rule in our lives and churches and is one of the blessings of covenantal dogmatics.

Baptist confessionalism informs and inspires the Baptist practices of covenant. As mentioned above, Baptists commit to the practice of covenants because of their confession drawn from the biblical text and biblical authority. The Great Ellingham Baptist Church (1699) wrote: "We likewise find in Holy Writ, that an explicit covenanting with, and giving up ourselves to the Lord and one another, is the formal cause of a particular visible gospel church."[69] Baptists confess their faith within the framework of a covenant community, the church, even as that confession compels them to go beyond the church's bounds.

Confessing the faith together within the commitment of a local covenanted body provides the setting for church members to submit to one another and to church leaders with the context of a shared faith. A covenant confession implies not only a believers' church but a congregational administration as well. The redeemed body, as a whole, commits to mutual care and mutual mission. Leaders are primarily disciplers and the members share the burdens of ministry and governance within a discipling community. The trajectory of the discipleship enterprise is informed by the authoritative Scriptures and accomplished in the covenant relationships of the church, where mutual submission among believers is an extension of the body's submission to Christ.

---

[69] George and George, *Baptist Confessions, Covenants, and Catechisms*, 181.

# CHAPTER 8

# THE ORDINANCES

## Stephen Lorance and Christine E. Thornton

Few doctrines define Baptists more clearly than the ordinances—not only in name, but also in practice. While Baptists have often reflected on the fact that God has commanded his church to observe these practices, we have not always reflected on their purpose, the significance of baptism across the biblical canon, and the role of baptism in Baptist theology. To begin to unfold a Baptist dogmatic approach to the ordinances, we will consider the purpose of the ordinances, uncover the significance of baptism in Bible interpretation, and conclude with the role of believer's baptism for Baptist dogmatic theology. In the process, we will provide an authentically Christian and distinctly Baptist understanding from within the *historic, ecclesial, covenantal,* and *confessional* framework of Baptist dogmatics.

## Ordained for God's Purposes, Accomplished by the Power of His Presence

God ordained the practices of baptism and the Lord's Supper to grow his church to Christian maturity, and he accomplishes this purpose through his presence in Christ by means of the Holy Spirit. The ordinances are not mere commands to be followed out of rote obedience. Rather, God uses these regular activities to grow us up into the fullness of Christ. In the words of early Baptist Thomas Helwys, "the Lord hath not given His word, sacraments and the discipline of the Church unto His people, to the end that they should satisfy themselves with the outward obedience thereof . . . but . . . to be made like to Jesus Christ in His life, sufferings, death, burial, resurrection and ascension, by being partakers with Him of one and the same spirit."[1] While Baptists have some distinguishing practices of the ordinances, we join the universal church in embodied confession of the crucified and risen Christ, even as we hunger and thirst for his return in glory and our own bodily resurrection with him.

Healthy churches must have a healthy practice of the ordinances—not cordoned off as a solitary component of God's ecclesial activity. Rather, they are one piece among many in the formal and informal ministries of the church. In the formal ministries of the church, they pair uniquely with the ministry of the Word. Together, Word and ordinance (sometimes called "sacrament" in other Christian traditions) compose the formal ministry of the church.[2] This pairing of the ministry

---

[1] Thomas Helwys, "A Declaration of Faith of English People Remaining at Amsterdam in Holland," "Helwys Confession, 1611," The Reformed Reader, https://www.reformedreader.org/ccc/helwysconfession.htm.

[2] In this section, we will use both "ordinance" and "sacrament" to describe baptism and the Lord's Supper because one of the purposes of this section is to demonstrate the universal reality of these practices. While Baptists may not share some of the sacramental convictions of our brethren from other traditions, when discussing these universal components, we have chosen to use "sacrament" at points because it is the more common term for the practices in the Christian tradition. Further, in the last decades, many Baptists have begun recovering the sacramental significance of the ordinances in a series of theological texts. Consider the following: Anthony R. Cross and Philip E. Thompson, eds., *Baptist Sacramentalism: Studies in Baptist History and Thought* (Eugene, OR: Pickwick, 2007); Anthony R. Cross, ed., *Baptist Sacramentalism 2* (Eugene, OR: Wipf and Stock, 2009); Anthony R. Cross, Philip E. Thompson, and Alec Gilmore, *Baptist Sacramentalism 3* (Eugene,

of the Word and the observance of baptism and the Lord's Supper extends back to the earliest days of the Christian church,[3] through the Reformation,[4] and outward across contemporary, cultural bounds. To be the Christian church is to observe the ministry of the Word and the ordinances together.

The ministry of the Word, baptism, and the Lord's Supper are essential components of the Christian faith because the Christ of our faith is himself both Word and sacrament. He is the eternal Word and inherent in God's being as Word. As John introduces his Gospel, "In the beginning was the Word and the Word was with God and the Word was God" (John 1:1). Therefore, it is necessary for our knowledge of him and the practice of his body to be articulate according to his revelation through the Word of the Scripture. The Word encountered in the preaching of the church is the Son of God. Further, the Lord Jesus Christ, the incarnate Son of God is himself the one, true sacrament.[5] He is the "one mediator between God and mankind" (1 Tim 2:5). There is no other. He alone is the place where God has entered his creation, and the one place in creation where we go to behold and encounter God. The sacrament encountered in the embodied practice of the ordinances is none other than Christ himself. With Christ as the true content of the ministries of

---

OR: Pickwick, 2020); Anthony R. Cross, *Recovering the Evangelical Sacrament* (Eugene, OR: Pickwick, 2012); Stanley K. Fowler, *More than a Symbol: The British Baptist Recovery of Baptismal Sacramentalism* (Eugene, OR: Wipf and Stock, 2007); Michael A. G. Haykin, *Amidst Us Our Beloved Stands: Recovering Sacrament in the Baptist Tradition* (Bellingham, WA: Lexham, 2022).

[3] Steven A. McKinion explains this connection from the earliest, historical Christian texts, *The Didache* and Justin Martyr's *First Apology*. On the latter, he explains that "worship consisted of reading the Scriptures, explaining what had been read, instructing the listeners in proper living, praying, and sharing in the Eucharist." See Steve McKinion, ed., *Life and Practice in the Early Church: A Documentary Reader* (New York: NYU, 2001), 45.

[4] For example, the Augsburg Confession states, "The Church is the congregation of saints, in which the Gospel is rightly taught and the Sacraments are rightly administered" (Augsburg Confession VII.1).

[5] Thomas F. Torrance, *Theological Science* (New York: T&T Clark, 2000), 150.

Word and sacrament, the nature of the church's worship accords with the One in and to whom we worship.

In this way, when the ordinances are efficacious to grow the church into Christian maturity, they are not so by their own means in some mechanical sense—from the elements or the action. There is no change of substance (transubstantiation) such that the church's worship depends and terminates upon the elements themselves. Rather, God works through the water, bread, and cup, making himself known and accomplishing his good purposes, and the church gazes through the elements to the true sacramental reality—the risen Christ.[6] Thus, the incarnate Word empowers the ministry of Word and sacrament by means of his presence in the power of the Holy Spirit. His power is not bound by the elements of the ordinances nor by the liturgical ministry of the church.

The efficacious presence of Christ occurs through the ongoing activity of the Holy Spirit. In this way, as we think of God's activity in the ordinances, he continually acts the same way he always does—from the Father in the Son through the Holy Spirit. In baptism and the Lord's Supper, the Spirit continues his work, making actual the finished work of Christ in his church by growing us up into maturity of Christ (Eph 4:13, 15). In other words, the ordinances play an essential role in Christian sanctification because God works through the acts he commanded of his church.

As such, the Lord Jesus Christ is the content of these formal church ministries by means of the Holy Spirit's power. As we hear the Word preached, we behold the Christ through the words of the text once inspired and now illumined by the Holy Spirit. In baptism, Christians die and rise with Christ (Rom 6:1–7) through the waters of the Holy Spirit. His death and resurrection is the true baptism in which Christians now participate. We continue to be formed in that baptism through the

---

[6] These ideas are a summary of what T. F. Torrance refers to as the "dimension of depth" in the sacraments. Thomas F. Torrance, *Theology in Reconciliation: Essays Towards Evangelical and Catholic Unity in East and West* (Eugene, OR: Wipf & Stock, 1996), 83.

waters of the church. In the Lord's Supper, Christians partake of his body broken and his blood poured out in the moment of our eating as we await his imminent return (1 Cor 11:23–26), upheld and preserved by the Spirit's power. To assert Christ as the content of the ordinances does not just assume that the church remembers the historical fact of his death and resurrection, though we should remember and confess that he really did die and rise from the dead. As the content of baptism and the Lord's Supper, though, we assert that the risen Christ himself is present and acting by means of his Spirit as we enter the waters and take the bread and cup. As in the words of the Second London Confession, as we partake of the ordinances "inwardly by faith" we "spiritually receive, and feed upon Christ crucified and all the benefits of his death."[7]

If these practices are separated from one another, they cease to maintain the holistic integrity of Christian worship. Without the ministry of the Word (in evangelism to the lost and preaching to believers)—baptism and the Lord's Supper devolve into ritual acts which lack the power of confession and proclamation. Without the embodied ordinances—the ministry of the Word can denigrate into mere abstract ideas which lacks mooring in the present reality of human existence.[8] The gospel we preach is real, and the ordinances are the church's embodied response in the real world. We preach the Word of God beholding the Christ of the text.

---

[7] William Lumpkin and Bill Leonard, *Baptist Confessions of Faith*, 2nd rev. ed. (Valley Forge, PA: Judson, 2011), 294.

[8] Gregory of Nyssa makes this argument in *Against Eunomius*. He explains that Eunomius and his cadre of heretics "affirm that the mystery of godliness does not consist in venerable names, nor in the distinctive character of customs and sacramental tokens, but in exactness of doctrine." He rebuts their argument by arguing for the necessity of "sacramental customs." He writes, "Having learned from the holy voice of Christ that except a man be born again of water and of the Spirit he shall not enter into the kingdom of God and that He that eats My flesh and drinks My blood, shall live for ever, are persuaded that the mystery of godliness is ratified by the confession of the Divine Names—the Names of the Father, the Son, and the Holy Ghost, and that our salvation is confirmed by participation in the sacramental customs and tokens." See Gregory of Nyssa, *Against Eunomius* (San Francisco, CA: Fig, 2013), 376–77.

Through the ordinances, the church responds to that preaching with our bodies. Some hear, confess Christ, and are born into the church through the waters of baptism. For members already born into the body of Christ, we hear the Word and respond by partaking of his broken body and poured out blood as we proclaim his death until he comes (1 Cor 11:26). All of this depends upon the church's real and present participation in Christ by the power of the Holy Spirit.

While in some sense, these assertions are true for all Christian observance of Word and ordinance/sacrament, Baptists have the unique opportunity to claim God's present ministry because of our core convictions regarding the church's ontology. For Baptists, the church must be comprised only of those who are united to Christ, submitted to his lordship, and who have passed through the waters of baptism as one truly risen to new life in Christ. As such, Baptists need not depend upon any other sacramental reality than Christ himself because *all* true members of Baptist churches have come to him as the mediator, beheld his glory as the only Son of the Father and are already united to him by the Holy Spirit. The Baptist distinctives of regenerate church membership and believers' baptism uniquely allow for Baptists to expect God's present activity in the ordinances with no need for a mediator other than Christ.

In fact, this type of conviction is peppered across the sources of our Baptist heritage. In one of the earliest Baptist confessions, the 1610 confession of Thomas Helwys's party, they confess that the "the baptism of water leadeth us to Christ, to his holy office in glory and majesty; and admonisheth us not to hang only upon the outward, but with holy prayer to mount upward, and to beg of Christ the good thing signified."[9] For Helwys, through practice of baptism, Baptist churches are led to Christ and ascend in prayer, begging of Christ the "good thing signified"—himself, the risen Lord. Later John Gill would make a similar claim that ordinances only nourish the church when we behold Christ in faith. He writes, "only when Christ is held forth, and seen in the galleries, and

---

[9] Lumpkin and Leonard, *Baptist Confessions of Faith*, 103.

shews himself through the lattices to faith, that the ordinances are amiable and lovely, or when he is fed upon by faith in them."[10] For Gill, the ordinances are truly efficacious, nourishing the church, but they are only so when Christ shows himself through the church's faith. In the twentieth century, W. T. Conner affirmed a similar line of thought when he wrote of baptism that "Christ is the one who baptizes in the Spirit."[11] Christ by means of the Holy Spirit is the agent of baptism. By his present act, the ordinance has shaping power to grow the church. We join this chorus of Baptist voices by asserting the presence and purpose of God in Christ by the Spirit through the ordinances.

This sanctification through baptism and the Lord's Supper occurs at both the individual and the communal level. As individuals, we are born again into Christ and willingly choose to participate in our new birth into the church by baptism. The call of the apostles in Acts 2:38 to "repent and be baptized," by and large, requires an individual choice of response empowered by the Holy Spirit. Further, as we approach the table we do so as individuals accountable for ourselves in the process, and so, Paul warns individuals to take the Supper in a worthy manner (1 Cor 11:27–32). At the same time, the ordinances are inescapably and necessarily communal. There is but "one baptism" (Eph 4:5) in which we all share communally. To be baptized is to die and rise as an individual in Christ and emerge from the waters as a member of his body. One cannot be born again into Christ without being essentially and eternally united to his body—not as a matter of choice but as a matter of our inward being in him. Further, one cannot partake of his broken body and blood poured out without sharing in the church's communion. Thus, Paul instructs us to "welcome one another" when we partake of the Supper (1 Cor 11:33). In the ordinances, we always participate in Christ and his body, the church (Eph 1:22–23). As such, we grow up together into Christ "until we all reach

---

[10] John Gill, *Complete Body of Doctrinal and Practical Divinity: Being a System of Evangelical Truths, Deduced From the Sacred Scriptures* (Andesite, 2015), 470.

[11] W. T. Conner, *Revelation and God* (Nashville: Broadman, 1936), 314.

unity in the faith and in the knowledge of God's Son, growing into maturity with a stature measured by Christ's fullness" (Eph 4:13).

The ordinances have teleological value by means of their Christological reality. God empowers our practices, making them effectual unto sanctification, both individual and communal. As covenanted Christians participate in these embodied rites, Christ is present and active through the presence of the Holy Spirit forming his church into Christlikeness. Thus, Christ himself is the true content of both baptism and the Lord's Supper, and the regenerate church, his body, is the true context for the ordinances.

## The Doctrine of Baptism: Biblical Exposition through Theological Interpretation

As God works through baptism and the Lord's Supper, these practices form and define Baptist churches. As we consider the formative aspect of Baptist practice of the ordinances, we naturally reflect on the biblical mooring of these practices. Consequently, in this section we turn our attention to the relationship between baptism and the Bible.

The Baptist practice of believers' baptism can only be understood against the backdrop of the confession of Christ "according to the Scriptures" (1 Cor 15:1–8), who himself is its content. In this way, we consider not only the Christian experience of beholding Christ in faith through the waters of baptism, but also the Christian hermeneutic where we behold the baptism of Christ through the entire canon of Scripture. For we hold that, as John Sailhamer describes, the Old Testament is properly understood as a stained-glass window, whose various pieces and parts not only reflect thematic light among themselves but ultimately form a unified picture of the Christ.[12]

---

[12] John Sailhamer, "The Messiah and the Hebrew Bible" *JETS* 44/1 (March 2001), 15–16. Sailhamer presents this line of interpretation in contrast with the atomistic hermeneutic of many that treat the Old Testament instead like a shattered mirror.

Irenaeus (ca. 130–202) offers a similar metaphor, describing Scripture as a "mosaic" of smaller images.[13] He also extends a helpful reminder: though we have all the pieces, we need the proper "hypothesis" to rightly arrange them into the correct picture.[14] Though we have in the Scriptures the "compendium" or "thesaurus" of images, words, and reports, we need the proper rule to interpret them rightly. That is, when we approach the Scriptures, we need the big picture in mind to behold the King through the constituent parts. This "rule of faith," however, is not a list, but is instead the personal revelation of the God of the gospel: The Father, in the Son, Jesus Christ, by the Spirit—according to the Scriptures. Our interpretation, then, is guided by this historical confession, with Irenaeus and the early church reminding that we proceed through the Scriptures in reverse: from the light of the glory of God in the face of Jesus, we see that the apostolic preaching of Christ is shaped by crucial Old Testament promises, which gather the refracted motifs in the Scriptures.[15] And the inverse is also true: that is, we preach Christ according to the Scriptures, *and* we read the Scriptures according to Christ.

What is more, Irenaeus claims it is in our baptismal confession (Matt 28:18–20) we have a concise articulation of the rule. Our baptismal confession can serve like a prism that gathers the refracted rays throughout the Old Testament of the light of Jesus Christ because in our baptism

---

[13] Compare to Irenaeus, *Against Heresies*, in *The Apostolic Fathers with Justin Martyr and Irenaeus*, vol. 1. Ante-Nicene Fathers, ed. Alexander Roberts and James Donaldson (Peabody, MA: Hendrickson, 1994), 1.8.1. (Designated hereafter as *AH*).

[14] Irenaeus criticizes the heretics for disregarding the "intrinsic order and connection" of the text, working to "dismember and destroy" the picture, so that they finally "rearrange the gems and so fit them together as to make them into the form of a dog or of a fox" instead of the king. *AH*, 1.9.1.

[15] We participate in what Richard Hays has called "reading backwards." This is a practice of "dialectical intertextuality" that takes into account the "paradigm-shattering implications of [the four Evangelists'] fresh encounter with Israel's Scripture in light of the story of Jesus." Cf., Richard Hays, *Reading Backwards: Figural Christology and the Fourfold Gospel Witness* (Waco, TX: Baylor University Press, 2016), xi.

the whole gospel is both participated in and summarized. In our baptism, then, we confess the three articles of our faith which accord with the three triune persons, and we epitomize the "order and connection of the Scriptures."[16] For we are baptized in the name of the Father, Son, and Spirit when we are baptized into the "one coming throughout the whole economy, recapitulating all things in himself."[17] In this way, we theologize to better articulate the gospel of our baptismal confession, and we begin Bible interpretation as baptized believers—one who has confessed Christ and passed through the waters of the Spirit to new life in God. Our baptism, then, is a summary confession of union with Christ, who in himself has summed up all things (Eph 1:9–10).

In view of the Christ according to the Scriptures, Christian baptism is primarily about the three themes: resurrection (life through death), reconciliation (cleansing of sin and separation), and illumination (presence and provision).[18] That is, in baptism we confess that Christ summed up in himself, in his dual baptism in the Jordan and at the cross, three key promises of the Scriptures:

1. The New Creation: integrating Creation, Flood, and Exile motifs
2. The New Temple: atoning for the moral and relational dimensions of our sin

---

[16] Irenaeus, *On the Apostolic Preaching*, trans. John Behr (Crestwood, NY: St Vladimir's Seminary Press, 1997), 102n11. Cf. also *AH* 1:8:1–10:3.

[17] *AH* 3.16.6.

[18] While this is certainly not an exhaustive list of all the images associated with baptism, it is an attempt at the most succinct. Two recent works group the images differently. Isaac Morales, *The Bible and Baptism: The Fountain of Salvation* (Grand Rapids, MI: Baker Academic, 2022), identifies four primary images from the Old Testament: life, death, freedom, and purity. Similarly, Peter Leithart, *Baptism: A Guide to Life from Death* (Bellingham, WA: Lexham, 2021), identifies four: washes, delivers, judges, and saves. Cf. Paul Bradshaw, *Early Christian Worship: A Basic Introduction to Ideas and Practice* (Collegeville, MN: Liturgical Press, 2010), for a survey of the different biblical images used in early Christian literature.

3. The New Exodus: leading his people from slavery to the land of promise

These threads also shape Baptist churches in being and practice, in that as we descend into and ascend out of the water (life through death), we are also baptized into one body (cleansing from sin and separation) and continually nourished along the way (presence and provision). The Baptist practice of baptism, then, is first and foremost a confession of Christ. It is the visible proclamation that Christ has gathered up the promises of God in himself (2 Cor 1:20) so that in him we participate in the new creation, the new temple, and the new exodus.

## Christ's Baptism, Resurrection, and the New Creation

In the clearest articulation of his theology of baptism, Paul employs the image of death and resurrection: "Or are you unaware that all of us who were baptized into Christ Jesus were baptized into his death? Therefore, we were buried with him by baptism into death, in order that, just as Christ was raised from the dead by the glory of the Father, so we too may walk in newness of life" (Rom 6:3–4). Paul, then, presents baptism as the sacramental picture to understand our union with Christ, and as such it can serve as a hermeneutical key to understand the Scriptures. As Paul reminds us, Christ was "buried . . . [and] raised on the third day according to the Scriptures" (1 Cor 15:3–4). That is, Jesus's descent and ascent gathers up two thematic threads of the Old Testament in his person— water as judgment (descent in the flood and exile) and life through death (ascent in the new creation).

In his descent through baptism into death, Jesus fulfills the theme from Scripture of water as judgment by reliving both the flood and the exile in "the sign of Jonah" (Matt 12:38–39; Luke 11:29). That is, just as the waters of God's judgment against sin swept across the world in the Flood (Gen 6:11), the nation in the exile (Isa 8:7–8), and Jonah in the sea

(Jonah 2:2), so now does the "baptism [Jesus] is to undergo . . . [consume him] until it is finished" (Luke 12:50). And just as the nation was thrown into exile (Isa 22:18) and Jonah thrown into the waters (Jonah 1:15),[19] so now also Jesus descends into the waters of his own baptism.[20] So that just as Jonah, the prophet in exile, represents the nation in exile, so now does Jesus stand for the people, the one man who descends to death for the many (John 11:50–51).

Therefore, the one greater than Jonah is here (Matt 12:41). For in a descent greater than Jonah's to Sheol (Jonah 2:1), Jesus has descended to the dead.[21] So that the very one who in creation "tread on the waves of the sea" (Job 9:8), and who "came toward [his disciples] walking on the sea" (Mark 6:48)—this one, Jesus, drowned under the judgment waters of God's wrath for sin. And just as, at the flood, God took man's breath (Gen 7:22), even so, on the cross Jesus, the "life-giving spirit" (1 Cor. 15:45), yielded up his Spirit (Matt 27:50; Luke 23:46). But in an ascent greater than Jonah, Jesus is raised from the dead. Just as Jonah was preserved in

---

[19] This is also said of Pharaoh and his army: "You divided the sea before them, and they crossed through it on dry ground. You hurled their pursuers into the depths like a stone into raging water" (Neh 9:11). Cf. also Exod 15:1.

[20] While we will visit Jesus as the new temple in the next section, we see this theme in summary via Mark 11. That even though the temple is a fruitless fig tree of the fruitless nation that remains in exile because of its lack of fruit (Isaiah 5), God has not forsaken us. He is the one who takes the curse of the fig tree on himself at the tree. He is the one who casts the temple of his body into the sea (Mark 11:23; John 1:21), burying our sins with him and treading them underfoot (Mic 7:19). So that when he emerges from death, he becomes the "house of prayer for all nations" (Mark 11:17). Therefore, he is the one with the authority to judge and cleanse (Mark 11:15–17), because of the "sign" of his baptism at the cross where he will throw down and raise the true temple back up in three days (John 2:18–19). Cf. Steve McKinion, "A House of Prayer: Mark 11:10–26" https://www .youtube.com/watch?v=EgMJNEke6Rk; accessed April 17, 2023.

[21] Following Matthew Emerson, *"He Descended to the Dead:" An Evangelical Theology of Holy Saturday* (Downers Grove, IL: IVP, 2019), 4, "the content of the original phrase [of the Apostles' and Athanasian Creeds] is more accurately rendered by *ad infernos* ('descended to the dead [ones]') than by *ad inferna* ('descended into hell')."

the "belly of the fish" (Jonah 1:17) and Noah survived the waters of death through an ark sealed with pitch (Gen 6:14; cf. also Moses in Exod 2:3), Jesus is kept in the sealed tomb, "the heart of the earth" (Matt 12:40; cf. Jonah 2:6). And just as Jesus comes up out of the water in the Jordan (Matt 3:16–17), God raised him up out of the grave by the Spirit (Rom 8:11).

In all this we see Jesus inaugurating the new creation in his very person. For, in the beginning, as Peter reminds, "The earth was brought about from water and through water" (2 Pet 3:5). That is, as God creates the heavens and the earth through his Word (John 1:3) with the Spirit "hovering over the surface of the waters" (Gen 1:3), he divides the water, and life emerges.[22] And after the flood God's Spirit blew over the earth (Gen 8:1), and Noah's dove came to rest on the new creation that arose from the flood waters. Similarly, in the Jordan, Jesus comes up out of the water and the Spirit descends to rest on *him* (Matt 3:16; Luke 3:22; Mark 1:10). And in the grave, the Spirit hovers over the darkness, but on the "first day of the week" (John 20:1) Jesus rises from the virgin tomb to a new garden (John 19:41; cf. also 20:15)—bringing the new creation with him.

It is in this way that Jesus is proclaimed to be the Savior of Isaiah 11—the one on whom the sevenfold Spirit rests (cf. Isa 11:2) both in the Jordan (John 1:32) and in his resurrection (Acts 2:32–33). He is the "servant" of the Lord (Isa 42:1–4)—the one who has passed through the waters and has not been overwhelmed (Isa 43:2). He is the one who will form a nation as in the womb (Isa 44:2; John 1:12–13), as water and the Spirit are poured out (Isa 44:3; John 1:33). He is the new Adam, from whose side life is taken in sleep.[23] Therefore, it is through the Lord's

---

[22] On the second day God separates the waters (Gen 1:6), and it is from this separation of waters that the Lord brings life: both the sea creatures that fill the waters and the living creatures with which he fills the dry land. What is more, it is from the waters that the dry land emerges (Gen 1:9–10), and Adam is "formed . . . out of the dust" of that dry land (Gen 2:7).

[23] "As Adam was a figure of Christ, Adam's sleep sketched out the death of Christ, who was to sleep a mortal slumber, so that from the wound inflicted on

passion that we see the fulfillment of the pattern from the beginning: God brings life *through* Christ's death and resurrection.

Our descent into the water, therefore, is both to proclaim Christ's own descent and to picture the truth that Jesus has so united us to himself by his Spirit that we have died with him to sin and our new life is now hidden with Christ in God (Col 3:3). That is, we have experienced beforehand God's judgment against sin. For those who are in Christ, "the old has passed away" (2 Cor 5:17) before heaven and earth "pass away" (Matt. 24:35) in God's eschatological judgment that will be like the Flood (2 Pet 3:6–7). And it is in our ascent out of the water that we re-enact and re-live how we have been raised with Christ, born again of water and Spirit (John 3:5) become, through Jesus, children of God (John 1:11–12), created anew in him (Eph 2:10). It is in this way that a Baptist Dogmatics approach to baptism begins with the confession of Christ and our union with him. Just as the words written over the entrance of ancient baptistries remind: *Janua vitae spiritualis.*[24] That is "the door of spiritual life" is personal participation in the baptism of Jesus himself, the resurrected one, who brings God's life through death.

## Christ's Baptism, Reconciliation, and the New Temple

Christ's baptism also gathers up key themes surrounding the promise of the new temple, namely cleansing from both sin and separation. In line with this point, the author of Hebrews describes the new life of the Christian with cultic language: "Therefore, brothers and sisters, since we have boldness to enter the sanctuary through the blood of Jesus—he has inaugurated for us a new and living way through the curtain (that is,

---

his side might be figured the true Mother of the living, the Church." Tertullian, as cited in John Behr, *John the Theologian and his Paschal Gospel: A Prologue to Theology* (Oxford: Oxford University Press, 2019), 187.

[24] Cf. Pierre Thomas Chamelot, *Spiritualité du Baptême* (Paris: Les Editions du Cerf, 1963), 11.

through his flesh)—and since we have a great high priest over the house of God, let us draw near with a true heart in full assurance of faith, with our hearts sprinkled clean from an evil conscience and our bodies washed in pure water" (Heb 10:19–22).

The language of our hearts being "sprinkled clean" clearly evokes the new covenant promises of Ezekiel 36, when the Lord promises to "sprinkle clean" water on us and give us a new heart (cf. Ezek 36:25–26). And the image of entering the sanctuary mimics Ezekiel's visionary tour of the new temple in Ezekiel 40–47, culminating in the river of life flowing from the holy of holies. From the perspective of the cross, we see that Jesus' body *is* the promised new temple in Ezekiel. And as the new-temple-in-person, he has inaugurated the new covenant so that with our baptism into Christ we have full and final reconciliation with both God and man.

For we are the people of God during the time of Ezekiel, languishing in exile because of our sin and unfaithfulness (Ezek 39:23). But when Jesus Christ ascends the cross, we like Ezekiel are brought to the mountain to see the New Temple (Ezek 40:2). That is, we see the temple of Christ's body on the hill of Calvary (John 2:21; cf. also Matt 12:6). And as Ezekiel, we are expecting the river of life to flow from this temple (Ezekiel 47), making fresh the Dead Sea (Ezek 47:8) and bringing life (Ezek 47:9) and healing (Ezek 47:12). For the one on the cross is the one who provides "living water" (John 4:10), and truly, when one of the soldiers pierced his side with a spear, "at once blood and water came out" (John 19:34; cf. also 1 John 5:6–7). It is for this reason that when Jesus, the Lamb of God, is slain on the tree, he "handed over the spirit" (John 19:30 NABRE).[25] He, then, is the one who has not only "sprinkle[d] clean water" (Ezek 36:25), but who has put his Spirit within us so that we are now delivered from uncleanness and are careful to obey (Ezek 36:27).

---

[25] John Behr criticizes the regular "mistranslation" ("he bowed his head and gave up his spirit") for two reasons: (1) "his" does not occur in the Greek, but rather a definite article, and (2) the Greek word translated as "gave up" really means to "hand over." The Greek text: *paredoken to pneuma.* Behr, *John the Theologian*, 135.

In John's Revelation we see again the confluence of water, the tree, and the lamb, when the "river of the water of life" flows from "the throne of God and of the Lamb" (Rev 22:1), with "the tree of life" on either side of the river (Rev 22:2). These images—water/Spirit, lamb, and tree—as John Behr reminds us, point backward, being "brought to realization at the crucifixion."[26] Therefore, it is at the cross where we see the glory of God enthroned, the true holy of holies.[27] And it is also from the new holy of holies, Jesus himself, that flows, as Luther calls it, the "saving Flood," which now fills the earth with cleansing.[28] Or as the early Christians engraved on their baptismal: "It is here, the source of life, which washed the entire earth, originating from the wound of Christ."[29] Our water baptism, then, is an embodied confession, a visible proclamation of our cleansing of sin through the blood of Jesus.

What is more, when Christ's body is torn on the cross, the curtain of the temple is "torn in two from top to bottom" (Matt 27:51; cf. Mark 15:38; Luke 23:45). That is, just as exile was a physical reminder of the separation caused by sin, so was the "keep-out curtain" of the temple a

---

[26] Behr, *John the Theologian*, 145. That is why, in John's Revelation, we will have no need of a temple building (Rev 22:22). For the Lamb himself is our temple, dwelling with us forever (Rev 21:3) and giving life to the nations (Rev 22:2).

[27] As Robert W. Jenson, *Ezekiel* (Grand Rapids: Brazos Press, 2019), 334, states of Ezekiel's river, "We are to suppose that the spring is under the most holy place." Similarly, Peter J. Leithart, "You Shall Judge Angels," in *The Gospel of John: Theological-Ecumenical Readings*, edited by Charles Raith II (Eugene, OR: Wipf and Stock, 2017), 194, describes the cross of Christ as the culmination of John's "tour of the tabernacle"—the holy of holies: "At the end of John's gospels, the glory of God announced in the Prologue is finally revealed in all its radiance. Broken and bleeding, Jesus crucified is Yahweh enthroned on the ark, hanging between two criminals who serve as cherubic throne-guards." John Behr, *John the Theologian*, 180, continues, "It is, moreover, here that the Lord makes himself known: 'I will be known . . . to you from there, and I will speak to you from above the mercy seat in between the two cherubim that are on the ark of witness' (Exod. 25:21). This is the moment about which Jesus had already spoken: 'When you have lifted up the Son of Man, then you will know that I AM' (8:28)."

[28] Cf. Martin Luther's baptismal hymn in Leithart, *Baptism*, 2–3.

[29] Chamelot, *Spiritualité du Baptême*, 11.

visible declaration of our separation from God.[30] But sin's separation has been done away with, as Hebrews reminds us, when the living way is opened through the curtain of his flesh (Heb 10:20). That is, "access to God is not ultimately granted by passing through a curtain. It is granted through the torn and bloody dead flesh of Jesus."[31] What is more, as Christ's body was divided at the cross, he "tore down the dividing wall of hostility" that separates us from one another (Eph 2:14). Therefore, Christ himself is our peace, both with God and man, reconciling us to God in one body through the cross (Eph 2:16). He, as the new temple, has cleansed us from both sin and separation.

Our baptism, then, shows this two-fold reconciliation: firstly, that our hearts are sprinkled, not with water, but by the blood of the Lamb through the Spirit, which is confessed as our bodies are washed in baptism. Baptism, then, is the visible proclamation of the spiritual reality that we have been washed, sanctified, and justified in the name of the Lord Jesus Christ and by the Spirit of our God (1 Cor 6:11). That is why the earliest Christians prioritized baptism in "living water,"[32] to show that we have been cleansed of sin by the blood of the Lamb (Isa. 1:18; Rev. 7:14). Or as we still sing in our Baptist churches, "There is a fountain filled with blood / drawn from Immanuel's veins /and sinners, plunged beneath that flood / lose all their guilty stains."[33]

The second aspect of reconciliation is cleansing from separation so that when we are baptized into Christ, we are united with both God

---

[30] Carl Laferton and Catalina Echeverri, *The Garden, the Curtain and the Cross Storybook: The True Story of Why Jesus Died and Rose Again* (Epsom, UK: The Good Book Company, 2016).

[31] Thomas R. Schreiner, *Commentary on Hebrews* (Nashville: Holman Reference, 2015), 316–17.

[32] *Didache* 7.1, 2 states, "Concerning baptism, baptize this way . . . in the name of the Father, and of the Son, and of the Holy Spirit (Matt 28:19) in living water. If you don't have living water, baptize in other water." Cf. Michael Holmes, *The Apostolic Fathers: Greek Texts and English Translations*, 3rd ed. (Grand Rapids: Baker Academic, 2007), 340–43.

[33] William Cowper (1731–1800), "There Is a Fountain Filled with Blood."

and man. It is by the cross of Christ that God has "reconciled you by his physical body through his death" (Col 1:22). And it is at his cross that he has united us to one another. In our baptism, we visibly show that we were "all baptized by one Spirit into one body" (1 Cor 12:13). Baptists believe this body is not primarily "some abstract metaphysical ecclesial entity," as Stephen Holmes reminds, "but the local fellowship of believers"[34]—and that being those united by the baptismal covenant. That is why Baptists have historically held baptism as the center point in our covenantal emphasis, the hinge between our identity as the people of God (the vertical covenant) and our commitment to one another (the horizontal covenant), the juncture of our participation in Christ and in his body.

## Christ's Baptism, Illumination, and the New Exodus

To summarize what has been covered to this point: Our baptism into Christ gathers up two primary threads of Old Testament promise—resurrection and reconciliation. He himself is the new temple—the "place" where we meet with God and dwell with man in peace,[35] and he inaugurates the new creation—the "world of Easter" toward which the narrative of the Old Testament has been "lean(ing) beyond its temporal realm."[36] This new thing Jesus has done, however, is cast in terms of the paradigmatic event of God's salvation in the Scriptures—the exodus. We see these three converge at Jesus' baptism in the Jordan: "When Jesus was

---

[34] Stephen R. Holmes, "Baptists and the Bible," *Baptist Quarterly*, 43, no. 7 (2010), 414.

[35] N. T. Wright, *The Resurrection of the Son of God* (Minneapolis: Fortress, 2003), 671–72, reminds that when one keeps John 20 with Jesus' words of the temple of his body in chapter 2, "the reader will understand that, with Jesus' resurrection, judgment has been passed on the Temple, and that Jesus himself is now the place where, and the means by which, the father's presence and forgiving love are to be known."

[36] James Wm. McClendon Jr., *Ethics: Systematic Theology*, vol. 1, rev. (Nashville: Abingdon, 2002), 189.

baptized, he went up immediately from the water. The heavens suddenly opened for him, and he saw the Spirit of God descending like a dove and coming down on him. And a voice from heaven said, 'This is my beloved Son, with whom I am well-pleased'" (Matt 3:16–17).

The heavens are opened, as for Ezekiel (Ezek 1:1), and we see the one who cleanses us from sin and separation, who will bring his people back from exile (Ezek 36:24). This is the servant of the Lord in Isaiah on whom the Spirit rests—the one who will bring the new creation by "extend(ing) his hand a second time to recover the remnant of his people who survive" (Isa 11:11; cf. also 11:15; 43:16–19). This is the true Son of God (cf. Exod 4:22) called out of Egypt (Matt 2:15; cf. Hos 11:1), the "Holy One among you" (Hos 11:9), who will bring his children home in the new exodus (Hos 11:10–11).

In his baptism, then, Jesus reenacts the exodus in himself. That is, *the long story of God and God's people becomes his story*. That is why on the mountain of transfiguration Jesus spoke with Elijah and Moses about "his exodus," which "he was about to accomplish in Jerusalem" (Luke 9:31).[37] He is the beloved Son of God, who is brought through the waters of judgment (cf. Exodus 14), and, in so doing, crushes the head of the serpent (Exod 15:6).[38] He is the one to make the bitter water sweet by means of the tree (Exod 15:22–25).[39] He is the bread from heaven (Exodus 16),

---

[37] While various contemporary English translations render the topic of their conversation as "his departure," the Greek clarifies: they were speaking "*tēn exodon autou.*"

[38] "Indeed, as the prophets interpreted the Exodus, the Lord "hacked Rahab to pieces" and "pierced the sea monster" (Isa 51:9), that is Pharaoh, "the great monster lying in the Nile" (Ezek 29:3). He is the one in Isaiah who "pierced the dragon" (Isa 51:9, ESV) when he himself is "pierced because of our rebellion, and crushed because of our iniquities" (Isa 53:5). Also, Melito of Sardis, *On Pascha* (New York: St. Vladimir's University Press, 2020), 76, thematically connects the Exodus with the Passover Lamb, noting that Jesus "cut the Red Sea open" as like a sacrifice.

[39] Tertullian, *On Baptism*, in *Ante-Nicene Fathers* vol. 3 (Peabody, MA: Hendrickson, 1996), 9. notes, "Again *water* is restored from its defect of 'bitterness' to its native grace of 'sweetness' by the tree of Moses. That tree was Christ,

the rock struck in the wilderness (Exod 17:6), "inviting the spiritually thirsty to drink from the 'living waters' of the Spirit which flow out of his heart."[40] What is more, he baptizes us "with the Holy Spirit and fire" (Luke 3:16; cf. also Acts 1:4–5), providing his protection and provision in our journey as in the pillar of fire in the wilderness (Exod 13:21–22), and his presence as at the mountain (Exodus 19). In Christ's baptism he accomplishes the New Exodus in his person.

For this reason, it is in our baptism into Christ that we participate in Christ's Exodus. That is, when we are in Christ, *his* story becomes *our* story. We are the ones rescued from Egypt, baptized in the sea, who now eat the spiritual food and drink from the rock of Christ (1 Cor 10:1–4). Revelation 12 shows us that, as with Christ, Satan has tried to drown the church (vv. 13–15), yet we have come through the waters (v. 16) so that we now live in Christ's victory as the "creatures of the desert" fed on the "crushed . . . heads of Leviathan" (Ps 74:13–14). And just as Israel (Exod 3:17) was brought through the waters to worship God on the mountain (Exod 3:17; cf. also Noah, Gen 8:1–20), so now the Lord has fulfilled his promise (Isa 2:3) and has brought us to Mount Zion (Heb 12:18–24), worshippers now in Spirit and truth (John 4:19–24).

That is why, as Wilken reminds of the early church, at their first Eucharist those recently baptized "received a cup of milk and honey"[41] to show that they had been baptized with the New Joshua in the River Jordan, to journey with Christ to the land of promise. This introduces an important theme in the early church: baptism as illumination.[42] It is in our baptism that the Spirit lifts the veil, so that we who contemplate

---

restoring, to wit, of Himself, the *veins* of sometime envenomed and bitter nature into the all-salutary *waters* of baptism."

[40] Paul S. Fiddes, *Tracks and Traces: Baptist Identity in Church and Theology* (Milton Keynes, UK: Paternoster, 2006), 116.

[41] Robert Louis Wilken, *The Spirit of Early Christian Thought* (New Haven, CT: Yale University Press, 2005), 29.

[42] Justin Martyr, *First Apology*, in *Ante-Nicene Fathers* vol. 1 (Peabody, MA: Hendrickson, 1996), 65. Justin designates the baptized as the "illuminated person."

the glory of God in the face of Christ are being transformed into that same image from one degree of glory to another (2 Cor 3:16–18). While the image certainly speaks to the instantaneous "transformation of life, the removal of slavery, the losing of chains,"[43] this theme also lends to the continuing ministry of Christ through our baptism—that is, as Paul S. Fiddes indicates, baptism as both journey and refreshment.[44] Or, as Gregory Nazianzus writes in full, "Like those who in the course of a long journey make a brief rest from labour at an inn, we should be enabled to accomplish the rest of the road fresh and full of courage. Such is the grace and power of baptism."[45]

Therefore, it is our confession of Christ in baptism that continues to give shape and sustenance to our ecclesial context—the "paradoxical pilgrimage" of the church "in the presence of God in Jesus Christ and through the Holy Spirit, as 'sojourners and strangers.'"[46] Along this road from slavery to final salvation, we do not forsake gathering together (Heb 10:25), but join the strangers and exiles who lived by faith (Hebrews 11), considering Christ—through the Word, in the water, and at the table—so that we do not lose heart (Heb 12:3), looking together for the city that is to come (Heb 13:14). Our baptism, then, also serves as a prolepsis of our ecclesial *telos*—we who have been baptized into one body (1 Cor 12:13), in our life together increasingly become his body, growing into maturity with a stature measured by Christ's fullness (Eph 4:13). Our ecclesial journey, then, is an increasing realization of our baptismal confession, where we, as his body, continue to grow up in every way in him, the head (Eph 4:15), so that in the end we will both be *with* him and be *like* him (1 John 3:2).

---

[43] Gregory Nazianzus, *Theological Orations* in *Nicene and Post-Nicene Fathers* vol. 1 (Peabody, MA: Hendrickson, 1995), 360.

[44] Fiddes, *Tracks and Traces*, 115–17,

[45] Nazianzus, *Theological Orations*, 40.7.

[46] Compare to Gregg R. Allison, *Sojourners and Strangers: The Doctrine of the Church* (Wheaton, IL: Crossway, 2012), 471.

# Baptist Dogmatics—Theology with a Baptismal Framework

As we weave together the threads of the experience of God's sanctifying activity in his church through the ordinances, and the baptismal framework through which we behold Christ in the biblical canon, a distinct vision for Baptist dogmatics begins to form. Following the early church and our Baptist forebears, baptism begins to play a much larger role than an occasional practice of Baptist churches. Baptist dogmatics begins to take on a baptismal framework of thought which results from the significance of believer's baptism within our ecclesial experience, the baptismal shape of our confession and missional context of our belief and practice. In this way, baptism not only defines Baptist church practices, but also, Baptist dogmatic theology.

As Baptist dogmatics emerges from the experience in Baptist churches, it takes on a baptismal shape. Baptists are defined, not only in name, but also in being by the practice of believer's baptism. Baptists uniquely hold that the church *is* those who are born again by water and Spirit. This is what John Hammett calls the distinctive Baptist mark of the church.[47] All members of Baptist churches have personally passed through the waters of baptism—in the Spirit and in the church's practice in that order. We are persons shaped by that ecclesial experience. Further, we are a people who continue to be shaped by that same practice as healthy Baptist churches baptize those who have been raised from death to life in Christ. These are the practices from which Baptist theology emerges—through the regular worship of Baptist churches. As Baptists

---

[47] See chapter 4 in John Hammett, *Biblical Foundations for Baptist Churches* (Grand Rapids: Kregel, 1994), 81: Hammett continues, "central to the Baptist vision of the church is the insistence that the church must be composed of believers only. This is the distinctive mark of the church for Baptists" (81). He also includes "others who fall within the stream of those who advocate what is sometimes called the gathered church, or more often today, the believers' church" (81).

we think within the shared experience of our own baptism as a believer and regular participation in the baptism of our new brothers and sisters in Christ. As a Baptist type of Christian theology, our theological voices contribute in a baptismal key because we are baptismal people.

Further, our ecclesial experience shapes our dogmatic reflection within a baptismal frame because baptism forms the covenant community of Baptist churches. Baptists have long held that the vertical horizon of our covenant with God intersects with the horizontal aspect of our covenant with one another in the practice of baptism. This intersection is shown in the Baptist connection of the baptismal pledge with the membership covenant. That is, Balthasar Hubmaier (1480–1528), who penned "one of the greatest defenses of believer's baptism in Christian history,"[48] described baptism as the "key" not only into the universal church, but the "baptismal commitment and pledge of love" to the local body.[49] Similarly, John Smyth (1554–1612) declares, "The true forme of the Church is a covenant betwixt God & the Faithful made in baptisme in which Christ is visibly put on."[50] The vast majority of Baptists have emerged from the waters of baptism into the interconnected covenant body of a local church. According to the Baptist Faith and Message 2000, being baptized

---

[48] Brian C. Brewer, "Introduction" in *Balthasar Hubmaier: Theologian of Anabaptism*, trans. and ed. H. Wayne Pipkin and John Howard Yoder (Robertsbridge, UK: Plough, 2019), x.

[49] Hubmaier, 412. Also, Hubmaier, 175, reminds us, "For through this, as through a visible door, by the public confession of faith, we must enter into the general Christian church, outside of which there is no salvation." *On Fraternal Admonition*, in the section "How to Admonish a Brother," Hubmaier commends, "Be mindful of your baptismal commitment and of your pledge of love which you made to God and the church publicly and certainly not unwittingly when receiving water and in breaking bread." Hubmaier, *Hubmaier*, 406.

[50] John Smyth, *The Character of the Beast*, in *Works* 2:645. Jason Lee describes this statement as a "considerable shift in Smyth's thinking." He elaborates, "As a Separatist, Smyth referred to the act of covenanting as the true form of the church. As a Baptist, Smyth adjusts his thinking to replace the church covenant with baptism." Jason Lee, *Theology of John Smyth* (Macon, GA: Mercer University Press, 2003), 152.

into this communion "is prerequisite to the privileges of church membership and to the Lord's Supper."[51] Baptist churches covenant in baptism
to God and one another and rehearse that covenant through the regular observance of the Lord's Supper. This Spirit-empowered experience
of living a covenanted life with a particular, local communion of saints
shapes who we are and how we think. By way of our covenantal distinc-
tiveness, then, Baptist dogmatics has a baptismal frame which emerges
from our ecclesial experience.

Baptist dogmatics takes a baptismal frame not only by the formative
nature of our shared ecclesial experiences, but also, by means of baptismal
confession and its articulate frame. As Christians enter the waters of baptism in Baptist churches, they confess Christ the Son of the living God in
the power of the Holy Spirit. In response to the preaching of Christ, we
confess him in baptism. We confess not mere ideas, but we confess Christ
as we are baptized in the name of the Father, Son, and Holy Spirit. In this
way, our confession is real—according with a real God and our real life
in him. This real confession of God in Christ emerges from our mouths
as Spirit-empowered words, such that through our words we confess the
Word of God. In baptism we confess the name of the Father, Son, and
the Holy Spirit—the living God. We speak of this God in Christ according to the Scriptures—the second Adam who has been given all authority
on heaven and earth; the offspring of Abraham who commands us to
go to all nations; the one who baptizes us in the name, the true exodus;
the lawgiver, whose commands we obey; the true temple, who is with us
always—even unto the end. Further, we speak within the community, the
body into which we are baptized (1 Cor 12:13). While Christians confess
Christ in contexts more broadly than baptism, our baptismal confession
serves as our starting place—the confession of our birth in Christ. As
such, our baptismal confession sets the trajectory of our Christian lives
through which we confess the whole of the gospel. As we rehearse the
living confession of our new birth in its trinitarian, Christological and

---

[51] BFM 2000, Article VII.

biblical framework, we grow up into the maturity into Christ our head. Baptist dogmatics is the corporate and continued reflection on our confession in baptism, and so, takes on a baptismal frame. As Baptists practice theology, we ought always to remember our baptism.

Finally, baptism shapes Baptist dogmatics by providing the missional context of our belief and practice. In fact, the practice of believer's baptism cannot be understood apart from the Great Commission. Baptists cannot isolate baptism in the name of the Father, Son, and Holy Spirit from the commission to make disciples of all nations. The very command to baptize comes as a component of God's great mission (Matt 28:18–20).[52] As such, the very observance of baptism reinforces our commitment to that mission. Those who are baptized do so having heard the gospel preached to them by the church and believed on Christ. As they emerge from the waters, they are sent to preach that same gospel and invite others to enter that same life-giving water. In fact, they hear in their own *confession* their own *commission*. William Carey (1761–1834), who launched the modern missions movement, did so upon obedience to the baptismal confession. He states of Jesus's commission in Mark, "It is as if our Lord had said, 'This is your message . . . go and proclaim it to all nations.'"[53] We all continually participate in this mission, proclaiming the Word to the world, reaping the harvest as people believed and are saved, and filling the tanks to celebrate baptism once more. As often as Baptist churches observe baptism, we rehearse the missional cycle of coming to the waters and going to offer the invitation to others. So, our theology takes a baptismal frame as Baptists locate baptism in its proper context of God's mission.

---

[52] And as Balthasar Hubmaier warns, "For a serious command demands serious obedience and fulfillment" (Hubmaier, *Balthasar Hubmaier*, 122). This word, then, is clearer in that it is spoken by the person of Christ, involved the triune name, *and* was a direct command. The Great Commission, then, contained "powerful and unfathomable words . . . nowhere else in the Old or New Testaments can we find such high words put together in such explicit and clear way."

[53] In Andrew Fuller, *The Gospel Worthy of All Acceptation* (London: Religious Tract Society, 1830), 63.

# Conclusion

One can scarce overstate the significance of the ordinances, and baptism in particular, in Baptist dogmatics. The ordinances remind us of God's continued presence with this people, and his ongoing work in the world, as God uses them to fulfill his good purposes to grow his body into the maturity of Christ. As Baptists reflect on these key practices, interpret the Bible, and theologize from within the baptismal frame of reference, we have the opportunity to retrieve the best of our Christian and Baptist heritage. In doing so, we draw more deeply into our embodied experience in the local church and catapult outward as we participate in God's mission.

**CHAPTER 9**

# ESCHATOLOGY

## Matthew Y. Emerson and Oren R. Martin

In Baptist thought, eschatology has not played as prominent a role as other loci, especially those related to Baptist distinctives. There are some exceptions to this in Baptist history, such as the association of some seventeenth century British Particular Baptists with the Fifth Monarchy Movement, or the more recent connection between pretribulational, premillennial positions on the interpretation of Revelation and the political and cultural turmoil of the last half century or more in the West. For the most part, though, eschatology is not among the theological loci, normally emphasized by Baptist theologians.

This is not to say that Baptist theologians find eschatology unimportant, or that they ignore it. Far from it. Along with other major Christian doctrines, Baptists have clearly, deliberately, and consistently held to the fundamental, orthodox positions related to eschatology. In this sense, it might be appropriate to identify Baptist eschatology along the lines of the first and fourth signposts of this Baptist dogmatics project, namely "historical" and "confessional." Baptist eschatology listens to the resources of the past and confesses what Christians have always believed in every time and place about eschatology, and we do both under the ultimate authority and judgment of Scripture. Baptist eschatology is, then, focused on the fundamentals of the doctrine of last things. These "eschatological fundamentals" can be found in one of the most ancient summaries of the Christian faith, the Apostles' Creed. In particular, four lines communicate basic Christian beliefs about eschatology: "maker of heaven and earth," "who will come again to judge the living and the dead," "the resurrection of the body," and, "the life everlasting."

While the latter three are obvious, the first line mentioned here, about creation, is also important for eschatology, since in the eschaton creation will be restored and renewed. And the others communicate the realities of final judgment, bodily resurrection, and the final state. Together, these four lines also teach about the four *novissima*, or last things, that typically organize systematic eschatologies: death, judgment, hell, and heaven. And these four lines cover both personal and cosmic eschatology. In other words, in these four short lines of the shortest of the three ecumenical creeds, we find a rich resource for teaching and understanding basic, fundamental Christian beliefs about the last things. As an attempt to engage eschatology along historical and, especially, confessional lines, as many Baptists before us have done, this essay will explore these four credal lines and what they teach about eschatology. This chapter will also relate these eschatological fundamentals to Baptist thought and, in particular, Baptist distinctives.

## Biblical Theology and Eschatology: From Creation to New Creation

As Irenaeus noted so long ago, the creation narrative of Genesis 1–2 points the reader forward to creation's end, namely its restoration and culmination through the work of the seed of the woman (Gen 3:15), the lion of Judah (Gen 49:8–12).[1] And, as biblical theologians so often note today, the Bible is the grand narrative of God's creation, humankind's fall, God's redemption of creation through the work of Jesus Christ, and the restoration of creation at Christ's return.[2] The movement of Holy Scripture is thus from creation to new creation, from protology (first things) to eschatology (last things).

## *The Creed's Eschatological Shape*

The three ecumenical creeds mirror this biblical pattern. With respect to the Apostles' Creed, it is shaped by three articles, each confessing one of the three persons of the one God and the particular works appropriated to them. The first article confesses that we believe in "God the Father Almighty," to whom it then appropriates the work of creation with the phrase, "maker of heaven and earth." The third article begins by confessing the person of the Holy Spirit and ends with eschatological works appropriated to him, namely "the resurrection of the body and the life everlasting." Thus, the creed as a whole, mirroring the Bible that it is intended to summarize doctrinally, moves from creation to new creation as well.[3]

But it is not just the first and third article that ends eschatologically; the second article, on the Son, also moves from beginning to end. The article opens with a confession of the Son's unique status as the Father's only son (Greek, μονογενῆ; *monogenē*); this is most likely a reference to his eternal generation from the Father and thus a confession of his full

---

[1] See, for instance, St. Irenaeus of Lyons, *On the Apostolic Preaching*, ed. John Behr (Crestwood: St. Vladimir's Seminary Press, 1997).

[2] See, for instance, Matthew Y. Emerson, *The Story of Scripture: An Introduction to Biblical Theology* (Nashville: B&H Academic, 2017).

[3] For a systematic introduction to the Apostles' Creed, including issues of textual criticism, theological rationale, and historical context, see Liuwe H. Westra, *The Apostles' Creed: Origin, History, and Some Early Commentaries* (Turnhout: Brepols, 2002).

and equal deity with the Father.[4] It then confesses the entirety of his divine mission, beginning with his incarnation; moving through his life, death, descent, resurrection, and ascension; and ending with his impending judgment of the living and the dead. The Apostles' Creed in both its broad shape and in the shape of its middle, longest, central article is eschatologically oriented. Again, this is a reflection of the Bible's own eschatological shape, both with respect to the grand narrative and to the central story of Jesus of Nazareth, God the Son incarnate.

Theologically speaking, the question at this point is, what do we do with this information? How does understanding that the Apostles' Creed, mirroring the Bible, is shaped eschatologically help us to understand and teach eschatology from a dogmatic perspective? Simply put, it teaches us eschatology's end, namely the restoration of God's creation through the person and work of Christ by the power of his Spirit.

As we mentioned in the introduction, traditionally the doctrine of eschatology has covered the four *novissima*, or "Last Things": death, judgment, heaven, and hell. But there is also another distinction used to cover the end of all things, namely personal eschatology and cosmic eschatology. From this vantage point, the shape of the Apostles' Creed teaches us cosmic eschatology: God's creation will be restored and renewed at the last day when Christ returns in glory and in the restorative power of his Spirit.

## Creation's Groan and Eschatology's End

The eschatological end of creation is for God's people to dwell in God's place in God's presence forever. This *telos* is taught from the beginning of Scripture. In Genesis 1 and 2, God's crown for his creation is his image

---

[4] On the use of μονογενὴς in the Nicene Creed and in ancient Christian literature to refer to eternal generation, rather than simply the Son's "uniqueness" in relation to the Father, see Charles Lee Irons, "A Lexical Defense of the Johannine 'Only Begotten,'" in *Retrieving Eternal Generation*, ed. Fred Sanders and Scott R. Swain (Grand Rapids: Zondervan, 2017), 98–116.

bearers, human beings. These representatives of God's authority are given four tasks by God, four ways to exercise and demonstrate their status as image bearers.[5] They are to (1) "be fruitful and multiply and fill the earth" (Gen 1:28 ESV); (2) "subdue [the earth], and have dominion" over all of God's creatures (Gen 1:28 ESV); (3) "work . . . and keep" God's place (Gen 2:15); and (4) obey God's law (Gen 2:17). The sense of Genesis 1 and 2 is that Adam and Eve, as God's image bearers, will exercise their representative authority and expand God's place to cover all of creation through multiplying more image bearers and obeying his law. This, then, is the eschatological end of creation—the whole of creation filled with image bearers of YHWH who obey his law and thus rule well over his earth. When the creed confesses in the opening article that God is the "maker of heaven and earth" and then closes with "the life everlasting," it echoes this eschatological shape and end found in the creation narrative.

Of course, the creed also is shaped by the intervening biblical story of redemption, the story made necessary by the events of Genesis 3. While Adam and Eve should have obeyed and fulfilled all four tasks, they instead disobeyed God's Word and thus failed to rule over his creation well by listening to the voice of the serpent and eating the forbidden fruit (Gen 3:1–8). This failure to obey and thus to rule also impacts their ability to perform their other two image-related tasks, to be fruitful and multiply and to work and keep the Garden. Regarding the former, God tells Eve that he will multiply her pain in childbearing and that she will have strife with her husband (Gen 3:16). Both her ability and her desire to procreate are thus affected by their failure to obey and rule. Regarding working and keeping God's place, Adam is told that "cursed is the ground because of" him. God adds, "In pain you shall eat of it all the days of your life; thorns and thistles it shall bring forth for you; and you shall eat the plants of the field. By the sweat of your face you shall eat bread, till you return to the ground" (Gen 3:17–19 ESV).

---

[5] For a biblical-theological introduction to the *imago Dei*, see Anthony R. Hoekema, *Created in God's Image* (Grand Rapids: Eerdmans, 1986).

The eschatological end of creation is thus seemingly thwarted by Adam and Eve's sin. Instead of the proliferation of life, Adam and Eve bring death into the world. Instead of all of God's creation, led by God's image bearers, singing God's praise, it now groans under the weight of the curse of Adam's disobedience. But God does not leave his people or his place without hope. In the midst of doling out punishment for their disobedience, God also promises Adam and Eve that he will redeem creation, including his image bearers, from Adam's sin through the promised seed of woman (Gen 3:15). Despite the darkness and death brought about by the disobedience of the first man, God promises to reverse the curse of Adam through the last man, Eve's seed.[6]

The story of the Old Testament, the story of Israel, is the story of the search for this seed of woman. It is therefore an eschatological story, one that remains incomplete until the arrival of this last man, the Messiah, Israel's true king. We do not have space to trace in detail this story here, but suffice it to say that it happens essentially in three stages. First, in the so-called primeval history of Genesis 1–11, Moses traces the genealogy of the seed from Adam through Noah to Abraham. In the story of Noah, we see hints of new creation in the fact that Noah is placed on "dry land" and then told to "be fruitful and multiply." But like Adam, Noah also fails to obey. Nevertheless, God calls out Abra(ha)m and his family in Genesis 12 to be the father of the nation of Israel. In the promises that God makes to Abraham when he establishes his covenant with him, we see promises to restore what Adam lost. Abraham will be the father of a multitude of nations, and thus God promises to fulfill Adam's task to be fruitful and multiply through Abraham's seed. Kings will also come from Abraham's line, and his progeny will inherit a land flowing with milk and honey, and thus God promises to fulfill Adam's task to rule over

---

[6] On the relation between Adam and Eve's tasks and their subsequent punishments post-fall, see, for instance, William J. Dumbrell, *The Faith of Israel: A Theological Survey of the Old Testament*, 2nd ed. (Grand Rapids: Baker Academic, 2002), 22–23; and Graeme Goldsworthy, *According to Plan: An Introduction to Biblical Theology* (Downers Grove, IL: IVP Academic, 1991), 102–11.

and work and keep God's place through Abraham's seed. And then God gives Abraham a law to obey. But like Adam and Noah, Abraham fails to obey. We are still waiting on his seed to fulfill Adam's tasks, including obedience to God's Word.[7]

Second, Israel's story from Abraham through David and Solomon redounds with the same basic plot structure. God calls someone or some group from Abraham's lineage—Isaac, Jacob, Israel at Sinai, Israel in Canaan, David, Solomon—and promises to fulfill his promises to Abraham and restore Adam's losses through them *if they obey*. But none of them do. The OT keeps pushing forward, waiting for Abraham's and Adam's Seed to arrive, ruling over God's people, cultivating and keeping God's creation, being fruitful and multiplying, and obeying God's Word. But this Seed never arrives. We are left waiting for Israel's Messiah, the Davidic King, the one who will restore God's place through rebuilding the temple and renewing the land, the one who will rule over Israel and the nations, the one who will lead God's people in obedience and worship.

This brings us to the third eschatological movement of the OT, from the Davidic kingdom through the exilic and post-exilic periods. In many ways, the expectations here are the same as we've already described. The primary difference is that what Israel once possessed as signs of God's promises to Abraham—temple, king, land, descendants, and so on—are now destroyed and scattered because of their inability to obey. Israel's hope is that one day the Messiah will come to restore what Adam and Israel have lost, and, crucially, to give them God's Spirit so that they can *finally* obey as God intended. Additionally, this Messiah will suffer on behalf of God's people and bring out the resurrection of the dead on the Last Day.

The Christian confession is that Jesus, God the Son in the flesh, does what Adam and Israel failed to do and thus fulfills God's promises

---

[7] On this cosmic scope of Christ's redemptive work, see Michael D. Williams, *Far as the Curse Is Found: The Covenant Story of Redemption* (Phillipsburg, PA: P&R, 2005), 276.

to Abraham. This is the message of the Gospels, that Christ Jesus renews God's place through his miracles and especially through his resurrection; that he rules over God's place through his authoritative teaching, his calling of new Israel around himself, his atoning death and victorious descent and resurrection, and his ascension into heaven; and that, crucially, he obeys where Adam, Israel, and we do not. Not only does he live, die, and rise on Israel's and the nations' behalf, but he also gives those who are united to him his Spirit who also enables them to obey. And Jesus is fruitful, and he multiplies his people by his Spirit through the proclamation of his gospel. We see this primarily in Acts, when the good news of Jesus goes to new places.[8]

The church, defined and exhorted in the New Testament letters, is the sign of Christ's kingdom, the restoration of God's people in God's place, until he returns in glory. Their new life in Christ, both individually as believers justified before God and communally as the New Testament people of God, are foretastes of eternal life. Individually, the new life each Christian has in Christ is a foretaste of resurrection life, and communally, the new life Christians have together in Christ in local churches is a foretaste of all the saints, from every tribe, tongue, and nation, dwelling together with the triune God in the new heavens and new earth. The church's governance, under the supreme authority of Christ and according to his Word, is a foretaste of the new heavens and new earth, where Christ sits centrally on his throne and where righteousness dwells forever. As local churches proclaim the gospel, baptize, and take the new covenant meal together, they display Christ's rule, his impending restoration of creation, his multiplication of his people through the gospel, and his gift of the Spirit through whom they obey. And when Christ finally does return in glory, his work will be consummated in the eschaton. Because of his vicarious life, penal substitutionary death, and victorious descent to and resurrection from the dead, there will be no more sin-fueled

---

[8] See G. K. Beale, *A New Testament Biblical Theology: The Unfolding of the Old Testament in the New* (Grand Rapids: Baker Academic, 2011), 187–226.

disobedience by the resurrecting power of the Holy Spirit, and Christ will rule over God's multiplied and restored people in God's renewed place forever. This is the end toward which creation groans and for which it was made. And it is this end toward which the creed points us through its eschatological shape.

# Final Judgment

The second phrase indicative of eschatology in the creed is found at the end of the second article, focused on Christ's work. The end of the Son's mission is final judgment: "he will come again to judge the living and the dead." The first part of this statement, "he will come again," indicates his bodily return at the end of time. We will discuss that aspect of eschatology in our third section below when considering the phrase, "the resurrection of the body." Nevertheless, we should begin here by noting that Christ's bodily return is the grounds and impetus for the general resurrection of the dead. Upon Jesus's return, all the dead, righteous and unrighteous, will be raised bodily—for the purpose of eternal judgment, our topic in this section.

The focus of this eschatological statement in the creed is on Christ's role as judge. While much of our focus tends to remain on the fate of those being judged, which in and of itself is an important biblical teaching that the creed notes and that we must not neglect, the primary eschatological point is that Christ is the judge of the living and the dead. It is he, through his death and resurrection as the Lamb who was slain and the Lion of Judah, who is worthy to stand in judgment over humanity. As the last Adam and the only obedient Adam, Christ both is the one who fulfills all righteousness and thus also the only one who is able to stand in righteous, perfect judgment over the rest of humankind.

It is important to relate this aspect of Christ's work to the eschatological thrust of Scripture that we discussed in the previous section. As judge, Christ stands at the climax of both Adam and Israel's story. Whereas the first Adam failed to obey because he failed to rule—that is, to judge—the serpent rightly, the last Adam, Jesus, rules perfectly because he obeyed perfectly. And, as the perfect, eternal ruler of God's renewed place, he initiates the final judgment and renewal of all things by judging the serpent, the devil by throwing him into the lake of fire (Rev 20:10). In other words, Christ's act of final judgment reverses Adam's failure and restores what Adam lost, and he does so in his final, eternal defeat of the serpent.

This judgment of the serpent (along with the beast and the false prophet; Rev 19:20) is followed by Christ's judgment of all humanity. Again, because Christ alone obeys where Adam, Israel, and we have not, he is worthy to judge the rest of humankind. Of course, because he is not just fully human but also fully divine, he is also worthy to judge because he is the second person of the Trinity incarnate, God the Son.[9] Revelation 20:11–15 describes the final judgment this way:

> Then I saw a great white throne and him who was seated on it. From his presence earth and sky fled away, and no place was found for them. And I saw the dead, great and small, standing before the throne, and books were opened. Then another book was opened, which is the book of life. And the dead were judged by what was written in the books, according to what they had done. And the sea gave up the dead who were in it, Death and Hades gave up the dead who were in them, and they were judged, each one of them, according to what they had done. Then Death and Hades were thrown into the lake of fire. This is the second death, the lake of fire. And if anyone's name was not found written in the book of life, he was thrown into the lake of fire. (ESV)

There are at least three points to make here. First, all the dead are raised. Again, we will discuss this more below in the section on "the

---

[9] On the relation between justification, final judgment, and Christ's fulfillment of Adam's tasks, see again G. K. Beale, *A New Testament Biblical Theology*, 469–526.

resurrection of the body," but for now it is important to note that this resurrection of all the dead is only possible because of Christ's own victorious resurrection, the first fruits of all the general resurrection at his return. Death, the ultimate penalty for sin, is overturned by Jesus' vicarious, righteous life, his penal substitutionary atoning death, his victorious descent into death and resurrection from it, and his glorious, bodily ascension into heaven. As a result of this last Adam's victory over death, all of Adam's descendants are raised.[10]

Second, although all the dead are raised, they are not raised to the same fate. Some, namely those whose names are written in the book of life, are raised to eternal life. All others, namely those whose names are not written in the book of life, are raised to eternal conscious torment. It is important once more to tie this to Christ as the climactic character in Scripture and to his work as the climactic event of the biblical story. Those whose names are written in the book of life are declared righteous not by their own merit but by their union with Christ through faith.[11] On our own, "none is righteous, no not one" (Rom 3:10 ESV; cf., Ps 14:3). On our own, "all have sinned and fall short of the glory of God" (Rom 3:23). In other words, left to our own devices and apart from Christ, all of us face perdition as our eternal fate. While God's intended *telos* for humanity was eternal life with him, because of Adam's and our sin, we are destined for the second death, the lake of fire.[12]

---

[10] On the relation between the general resurrection and God's restoration of the cosmos (i.e. all that Adam's sin affected), see Richard Bauckham, *The Theology of the Book of Revelation* (Cambridge: Cambridge University Press, 1993), 48–49.

[11] Craig R. Koester, *Revelation and the End of All Things* (Grand Rapids: Eerdmans, 2001), 189–91.

[12] On the OT background for the description of the final judgment in Rev 20:11–15, see Richard Bauckham, *The Climax of Prophecy: Studies on the Book of Revelation: A Commentary on the Greek Text* (London: T&T Clark, 1993), 208–9; and G. K. Beale, *The Book of Revelation*, NIGTC (Grand Rapids: Eerdmans, 1999), 1031–38.

"But God, being rich in mercy, because of the great love with which he loved us, even when we were dead in our trespasses, made us alive together with Christ" (Eph 2:4–5 ESV). For those who are in Christ—that is, those who are united to him by faith—they have been raised with Christ, seated with him in the heavenly places, "so that in the coming ages he might show the immeasurable riches of his grace in kindness toward us in Christ Jesus" (Eph 2:6–7 ESV). It is these coming ages to which John refers in his description of the new heavens and new earth in Rev 21:1–22:5. Christ's work of judgment is thus also his work of salvation for those whose names are written in the book of life, in that he secures God's place, the new heavens and new earth, for God's people, those who are united to Christ, by ruling well through subduing the serpent and all who follow him.

We should also note, thirdly, that these eternal fates, dwelling with Christ or the second death in the lake of fire, are foreshadowed by the experience of human souls upon bodily death in the intermediate state. Those in Christ remain with him, via their human souls, in heaven, awaiting their bodily resurrection when Jesus returns and brings heaven to earth. Those who die apart from Christ await his return in a state of torment in Hades. Salvation has always been by grace through faith in Israel's Messiah, and the intermediate state is merely a waiting room that foreshadows what eternity will be when all humanity is raised bodily. Those who wait in Hades will be raised to eternal torment and those who wait in heaven will be raised to eternal life.[13]

## The Resurrection of the Body

The resurrection of the body is part of the essential fabric of the church's faith. After all, proclaims the apostle Paul, if Christ has not been raised

---

[13] On the intermediate state, see John W. Cooper, *Body, Soul, & Life Everlasting: Biblical Anthropology and the Monism–Dualism Debate* (Grand Rapids: Eerdmans, 1989).

then preaching is in vain, faith is futile, the dead are not raised, those who have fallen asleep in Christ have perished, and Christians of all people are most to be pitied (1 Cor 15:12–19). In other words, the resurrection of the body arises in the wake of Christ's bodily resurrection. All Christians—from the early church to the present—declare the hope of the resurrection.[14] Creeds and confessions consistently confess that all the dead, both the just and unjust, will be raised.[15] Though Scripture speaks of an intermediate state of both believers and unbelievers (2 Cor 5:1–8; 1 Thess 4:16)—that is, the temporary "condition of people between their physical death and the return of Jesus Christ (with the accompanying event of bodily resurrection)"—the spotlight of Scripture shines on the final resurrection of believers as restoration of the whole person, body (material) and soul (immaterial).[16] In fact, the resurrection of believers is a microcosm of what will happen on a cosmic scale, when God will make all things new.

---

[14] This common hope, however, acknowledges disagreements over the precise material "stuff" of the resurrection. For example, Brian Daley notes controversy throughout the Patristic period "on the *materiality and physical character of the resurrection* . . . Discussion of the qualities of the risen body by the Latin scholastics in the high Middle Ages, and even renewed discussion in our own time, point up just how mysterious and unclear in content the notion of bodily resurrection remains, despite its unquestioned acceptance by Christians as an article of faith and hope." Brian E. Daley, *The Hope of the Early Church: A Handbook of Patristic Eschatology* (Grand Rapids: Baker, 1991), 222.

[15] See Chad Van Dixhoorn, *Creeds, Confessions, and Catechisms: A Reader's Edition* (Wheaton, IL: Crossway, 2022).

[16] Gregg R. Allison, *Embodied: Living as Whole People in a Fractured World* (Grand Rapids: Baker, 2021), 247–48. Joseph Ratzinger writes, "The New Testament as a whole, in consonance with the Jewish world of belief in the period, yet transforming the inherited faith by a Christological revolution, maintained that there is an 'intermediate' state of being with Christ, something to be expected immediately after death as a continuation of life with Christ." *Eschatology: Death and Eternal Life*, 2nd ed., trans. Michael Waldstein (Washington, DC: Catholic University of America Press, 1988), 168.

## Centrality of Jesus's Death and Resurrection

Like other doctrines of the faith, the resurrection is the outworking of the triune God's decisive work in Christ by the Spirit, as God's ultimate purpose for his creation is to "unite all things in Christ, things in heaven and things on earth" (Eph 1:10 ESV). In the fullness of time God sent forth his Son (Gal 4:4), the Word who became flesh (John 1:14), an eschatological event that inaugurated the last days. In the Gospels, Christ cast his own arrival within the framework of eschatology (Luke 4:16–21). He cast out demons (Matt 12:28; Luke 11:20), demonstrated victory over Satan (Luke 10:18), performed miracles (Matt 11:2–5), bestowed forgiveness (Mark 2:10; cf. Isa 33:24; Mic 7:18–20; Zech 13:1), and proclaimed that the eschatological promises of the kingdom had come (Matt 11:5; Mark 1:15). His ministry and miracles demonstrated that the kingdom of God had invaded the present, for the long-awaited king stepped into history. His words and works revealed his kingly authority over sin, Satan, and death. And though his authoritative rule began in time at his miraculous incarnation by the Spirit (Luke 1:35)—the same Spirit who was at work in the first creation (Gen 1:2)—it summitted in his death-destroying death and resurrection (Matt 28:18–20).

Similarly, outside of the Gospels the NT reveals the in-breaking of the kingdom as a result of the risen and ascended Christ (e.g., 1 Cor 4:19–20; 15:20–28; Col 1:18). The good news is the message that "Christ died for our sins according to the Scriptures, that he was buried, that he was raised on the third day according to the Scriptures, and that he appeared to Cephas, then to the Twelve" (1 Cor 15:3–5). Without the death of Christ there is no salvation, but neither is there salvation without the resurrection. Under Christ's cosmic authority, the church must proclaim the gospel to every creature under heaven as God delivers his people from the domain of darkness and transfers them to the kingdom of his beloved Son (Col 1:12–23). Furthermore, Paul's emphasis on the new creation fits with the tension of the already-not yet. Believers are *now* new creatures in Christ (2 Cor 5:17; Gal 6:14–15), yet they live in the present evil age

(Gal 1:4; Rom 8:18–25) as they await the resurrection of their bodies (2 Cor 5:1–10). In Hebrews, believers have presently received the kingdom that cannot be shaken, but a day is coming when things on earth and heaven will be shaken and removed, and the consummation of God's purposes will be complete (Heb 12:26–28). For Peter, believers have been born again to a living hope through the resurrection of Jesus Christ from the dead and wait for the coming of the day of God, for the new heavens and a new earth in which righteousness dwells (1 Pet 1:3; 2 Pet 3:12–13). For this reason, Christian hope is thoroughly Christological, for it arises from the death and resurrection of the ascended Jesus, who is "the resurrection and the life" (John 11:25).

## *Reality and Nature of Death for Humanity*

Before giving attention to the hope of the resurrection, the enemy of death must be faced. In the opening chapter of Genesis, the pinnacle of creation is humanity. God's creative work through the first five days shifts from the cosmological to the anthropological. Mankind is related to, yet distinct, from the rest of God's good creation. Into no other created thing, inanimate or animate, has God breathed his own breath, giving it life. Humanity received life from God and became a living creature.

However, the blissful scene at the end of Genesis 2 is followed by the fatal events of Genesis 3.[17] In Gen 2:16–17, man's promised death upon

---

[17] The theological doctrine of "the fall" has fallen on hard times in critical scholarship. Brevard Childs, *Biblical Theology of the Old and New Testament: Theological Reflection on the Christian Bible* (Minneapolis: Fortress, 1992), 571 writes, "Some have seen the story as a primitive account of the effects of the growth of human civilization (Wellhausen). Others have interpreted the story as a type of parabolic explanation of human existence as one of limitation and restriction (Westermann). Finally, these chapters have been interpreted philosophically as an ontological description of frailty and finitude which is constitutive of human existence (Tillich)." Despite these objections, says Childs, the traditional terminology of the fall should continue to be used because "both in form and function chapter 3 is at pains to stress the full anthropological and

disobedience was the result of sin. In light of the rest of Scripture, death is real, universal, and inevitable (Eccl 3:1–2; 9:2–3; Heb 9:27). Furthermore, death must be understood as meaning more than just physical death. The ensuing story moves from creation to decreation, from harmony to conflict, from life with God to separation from God. Man is a totality, composed of both body and soul with material and immaterial aspects (Gen 2:7; Eccl 12:7; Jas 2:26). Therefore, the curse of sin is multifaceted, and death signifies both the undoing and temporary separation of the material and immaterial aspects of human nature. Since in Scripture the fullest meaning of life is found in fellowship with God, the deepest meaning of death must be separation from this fellowship. Death, then, includes both physical and spiritual, temporal and eternal, death. Indeed, death as the great enemy is vividly displayed in the separation of soul and body. Death is a tangible reminder that things are not the way they are supposed to be.

In Gen 3:19 (ESV), the words "till you return to the ground" and "to dust you shall return" are the climax of the punishment that falls on mankind. Death is the punishment inflicted for disobedience, which Paul confirms in Rom 5:12–21 and 1 Cor 15:21. Death is *not* the 'natural' end for man. So just as man was taken from the ground, so now he must return. He originates from the earth, and in the end that is what he again becomes. In the wake of Adam and Eve's sin, death ensues, beginning with their immediate offspring (Genesis 4) and thereafter flooding the whole biblical narrative.[18]

---

cosmological effects of the disobedience. The aetiological form of the curses makes clear that the events were not simply regarded as entertaining stories from the past, but rather offered a theological interpretation of man's miserable condition, both in the world and before God. Moreover, chapters 2–3 are carefully linked literarily to the larger primeval history of Genesis (1–11), and indeed provide the key for their interpretation." For a thorough treatment of the doctrine of sin, see Hans Madueme and Reeves, eds., *Adam, the Fall, and Original Sin: Theological, Biblical, and Scientific Perspectives* (Grand Rapids: Baker, 2014).

[18] James P. Boyce lists several benefits for believers concerning the reality and prospect of death. First, contemplating death brings sanctification. Second,

However, the darkness of death from Adam is lifted with the light of Christ, the Savior and Judge. First Corinthians 15 presents Jesus as the life-giving Spirit in contrast to the death-bringing Adam. In the vindication of Jesus (1 Tim 3:16), the judgment of all humanity has been given to him by his Father (John 5:25–29). It is at the voice of the Son of God that every person will be resurrected, both the righteous and the wicked. Though the timing of the resurrection of the righteous and the wicked has been disputed, Christians agree that all the dead will rise.

## *Bodily Resurrection*

Though death may be the last enemy, it does not have the last word. The day of the Lord will bring the resurrection of the dead as a living display of the death of death. God promised in Gen 3:15 that through Eve would come an offspring who would crush that serpent, Satan, and God kept his promise through the person and work of Christ (Luke 10:18; Rev 12:10–11).

The cause of the resurrection is the triune God. As the Father, Son, and Holy Spirit are inseparable, they act inseparably in the resurrection. God the Father initiates this work through God the Son, who is from the Father and has life in himself from the Father (John 5:26), and brings this work to completion in God the Spirit, raising Christ Jesus from the dead and ultimately giving life to believer's mortal bodies (Rom 8:11). That is, this work flows from the nature and character of God. As John Gill writes, "though the doctrine of the resurrection is above reason, it is not contrary to it; though it is out of the reach of the light of nature to discover it, yet being revealed, it is not repugnant to it; it is entirely

---

the prospect of death looks forward to final freedom from sin. Third, death is a pathway to eternal life. Fourth, death provides opportunities to bear witness to Christ. And finally, death is the pathway into the believer's personal presence with their Savior. James P. Boyce, *Abstract of Systematic Theology* (Hanford, CA: Den Dulk Christian Foundation, 1987), 441.

agreeable to the perfections of God."[19] First and foremost, perhaps, is God's omnipotence. "If God could, out of the dust of the earth, form the body of a man first, and infuse into it a living soul; then much more must he be able to raise a dead body, the matter and substance of which now is, though in different forms and shapes; and reunite it to its soul, which has a real existence."[20] The God of creation who has life in himself is the God of resurrection who gives life from himself.

There are hints of the resurrection in the Old Testament (Job 19:25–27; Ps 16:9; 17:15; Isa 25:8; 26:19; Dan 12:2), but it is more clearly revealed in the New Testament. And though Scripture teaches a general resurrection of all humanity, a resurrection of both the just to eternal life and the unjust to eternal punishment (Dan 12:2; John 5:25–29; Acts 24:15; Rev 20:12–13), the focus is on the resurrection of believers.[21] For believers, their resurrection is intimately connected to Christ's resurrection, for since "Jesus died and rose again, in the same way, through Jesus, God will bring with him those who have fallen asleep" and "the dead in Christ will rise first" (1 Thess 4:14–16). Indeed, the resurrection of Christ as "the firstborn from the dead" (Col 1:18; Rev 1:5) is central to the hope of the resurrection of believers.

In terms of its goal, the resurrection of believers is viewed as the completion of redemption (Romans 8). As the recreative work of the Spirit,

---

[19] See John Gill, *A Body of Doctrinal Divinity*, The Baptist Faith Series, no. 1 (Paris, AR: The Baptist Standard Bearer, 2000), 602–4. Gill considers (1) the omniscience of God, who knows all things and for whom, therefore, "it is not impossible nor improbable that the dead should be raised; since he knows all the particles of matter bodies are composed of," (2) the goodness of God, "for by this he does no injury to any of his creatures", and (3) the justice of God, which "seems to make it necessary that the bodies both of the righteous and the wicked should be raised; that being united to their souls, they may partake with them of the glory and happiness provided for the one, and they are made meet for; and of the punishment justly inflicted on the other."

[20] Gill, 603–4.

[21] Herman Bavinck, *Reformed Dogmatics: Holy Spirit, Church, and New Creation*, vol. 4, ed. John Bolt, trans. John Vriend (Grand Rapids: Baker, 2008), 693.

their bodies, once beset by the effects of the fall, will once and for all be made alive in redeemed, glorified bodies. Christ will return and transform their lowly bodies "to be like his glorious body, by the power that enables him even to subject all things to himself" (Phil 3:21 ESV). The clearest passage on the nature of this body is 1 Corinthians 15 (though also see Rom 8:11; 1 Cor 6:14; 2 Cor 4:14). Like the post-resurrection appearances of Christ, believer's bodies will be raised imperishable, in glory, in power, and spiritual.[22] In other words, there is a substantial unity as well as a qualitative distinction between present and future bodies.[23]

The resurrection is not merely a reunion of body and soul, but an event flowing from Christ's resurrection that reverses the curse of sin and completely restores what was lost in Eden. Furthermore, it is the final act in which faith gives way to sight and God's children shall be like him, because they shall see him as he is (1 John 3:2). Because of Christ, God guarantees the resurrection of the dead, the renewal of all things, and the coming of his perfect kingdom in righteousness and glory.

## Life Everlasting

The Bible begins with creation (Genesis 1–2) and ends with a description of a more glorious creation (Revelation 21–22). Between these two

---

[22] Though there are various interpretations of what a "spiritual body" is, all agree that it will not be changed into another substance, namely, a spirit. Rather, as Gill argues, "it will be different from what it is now, as to its qualities, but not as to its substance . . . and though the body will be raised a spiritual one, yet it will not be changed into a spirit, and lose its former nature; but will be subject and subservient to the soul or spirit, be employed in spiritual services, and delight in spiritual objects." Indeed, says, Gill, "If the body was a new, aerial, celestial body, different in substance from what it is, it would not be a resurrection, but a creation" (Gill, *A Body of Doctrinal Divinity*, 610). As J. van Genderen and W. H. Velema write, "the mystery of continuity does not lie within our human essence, but in the life-giving Spirit." Genderen and Velema, *Concise Reformed Dogmatics* (Phillipsburg, NJ: Presbyterian & Reformed, 2008), 868. For a similar point, see Bavinck, *Reformed Dogmatics*, 694.

[23] Bavinck, *Reformed Dogmatics*, 696.

accounts lies the drama of redemption.[24] The correspondence between the beginning and the end is revealing, for the vison of the new heaven and new earth in Revelation 21–22 is cast in grammar of creation made whole again.

Revelation 21–22 presents a grand picture of the climax of redemptive history. John's vision captures the consummation of all of God's redemptive purposes—which began in Eden, was promised in the Old Testament, inaugurated by the person and work of Christ at his first coming, and will be consummated at his final return. In other words, John's vision beautifully captures the new creation won by Jesus Christ.[25] The description of the new covenant, new temple, new Jerusalem, and new people of God in Christ affirms the future fulfillment of the main prophetic themes of the Old and New Testaments that culminate in the new creation.

In Rev 21:1–5, John described the divine *telos* of God's cosmological and eschatological plan:

> Then I saw a new heaven and a new earth, for the first heaven and the first earth had passed away, and the sea was no more. And I saw the holy city, new Jerusalem, coming down out of heaven from God, prepared as a bride adorned for her husband. And I heard a loud voice from the throne saying, "Behold, the dwelling place of God is with man. He will dwell with them, and they will be his people, and God himself will be with them as their God. He will wipe away every tear from their eyes, and death shall be no more, neither shall there be mourning, nor crying, nor pain anymore, for the former things have passed away."

---

[24] Bavinck, 40.

[25] The use of the Greek term "new" commonly implies a qualitative superiority in comparison with the old. See Walter Bauer et al., *A Greek-English Lexicon of the New Testament and other Early Christian Literature*, 3rd ed., rev. and ed. Fredrick William Danker (Chicago: University of Chicago Press, 2000), 497.

And he who was seated on the throne said, "Behold, I am making all things new." (ESV)

In John's final vision, the Jerusalem from above is now the symbolic center of the new creation. It is the place of God's people where all of their enemies are defeated and where sin and death will be no more. Furthermore, the nations come within its gates and the waters of paradise flow from the throne of God and of the Lamb through its streets. In other words, the new creation is a new and better Eden, for what was lost by Adam is gained by the last Adam, Jesus. Finally, God's kingdom has come on earth as it is in heaven.

Edenic imagery saturates the description of the new creation. As the final place of God's people, the new Jerusalem is at once a paradise, a holy city, and a temple.[26] At the end of Isaiah, God declares, "For behold, I create new heavens and a new earth, and the former things shall not be remembered or come into mind" (Isa 65:17), and this new creation will remain before him forever (Isa 66:22). In contrast to Greek dualism, which emphasizes the escape from physicality, redemption involves the whole man and finally places him on a redeemed earth.[27] In N. T. Wright's terms, this final state is "transphysical."[28] Heaven, the dwelling place of God that had become separated from creation due to sin, "comes down" out of heaven in a dramatic image of restored unity and harmony between the Creator and what he has created.[29] The new creation, then, is a restoration of Eden, for the kingdom of the world becomes the kingdom of our Lord and of his Christ, and he shall reign forever and ever (Rev 11:15).

---

[26] Bauckham, *The Theology of the Book of Revelation*, 132.

[27] Ladd, *The Presence of the Future*, 63, 317–20.

[28] N. T. Wright, *The Resurrection of the Son of God* (Minneapolis: Fortress, 2003), 477. In describing this mode of embodiment, Wright points out that the early Christians envisaged a body which was "still robustly physical but also significantly different from the present one." Wright, 478.

[29] Craig G. Bartholomew and Michael W. Goheen, *The Drama of Scripture: Finding Our Place in the Biblical Story* (Grand Rapids: Baker, 2004), 208.

Furthermore, the presentation of the new Jerusalem at the end of Revelation includes in its picture the new people of God. For example, John says that "the names of the twelve tribes of Israel's sons were inscribed" on the gates of the new Jerusalem, and "the city wall had twelve foundations, and the twelve names of the twelve apostles of the Lamb were on the foundations" (Rev 21:12, 14). In this description, the history of both Israel and the church comes to fulfillment. That is, both the Israel of the Old Testament and the church of the New Testament have their place as the people of God *in Christ*. To consummate God's teleological plan, then, the new creation is established to accommodate God's multinational people.

## Millennial Views

When it comes to tertiary issues in eschatology, such as the timing of the millennium in relation to the second coming of Christ, there are a variety of millennial views consistent with Baptist theology, including amillennialism, postmillennialism, historic premillennialism, and dispensational premillennialism. Though Baptists in the past (and present!) disagree on this topic, all agree that Christ will return to judge the living and the dead—the wicked to eternal punishment in hell and the righteous by faith in Christ to heaven—and to usher in the new heaven and new earth. Nevertheless, each view will briefly be described and a selection of Baptist representatives will be given.

Amillennialism, or realized millennialism, identifies the millennium as the present age between the first and second comings of Christ, during which time the gospel advances despite opposition, the church is established and strengthened, and Satan has limited authority to deceive the nations. At the end of the age, Christ will return to finally defeat Satan, usher in the final judgment, raise the wicked to eternal judgment and the righteous to eternal life, and (re)create the new heaven and new earth.

Postmillennialism holds that Christ will return after the millennium, which is an age of increasing peace, righteousness, and prosperity on earth as a result of the success of the gospel, so much so that the world will be significantly Christianized. At the end of the age, Christ will return for final judgment and the resurrection of the just and unjust, and usher in the new heaven and new earth.

Historic premillennialism, or post-tribulational premillennialism, is the consensus premillennial view of the church. This view holds that after the great tribulation toward the end of history, Christ will return before the millennium, which is a (literal or non-literal) thousand-year reign of Christ on the earth with the church, composed of both Jews and Gentiles in Christ, and Satan is bound. At the end, Satan is defeated, Christ executes final judgment and resurrection, and ushers in the new heaven and new earth.

Dispensational premillennialism, or pretribulational premillennialism, came into prominence in the mid-nineteenth century. This view holds that Christ will return before the millennium, which is a thousand-year reign of Christ on the earth, and secretly rapture, or remove, the church from the great tribulation so that he can deal with the nation of Israel in the seven-year tribulation. After the tribulation, Christ will return to establish his kingdom on the earth with Jews and Gentiles (some dispensationalists hold that during this time the temple will be rebuilt, and circumcision and the sacrificial system will be reinstituted). At the end of this time, Satan will be defeated and Christ will execute final judgment, the wicked to hell and the righteous to eternal life, and usher in the new heaven and new earth.

When it comes to Baptist views, as we have noted regarding the four signposts of a Baptist dogmatics, Baptists have been throughout their history focused on maintaining historic and confessional positions on the issues at hand. This does not mean, though, that there is not variety or disagreement on matters secondary and tertiary to the fundamentals of eschatology. This is especially true on the issue of the millennium. As David Dockery rightly notes, "[t]he eschatology of key Baptist leaders in the nineteenth century tended to be predominantly postmillennial. At the end of the twentieth century, the large majority of Southern Baptists leaders could be characterized as premillennial. But the early and middle years of the twentieth century were generally championed by amillennialists. Mullins, Conner, Ray Summers, as well as Hobbs, and several others articulated an amillennial eschatology."[30] Baptist leaders such as B. H. Carroll were postmillennial, with Carroll leveling strong critiques against his premillennial brothers, such as C. H. Spurgeon and D. L. Moody.[31] Along similar lines, James Leo Garrett writes:

> Baptists of the preceding centuries had affirmed eschatological doctrines such as the second coming of Christ, resurrection, judgment, hell, and heaven, and among them were to be found both postmillennialists and premillennialists, but eschatology had never been the area for differentiating Baptists from other Christian denominations. Dispensationalism as a system of teaching provides not only specific and peculiar eschatological teachings but also a distinctive hermeneutic and periodization for the Old and New Testaments. The embrace of dispensationalism by certain Baptist leaders, especially in the twentieth century, was at times divisive. Its utter separation of Israel and the Church threatened the reconciliation of believing Jews and Gentiles in the "one body" of Christ and the creation of "one new man" (Eph. 2:14–18).[32]

---

[30] See, e.g., E. Y. Mullins, *Baptist Beliefs* (Louisville: Baptist World Publishing, 1912); Mullins, *The Christian Religion in its Doctrinal Expression* (Philadelphia: Roger Williams Press, 1917); W. T. Conner, *Christian Doctrine* (Nashville: B&H, 1937); Ray Summers, *Worthy is the Lamb: Interpreting the Book of Revelation in Its Historical Background* (Nashville: B&H, 1999); Hershael Hobbs, *The Cosmic Drama: Studies in Revelation* (Waco: Word, 1971). David S. Dockery, "Hershel H. Hobbs," in *Theologians of the Baptist Tradition,* eds. Timothy George and David S. Dockery (Nashville: B&H, 2001), 229.

[31] See, e.g., B. H. Carroll, *The Day of the Lord,* comp. J. W. Crowder, ed. J. B. Cranfill (Nashville: B&H, 1936). For a survey of Carroll's theology, see James Spivey, "Benajah Harvey Carroll," in *Theologians of the Baptist Tradition,* 176–77.

[32] See, e.g., Craig A. Blaising and Darrell L. Bock, *Progressive Dispensationalism* (Grand Rapids: Baker, 1993); Blaising and Bock, eds. *Dispensationalism, Israel*

Despite differences on tertiary matters, Baptists have agreed that Christ will finally return bodily, powerfully, visibly, and gloriously to judge the living and the dead, consign unrepentant sinners to eternal judgment, and make all things new to dwell with his people in the new creation.

## *The Beatific Vision*

The fulfillment of faith, hope, and love rests upon the One who gave himself *for us*, that we might be *with him*. More than deliverance from the effects of sin and restoration of earthly life awaits believers. Indeed, Christians eagerly await the (im)mediate vision and experience of God's blessed presence.[33] First John 3:2 says, "Beloved, we are God's children now, and what we will be has not yet appeared; but we know that when he appears we shall be like him, because we shall see him as he is" (ESV). As Herman Bavinck writes, "Now, as we look into the mirror of God's revelation, we only see his image; then we will see him face to face and know as we are known."[34] In traditional theological language, the blissfulness of heaven will consist in contemplation (*visio*), knowledge (*comprehensio*), and enjoyment (*fructio*).[35] When Christians see God face to face in the life to come, and know him even as they are known, their joy in God will be full forever.

---

and the Church: The Search for Definition (Grand Rapids: Zondervan, 1992). James Leo Garrett, *Baptist Theology: A Four-Century Study* (Macon, GA: Mercer University Press, 2009), 570.

[33] For a retrieval of Aquinas' theology of beatitude, see Richard Hütter, *Bound for Beatitude: A Thomistic Study in Eschatology and Ethics* (Washington, DC: Catholic University of America Press, 2019); for Protestant retrievals, see Michael Allen, *Grounded in Heaven: Recentering Christian Hope and Life on God* (Grand Rapids: Eerdmans, 2018), and Hans Boersma, *Seeing God: The Beatific Vision in Christian Tradition* (Grand Rapids: Eerdmans, 2018).

[34] Bavinck, *Reformed Dogmatics*, 722.

[35] Allen, *Grounded in Heaven*, 62.

# A *QUO VADIS* MOMENT?
# AN AFTERWORD ON THE BAPTIST
# DOGMATICS PROJECT

### Keith Harper

*I was honored—and mildly surprised—when the editors of this volume
asked me to write a brief afterword offering historical perspective on the
project. I know the contributors, and I support the project's goals, but I was
not sure what I might bring to the discussion. I confess, I am not a theologian. By training I am an American historian who has spent his career
studying Baptists. There are many "limbs" on the Baptist family tree, but
I have spent most of my time studying Southern Baptists. I will, therefore,
base my comments on the limb I know best.*

In 1976 Americans were looking for some good news—*any* good news.
The nation was recovering from the violence of the late 1960s and dis-
illusionment stemming from both the Watergate Scandal and life after
Vietnam. The "born again" phenomenon was sweeping the nation as new

believers seemingly came out of nowhere. In that year, a peanut farmer and Southern Baptist Sunday school teacher from Plains, Georgia, won the US presidency. His name was Jimmy Carter and his sister, Ruth Carter Stapleton, was an outspoken Christian evangelist. For a moment, religiously minded Americans might have been tempted to believe they had returned to a simpler era, especially when magazines like *Newsweek* and *Christianity Today* proclaimed 1976 as "The Year of the Evangelical."[1]

Professing evangelicals could scarcely ponder the possibilities of a religious awakening before fault lines that had always been present began to widen. Harold Lindsell warned that a "Battle for the Bible" was underway. Before long the battle spilled over into partisan politics and all out cultural warfare. Although partisans may disagree on particulars, it is safe to say that this battle carried profound consequences. It was not a singular battle that pitted God-fearing folk against godless infidels. This battle occurred over many fronts and assumed different forms, many of which were intradenominational; all of which struggled to define acceptable bounds of conduct in the public square. Some Baptists did what generations of their forebearers would have deemed unthinkable: they turned to party politics to protect "traditional family values." Whatever optimism that existed in 1976 was soon squelched by bitter infighting, denominational schism, and simmering animosity that lingers into the twenty-first century.[2] So . . . what happened?

A variety of historical circumstances led to the Baptist Dogmatics Project (BDP), too many, in fact, to address in an afterword. The

---

[1] Jimmy Carter's rural roots and ties to evangelical Christianity must never overshadow the fact that he was a Democratic stalwart in Georgia and served as the state's governor before his election to the presidency. For a well-rounded work on Jimmy Carter see Jonathan Alter, *His Very Best: Jimmy Carter, A Life* (New York: Simon and Schuster, 2021). Works on the 1960s are legion, but Allan J. Matusow's *The Unraveling of America: A History of Liberalism in the 1960s* (Athens, GA: University of Georgia Press, 2009) is a good overview.

[2] See Harold Lindsell, *The Battle for the Bible* (Grand Rapids: Zondervan, 1976) and *The Bible in the Balance* (Grand Rapids: Zondervan, 1979).

personalities and events that laid the foundation for Southern Baptist life in the twenty-first century are open to sustained inquiry and doubtless would lead to multiple volumes. Nonetheless, a brief historical overview may be helpful in establishing the context for the BDP.

# Background

Southern Baptists entered the twentieth century already at odds with the nation's emerging scientific revolution. Darwinian evolution was challenging the Genesis account of creation, and biblical criticism was eroding confidence in the Bible's credibility, especially among college-educated Americans. Whose voice rang truest? Denominational leaders appeared to be at a crossroads. Should they opt for modernism or stay with "the Old Time Religion," as the song says?

Baptist leaders, North and South, sought a sound path through the intellectual challenges of modernity. Respected theologian and president of Rochester Divinity School, Augustus Hopkins Strong, struggled with modernism before opting for a more conservative path.[3] As A. H. Strong struggled to square the Bible with scientific trends and changing cultural patterns, Edgar Young Mullins faced similar difficulties. Mullins served as president of The Southern Baptist Theological Seminary in Louisville, Kentucky, from 1899 until his death in 1928. He remained committed to biblical conservativism, but he emphasized individualism and experientialism in the Christian's life.[4]

It is no exaggeration to say that E. Y. Mullins ranks as the most influential Southern Baptist thinker of the twentieth century. Among his many accomplishments, Mullins was one of the leading voices in calling for the first denomination-wide confession of faith, the Baptist

[3] Grant Wacker, *Augustus H. Strong and the Dilemma of Historical Consciousness* (Macon, GA: Mercer University Press, 1985).

[4] See E. Y. Mullins, *The Axioms of Religion* (Philadelphia: American Baptist Publication Society, 1908) and *The Christian Religion in its Doctrinal Expression* (Philadelphia: Roger Williams Press, 1917).

Faith and Message (BFM) in 1925. The BFM 1925 was never intended to ensure absolute theological agreement across the denomination, nor could it. Historian Bill Leonard argues that from its beginnings, the Southern Baptist Convention (SBC) operated according to the "Grand Compromise," whereby early Southern Baptist leaders agreed to lay aside theological differences for the sake of missions. Thus, it was not necessary for cooperating Southern Baptists to march in theological lockstep. A loose, general doctrinal agreement allowed for a measure of theological diversity, which in turn provided the foundation for a missionary consensus.[5]

In the broader culture, 1925 marked the year that cemented biological evolution as an accepted feature of American secondary and higher education. Fundamentalists appeared to suffer a humiliating defeat in the Scopes Trial, and while it may have been tempting to think that biblical fundamentalism would fade away, historian Joel Carpenter maintains that fundamentalists regrouped. By 1950 they had reemerged with new networks, institutions, and the like.[6] Americans had survived two world wars, with the Great Depression sandwiched in between them, and fundamentalists were prepared to fight for their denominations.[7]

The Scopes Trial was more than a controversy over human origins. Religious conservatives had been sparring with modernists since the late-nineteenth century over the Bible's trustworthiness. These disputes

---

[5] Bill J. Leonard, *God's Last and Only Hope: The Fragmentation of the Southern Baptist Convention* (Grand Rapids: W. B. Eerdmans, 1990); For E. Y. Mullins and modernity, see Curtis W. Freeman, "E. Y. Mullins and the Siren's Song of Modernity," *Review and Expositor* 96, no. 1 (1999): 23–42; For contrasting views of Mullins's theology see C. Douglas Weaver's introduction in *E. Y. Mullins: The Axioms of Religion*, ed. C. Douglas Weaver (Macon: Mercer University Press, 2010), 1–35 and R. Albert Mohler's introduction in E. Y. Mullins, *Axioms of the Christian Religion*, compiled by R. Albert Mohler (Nashville: B&H, 1997).

[6] Joel A. Carpenter, *Revive Us Again: The Reawakening of American Fundamentalism* (New York: Oxford University Press, 1997).

[7] Thomas S. Kidd and Barry Hankins, *Baptists in America: A History* (New York: Oxford University Press, 2015).

actually triggered the rise of American fundamentalism and revealed a significant division among American Protestants with respect to episte-mology.[8] The Scopes Trial signaled the increasing importance of science and technology in framing American culture and values. It also demon-strated clear fragmentation among American Protestants, a fragmenta-tion that would only increase throughout the twentieth century.

If Baptist theologians struggled to find a voice after the Second World War, they were not alone. Sociologist Robert Wuthnow claims that American religion has been experiencing a "restructuring" since the War's end. That is, religion has not succumbed to secularization. Rather, it had been altered, assuming new forms.[9] One might go a bit further and argue that America's religious restructuring resulted from its fragmenta-tion. Fundamentalists clamored for a hearing, as did religious liberals. Likewise, neo-orthodox and neo-evangelical theologians who were nei-ther fundamentalists nor liberals, insisted on cultural and institutional space for their beliefs. These thinkers attempted to bring discussion of religion and culture back to a more moderate religious center, but they pleased neither religious liberals from the left, nor fundamentalists from the right.

As intradenominational battle lines were being drawn, many Baptists became increasingly preoccupied with defending Scripture from per-ceived biblical naysayers. But, in 1947, Carl F. H. Henry added another dimension to the discussion. Henry's remarkably perceptive book, *The Uneasy Conscience of Modern Fundamentalism,* raised a challenging issue. Given the Bible's teachings on wealth and power, how would postwar fundamentalists address issues such as poverty, justice, and civil rights?[10]

---

[8] I am indebted to Daniel K. Williams for this insight. On the rise of fun-damentalism, the best work remains George Marsden, *Fundamentalism and American Culture* (New York: Oxford University Press, 2022)

[9] See Robert Wuthnow, *The Restructuring of American Religion: Society and Faith Since World War II* (Princeton: Princeton University Press, 1988).

[10] Carl F. H. Henry, *The Uneasy Conscience of Modern Fundamentalism* (Grand Rapids: Eerdmans, 1947).

Henry could scarcely know it at the time, but his small book posed a straightforward question that continues to vex fundamentalists: How should one apply the Scripture's social teachings? One answer came when the *Brown v. Board* decision desegregated public schools in 1954. Angry whites, many of whom claimed to be fundamentalists, responded by preventing their children from attending integrated schools. In some cases, fundamentalists created all white academies. By 1955 the answer to Henry's questions was clear. Many Baptists proved more willing to defend the Bible's literal truth than live out its mandate to love others.

Americans entered the 1960s with an increasing measure of fear. In addition to the Cold War and the threat of nuclear annihilation, the US government escalated its military involvement in Southeast Asia, and social unrest was increasing. Meanwhile, internal disfunction threatened the SBC family in 1961 when Southern Baptists learned that Ralph Elliott, an Old Testament professor in the newly created Midwestern Baptist Theological Seminary, taught the Bible according to higher critical methods. Elliott was eventually fired from Midwestern, but the issue of how one should properly read and teach the Bible became the crucial issue for the Convention. Other issues followed, and by 1979 the SBC was poised for a showdown.[11] Ironically, the negation of any social ethic accelerated America's religious fragmentation, and American religion was fragmenting as quickly as American culture.

## Biblical Inerrancy and the Controversy

Between 1979 and 1991 Southern Baptists were embroiled in what is usually referred to as "the Controversy." The SBC was not the only denomination to endure turmoil in the latter twentieth century, but they

---

[11] See Ralph Elliott, *The Message of Genesis: A Theological Interpretation* (Nashville: Broadman Press, 1961). Thirty years later, Elliott discussed his early career and termination from Midwestern in *The Genesis Controversy and Continuity in Southern Baptist Chaos: A Eulogy for a Great Tradition* (Macon, GA: Mercer University Press, 1992).

were arguably the most vocal. Details of this period are well chronicled and need not be rehashed here.[12] It is important to note that by the end of the 1980s significant differences could be seen among Southern Baptists, ranging from denominational leaders to rank-and-file church members.[13]

Historian and pastor Jerry Sutton's assessment of the Controversy as a "Baptist Reformation" is surely an overstatement. The Controversy amounted to replacing Leonard's Grand Compromise with inerrancy as the focal point of Southern Baptist thought and action.[14] But as a subsequent generation of SBC leaders soon discovered, inerrancy may reinforce a score of theological tenets, but it is not a theology unto itself.

For Baptists, the Battle for the Bible revealed differences of opinion with respect to revelation and application. Precisely what is the Bible and how did humanity come to have it? Did human authorship somehow diminish the Bible's trustworthiness? How should Southern Baptists approach Scripture? Biblical inerrancy quicky became the buzz phrase of the 1980s, and numerous books rushed to describe and defend the Bible's truthfulness, but few Baptists wrote on biblical holiness.[15]

---

[12] David Morgan's *The New Crusades, the New Holy Land* (Tuscaloosa: University of Alabama Press, 1996) remains the best single volume treatment of the controversy. See also Jerry Sutton, *The Baptist Reformation: The Conservative Resurgence in the Southern Baptist Convention* (Nashville: B&H, 2000).

[13] Nancy Tatom Ammerman, *Baptist Battles: Social Change and Religious Conflict in the Southern Baptist Convention* (New Brunswick: Rutgers University Press, 1990).

[14] To be clear, Southern Baptists did not abandon their missionary endeavors. The point here is to note that inerrancy assumed an emphasis that unseated missions and the SBC's primary focus.

[15] For inerrancy, see Benjamin Breckinridge Warfield's classic, *The Inspiration and Authority of the Bible*, ed. Samuel G. Craig, with introduction by Cornelius Van Til (Phillipsburg, PA: P&R, 1979). For more recent assessments see Norman Geisler, ed., *Inerrancy* (Grand Rapids: Zondervan, 1980) and Norman L. Geisler, ed., *Biblical Errancy: An Analysis of its Philosophical Roots* (Grand Rapids: House, 1981). For a variety of views see James R. A. Merrick and Stephen M. Garrett, eds., *Five Views on Biblical Inerrancy* (Grand Rapids: Zondervan, 2013).

Southern Seminary president Al Mohler once described the Controversy as a contest between "the truth party" and "the freedom party."[16] Moving beyond 1991, however, the issue became less about "truth" in the abstract, and more about advancing propositional apologetics. The SBC became increasingly linked to the Council of Biblical Manhood and Womanhood, an organization dedicated to fighting feminism and reestablishing what they described as biblical gender norms. This affiliation culminated with a new confession of faith, BFM 2000, which noted that women should "graciously submit" to their husbands.

## The Baptist Dogmatics Project

Establishing biblical inerrancy as normative for Southern Baptists did not solve the SBC's problems. Arguably, the inerrancy controversy inadvertently created a crisis of application. Scandal in the post-Controversy SBC, especially against a backdrop of nationwide denominational decline, raises a host of important questions. What does one do with an inspired Bible? What does the Bible mean when it is says believers are to "contend for the faith"? Is there value in an inerrant Bible that is interpreted incorrectly? If inerrancy is pushed to its extreme, does it reduce the "faith once delivered" to mere assent to propositionalism?

The Latin phrase, *quo vadis*, literally means "where are you going"? Given the turmoil generated by the Controversy and the moral crisis of SBC leadership, it seems fair to ask if Southern Baptists are at a *quo vadis* moment. Where are Baptists going? If there is a proper way forward, what is it? Assuming the highest possible view of Scripture, the contributors to this volume believe the Baptist Dogmatics Project (BDP) *is* a way forward through a renewed theological vision.

---

[16] For "truth party" versus "freedom party," see R. Albert Mohler, "A Call for Baptist Evangelicals and Evangelical Baptists: Communities of Faith and a Common Quest for Identity," in *Southern Baptists & American Evangelicals: The Conversation Continues*, ed. David S. Dockery (Nashville: B&H, 1993) 224–39.

The BDP is not concerned with merely defining what the Bible is, for we have an established position on its inspiration, veracity, and authority.[17] Neither is the BDP concerned with refashioning systematic theology. Rather, the contributors to this volume are more interested in why God revealed himself to humanity and how we may fully partake in the riches of redemption in Christ. That is, the BDP is concerned with a transformative kind of Christianity, one that focuses on the kind of reflection and spirituality expressed in J. I. Packer's observation: "A little knowledge of God is worth more than a lot of knowledge about God."[18]

The BDP is concerned with transformational Christianity in at least two separate spheres. On one hand, there are numerous admonitions in Scripture for Christ's disciples to be transformed by the Holy Spirit's inner work (Rom 12:1–2). Unfortunately, Baptists tend to be notoriously weak in pneumatology, and the increasing emphasis on propositionalism throughout the twentieth century only amplified that weakness. Moreover, God draws people to himself in different ways. As Richard Baxter observed, "God breaketh not all men's hearts alike."[19] The BDP

---

[17] The historic Baptist confessions of faith all hold a very high view of biblical inspiration. Most recently the BFM 2000 begins with the article, "The Scriptures," and says, "The Holy Bible was written by men divinely inspired and is God's revelation of Himself to man. It is a perfect treasure of divine instruction. It has God for its author, salvation for its end, and truth, without any mixture of error, for its matter. Therefore, all Scripture is totally true and trustworthy. It reveals the principles by which God judges us, and therefore is, and will remain to the end of the world, the true center of Christian union, and the supreme standard by which all human conduct, creeds, and religious opinions should be tried. All Scripture is a testimony to Christ, who is Himself the focus of divine revelation."

[18] J. I. Packer, *Knowing God* (Downers Grove, IL: InterVarsity Press, 1973) 21.

[19] For a recent assessment of Baptists and the Holy Spirit, see C. Douglas Weaver, *Baptists and the Holy Spirit: The Contested History with Holiness-Pentecostal-Charismatic Movements* (Waco, TX: Baylor University Press, 2019); The Baxter quote is from Richard Baxter, *Reliquiae Baxterianae, Or, Mr Richard Baxter's Narrative of the Most Memorable Passages of his Life and Times*, ed. N. H. Keeble et al. (Oxford: Oxford University Press, 2020), Part 1, 7.

sees discipleship as a community venture where believers invest in one another unto growth in the Spirit unto useful service to God and humanity. As the BDP manifesto notes, "Baptist Dogmatics enables us to recognize God's work for humanity and his ongoing work among human beings as relevant to the present human challenges and as the basis for future hope" (see chapter 1).

Beyond spiritual growth and maturity, the BDP is concerned with manifesting a holy witness before the world. In *The Analogical Imagination: Christian Theology and the Culture of Pluralism*, theologian David Tracy maintains that theologians engage three publics, namely, the church, the academy, and a broader "society." He further divided society into three realms: (1) the realm of technoeconomic structure; (2) the realm of polity bearing on "social justice and the use of power"; and (3) the realm of culture. "Whether or not particular theologians are explicitly involved in the tasks of responsible citizenship in so complex a society," Tracy observes, "they are clearly affected by specific roles in that society."[20]

The BDP is concerned with addressing the church, academy, and culture with a sound, Christ-centered witness. Again, Tracy notes, "Christians believe *in* Jesus Christ *with* the apostles as witnesses to Jesus Christ and thereby in the tradition which mediates that belief in belief in Jesus Christ *with* and *through* the apostolic witness. A central sign of the tradition's fidelity to that witness, and thereby to its own religious as prophetic reality, is the tradition's own self-reformation."[21] In Christianity, Tracy sees deep connections with the past that continuously inform the present and point to the future with hope in Christ.

If Tracy is correct, theology proper requires an ongoing reevaluation or recalibration of one's beliefs and practices in relation to its host society and the larger Christian tradition. It was not wrong for Baptists of the 1970s and '80s to clarify and articulate a position on Scripture. But

---

[20] David Tracy, *The Analogical Imagination: Christian Theology and the Culture of Pluralism* (New York: Crossroad, 1981) 237, italics in original.

[21] Tracy, 237, emphasis original.

stopping short of a thoroughgoing reconsideration of individual and corporate spirituality failed to uphold the authority and sufficiency of the Scriptures. Consequently, the BDP is dedicated to discipleship in the local church. Perhaps the manifesto offers the best summary of the BDP when it says, "The two-testament revelation of God (*covenant theology*) which is proclaimed in summary form in the preached gospel, brings the offer of relationship (*covenant soteriology*) with the triune God. Believers are called to live this life in unified relationships with other believers as a church (*covenant ecclesiology*)."[22]

The Scriptures are abundantly clear and almost too numerous to cite here. Nonetheless, the apostle Paul told the church at Corinth, "That is, in Christ, God was reconciling the world to himself, not counting their trespasses against them, and he has committed the message of reconciliation to us" (2 Cor 5:19). The Scriptures attest to a God who is reconciling the world to himself through his only begotten Son, Jesus. Moreover, that God, the only true God, has given us a ministry of reconciliation. It is more than forgiveness; it is life in the Spirit lived in community with others who have been translated from a kingdom of darkness into a kingdom of light. It is past time for a denomination-wide self-examination and reevaluation of our faith *and* praxis. It is fair to say that since the Controversy, Southern Baptists have assumed a defensive posture, an "us against the world" mentality fueled in large part by the politics of fear.[23] The BDP is not an attempt to redefine orthodoxy. Rather, it is an exploration of transformational Christianity in a Baptist tradition.

---

[22] See preface.

[23] On the politics of fear see Edward R. Crowther, "'The Most Distressing Thing in Our Baptist Life': Southern Baptists and the Politics of Fear" in *Southern Baptists Re-Observed: Perspectives on Race, Gender, and Politics*, ed. Keith Harper (Knoxville, TN: University of Tennessee Press, 2022), 142–72. See also James Guth, "Southern Baptist Clergy, the New Christian Right, and Political Activism in the South," in Glenn Feldman, ed., *Politics and Religion in the White South* (Lexington: University Press of Kentucky, 2005): 187–213.

# AUTHOR INDEX

## A

Abelard, Peter, 220
Akin, Daniel L., 228
Alarcón, E., 95
Alexander, Frank S., 154
Allen, David L., 222
Allen, R. Michael, 46, 84, 184, 186, 367
Allison, Gregg R., 271, 337, 355
Alter, Jonathan, 370
Ames, William, 246
Ammerman, Nancy Tatom, 375
Anatolios, Khaled, 90, 118, 121, 125,
  173
Anselm of Canterbury, 96–97, 104, 217
Arlig, Andrew, 106
Athanasius, 118, 122, 181, 215
Augustine of Hippo, 62, 96, 98, 104,
  112, 172, 179, 183, 211, 290
Averbeck, Grant, 119
Ayres, Lewis, 118

## B

Backus, Isaac, 242–43
Bainton, Roland, 153, 196
Barrett, Jordan P., 94
Barth, Karl, 19–20, 173, 198
Bartholomew, Craig G., 363
Basden, Paul, 274
Basil of Caesarea, 112, 122
Battles, Ford Lewis, 97, 265
Bauckham, Richard, 86, 353, 363
Bauer, Walter, 362

Bavinck, Herman, 106, 113, 173, 182,
  186, 286, 289, 360–62, 367
Baxter, Richard, 377
Beale, G. K., 120, 258, 263, 350, 352–53
Beckwith, Carl L., 104
Beeke, Joel R., 105
Beeley, Christopher A., 174
Behr, John, 63, 126, 201, 215, 330–32,
  345
Berkhof, Louis, 108
Bingham, Matthew, 34
Blaising, Craig A., 366
Boa, Ken, 256
Bock, Darrell L., 366
Boersma, Hans, 367
Bolt, John, 106, 289, 360
Bonaventure, 105, 123, 202
Bowman, Robert M., Jr., 86
Boyce, James P., 237, 359
Bradshaw, Paul, 326
Brakel, Wilhelmus à, 196
Brewer, Brian, 339
Broadus, John A., 156, 273
Browne, Charles Gordon, 102
Brown, J. Newton, 277
Bruce, F. F., 296–97

## C

Calvin, John, 97, 221, 265
Carey, William, 311
Carmichael, Casey, 185
Carpenter, Joel A., 372

381

# SUBJECT INDEX

Roman Catholic Church and traditions, 30

Romanian Baptist Church of Akron, 11

## S

Sabbath, 141

Sabellianism, 71, 102–7

sacrament, 31–32, 35, 41, 123–24, 236, 260, 284, 286, 309, 318–22, 327

Sailhamer, John, 324

salvation, 4–5, 19, 23, 41, 48–49, 59, 62–63, 69, 71, 73, 77, 87, 113, 122, 126, 142, 146, 172, 179, 183–84, 187, 189, 198, 202, 207–10, 212, 214–22, 227–39, 243, 263, 266, 276, 279, 294, 314, 321, 334, 337, 339, 354, 356, 377. *See also* soteriology

sanctification, 5, 113, 148, 208–9, 232, 236–39, 248–49, 254–57, 260–64, 266, 268–70, 272–74, 277–78, 280, 320, 358

    Baptists and, 270–80

    of believers, 37, 309

    by the Holy Spirit, 43, 113, 323–24

Satan, 30, 60, 160, 229, 336, 356, 359, 364–65

Scarborough, Lee Rutland, 9, 159

Schreiner, Tom, 256

Scopes Trial, the, 372–73

Scripture, 55–81. *See chapter 1, "Scripture"* (55–81)

    allegorical sense of, 67–68

    authority of, 3–4, 15–16, 25–28, 53–81, 272

    creeds and, 68–72

    interpretation of, 25–28, 60–68

    as ruled by the gospel, 79

    ruled readings of, 55–73, 76, 79

    as the Supreme Judge, 25, 70, 76

sectarianism, 25, 77

self-reformation, 378

self-revelation of God, 19, 59, 80–81

Sermon on the Mount, the, 143, 149

sermons, 19, 159, 229

Shema, 85–86

Simons, Menno, 197

simplicity, divine, 94–97, 105–6, 117, 129

Sinai, 56, 119–20, 140, 349. *See also* Mosaic covenant

sinfulness, 139, 152, 160, 172, 198, 216, 219, 225, 229–30, 236–37, 254, 257, 265, 353

slavery, 134, 140, 150–51, 155–56, 164–65, 220, 229, 327, 337

Smith, Brandon, 3, 14

Smyth, John, 38–39, 271, 297, 313, 339

social covenants, 145–46

*sola Scriptura*, 70, 242

soteriology, 5, 38–42, 70, 299, 304, 314–16, 379. *See also chapter 5, "Soteriology"* (207–44); salvation

Soulen, Kendal, 86

*Southeastern Theological Review*, 6, 14

Southern Baptist Convention, 11, 158, 164–67, 372–76. *See also* International Mission Board of the SBC

Southern Baptist Theological Seminary, 11, 155, 371

Spivey, Jim, 159

Sproul, R.C., 247

Spurgeon, Charles H., 225, 255, 289, 366

Stamps, Luke, 4, 14

Stapleton, Ruth Carter, 370

Strickland, Walter, 6

Strong, Augustus Hopkins, 371

submission, 36–37, 42, 55, 70, 75, 268, 293, 301, 304–5, 308, 315–16, 322

subordinationism, 173

suffering, 44, 101, 189, 191, 218, 220, 228, 264, 266, 280, 311–12, 318

Summers, Ray, 366

Sutton, Jerry, 375

Swain, Scott, 6, 46, 88, 102, 113

systematic theology, 1, 3, 17–53, 149, 234, 377. *See also section, "The Method, End, and Terrain of Baptist Dogmatics"* (17–54)

## T

*Te Deum*, 192. *See also* virgin birth, the

temptation, 60, 139, 160, 174, 191

Ten Commandments, 69. *See also* human dignity: Law and the Prophets, the

Tertullian, 218

# SCRIPTURE INDEX